ANIME STUDIO 6: THE OFFICIAL GUIDE

Kelly L. Murdock

Course Technology PTR

A part of Cengage Learning

COURSE TECHNOLOGY
CENGAGE Learning™

Australia, Brazil, Japan, Korea, Mexico, Singapore, Spain, United Kingdom, United States

COURSE TECHNOLOGY
CENGAGE Learning™

Anime Studio 6: The Official Guide
Kelly L. Murdock

Publisher and General Manager,
Course Technology PTR:
Stacy L. Hiquet

Associate Director of Marketing:
Sarah Panella

Manager of Editorial Services:
Heather Talbot

Marketing Manager:
Jordan Casey

Acquisitions Editor:
Heather Hurley

Project and Copy Editor:
Marta Justak

Technical Reviewer:
Steve Yatson

Interior Layout:
Shawn Morningstar

Cover Designer:
Mike Tanamachi

DVD-ROM Producer:
Brandon Penticuff

Indexer:
Larry Sweazy

Proofreader:
Brad Crawford

For product information and technology assistance, contact us at
Cengage Learning Academic Resource Center, 1-800-354-9706

For permission to use material from this text or product,
submit all requests online at **cengage.com/permissions**
Further permissions questions can be emailed to
permissionrequest@cengage.com

Anime Studio is a trademark of Smith Micro Software, Inc.
All other trademarks are the property of their respective owners.
All images © Cengage Learning.

Library of Congress Catalog Card Number: 2009941739

ISBN-13: 978-1-4354-5561-0

ISBN-10: 1-4354-5561-4

Course Technology
20 Channel Center Street
Boston, MA 02210
USA

Cengage Learning is a leading provider of customized learning solutions with office locations around the globe, including Singapore, the United Kingdom, Australia, Mexico, Brazil, and Japan. Locate your local office at: **international.cengage.com/region**

Cengage Learning products are represented in Canada by Nelson Education, Ltd.

For your lifelong learning solutions, visit **courseptr.com**

Visit our corporate website at **cengage.com**

Printed in Canada
1 2 3 4 5 6 7 11 10 09

My son, in karate, was recently enrolled,

"It's great discipline," I was thinking quite bold.

But now I'm having to rethink my decision,

'Cause practice at home isn't what I envision.

Every day when from class he's returned,

He's anxious to show me the moves that he's learned.

I cringe when he asks me to grab him from behind

Because I usually end up on ground in a bind.

Playing with my son now leaves me with bruises,

And I'm running out of ways to dodge with excuses.

There must be a way I can counter his attack,

Without always ending up flat on my back.

I've been watching TV to find a solution,

To counter his moves with bold retribution.

After studying long, I'm ready for his blows,

By trying out what I've learned from the wrestling pros.

—To Thomas, 2009, who is black belt bound.

Acknowledgments

After writing the successful official guide for Smith Micro's Poser, the Smith Micro guys seemed to be rather happy about the results, so happy that when we presented the idea of covering yet another one of their products, they were quick to lend all the support that we needed. What a great team to work with.

Along with my praises for the Smith Micro personnel, I need to quickly extend my thanks and adulation to the Cengage Learning people. This is a great group that I'm happy to call my friends. First on the list for this project is Heather, who was quick to get the new version approved and under way.

Thanks also to the various editors who helped along the way, including Steve Yatson, who has shared his expertise as the technical editor.

I've also really enjoyed working closely with the team at Smith Micro. I got a chance to spend some time with them at Siggraph and was impressed with their dedication to the product and their willingness to address any issues or questions I had. Huge kudos to Steve Cooper, Steve Rathmann, and Steve Yatson.

A huge thanks also to Mike Clifton, the creator of Anime Studio, for his dedication and tireless work in helping the program to be what it is—an amazing piece of software. Thanks also to the various forum members on the Lost Marble site. Whenever I was stuck or lost, I could turn to the forum to find the answers I needed.

As always, I'd like to thank my family, without whose support I'd never get to the end of a book. To Angela, for her patience—maybe we should work on finishing the basement now, eh? To Eric, who needs my help to finish *Half Life* and *Metal Gear Solid*, and to Thomas, who is busy with karate practice and a great job on getting straight A's.

About the Author

Kelly L. Murdock has a background in engineering, specializing in computer graphics. This experience has led him to many interesting experiences, including using high-end CAD workstations for product design and analysis, working on several large-scale visualization projects, creating 3D models for several blockbuster movies, working as a freelance 3D artist and designer, 3D programming, and a chance to write several high-profile computer graphics books.

Kelly's book credits include eight editions of the *3ds Max Bible, Edgeloop Character Modeling for 3D Professionals Only, Poser 6, 7,* and *8 Revealed, LightWave 3D 8 Revealed, Maya 6* and *7 Revealed,* two editions of the *Illustrator Bible,* and four editions of the *Adobe Creative Suite Bible, Adobe Atmosphere Bible, gmax Bible, 3d Graphics and VRML 2.0, Master Visually HTML and XHTML,* and *JavaScript Visual Blueprints.*

In his spare time, Kelly enjoys playing basketball.

Author Vision

Anime Studio is an amazing piece of software, but it isn't overwhelming. Every feature is covered, providing you with a reference that you can use whenever you get stuck or to give you some creative inspiration.

Although there are many different ways to learn, I've tried to write a book that appeals to those who learn by doing as well as those who can read a concept and understand it. I'd love to hear your feedback, so sign up as a fan on my Facebook page and maybe see some of my latest work.

Thanks,

Kelly L. Murdock

Contents

Part IX   Rendering and Exporting

Part X   Extending Anime Studio with Scripts

Introduction

When I first took a look at Anime Studio, I thought, "Wow, this simple little vector package has a bones system." I'm quite familiar with using bones within a 3D package to animate 3D figures, but this was something unique to see them in a simple 2D package. As I've dug deeper into the package, I've noticed many other cool features that really separate this package from many others that are similar. No wonder it is getting a following.

If you're new to Anime Studio, don't be put off by the simplicity of the program. Beneath the slick, uncluttered interface is a powerful piece of software that can be used to create, render, and animate entire scenes and projects. The deeper you dig into the software, the more useful it becomes. My goal with this book is to help you discover the hidden gems in the software.

What You'll Find in This Book

Throughout the book, several special icons are used to highlight special comments, including **Notes**, **Cautions**, and **Tips**. These comments provide a way to present special information to you the reader. Be sure to watch for them. Since this is a second edition, I've also included a **New Feature** element throughout the book, along with a section on the following page that highlights all the features that are new to this edition.

Along with every discussed task are several step-by-step tutorials that show you a simplified example of the discussed topic. Each of these examples was created to be extremely simple to keep the number of steps to a minimum. I've added some variety here and there, but none of these examples should be overwhelming (or will win a prize at the county fair). The real creative work is up to you, but these examples will be enough to show you how to use a feature and give you some practice.

Each tutorial example begins from the default setting that appears when the program is first loaded, but you don't need to close and reopen the software to begin each example; just select the File, New menu command, and you'll be ready to go. For some of the more complex examples, the steps instruct you to open an example file. You can access every file that is used in the tutorial examples from the book's attached DVD, or you can use your own files as a beginning point.

Also included with the DVD files are the final saved files from each example. These are available for you to compare with your own work to learn where you might have made a mistake.

Who This Book Is For

Anime Studio isn't a huge software package, but some of its features can be a little tricky. This book is really intended for those who are new to animation and to the software. I've tried to cover the software completely, so all the default features are covered. If you aren't new to Anime Studio, but are new to the latest version, then you'll be happy to know that I've highlighted the new features, making them easy to find and learn.

How This Book Is Organized

This book has been organized in a manner that is similar to the common Anime Studio workflow, starting with the simpler layer types and working up to the more complex ones. Along the way, I've elected to present a larger number of smaller, focused chapters than fewer larger, complex chapters. The result of this approach is some smaller chapters that make it easier to find what you're looking for.

The DVD also includes several example animation pieces provided by several professionals who use Anime Studio in their production pipelines. These examples show at a professional level what is possible with the software, and they are an inspiration to me.

Companion Web Site Downloads

You may download the companion Web site files from www.courseptr.com/downloads. You may also download Appendix A, "Anime Studio Keyboard Shortcuts" from the Web site.

DVD Downloads

If you purchased an ebook version of this book, and the book had a companion DVD, we will mail you a copy of the disc. Please send ptrsupplements@cengage.com the title of the book, the ISBN, your name, address, and phone number. Thank you.

What's New with Anime Studio 6

If you're familiar with previous versions of Anime Studio, then you'll want to see a quick list of the new features. Here are the features new to version 6, as well as a cross-reference to each individual chapter that covers these features in more detail.

> **Note**
>
> Several of these new features are only available within Anime Studio Pro.

Interface Palettes

The interface has been modified to allow all control palettes to be either floating or docked. Floating palettes can be made into docked palettes using the Window menu. You can also resize the docked palettes by dragging on the border between palettes. More on the interface changes is covered in Chapter 2, "Exploring the Anime Studio Interface."

Consolidated Style Palette

The Style palette has been consolidated to display only the main features, including a 24-bit color palette. An expanded set of controls is available by clicking the Advanced button at the bottom of the Style palette. The Style palette changes are covered in Chapter 15, "Setting Object Strokes."

Hiding Shapes

Menu options to Hide Shape and Show All Shapes have been added to the Draw menu. This allows you to quickly hide those shapes that are in the way of your current work. The ability to hide shapes is covered in Chapter 13, "Filling Shapes and Using Strokes."

Library Palette

The new Library palette opens a window displaying all the content included with the default install. Each piece of content is displayed as a thumbnail, making it easy to pick the correct item. The new Library palette is covered in Chapter 6, "Working with the Content Library."

Auto Shading

Within the Layer Settings dialog box is an option to set an Auto Shading Radius. By entering a value, you can quickly shade all objects on the layer. This provides an easy way to get great shading results that are consistent. You can learn more about this feature in Chapter 4, "Working with Layers."

Layers Palette Improvements

The Layers palette has been improved in several ways. The palette now allows multiple layers to be selected at once. This enables all selected layers to be moved or rotated together. You can also reorder multiple layers in one move. To the right of the selected layer is an arrow icon that you can click to immediately access a pop-up menu of layer settings. The changes to the Layers palette are covered in Chapter 4, "Working with Layers."

Scatter Brush

The Tools palette includes a new Scatter Brush used to spread an existing shape around the scene as you paint. You can randomly set the orientation, spacing, and color of the objects. More on the Scatter Brush is covered in Chapter 14, "Using the Scatter Brush."

Improved Gradients and Texture Placement

The Gradient style effect has been improved to allow you to control the number of color stops and transitions. You can also interactively control the placement, orientation, and scale of applied gradient fills. This same interactive placement can also be used to control texture placement. More of new gradients and texture placement is presented in Chapter 13, "Filling Shapes and Using Strokes."

Eyedropper Tool and Brush Improvements

For quickly reusing existing fill and stroke colors, you can use the new Eyedropper tool. Brushes are no longer limited to 128-pixel wide grayscale brushes. Anime Studio 6 supports color brushes up to 512 pixels wide. The Eyedropper tool and brush improvements are both presented in Chapter 13, "Filling Shapes and Using Strokes."

Multitrack Audio Sequencer

The Timeline palette includes a new Sequencer tab that allows multiple sound effect and music track files to be loaded and manipulated into a single scene. The Sequencer also enables multiple video tracks to be loaded. This powerful new feature is covered in Chapter 19, "Working with Sound."

Video Tracking

Loaded background video files can be motion tracked so that a set of bones closely follows the background video. This innovative new feature can make animating a character based on a video easy and quick. This feature is covered in Chapter 28, "Using Video Tracking."

Timeline Palette Improvements

The Timeline palette has been simplified so that only the channels that are animated are displayed in the Timeline palette. Within the Animation Controls are two new buttons for navigating between the previous and next keyframes. Anime Studio 6 also allows nonlinear animation. These improvements to the Timeline palette are covered in Chapter 17, "Working with the Timeline."

Lip-Sync

The lip-sync features in Anime Studio 6 allow lip-syncing by simply dragging resources from the Library and aligning them with the loaded lip-sync file. These features are covered in Chapter 20, "Using Lip-Sync."

Morphing

Morphing between established morph targets is possible in Anime Studio 6. These features are covered in Chapter 21, "Morphing Objects and Using Actions."

Upload to YouTube

Animated scenes can be loaded and posted directly on YouTube. This feature is covered in Chapter 34, "Exporting to the Web."

Other Improvements

In addition to the major new features listed above, Anime Studio 6 also includes a number of minor improvements such as the following:

- **New Resolution Presets:** The Project Settings dialog box includes several new resolution presets, including NTSC and PAL Widescreen, HDTV 1080p, VGA, and YouTube.

- **Construction Curves toggle:** A checkbox to display or hide the Construction Curves has been added to the bottom of the Document Window.

- **Use Spacebar for Panning:** Holding down the Spacebar allows the content in the Document Window to be panned.

- **Animatable Shape Effects:** All shape effects, including gradients and halos, can be animated.

- **Simplified Timeline channels:** Only channels that are animated are displayed in the Timeline palette.

- **Copy and paste bones:** Selected bones can be copied and pasted between layers using the Edit, Copy and Edit, Paste menu commands.

- **HD Video import and export:** HD video can now be imported into Anime Studio 6. The software can also export using this format.

- **Lua 5.1 support:** Anime Studio 6 includes support for the latest version of Lua.

Part I

Getting Started with Anime Studio 6

Understanding Anime Studio 6

- ■ Highlighting the history of animation and anime
- ■ Discovering the history of Anime Studio
- ■ Understanding the product line
- ■ Knowing where Anime Studio is used

Welcome to *Anime Studio 6: The Smith Micro Official Guide*. If you're reading this book, you must have some interest in Anime Studio or in anime, or maybe your Auntie Maude just sent you this book for grins, and you have nothing better to do while you sit on the beach during your vacation. If the latter is your excuse, then put down this book immediately and go play in the water—vacations don't come around that often after all.

If you're reading this book because you want to create fun or complex animations to share with your friends or bosses, then try to stay awake as we slog through this introductory material or feel free to jump forward to whichever chapter looks interesting.

The History of Animation

The history of animation is a broad enough topic to be its own book, but it all boils down to those perceptive people who discovered that if you flip quickly through several similar images that have only small changes between each one, the resulting objects seem to come alive.

The historical discussion then turns to a number of interesting technical machines that make the process of flipping through frames easy and consistent. These early machines included odd-named wonders like the Magic Lantern, the Thaumatrope, the Zoetrope, the Praxinoscope, Thomas Edison's Kinetscope, and Louis Lumiere's Cinematograph. With these machines came an interest and a curiosity that took animation from novelty to a viable commercial form of entertainment.

One of the first animated pieces was *Humorous Phases of Funny Faces* by James Stuart Blackton in 1906. Other early animation films included *Fantasmagorie* (France) in 1908, *The Beautiful Lukanida* (Russia) in 1912, *El Apostol* (Argentina) in 1917, *Adventures of Prince Achmed* (Germany) in 1926, and *Snow White and the Seven Dwarfs* in 1937.

Early animation works included the works of Winsor McCay (*Gertie the Dinosaur*), Max Fleischer (*Koko the Clown*), Earl Hurd (*Bobby Bumps*), Otto Messmer (*Felix the Cat*), and John Bray (*Col. Heeza Liar*) in the 1920s. Throughout the 1930s and 1940s, Disney studios were introducing the world to Mickey Mouse, Donald Duck, and Silly Symphonies; Fleischer Studios were animating Betty Boop and Popeye; Walter Lantz was animating Woody Woodpecker; and the teams at Warner Bros. including Tex Avery, Friz Freleng, and Chuck Jones were releasing Looney Tunes shorts starring Bugs Bunny, Daffy Duck, and their friends. Tex Avery later moved on to do animations for MGM.

In the mid-1950s, cartoons moved to the television market with the help of Hanna-Barbera Productions, which produced the first animated television series. Other notable series included *Huckleberry Hound, The Flintstones, Scooby-Doo*, and *The Jetsons*.

Another popular form of animation was created using stop-motion techniques. This involved moving clay models slightly for each frame of the animation. This type of animation was used in the 1933 version of *King Kong* and was mastered by Ray Harryhausen for such films as *The 7th Voyage of Sinbad* and *Clash of the Titans*. Stop-motion animation is still alive and doing well thanks to Nick Park and Aardman Studios with their Wallace and Gromit characters and by Tim Burton on his *Nightmare Before Christmas* feature.

Traditional animation was accomplished by hand-drawing individual frames, but in the later 1980s, computers were being used to produce animation sequences. Advances in both software and hardware led to Pixar's 1995 release of *Toy Story*, the first feature-length computer-generated film. Today, most animated features are produced using computers.

While each animation studio developed its own unique style, many of the commercially viable animated forms were cartoons developed for younger audiences. As animated television series became more and more popular in the late 1960s and 1970s, most series were aired on Saturday mornings, an off-peak time slot that catered to children. But a different story was happening in other parts of the world. Japan, for instance, was embracing a new, unique, and edgy style (also developed in Japan) that was geared more for adult audiences. This genre is called *anime*.

The History of Anime

Anime is a Japanese export and represents a distinctive style of animation. In fact, the early masters of anime developed recognizable characters and an entire language of shots that make it easy to recognize.

One of the earliest examples of anime was *Astro Boy*, created by Osamu Tezuka in 1963. For many years, anime was popular in Japan as a key form of entertainment, but it had little impact in the West. Some of the early anime successes included *Lupin III* and *Mazinger Z*. Mazinger Z presented a common anime theme of *mecha*, based on mechanized robots and machines. Another early popular mecha-based anime feature was *Mobile Suit Gundam*.

In 1988, *Akira* was released, and it captured the attention of many viewers in the West who embraced this cutting-edge animation style that catered to adults. Another milestone feature was *Ghost in the Shell*, which included cyberpunk themes of futuristic technology.

One of the key anime directors today is Hayao Miyazaki, whose films *Princess Mononoke* and *Spirited Away* have set box-office records in Japan and have earned favorable reviews and an Academy Award in 2003. Other notable anime works include *Sailor Moon, Dragonball Z, Ranma 1/2, Neon Genesis Evangelion,* and *Cowboy Bebop*.

Today most anime feature films are released in Japan along with the West, and many of the older anime features have been translated to English and many other languages.

The History of Anime Studio

Anime Studio is simply a software package that enables users to animate characters in 2D using advanced control mechanisms, such as bones, and special features, such as particles. It supports the integration of 3D objects and even allows the camera to be transformed in 3D space. These features make it a good choice for studios and individuals who want to animate scenes in the anime style. But the product is in no way limited to this style. It is simply a tool that can quickly and easily animate scenes, regardless of your chosen style.

Anime Studio, the software, started out as a simple product named *Moho* that was created by a single developer, the amazing Mike Clifton. This product went through several revisions until it was acquired by e frontier in 2006 and named Anime Studio. e frontier had also acquired several other impressive packages, including Shade, Poser, and an interesting package called *Manga Studio*. In 2008, Anime Studio was acquired by Smith Micro along with several other e frontier products.

Manga Studio is a software package that enables users to compose, ink, and publish manga-style cartoons, another Japanese export. Along with the Manga Studio package came a relationship with TokyoPop, a popular manga publisher in Japan. With the connection between e frontier and TokyoPop came the idea to rename Moho as Anime Studio and to push it as the premiere animation tool for creating anime-style animations.

The success of Anime Studio has been outstanding, with units flying off the shelves. Smith Micro has promised continued support and development of the product with new features.

Understanding the Product Line

Currently, Anime Studio is available in two different versions: a beginning-level product named simply *Anime Studio* and a professional-level version called *Anime Studio Pro*. The current version is release 6.

Note

All features new to the latest version are summarized in Appendix A, "What's New with Anime Studio 6."

Anime Studio Debut

The Anime Studio Debut product, shown in Figure 1.1, includes several drawing tools; the capability to work with layers, fills, and outlines; the capability to control vectors and images using bones; camera controls; and basic animation capabilities. It also allows the importing of JPEG, BMP, PSD, Targa, and PNG image files and the ability to export animations to the SWF, YouTube, AVI, and QuickTime formats.

Anime Studio Pro

Anime Studio Pro, shown in Figure 1.2, offers all the tools and features found in the base package plus additional tools, such as Arrow, Noise, and Magnet. It also offers the capability to load and manipulate 3D objects and transform cameras in 3D space. Other advanced features include particle layers, styles, and pattern brushes, support for importing Illustrator and EPS files and HD Video, and a Lua-based scripting engine for writing custom scripts.

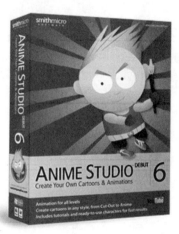

Figure 1.1
Anime Studio Debut.

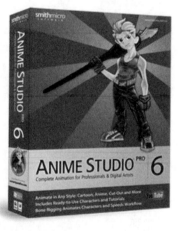

Figure 1.2
Anime Studio Pro.

Trial Version

Trial versions of Anime Studio Debut and Anime Studio Pro are freely available from the Smith Micro Web site. The trial version of Anime Studio Debut is located at http://my.smithmicro.com/downloads/index.html and the trial version of Anime Studio Pro is located at http://my.smithmicro.com/win/anime/trial.html for Windows and http://my.smithmicro.com/mac/anime/trial.html for Mac. These trial versions will run for 30 days.

The limitations of the trial version are that it cannot import any external files or export animations. However, you can save your files and access them again with a licensed version of the software.

An Anime Studio license can be purchased online at the Smith Micro Web site at http://store.smithmicro.com. Upgrades between previous versions and the Debut and Pro versions are also available.

Differences Between the Debut Package and the Pro Package

If you break down the feature sets of the base and Pro packages into a table, it looks like Table 1.1.

Table 1.1   Debut Versus Pro Features

Feature Category	Anime Studio Debut Feature List	Anime Studio Pro Feature List (includes all of the Anime Studio Debut features plus the following)
Drawing Tools:	Insert Text, Select Points, Translate Points, Scale Points, Rotate Points, Add Point, Scatter Brush, Delete Edge, Curvature, Freehand, Draw Shape (rectangle, oval, triangles, stars, spirals)	Shear Points X and Y, Perspective Points H and V, Bend Points H and V, Noise, Magnet tool
Fill and Style Tools:	Select Shape, Create Shape, Paint Bucket, Delete Shape, Eyedropper, Line Width, Hide Edge	
Bone Tools:	Select Bone, Translate Bone, Scale Bone, Rotate Bone, Add Bone, Reparent Bone, Bone Strength, Manipulate Bone, Bind Layer, Bind Points, Offset Bone	
Layer Tools:	Set Origin, Translate Layer, Scale Layer, Rotate Layer Z, Switch Layer, Video Tracking (Three Points)	Rotate Layer X and Y, Shear Layer X and Y, Particle Layer, Video Tracking (Unlimited Points)

cont.

Table 1.1   Debut Versus Pro Features *(continued)*

Feature Category	Anime Studio Debut Feature List	Anime Studio Pro Feature List (includes all of the Anime Studio Debut features plus the following)
Layer Types:	Vector, Image, Bone, Switch, Audio	Group, Particle, 3D, Note
Camera and Workspace Tools:	Track Camera, Zoom Camera, Roll Camera, Pan/Tilt Camera, Pan Workspace, Zoom Workspace, Preferences, Edit Dimensions, Background Color	Rotate Workspace, Orbit Workspace, Editor and GUI Color Preferences, Tracing Image, Depth of Field, 3D Camera, Stereo Rendering, Sort Layers by Depth, Sort by True Distance, Noise Grain, Grid, Grid Size, Multiple Pane View, Display Quality
Export Options:	Save Project Settings, Edit Dimensions, Background Color, Max of 768 by 768 Resolution	Max of 9000 by 9000 Resolution
Animation Features:	Keyframes, Playback Controls, Animation Channels, Ruler, Blend Morph Targets, Max of 120 fps and 3000 Frames	Onionskins, Graph Mode, Create and Blend Morph Targets, Unlimited Frames
Audio and Lip Sync:	Sequencer with 2 Audio/1 Video Track, Amplitude Only Lip Sync	Multi-track Audio and Video Sequencer, Production Lip Sync Library
Action and Scripting:		Store, Edit, and Delete Reusable Animation, Pre-built Scripts
Content Library:	Categorized Content	User Samples, 3D Objects
Import Formats:	JPEG, BMP, PSD, PNG, Targa, WAV, AIFF, QuickTime (MOV), AVI, Moho	Illustrator (AI), EPS, 3D Objects (OBJ), HD Video
Export Formats:	QuickTime (MOV), AVI, SWF, YouTube Upload	JPEG, BMP, PSD, PNG, Targa, Sequential Image Export, Batch Movie Export, HD Video

Where Is Anime Studio Used?

Anime Studio is used in many different places. Some studios have adopted it as the tool of choice for producing online animation content for the Web, while other studios are using it in production environments. Another huge group of users is hobbyists who want to create quick and delightful animations for entertaining friends and associates. Some examples of how Anime Studio animations are used can be found by looking through the User Samples section in the online Content Library.

Anime Studio on the Web

Because of the small file sizes that result from working with vectors, it is no surprise that Anime Studio animations are common on the Web. Anime Studio has the capability to export animations to the Flash format and to upload animations directly to YouTube and Facebook. Anime Studio is used frequently to create the Jib-Jab type animations that are popular on the Web.

Anime Studio in Email

Exported Anime Studio animation files can be attached easily to an email. When received, the animation can be played in a Flash player, which is integrated seamlessly into most email clients.

Anime Studio on CD and DVD

Ambitious Anime Studio projects can be saved to CD or DVD to be used as cut scenes for training materials, presentations, and games.

Anime Studio in Production

Some studios use Anime Studio Pro in their production pipeline to create movies, commercials, and other commercial products. The product is only limited by the creativity of the artists who use it. For a great example of this type of work, check out Freakish Kid at http://freakishkid.com.

Chapter Summary

This chapter was a quick introduction to Anime Studio, showing its history and product breakdown. The chapter included a brief intro to animation and anime and showed the legacy of work that Anime Studio is extending. The chapter also highlighted a list of the features found in the Debut and Pro versions. Throughout the book, all features of both the Debut and Pro versions are covered, and if the feature is exclusive to the Pro version, a note identifies it as such.

In the next chapter, we'll look into the interface used to work with Anime Studio.

2

Exploring the Anime Studio Interface

- ▧ Learning the interface elements
- ▧ Interacting with the interface
- ▧ Using keyboard shortcuts
- ▧ Hiding and viewing interface windows
- ▧ Rearranging the interface

Before you can use Anime Studio effectively, you need to learn to use its interface. The Anime Studio interface is composed of a series of docked palettes. These individual palettes can be undocked and moved around the interface to where you need them to be. It feels a lot like an Adobe product in that it has plenty of palettes and windows. If you're familiar with any of the Adobe products, then you should feel right at home with the Anime Studio interface. But even if you are comfortable with the interface, there are some "under the hood" details that will help you use the software even more efficiently if you take the time to learn them.

The key to being efficient in the interface is to realize that there are several ways to accomplish a task. You could select a menu item, click a toolbar icon, or use a keyboard shortcut. All of these methods would accomplish the same task, but which is the fastest method depends on your preference. Often, keyboard shortcuts are the fastest method, but they take some learning to master.

Learning the Interface Elements

The entire interface is composed of the main window and four docked tool palettes. Each palette surrounds the main window. You can undock any of the palettes from the interface and move it by clicking and dragging its title bar. You can also resize most of the palettes, with the exception of the Tools palette, by dragging on either its border edge or one of its corners (it works for either docked or floating palettes).

The Main Window

All the drawing and creative work is displayed in the main window, also called the *working area*, as shown in Figure 2.1. There are multiple configuration options available for the main window, including the ability to split the window into multiple panes and to change the display quality. You will learn more about configuring the main window in Chapter 3, "Managing and Configuring the Workspace."

Title bar   *Menu bar*   *Status bar*   *Tool Options bar*   *Working area*

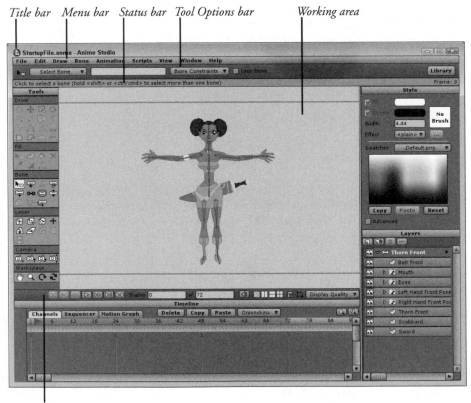

Figure 2.1
Anime Studio's main window.

Working area controls

> **Note**
>
> When Anime Studio is first started, a default file named *StartupFile* is opened auto-matically, rather than simply a blank page. This file is located in the Startup folder where Anime Studio is installed.

The main window also has several additional interface elements that control the entire interface, including the title bar, menu bar, tool options bar, and the work-ing area.

Title Bar

The title bar displays the name of the open project file. If a new file is created, then the title bar lists *Untitled.anme* until the file is saved. Clicking the Close icon in the upper-right corner of the main window will close the program, but it offers you a chance to save your current work before exiting.

> **Tip**
>
> For a Windows system, double-clicking the main window title bar will expand the main window to fill the entire screen. Double-clicking a second time returns it to its previous size and location. For a Macintosh system, double-clicking the main window title bar sends the application to the Doc and hides the application. Click the Doc icon to restore the window.

Menu Bar

Of the available interface palettes, only the main window has menus. These menu commands control the entire program. Many of the menu commands can be accessed in other ways, such as keyboard shortcuts.

Tool Options Bar

In addition to menus, the main window also includes a bar of tool options. These buttons, which typically include checkboxes and a pull-down menu, are located along the top of the main window directly below the menus. They provide quick access to relevant options and parameters for the current tool. The available options will change depending on the currently selected tool. Note that some tools (Delete Edge, Select Shape, Delete Shape, Eyedropper, Hide Edge, Manipulate Bone, and Bind Layer) have no options.

Tip

You can always identify the current tool by looking at its icon that appears at the left end of the Tool Options bar. Moving the mouse over this icon reveals its name in a tooltip.

At the right end of the Tool Options bar is a Library button used to access the Library palette. This button is always available, regardless of the selected tool.

Status Bar

Underneath the Tool Options bar is the status bar. This bar provides information on how to use certain commands and describes what the interface expects you to do next. If you get stuck, you can look to the status bar for helpful information. For example, when the Add Points tool (A) is selected, the status bar reads "Add a point (press <space> to weld, hold <alt> to disable auto-welding)."

Note

Within the Preferences dialog box is an option to display the status bar at the top of the window. If this option is disabled, then the status bar will appear at the bottom of the interface.

Working Area Controls

Along the bottom edge of the main window are controls for playing back animations and changing the layout and view of the working area. These controls are explained in more detail in Chapter 3, "Managing and Configuring the Workspace."

Tools Palette

The Tools palette, shown in Figure 2.2, includes a set of grouped buttons that execute specific tasks and work with the content in the main window. This palette is docked to the left side of the interface. The Tools palette for Windows doesn't include a Close icon when floating because it is intended to remain open at all times, but you can dock and undock the Tools palette with the Window, Tools menu.

Figure 2.2
The Tools palette divides all the tool buttons into different groups.

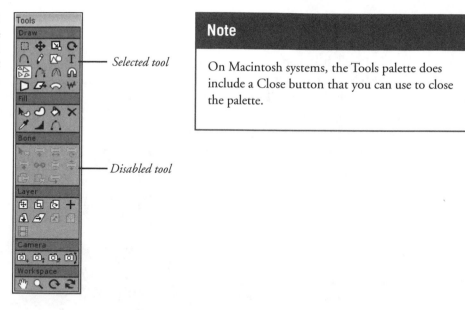

Selected tool

Disabled tool

Note

On Macintosh systems, the Tools palette does include a Close button that you can use to close the palette.

The tools in the Tools palette are divided into several groups: Draw, Fill, Bone, Layer, Camera, and Workspace. The tools within these groups are covered in their respective chapters that follow. The active tool is easy to identify because it is highlighted yellow in the Tools palette.

Most tools have an associated keyboard shortcut that can be used to select the tool quickly. The tool's name and its shortcut are displayed in a tooltip if you move the cursor over the top of the tool button.

As you select different objects in the main window or as you select one of the different layers, some tools are disabled and others are enabled. Only those tools that can be selected and used on the current object or layer are enabled. Enabled tools can be selected by clicking them with either the left or right mouse button.

Tip

Anime Studio lets you edit and modify the tools used in the Tools palette and even add your own scripted tools. This advanced feature is covered in Chapter 36, "Customizing the Interface."

Style Palette

The Style palette, shown in Figure 2.3, includes options for setting the Fill and Stroke colors, width, and effect for the selected shape. It is docked to the upper-right corner of the interface. The Style palette can be docked and undocked using the Window, Style menu or the Ctrl/Cmd+] keyboard shortcut. Much of the Style palette is covered in Chapter 15, "Setting Object Style."

Figure 2.3
The Style palette holds the object's fill, outline, and colors.

Layers Palette

The Layers palette, shown in Figure 2.4, displays a list of the available layers in the current project. It is docked in the lower right-hand corner of the interface. It provides an easy way to quickly select from the available layers. You can also hide and unhide layers with a single click. The Layers palette can be docked and undocked with the Window, Layers menu. A general discussion of layers is presented in Chapter 4, "Working with Layers."

Figure 2.4
The Layers palette lists all the available layers.

Timeline Palette

The Timeline palette, shown in Figure 2.5, includes the controls used to animate objects. The animation keyframes are displayed as dots on the Timeline palette, and the number of frames runs along the top of the palette. The Timeline palette is docked along the bottom edge of the interface. The Timeline palette is covered in detail in Chapter 17, "Working with the Timeline." The Timeline palette can be docked and undocked using the Window, Timeline menu or the Ctrl/Cmd+[keyboard shortcut.

> **Note**
>
> The docked Timeline palette is always reduced in size when the Layers palette is docked, but the docked Timeline palette will run across the entire bottom interface edge when the Layers palette is floating or closed, even if the Style palette is docked.

Figure 2.5
The Timeline palette holds all the animation keys.

Frame numbers   *Animation key*

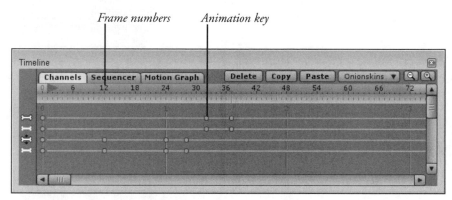

Actions Palette

The Actions palette, shown in Figure 2.6, records sequences of commands that can be replayed, and it is a huge time-saver if used correctly. (Actions are covered in more detail in Chapter 21, "Morphing Objects and Using Actions.") All palettes are visible by default when Anime Studio is started, with the exception of the Actions palette. The Actions palette is opened and closed using the Window, Actions menu or the Ctrl/Cmd+K keyboard shortcut.

Figure 2.6
The Actions palette automates repetitive tasks.

> **Note**
>
> The Actions palette is only available in Anime Studio Pro.

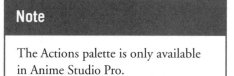

Library Palette

The Library palette, shown in Figure 2.7, displays folders full of content that is ready to use in Anime Studio. Double-clicking a folder will open it to reveal thumbnails of content contained therein. Double-clicking a piece of content loads it into the interface. The Library palette is opened and closed using the Library button at the right end of the Tool Options bar. You can also open and close the Library palette with the Window, Library menu, or the Ctrl/Cmd+Shift+L keyboard shortcut. You can learn more about using the Library palette in Chapter 6, "Working with the Content Library."

New Feature

The Library palette is new to Anime Studio 6.

> **Note**
>
> The Library palette (and the Actions palette) cannot be docked to the main interface, and it is always floating.

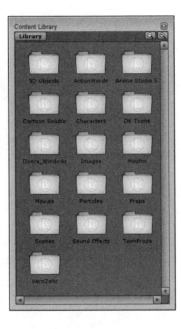

Figure 2.7
The Library palette contains content that may be used within Anime Studio.

Interacting with the Interface

If you use any other computer programs, then you're probably familiar with using menus and the mouse. Anime Studio uses the standard paradigm for interacting with the interface, but there are some interface controls that may be new to you.

Accessing Tooltips

If you ever get confused trying to identify a specific tool or button in the interface, you can use the available tooltips to discover a button's name. Tooltips are text bubbles, as shown in Figure 2.8, that appear when you hold the mouse cursor still over the top of a button; they reveal the button's name and keyboard shortcut, if it has one. If the tooltips get annoying after a while, that's just too bad, as there is currently no way to disable them.

Using Keyboard Shortcuts

Many, but not all, commands have keyboard shortcuts that allow you to execute specific commands by pressing a keyboard key. These shortcuts provide direct access to a tool, view, or command. On menus, keyboard shortcuts are listed to the right of the menu command, and tools with keyboard shortcuts list them in the tooltip. You can find a comprehensive list of keyboard shortcuts in Appendix B, "Anime Studio Keyboard Shortcuts," which is located online at www.courseptr.com/downloads.

Floating Palettes

Most of the default palettes are docked to the interface by default, but you can use the Window menu to make several palettes into floating palettes. Simply select the palette from the Window menu or use its keyboard shortcut and the palette will float free of the interface.

Caution

Each of the docked palettes has its own place, and you cannot change where each palette is docked.

Figure 2.8
Tooltips reveal the button's name.

Tooltip

Tip

Learning to use keyboard shortcuts will enable you to work much quicker than having to repeatedly move the mouse to a specific interface palette or menu.

Floating palettes can be positioned anywhere on the desktop by dragging their title bar. Floating palettes are marked by a checkbox to the left of their name in the Window menu. Selecting the palette again in the Window menu will dock it to the interface again.

New Feature

The capability of palettes to float free of the interface is new to Anime Studio 6.

Hiding and Viewing Interface Windows

Most of the palette windows can be closed or hidden when floating by clicking the Close icon located in the upper-right corner on Windows systems or in the upper-left corner on Macintosh systems. The Tools palette is the only one that cannot be hidden. Hidden palettes can be reopened using the Window menu. Figure 2.9 shows the main window after all palettes have been made into floating palettes.

> **Note**
>
> Clicking the Close icon button in the main window exits the program.

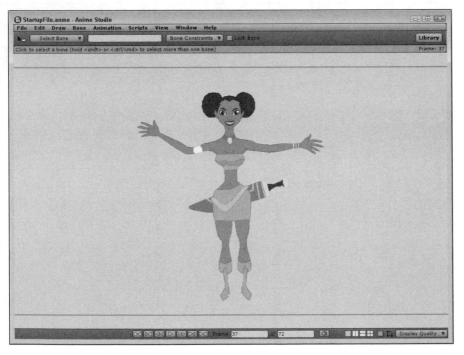

Figure 2.9
If all palettes are floating, then the main window is maximized.

Rearranging the Interface

If you drag a floating palette's title bar, you can relocate the selected palette to a new location. You can resize some of the floating palettes by dragging their edges or corners. You can also resize docked palettes by dragging the edges between adjacent palettes. Docked palettes are maximized automatically to fill the current screen space. This will reduce the size of the adjacent palette. Figure 2.10 shows the interface with increased Style and Layers palettes and a decreased Timeline palette.

> ### Note
>
> All floating palettes—including the main window—can be resized, except for the Tools and Style palettes.

Figure 2.10
Docked palettes can be resized.

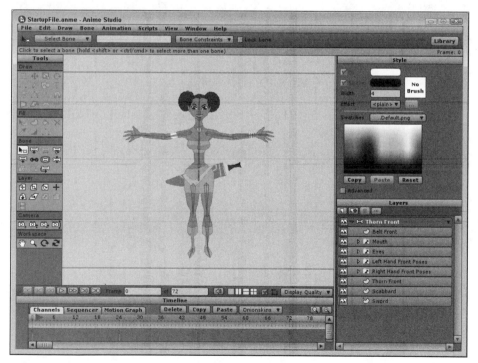

New Feature

The ability to resize docked palettes is new to Anime Studio 6.

Using the Right-Click Mouse Button

In some locations within the Anime Studio interface, you can access a pop-up menu by clicking the right mouse button. For example, if you right-click the Timeline palette, you can add a keyframe or change a key's interpolation method. Right-clicking a switch layer lets you choose the active sublayer.

The right-click button is also helpful in certain situations. For example, in the Style palette, clicking a color swatch with the left mouse button selects the fill color and clicking a color swatch with the right mouse button selects the outline color. Dragging in the working area with the right mouse button will pan the view.

Using the Scroll Wheel

In addition to the right mouse button, you can also take advantage of the mouse's scroll wheel. Scrolling in the working area will zoom the view in and out. Scrolling the mouse wheel up and down in the Timeline palette moves the Time Slider back and forth between the different frames. Finally, scrolling through the Layers palette moves you up and down through the list of layers. You can also use the scroll wheel to change a parameter value quickly.

Changing Values with the Mouse

Whenever a parameter field is selected, you can type a new value by using the keyboard, but another way to alter the value is with the scroll wheel on the mouse. Scrolling up will increase the parameter value and scrolling down will decrease it. You can also change the parameter value by right-clicking and dragging with the mouse. Dragging to the right increases the value and dragging to the left decreases it.

Chapter Summary

This chapter introduced the Anime Studio interface, including the various palettes and the main window. It also explained how to work with the interface, including a number of tricks for making you work more efficiently.

The next chapter explores the main window in more detail and shows how it can be configured.

3

Managing and Configuring the Workspace

- Creating a new project
- Opening and saving projects
- Panning and zooming the view
- Changing the working area
- Changing the display quality
- Loading a tracing image
- Changing project settings
- Setting preferences

Before jumping into the drawing tools, it is helpful to first learn how to open and save project files. It is also helpful to know how to configure and work with the main view window. Anime Studio includes multiple settings for controlling the layout, size, background color, and display quality. There are also tools for panning and zooming the working area, loading a tracing background image, and setting preferences for the entire interface. All of these features will help configure the interface and your projects to meet your needs.

Creating a New Project

New projects are created using the File, New menu command (Ctrl/Cmd+N). This opens a blank project in the main window. Anime Studio Pro allows only one project to be open at a time, but you can start multiple copies of Anime Studio if you want to work with multiple projects simultaneously. If your current file hasn't been saved, then a warning dialog box appears asking if you want to save the current project before opening a blank project.

> **Tip**
>
> When Anime Studio is first started, the StartupFile.anme project file, located in the Startup folder, is automatically loaded by default. If you are using a template as a starting point for your projects, you can overwrite this startup file to make the new template appear by default.

Opening and Saving Projects

The File, Open menu command (Ctrl/Cmd+O) opens a file dialog box, shown in Figure 3.1, where you can choose the project file to open. All Anime Studio files are saved using the .ANME file extension. At the bottom of the file dialog box is a File Name drop-down list. This list holds all the recently opened files for quick retrieval.

> **Tip**
>
> The file dialog box is resizable. If you have a folder containing a large number of files, then making the dialog box larger will make it easier to locate and select files to open.

You can also open a saved file by dragging it from the Finder or from Windows Explorer and dropping it on the working area.

If you select the File, Close menu command (Ctrl/Cmd+W), the current project file will be closed, and the working area will appear dark.

Figure 3.1
Open dialog box.

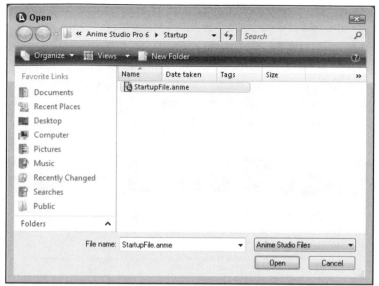

The File, Save menu command (Ctrl/Cmd+S) saves the current project automatically. If the project hasn't been saved yet, a file dialog box appears in which you can specify a location and a name for the project file. New projects are named Untitled.anme until they are given a name. The file name is listed on the title bar of the current window. If the file has already been saved, then you can use the File, Save As menu command to save the file with the different name.

If you decide to close the current project or exit Anime Studio, then a warning dialog box, shown in Figure 3.2, appears if the file has changes that have not yet been saved. Clicking the Yes button saves the current changes or opens the file dialog box where you can save the current project. Clicking the No button closes the project or exits the program without saving the recent changes; clicking the Cancel button returns to the program and the file remains open.

Figure 3.2
Save changes warning
dialog box.

Working with the Working Area

When a new working area is loaded, two crossing arrows are displayed at the center of the area. These arrows are called the *origin*, as shown in Figure 3.3, and they denote the center of the working area. It is about the origin that the current layer is scaled and rotated. All coordinate values are also measured from the origin. The Layer category in the Tools palette includes a tool for moving the origin.

Tip

The area outside of the visible region can be used as a holding area for objects that aren't currently in the scene. Objects outside of this region are not rendered.

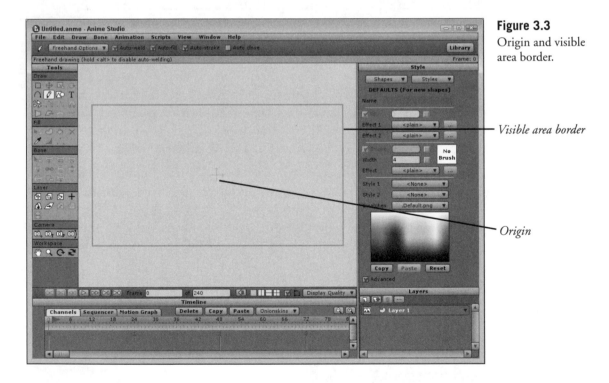

Figure 3.3
Origin and visible area border.

Visible area border

Origin

The working area also includes a blue rectangle that marks the edges of the visible region. Only objects contained within this visible region are visible in the final animation. You can change the size of the visible region using the File, Project Settings dialog box, which is covered later in this chapter.

You can hide the entire area and all objects outside of the visible region using the View, Show Output Only menu command (Ctrl/Cmd+J).

Navigating the Workspace

Even though the visible area is the only area that is rendered for the final output, you can use the entire working area for positioning and working with your objects. In order to access the area beyond the visible region, you'll need to pan or zoom the workspace. The Tools palette includes four tools in the Workspace category, listed in Figure 3.4, for navigating the working area.

Figure 3.4
Workspace tools.

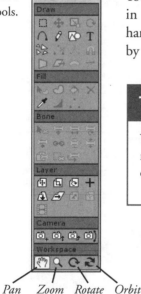

Pan   Zoom   Rotate   Orbit

You can pan the working area using the Pan tool, which is found in the Workspace category of the Tools palette (it looks like a hand). Selecting the Pan tool lets you reposition the visible region by dragging with the left mouse button.

> **Tip**
>
> You can also pan the working area by dragging with the right mouse button, regardless of which tool is selected, or by holding down the Spacebar while dragging the mouse.

The Zoom tool (which looks like a magnifying glass) is used to zoom in and out of the working area by dragging the left mouse button left and right. This tool is located next to the Pan tool in the Workspace region of the Tools palette. The Zoom tool always zooms in straight to the center of the main window, regardless of where your mouse cursor is located. To zoom in on a particular object, you should first pan the working area so that the object is located in the center of the main window before zooming

You can control the exact place where the zoom takes place by dragging over the area that you want to zoom on if you enable the Zoom with Drag Box option in the Preferences dialog box. Once enabled, you can drag to specify a rectangular region to zoom in on.

Tip

You can also zoom in and out of the working area by dragging with the right mouse button while holding down the Shift key or by rolling the mouse scroll wheel back and forth. These shortcuts for zooming will work no matter which tool is selected.

Tip

Being able to pan and zoom with the mouse are the first shortcuts that you should memorize. They will allow you to quickly navigate the working area as you draw and work with objects.

Although not as important as panning and zooming, the Rotate Workspace tool (8) lets you spin the entire working area about the center of the main window. If you find it easier to draw vertical lines by dragging the mouse side to side, then you can rotate the working area to do this. Figure 3.5 shows a scene rotated to the side.

Tip

The shortcut for the Rotate tool is to hold down the Ctrl/Cmd key while dragging with the right mouse button. This shortcut works regardless of the selected tool.

The Orbit Workspace tool (9) lets you rotate the working area into 3D space causing the flat 2D drawings to be tilted at an angle, as shown in Figure 3.6. When rotating the project into 3D space, the visible region border disappears, but a blue view icon appears showing the 3D location of the default view. The Orbit tool can rotate 360 degrees about the center of the working area. The Orbit tool is especially helpful when you have some 3D objects added to your scene because it lets you rotate about them in 3D space seeing them from all angles. Holding down the Alt/Opt key while dragging with this tool moves the camera closer or farther from the center.

Figure 3.5
Rotated working area.

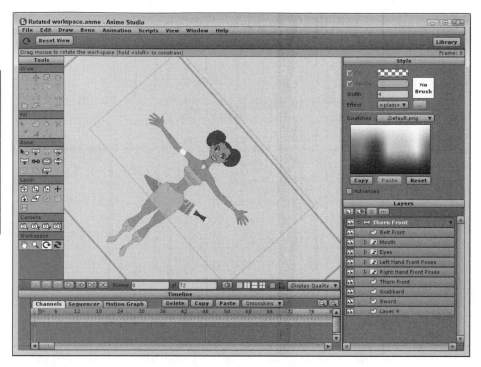

Figure 3.6
An orbited
working area.

Default view icon

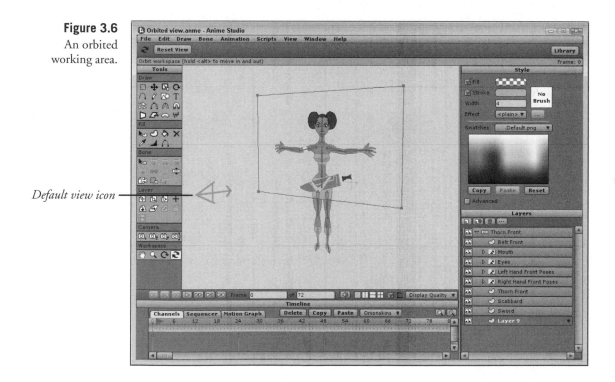

Resetting the View

When any of the Workspace tools are selected, you can return the view to its default size and position by clicking the Reset View button located in the Tool Options bar. This same feature can be accessed using the View, Reset menu command or by pressing the Escape or Home keyboard keys. This button centers the entire visible region within the main window.

Tip

The Home key is another good shortcut to learn because it lets you get back to the default view quickly.

Using Grids

The Enable Grid menu and the Grid Spacing menus are located in the View menu. Selecting the Enable Grid menu makes an infinite grid appear in the main window, as shown in Figure 3.7. You can change the density of the grid using the Grid Settings menu, which opens the Grid Settings dialog box, shown in Figure 3.8. The Grid Spacing value is measured in pixels.

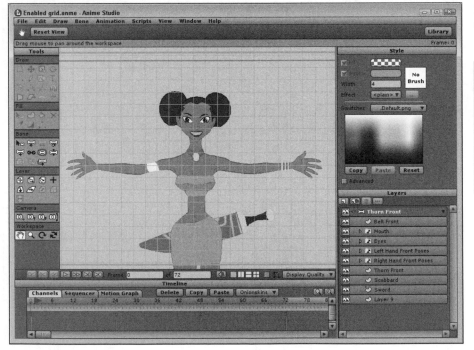

Figure 3.7
Grid enabled.

Note

Grids are only available in Anime Studio Pro.

Figure 3.8
Grid Spacing
dialog box.

Grids are great for visually lining up points when drawing on a vector layer, but they offer more flexibility than just visually lining up objects. If you begin drawing curves and shapes with the grid enabled, then any points you create will snap automatically to the closest grid point. This is convenient if you want to draw precise shapes such as perfect squares and circles. But it can be annoying if you want your objects to have a more freehand look to them.

Caution

If you zoom way in on a snapped point, you'll notice that the point doesn't line up exactly with the grid and that all curves are slightly bowed, but the spacing is consistent so all snapped points will be equally spaced and at the normal view these odd effects aren't noticeable.

You can disable grid snapping while keeping the grid active is with the View, Disable Grid Snapping menu command. This is a simple toggle command that can be on or off. When enabled, snapping to grid points is suspended.

If you have an existing freehand curve or object that you want to snap to the nearest grid point, you can use the Draw, Snap to Grid menu command (Ctrl/Cmd+G). If you've drawn a freehand curve, be cautious in using the Snap to Grid command because it could distort the curve you've drawn, as shown in Figure 3.9, which shows a smooth freehand letter on the left and the same letter on the right after the Snap to Grid command was used.

Figure 3.9
Snap to grid
distortion.

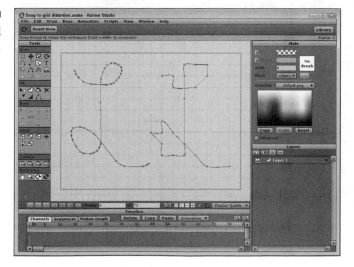

You should also be aware that the grid will move with the current layer. If you want to have a grid that doesn't move, which is useful as a visual reference when animating, then you can simply create your own grid on a lower layer or screen capture the grid and load it into an image layer. By placing a grid image or drawing on its own layer, it will stay stationary as the other layers move.

Enabling Multiple Views

To the right of the Mute Sound toggle at the bottom of the main window are four boxes. These icons are used to show multiple views of the scene in the working area. The enabled option is highlighted darker than the other options. The four options, from left to right, are as follows:

- ■ **Single View:** Displays a single view in the main window.
- ■ **Side by Side:** Displays two vertically stretched views in the main window.
- ■ **Over and Under:** Displays two horizontally stretched views in the main window.
- ■ **Four-way View:** Displays four views in the main window, one in each corner.

Figure 3.10 shows the main window divided into four separate views with the Four-way button. Each view can be configured and navigated independently of the others.

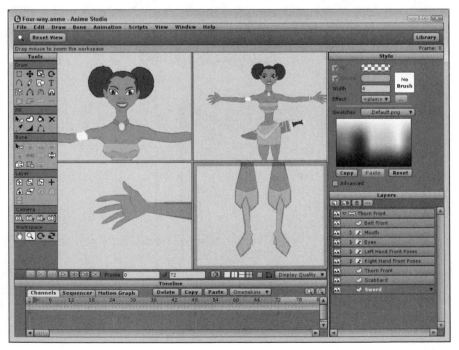

Figure 3.10
Four-way view.

> **Note**
>
> Multiple view layouts are only available in Anime Studio Pro.

When multiple views are available, the current view is indicated by the view that has a gray border around it. The display quality options, covered in the next section, only apply to the current view window. When an animation is played, it is played equally in all windows. The grid and the Fast Buffer display quality option also apply to all view windows.

Using multiple views is helpful when you are working in several different places at once. For example, if you have a character open, one view can focus on the head and another on the hands. The drawback to this is that if you switch back to a single view and then return to the four-window view, all of the zoomed views are reset each time you reopen the four-view window.

Displaying Paths

To the right of the Multiple View icons is a single checkbox for displaying or hiding Construction Curves, which are also known as *paths*. When enabled, all the lines and points for the selected object are displayed allowing you to move and edit them. When disabled, these paths are hidden showing only the object and its fill. Figure 3.11 shows the default project with paths enabled.

New Feature

The checkbox in the main view window to turn paths on and off is new to Anime Studio 6.

> **Note**
>
> Toggling paths on in the main window is the same as enabling the Paths option in the Display Quality pop-up dialog box.

Changing the Display Quality

At the bottom-right corner of the main window is a pop-up set of options for setting the display quality, as shown in Figure 3.12. As your scene gets more and more complex, using these options makes it easy to find and select specific elements, and it also speeds the redrawing of the scene.

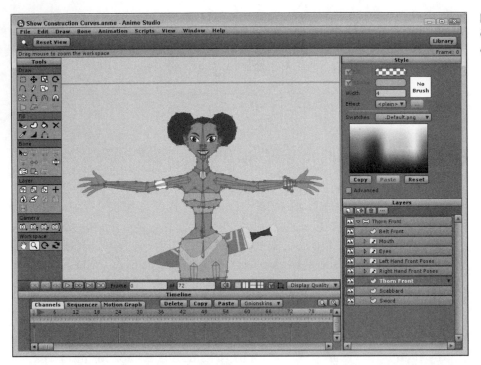

Figure 3.11
Construction Curves enabled.

Note

The Display Quality settings are only available in Anime Studio Pro.

Figure 3.12
Display Quality options.

The buttons on the left are presets that selectively enable several of the options on the right. The preset buttons include Wireframe, Low, Medium, High, and Preview. The Wireframe preset enables only the Paths option, the Low preset adds Fills and Images, the Medium preset shows all the images as smoothed and adds in Strokes and Masking, the High preset adds the Shape Effects, Transparency and Brush options, and the Preview preset hides the Paths option. This shows the scene without any editing controls, just as if the scene were output.

The available options in the Details section include:

- Fast Buffer: Enables the fast method for redrawing the scene, but note that choosing this option can result in inaccurate colors.

- Paths: Displays all points and curves for vector layers.

- Fills: Displays all the vector shape fill colors.

- Strokes: Displays the outlines for all vector layers.

- Shape Effects: Displays any applied effects added in the Style palette to a fill.

- Images: Displays all imported images.

- Smooth Images: Displays all images with alpha blending.

- Masking: Displays all masking effects.

- Transparency: Displays transparency.

- Brushes: Displays all brush effects applied to strokes.

- Antialiasing: Displays vectors without any jagged edges due to aliasing.

Figure 3.13 shows a character in the side-by-side view layout. The left view window has the Wireframe preset selected. This lets you work with the points, edges, and bones without any distractions. The right view window has the Preview preset selected, which shows the character without any bones.

> **Tip**
>
> You can close the Display Quality pop-up dialog box by right-clicking in the working area away from the dialog box.

> **Tip**
>
> Each layout pane can have its own Display Quality settings.

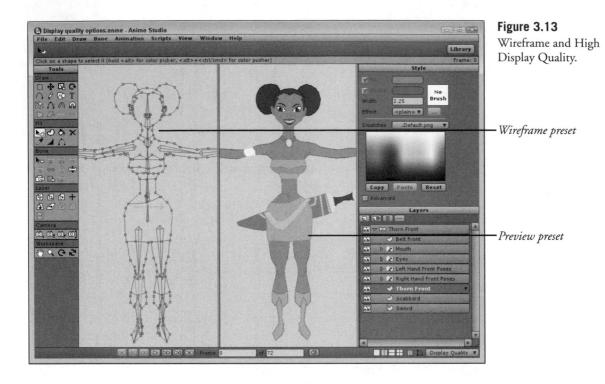

Figure 3.13
Wireframe and High
Display Quality.

The Display Quality buttons are helpful when your project becomes more complicated, but it can also cause trouble if you forget about your current settings. For example, if you disable the Paths option, then any points or curves you draw in the working area won't be visible even though they are created. This same problem happens if you draw a curve with the Add Points tool when the Preview display preset is selected.

Concerning the Transparency display option, this only applies to transparent vector objects. Image layers can be made transparent, but you'll need to render the project in order to see transparent images. You can render the project with the File, Preview menu command (Ctrl/Cmd+R). One work-around for this is to save the image using the .PNG format with transparency. Transparent .PNG images will appear transparent in Anime Studio if the Smooth Images display option is enabled.

Note

Many of these same Display Quality settings are available for individual layers using the Current Layer pop-up list.

Enabling Video Safe Zones

When an animation sequence is displayed on a television set, the pixels at the edges of the display can appear distorted, blurred, or even chopped off. It would be tragic to have the opening text of your animation that says, "To Everyone, Hello," end up with the last *o* chopped off, thus making your cheerful greeting into something offensive.

To prevent this, you need to keep any text or pixels you don't want to lose in the center of the screen. To know exactly which areas are safe, you can enable the View, Video Safe Zones (Ctrl/Cmd+F) menu command. This shows the safe areas as two light brown rectangles, as shown in Figure 3.14. The inner rectangle shows the safe area for titles and the outer rectangle shows the safe area for action.

> **Note**
>
> The Video Safe Zones feature is only available in Anime Studio Pro.

Figure 3.14
The light brown rectangles show the video safe zones.

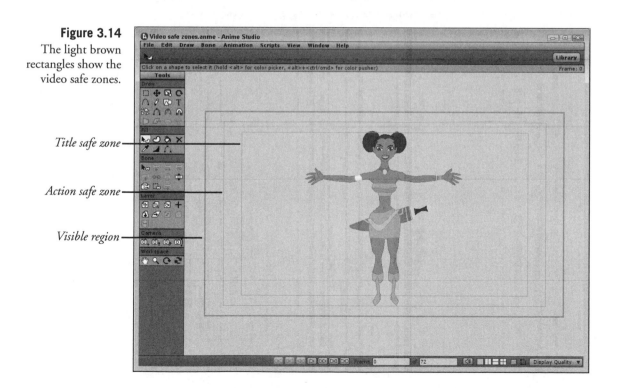

Title safe zone

Action safe zone

Visible region

Loading a Tracing Image

If you have a scanned, sketched image or a digital snapshot that you want to use as a template so that you can trace the artwork, you can use the View, Select Tracing Image (Ctrl/Cmd+Y) or the File, Import, Tracing Image menu command. This loads and centers the selected image within the main window and dims the image to allow you to trace it easily using the various drawing tools. Figure 3.15 shows an image loaded as a tracing image.

Note

The Tracing Image features are only available in Anime Studio Pro.

Tip

If you drag and drop an image onto the main window, a dialog box appears with options to make the image a Tracing Image, a New Image Layer, or to Cancel.

Figure 3.15
Tracing images are dimmed in the main window.

The background tracing image can be hidden using the View, Show Tracing Image (Ctrl/Cmd+U) menu command. This command toggles the tracing image on and off, but doesn't remove it from memory.

> **Caution**
>
> Tracing images are not saved with the project file. If you save, close, and then reopen a file, you'll need to add the tracing image again. Also, if you switch between different views using the layout buttons at the bottom of the main window, the tracing image is lost.

If you don't want to use the Tracing Image feature, then you can create your own tracing layer by adding a vector layer above the image you want to trace, creating a large white rectangle and setting its Opacity setting to 75% in the Layer Settings dialog box. You'll need to make sure that the Transparency setting in the Display Settings is enabled in order to see through the white rectangle. This method also gives you the option to move the image or the vector layer. It also gives you the chance to change the Opacity if the image is too dim.

Changing Project Settings

Each project file has configuration settings that you can change to customize the project. These settings are located in the Project Settings dialog box, shown in Figure 3.16, which is opened using the File, Project Settings (Ctrl/Cmd+Shift+P) menu command. Several of the settings, including Frame Rate and Depth of Field, will be covered in later chapters.

If you click the Save As Defaults button, the current settings are retained for all future projects. If you have a specific size of project that you work with, then setting that size and saving it as a default will make that size appear automatically when new projects are created. The factory defaults can be restored at any time using the Restore Defaults button.

Changing Output Dimensions

The Project Settings dialog box includes Width and Height settings that control the size of the blue visible region in the working area. This area also defines the size of the final output. The Presets drop-down list includes options for setting the output dimensions to NTSC D1, NTSC D1 Widescreen, PAL D1/DV, PAL D1/DV Widescreen, HDV/HDTV 720p, HDV 1080p, HDTV 1080p, VGA, Web, Web Widescreen, YouTube, and YouTube HD.

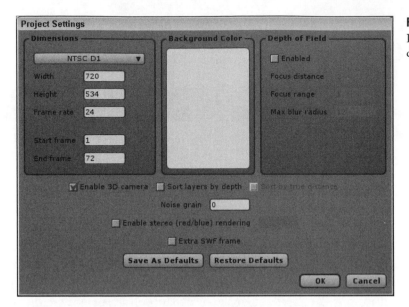

Figure 3.16
Project Settings
dialog box.

Note

The NTSC aspect ratio of 720 by 534 is common in the U.S. and the PAL standard of 768 by 576 is common in Europe. The Web standard is 320 by 240, while the VGA and YouTube standards are 640 by 480.

New Feature

Several resolution presets, including YouTube, are new to Anime Studio 6.

Be aware that Anime Studio is built to animate objects and is not intended to create output for printing. That is why you won't find a Dots-Per-Inch (dpi) setting. Anime Studio can only output images at the standard 72 dpi. However, if you want to create an image that will be printed at 300 dpi, you simply need to increase the image resolution to compensate for the higher dpi setting. You can then use an image editing package like Photoshop to convert the Anime Studio image to the correct size with the correct dpi.

> **Note**
>
> Anime Studio Debut has a maximum resolution setting of 788 by 768 pixels. Anime Studio Pro has a maximum resolution of 9000 by 9000.

Changing Background Color

If you click the Background Color swatch in the Project Settings dialog box, a Color Picker dialog box appears in which you can select a new color for the project background. However, don't expect this background color to appear within the main window. The background color is only displayed when you render the project with the File, Preview command (Ctrl/Cmd+R). You can change the interface background color using the Preferences dialog box, which is covered next. Figure 3.17 shows the default character rendered with a bright blue background.

Figure 3.17
Altered background color.

Setting Preferences

The Preferences dialog box, shown in Figure 3.18, is opened using the Edit, Preferences menu command. The Preferences are divided into four panels: Options, Video Uploads, Editor Colors, and GUI Colors. Most of these options are covered in later chapters.

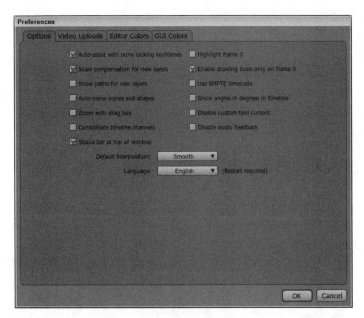

Figure 3.18
Preferences dialog box.

Changing Language

One setting in the Options panel of the Preferences dialog box that directly impacts the interface is the Language setting. This drop-down list lets you switch the interface language to English, German, or French and a restart of the program is required. Figure 3.19 shows the interface with the French language selected. Notice how the language change doesn't change the named layers, only the interface strings.

Note

The language preference was a feature added to Anime Studio 6.1. You can upgrade from Anime Studio 6.0 to 6.1 using the Smith Micro Web site.

Figure 3.19
French language
interface.

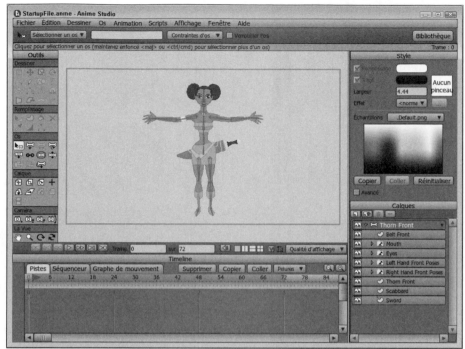

Changing UI Colors

The Editor Colors panel in the Preferences dialog box is used to change the default colors used to denote when an object is selected or inactive. It also shows the colors for the object, background, default fill, and edge. You can change any of these colors as needed by simply clicking the color swatch you want to change. Figure 3.20 shows the Editor Colors panel of the Preferences dialog box.

Tip

If you change the custom interface colors, be sure to use subtle colors for the background. Bright saturated colors will make it hard to see the details.

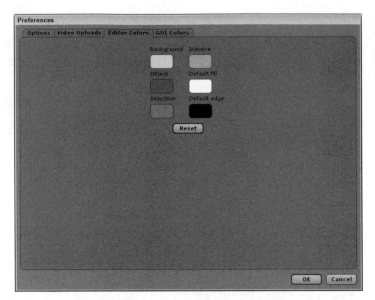

Figure 3.20
The Editor Colors panel in the Preferences dialog box.

The GUI Colors panel, shown in Figure 3.21, shows the colors for the various interface controls. For example, the default text color is black, but you can set it to whatever color you want. The Sample Widgets section shows what the various controls look like with the currently selected colors. The Reset button is used to restore the original colors.

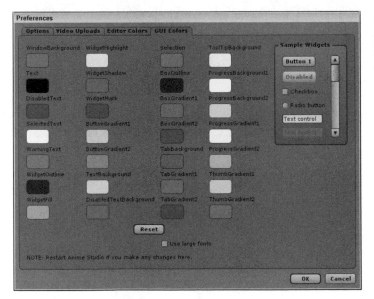

Figure 3.21
GUI Colors panel in the Preferences dialog box.

If you select the Use Large Fonts option, then all the interface text is displayed using a larger font size, which is helpful if you find the interface text hard to read.

Note

If you make any changes to the GUI Colors settings, you'll need to restart Anime Studio before the new colors are used.

Although Anime Studio by default uses a white background with black text, many users prefer to have the opposite contrast with a black background and white text. Using the GUI Colors panel, you can easily make this change. Figure 3.22 shows the interface with these types of colors. The interface also uses the Large Fonts option.

Figure 3.22
A project with custom interface colors.

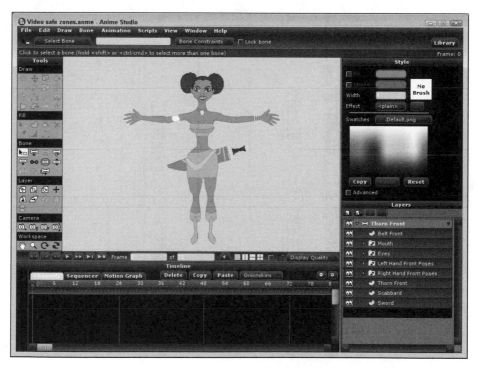

Chapter Summary

This chapter focused on the configuration details of the main window. You should now have a good grasp of the Anime Studio interface, including configuring the working area and setting project settings and preferences.

The next chapter tackles the key concept of layers.

4

Working with Layers

- Understanding layers
- Working with layers
- Using the layer settings
- Using the layer tools

Now that you've learned about the interface and are comfortable with where the various features and tools are located, you can learn how content in Anime Studio is organized. The big answer to this question is layers. All Anime Studio content is located on layers. Learning to create, manage, and work with effectively layers is the key to being able to create animations without the headaches.

Understanding Layers

Understanding layers is a key concept in Anime Studio. Every piece of content, whether it is vector lines, bones, or particles, is contained on a layer. There are multiple different types of layers and each type holds a different kind of content. Each layer type has an icon that identifies its type in the Layers palette. All layers are managed using the Layers palette, which is shown in Figure 4.1.

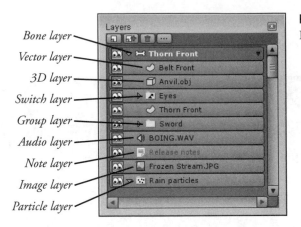

Figure 4.1
Layers palette.

Bone layer
Vector layer
3D layer
Switch layer
Group layer
Audio layer
Note layer
Image layer
Particle layer

Layers provide a way to organize sets of content. For example, you could include all the background content on one layer and the foreground character on another layer. Layers can move, rotate, and scale independent of the other layers, so you could use them to create some advanced scenes. For example, you could draw a character's body on one layer and its arm on another layer. Then by locating the arm's layer center at the connection point, you could rotate the layer to make the arm move. This is just a simple example of how layers can be used.

In addition to organization, layers are also used to define the stacking order of objects in the scene. Objects on layers positioned at the top of the Layers palette will appear in front of overlapping objects that are on a lower layer.

The Available Layer Types

Each layer can contain a unique type of content. You can identify each layer type by the icon to the left of the layer name in the Layers palette. The available layer types include the following:

 Vector Layer: Vector layers hold all 2D vector-based lines, curves, shapes, and text. Vector layers are covered in more detail in Chapter 8, "Using Vector Layers."

 Image Layer: Image layers hold loaded pixel-based images imported from an external file. Image layers are covered in more detail in Chapter 22, "Adding Image Layers."

 Group Layer: Group layers hold several layers together for easy selection. Group layers are only available in Anime Studio Pro and are covered in more detail in Chapter 23, "Organizing Layers into Groups."

Bone Layer: Bone layers hold all bone objects that are used to move a selected group of points. Bone layers are covered in more detail in Chapter 26, "Creating and Binding Bones."

Switch Layer: Switch layers contain several sublayers, like the Group layer, except only one of the sublayers is visible at a time. This layer type provides a way to control interactively what is displayed. Switch layers are covered in more detail in Chapter 24, "Using Switch and Note Layers."

Note Layer: Note layers let you leave comments on your current project such as a reminder to finish a particular effect. Note layers are only available in Anime Studio Pro and are covered in more detail in Chapter 24, "Using Switch and Note Layers."

3D Layer: 3D layers hold 3D objects created and imported from a 3D package. 3D layers are only available in Anime Studio Pro and are covered in more detail in Chapter 29, "Using 3D Layers."

Particle Layer: Particle layers hold a large number of small objects called particles that act and move as one object. Particle layers are only available in Anime Studio Pro and are covered in more detail in Chapter 31, "Using Particle Layers."

Audio Layer: Audio layers hold any imported sound objects that appears in the Sequencer. Audio layers are covered in more detail in Chapter 19, "Working with Sound."

New Feature

Audio layers are new to Anime Studio 6.

Note

Group, Note, 3D, and Particle layers are only available in Anime Studio Pro.

Working with Layers

All the commands for creating and working with layers are available in the Layers palette. Each layer has a layer name and its own unique settings that define how the layer interacts with other layers. The layer type is identified by the appropriate icon to the left of the icon name.

Note

There is no way to convert layers to a different type. Each layer holds a unique set of content.

Creating a New Layer

When you click the New Layer button at the top of the Layers palette, a small pop-up menu, shown in Figure 4.2, appears from which you can select the type of layer you want to create. When a new layer is created, it is automatically added directly above the currently selected layer. New layers are automatically named *Layer* followed by a sequential number.

New layer

Duplicate layer

Delete layer

Layer settings

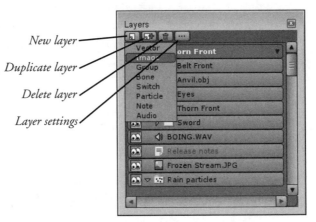

Figure 4.2
New Layer selection list.

Tip

If the number of layers exceeds the space available in the Layers palette, then a scroll bar appears that you can use to access the layers on the bottom of the palette. When the mouse cursor is over the Layers palette, you can use the scroll wheel to move the layer list up and down.

Selecting a Layer

To select a layer, simply click it. The selected layer in the Layers palette is colored blue. If you hold down the Shift or the Ctrl/Cmd key while clicking on layers in the Layers palette, you can select multiple layers at once, but only one layer can be active at a time. The active layer is colored darker than the rest and has the down arrow to the right for accessing the pop-up menu. All selected layers are highlighted in blue and double-clicking the selected layer makes the Layer Settings dialog box appear for the active layer.

New Feature

The ability to select multiple layers at once is new to Anime Studio 6.

Changing Layer Visibility

In the left column of the Layers palette is an icon for controlling the visibility of each layer. If the layer is visible, then an icon showing a pair of googly eyes is visible. If the icon is blank, then the layer is hidden. Hidden layers can be made visible by simply clicking the visibility icon.

Using this visibility option only affects whether the layer is visible in the working area and cannot be animated. Within the Layer Settings dialog box is another Visible setting that can be animated.

Note

The current selected layer is always visible while it is selected, even if the Layer Visibility toggle is disabled.

Tip

If you hold down the Alt/Opt key while clicking the visibility icon, all layers on the same level are hidden and the layer that you clicked remains visible. This provides a quick way to hide everything but the current layer.

Renaming Layers

To rename the current layer, simply double-click the layer to open the Layer Settings dialog box. In the General panel of the Layer Settings dialog box is a Name field that you can use to rename the current layer. The Name field is also available in the Layer pop-up menu. When the Layer Settings dialog box is opened, the Name field is already selected, so you can begin typing the new name immediately without having to click the Name field to select it. Layer names aren't restricted to specific characters and can include spaces, upper- and lowercase letters, and symbols like the $, #, and *. However, some of these symbols may cause trouble if you try to use them in a script.

Tip

Renaming layers is helpful as a project gets more and more complex. A project with unnamed layers makes it hard to locate objects and difficult to interpret scripts that access layers.

The layer name can also be found and changed using the pop-up menu shown in Figure 4.3, which appears when you click the down arrow located to the right of the layer name for the selected layer. This menu also includes some of the same options found in the Layer Settings dialog box, which is explained later in this chapter along with many of the display quality settings found in the Display Quality pop-up menu that are discussed in Chapter 3, "Managing and Configuring the Workspace." The difference between the Display Quality pop-up menu and the Current Layer display settings is that the latter are applied only to the current layer.

The Current Layer pop-up menu can be closed by right-clicking in the working area away from the menu.

Caution

The Layers palette allows you to name two different layers with the same name. Naming two layers the same could cause problems for any scripts that access those layers. Two layers with the same name also will not work in a Switch layer.

Figure 4.3
Current Layer
pop-up menu.

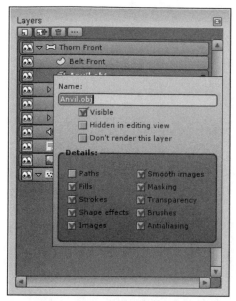

Duplicating a Layer

When you click the Duplicate Layer button at the top of the Layers palette, a copy of the currently selected layer is added to the Layers palette directly above the current layer. The new copy is named the same as the original layer but with a sequential number. For example, if you select a layer named Arm, then the new duplicated layer will be named Arm 2. Duplicating a layer that includes sublayers creates a copy of all the sublayers also.

Reordering Layers

Remember that in the Layers palette if the content on two layers overlaps in the working area, then the layer that is closest to the top in the Layers palette appears on top of the other one, so it becomes important to order your layers correctly and make sure that any background objects are on layers positioned at the bottom of the Layers palette. If you need to reorder any layers, you can do it directly in the Layers palette.

If you drag a layer or multiple layers in the Layers palette, a red line appears in between the existing layers. If you drop the layer when this red line is visible, then the dragged layer or layers are moved to a new position where the red line appeared.

> **Note**
>
> The action of moving layers cannot be animated. If you move a layer at any frame other than frame 0, no keys are set. If you need to change the stacking order, you can animate the Raise and Lower Shapes commands in the Draw menu.

Creating Sublayers

Some layers can hold sublayers, including the Group, Switch, Bone, and Particle layers. Layers that can hold sublayers are also identified by a small arrow icon located to the left of the layer type icon. This small arrow icon is used to expand and contract all the sublayers. When you drag a layer over a layer type that can have sublayers, then the entire layer is highlighted red. If you drop the layer when the layer is highlighted, as shown in Figure 4.4, then the dropped layer becomes a sublayer of the highlighted layer. Sublayers are indented under the layer that contains them.

> **Caution**
>
> You can only drop sublayers onto a layer that is expanded to show all its sublayers. Anime Studio doesn't allow you to drop sublayers onto a contracted layer. This is also a simple way to lock a group so that new sublayers aren't added to it by accident.

Expand/contract sublayers ——

Highlighted layer ——

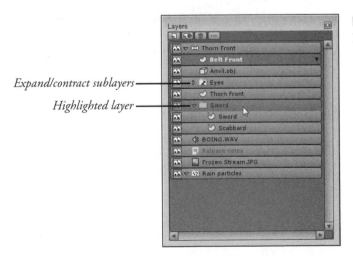

Figure 4.4
Highlighted layer.

Deleting Layers

To delete a layer or a sublayer, simply select the layer and click the Delete Layer button at the top of the Layers palette. This button causes a warning dialog box to appear that warns that this action cannot be undone. When a layer containing sublayers is deleted, all its sublayers are deleted also.

> **Note**
>
> When you click the Delete Layer button, only the active layer is deleted, even if multiple layers are selected.

To practice working with layers in the Layers palette, follow these steps:

1. Open the Award.anme file from the Chapter 4 folder on the included CD. This file includes three layers with a plaque, some text, and a star.

2. If you render the opened file with the File, Preview (Ctrl/Cmd+R) command, only the wood plaque is visible. Drag the text and the star layers above the plaque layer in the Layers palette. The star and text are now visible.

3. To edit this award to be a four-star award, select the star layer and click the Duplicate Layer button at the top of the Layers palette three times to create four star layers.

4. With one of the star layers selected, choose the Translate Layer tool (1) in the Tools palette and drag in the working area to reposition one of the stars. Select each of the other star layers and move them into a line of stars under the text.

5. Click the New Layer button in the Layers palette and select the Group option from the pop-up menu. Double-click the new layer and name the layer *stars* in the Layer Settings dialog box. Then drag each of the star layers and drop each one on the new group layer.

Figure 4.5 shows the resulting four-star award along with its layers. With all the star layers grouped together in a group layer, you can move all the stars together, and it helps to keep the content organized.

Figure 4.5
An award created by
manipulating layers.

Using Layer Settings

Clicking the Layer Settings button at the top of the Layers palette or double-clicking
a layer opens the Layer Settings dialog box shown in Figure 4.6. The Layer Settings
dialog box includes several panels of options. The available panels depend on the
type of layer that is accessed, but all layers include a General, Shadows, Motion
Blur, and Masking panel. Enabling shadows is covered in Chapter 33, "Rendering
the Final Scene," motion blur is covered in Chapter 32, "Using Motion Blur and
Depth of Field," and masking is covered in more detail in Chapter 13, "Filling
Shapes and Using Strokes."

Setting Display Options

Directly under the Name field in the General panel are three options for controlling the display of the current layer. The Hide in Editing View option causes
the layer to be hidden when it is not selected. This option is different from the
Visibility icon in that the layer will still be rendered when the scene is output. This
option is intended to simplify the working area while editing and helps keep content out of the way while you work on other objects. When this option is enabled,
the layer name appears dimmed out and italicized, as shown in Figure 4.7.

Figure 4.6
Layer Settings
dialog box.

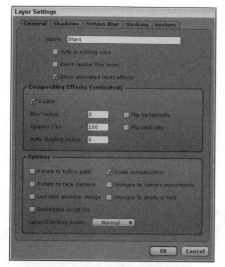

Tip

If you have any particle layers in your project, consider enabling the Hide in Editing View option for the particle layer as those layers can slow down the redraw considerably.

Figure 4.7
Layer names are
dimmed when the
Hide in Editing
View or the Don't
Render This Layer
option is enabled.

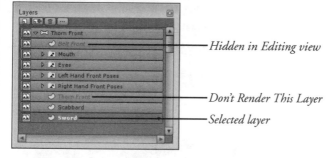

The Don't Render This Layer option causes the layer to be ignored when the file is output or rendered. For example, the Note layer has this option enabled by default. This option is useful for layers that are used to hold reference images. Layer names for layers with this option enabled are dimmed (but not italicized) in the Layers palette.

Both the Hide in Editing View and the Don't Render This Layer options can also be found in the current layer pop-up menu.

The Allow Animated Layer Effects option provides a way to keep any applied layer effects from affecting layers that you don't want it to affect. Using this option, you specifically must request that a layer effect is enabled in order for it to show up in the animation. Most of the layer effects are available in the Compositing Effects section of the Layer Settings dialog box, but a couple additional layer effects are located in the Scripts menu.

New Feature

The Allow Animated Layer Effects option in the Layer Settings dialog box is new to Anime Studio 6.

Specifying Compositing Effects

The Compositing Effects section of the General panel in the Layer Settings dialog box includes settings for controlling the layer's visibility, blur radius, and opacity for the given frame. There are also settings for flipping the layer horizontally and vertically.

Caution

The Visible setting in the General panel of the Layer Settings dialog box is different from the Visibility icon located in the Layers panel (the googly eyes). The Visible setting in the Layer Settings dialog box controls whether the layer is visible for the given frame when rendered and is a property that can be animated.

Using the Visible setting, you can have layers turn on and off during an animated sequence.

Note

The Visible option in the Layer Settings dialog box is an exception. Its setting is animated regardless of whether the Allow Animated Layer Effects option is enabled or disabled.

The Blur Radius value is a setting used to blur the entire layer. It is measured in pixels and the higher the value, the greater the blur. This is useful if you want to create a depth of field effect by blurring a background layer. This value can also be animated over several frames to simulate objects in the layer slowly coming into focus. You can learn more on blurring and depth of field effects in Chapter 32, "Using Motion Blur and Depth of Field." The blurring effect can only be viewed if the project is rendered. Figure 4.8 shows four lines of text with varying degrees of blurriness. The Blur Radius value from the top to the bottom line of text is 0, 10, 20, and 40.

Figure 4.8
Varying Blur
Radius values.

The Opacity setting determines how transparent the layer is. A value of 100 has no effect on the layer and a value of 0 makes the layer totally transparent. The Opacity settings can likewise be used to gradually have objects fade away over a set number of frames. More on animating attributes such as visibility and opacity is covered in Chapter 16, "Understanding Keyframes and Tweening."

Transparency effects for vector layers can be viewed in the working area if the Transparency option in the Display Quality pop-up menu is enabled. Image layers don't appear transparent until they are rendered. Figure 4.9 shows some semi-transparent text in the working area. Notice how you can see the image through the text.

You can also change the transparency of a layer's objects by changing the Alpha value for the fill or outline color. The big difference is that the Opacity value in the Layer Settings dialog box changes the transparency for all objects in the layer.

Note

Don't be confused by the term *opacity*. Opacity is just the opposite of transparency, and it describes how visible the object is. For example, a layer with an Opacity value of 60 is only 40% transparent and a layer with an Opacity value of 0 is completely transparent.

Figure 4.9
Semi-transparent text is visible in the working area.

The Auto Shading Radius value causes the objects drawn on the current layer to be shaded automatically when its value is set to a value other than 0. Larger radius values cause the objects to be shaded a greater distance from the edge. The shading color is always set to gray and cannot be changed. Figure 4.10 shows a simple collection of shapes with an Auto Shading Radius value of 50.

New Feature

The Auto Shading Radius value in the Layer Settings dialog box is new to Anime Studio 6.

The Flip Horizontally and Flip Vertically options can be used to create a mirror image of the current layer. Sometimes, image layers are imported flipped, and this setting can correct them. These settings can also be animated, making it possible to simulate an object flipping back and forth like the lights at a railroad crossing.

Using General Layer Options

The final section in the General panel of the Layer Settings dialog box holds several miscellaneous options that are applied at a layer level.

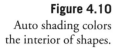

Figure 4.10
Auto shading colors the interior of shapes.

These options include the following, but many of the details on several of these options are covered in later chapters:

■ **Rotate to Follow Path:** This option causes the layer to be rotated to align to the transformation path direction. For example, if you have an arrow shape, this option will cause the arrow to automatically be oriented to follow the translation path instead of maintaining its current orientation. More on this option is covered in Chapter 17, "Working with the Timeline."

■ **Rotate to Face Camera:** This option is used to make the layer a *sprite*, which is an object that always faces the camera. This happens by rotating the layer about its vertical axis so that it is always perpendicular to the camera's aiming axis. More on this option is covered in Chapter 25, "Changing the View with Cameras."

■ **Use HSV Modifier Image:** This option lets you specify an HSV modifier image that is used to distort the camera lens much like adding filters to the lens of a movie camera would do. Several default HSV images are included with the Anime Studio installation in the Samples\HSV Modifiers Images folder. More on using image layers and HSV modifiers is covered in Chapter 22, "Adding Image Layers."

■ **Embedded Script File:** Enabling this option automatically opens a file dialog box where you can select a script file to run on the current layer. More on creating and using scripts is covered in Chapter 37, "Using Scripts and Lua."

■ **Scale Compensation:** When a layer is scaled with this option selected, its lines are automatically made thinner or thicker based on the scale amount. This helps keep the layer objects in check. More on this option is covered in Chapter 13, "Filling Shapes and Using Strokes."

■ **Immune to Camera Movements:** This option causes all objects on the layer to remain constant regardless of how the camera is moved. This is helpful when used on title screens or logos that are positioned in the corner of the project. General camera movements are covered in Chapter 25, "Changing the View with Cameras."

■ **Immune to Depth of Field:** A depth of field effect causes one specific area to be in focus and the rest of the layers to be blurry. By enabling this effect, you can exclude a layer from this effect, such as a logo or title that remains clear even though the other layers are blurred. Using a depth of field effect is covered in Chapter 32, "Using Motion Blur and Depth of Field."

■ **Layer Blending Mode:** The blending mode drop-down list lets you select how different semi-transparent layers are combined. The options include ways to combine the colors together, subtract one color from another, and create a color based on the luminosity value. The various blending modes are examined in the next section.

Using Blending Modes

Blending modes are only used when two layers are overlapped and the top layer is at least semi-transparent. By changing between the various blending modes, you can change the shading effect of the various layers that are blended. The available blending modes include the following:

> **Note**
>
> Blending mode changes are only visible when the file is rendered. They are not visible in the working area.

■ **Normal:** The default blending mode. This mode simply replaces the color on the lower layer with the color on the upper layer. The results are what you'd expect when combining the colors of two layers together.

■ **Multiply:** This blending mode multiplies the colors on both layers together resulting in a darker final color. Using this blending mode with black results in black regardless of the other color and using this mode with white leaves the other color the same. This happens because black has a value of 0, and 0 times any color value is still 0. White has a color value of 1, and 1 times any color value yields the same color value. This blending mode is useful if you are using an image that is too light and the details are washed out.

■ **Screen:** This blending mode multiplies the inverse of the lower layer colors with the upper layer colors resulting in a result that is the opposite of the Multiply blending mode, thereby causing the colors to get lighter. This blending mode is used to lighten a layer that is too dark.

■ **Overlay:** This blending mode is based on the lower layer colors. If the color is darker than 50%, then the layers are multiplied together, but if the lower layer color is lighter than 50%, the layers are screened together. This blending mode increases the layer's contrast causing the dark layers to become darker and the light colors to become lighter.

■ **Add:** This blend mode simply adds the two colors together resulting in a brighter color. It works by lightening each lower layer pixel by the brightness of the upper layer pixel up to white. Darker pixels on the upper layer result in objects being less visible. The Add blending mode works like the Screen blending mode, but it is more extreme.

> **Note**
>
> Photoshop doesn't include a blending mode called Add, but the Add blending mode in Anime Studio works exactly like the Linear Dodge blending mode in Photoshop.

■ **Difference:** This blend mode simply subtracts the two colors from each other resulting in a darker color. This results in changing the luminance of the upper layer pixels based on the difference between the two colors, so black and white will appear white, black on black will appear black, and white on white will appear white. One useful use of the Difference blending mode is to create an inverted relief look by offsetting the upper layer from a duplicate of the lower layer by a few pixels. This highlights all the edges in the images, as shown in Figure 4.11.

Render...done!

Save As... ▼

Figure 4.11
Edges are highlighted by offsetting and Difference blending a duplicate layer.

- **Hue:** This blending mode combines the hue of the upper layer color with the saturation and luminance of the lower layer color. It is used to change the color of specific objects like the color of a cat's eyes in a background image.

- **Saturation:** This blending mode combines the luminance and hue of the lower layer color with the saturation of the upper layer color. This mode is used to pump up the color saturation of the lower layer. It can also be used to reduce the lower layer's saturation if the upper layer has a low saturation value.

- **Color:** This blending mode combines the luminance of the lower layer color with the hue and saturation of the upper layer color. This is used to colorized black and white images. It is also used to apply a colored tint to the layer.

Tip

To make your output black and white, simply cover the entire project with a black rectangle and set its Layer blending mode to the color option and render.

■ **Luminosity:** This blending mode only uses the luminosity of the upper layer color. It is used to convert the upper layer of a grayscale image.

Figure 4.12 shows the various blending modes available in the Layer Settings dialog box. The lower layer contains the blue accent symbols and the upper layer contains the various gradient colored rectangular bars.

Figure 4.12
Blending modes.

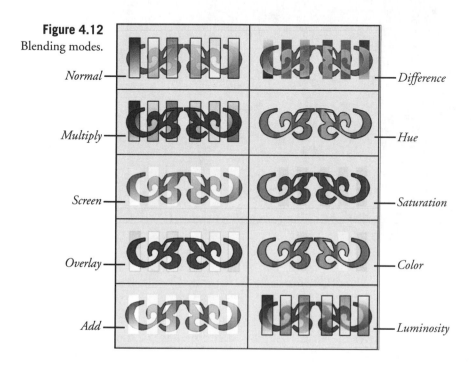

Normal

Multiply

Screen

Overlay

Add

Difference

Hue

Saturation

Color

Luminosity

To use the Add blending mode, follow these steps:

1. Open the Beachfront.anme file from the Chapter 4 folder on the included CD. This file includes a single image layer with a loaded image of a beach.

2. Click the New Layer button in the Layers palette and select the Image option in the pop-up menu. In the File dialog box that opens, select the Rendered sun.jpg file. This image is of a fiery sun set on a black background.

3. Select the Scale Layer tool (2) and drag in the working area to reduce the size of the new image layer. Then use the Translate Layer tool (1) to position the sun layer in the upper-left corner of the working area, as shown in Figure 4.13.

Figure 4.13
Overlapping
image layers.

4. Double-click the top layer in the Layers palette to open the Layer Settings dialog box. Then select the Add option as the Layer blending mode.

5. Select the File, Preview menu command (Ctrl/Cmd+R) to render the project. The Add blending mode removes the black background and blends the sun into the sky, as shown in Figure 4.14.

Figure 4.14
Blended sun
with Add.

To see more of the sun details, you can use the Screen blending mode instead of the Add blending mode. Double-click the sun layer to open the Layer Settings dialog box again and switch to the Screen blending mode. The rendered results are subtler, as shown in Figure 4.15.

Figure 4.15
Blended sun with Screen.

> **Tip**
>
> Blending modes can also be used to create a variety of textures. More on textures is covered in Chapter 15, "Setting Object Style."

Using Layer Masks

A layer mask is a layer that is used to define the visible region of the project. It can also be used to hide all objects on layers underneath it. These masks are used, for example, to only display objects within a specific area or to hide and slowly reveal objects. They also work to introduce a character in the middle of the scene during an animation. All layer masking options are available in the Masking panel in the Layer Settings dialog box, as shown in Figure 4.16.

Objects on a layer mask either can be visible or invisible. When a simple mask is applied, its results are displayed in the working area. However, if the mask sublayer is selected, then the results will not be correct since all the sublayer objects are visible when the layer is selected. More on masking is presented in Chapter 23, "Organizing Layers into Groups."

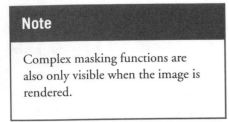

Note

Complex masking functions are also only visible when the image is rendered.

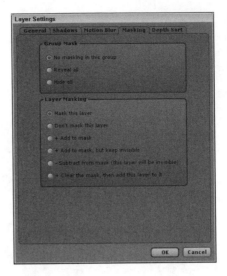

Figure 4.16
Masking panel
of the Layer Settings
dialog box.

The following options are available in the Masking panel:

- **Mask This Layer:** The default option. This option causes the current layer to be masked by a mask layer if a mask layer is available.

- **Don't Mask This Layer:** This option causes the current layer to ignore the layer mask resulting in all layer objects being visible.

- **+ Add to Mask:** This option adds all objects to the mask so that they hide all layers underneath them.

- **+ Add to Mask, but Keep Invisible:** This option also adds the current layer objects to the mask, but makes all objects invisible.

- **- Subtract from Mask (This Layer Will Be Invisible):** This option removes the objects on the current layer from the layer, thereby making objects underneath this layer's object visible.

- **+ Clear the Mask, Then Add This Layer to It:** This option uses the transparency of the current value as the mask.

For Group and Bone layers, some additional options are available:

- **No Masking in This Group:** This option is only available for Group and Bone layers. It causes the current group of layers not to be masked.

- **Reveal All:** This option is only available for Group and Bone layers. This option enables masking and makes all sublayers for this group visible.

- **Hide All:** This option is only available for Group and Bone layers. This option enables masking and makes all sublayers for this group invisible.

Layer masks only work with object transparency. You can think of it as a black-and-white filter for the project. All black areas of the mask mark those areas that are completely hidden, white areas are fully visible, and any gray areas are partially hidden.

Caution

When using a vector layer as a mask, the object's entire shape becomes a mask, even if the shape is filled with a semi-transparent color or gradient fill.

Masks will only work when placed within a group or bone layer. If you're using Anime Studio Debut, which doesn't have group layers, you can use a bone layer as a group layer. The order of the sublayers is also important with the mask sublayer placed below the object that is masking.

When the Reveal All group option is selected, then the entire mask is set to white, which makes all sublayers visible. You can hide overlapping areas by setting a sublayer that you want to remove to Subtract from Mask. Figure 4.17 shows a background layer with a key shape that has been removed using the Subtract from Mask option.

Note

Using the Add to Mask option when the Reveal All group option is enabled does nothing.

When the Hide All group option is selected, then the entire mask is set to black and sublayers can be made visible with the Add to Mask option. Figure 4.18 shows a key where the entire mask has been set to Hide All and then striped portions of the key are made visible with the Add to Mask option.

Note

Using the Subtract from Mask option when the Hide All group option is enabled does nothing.

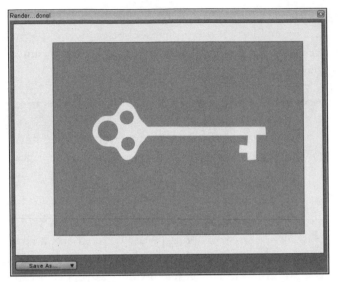

Figure 4.17
Subtracting from
a Reveal All mask.

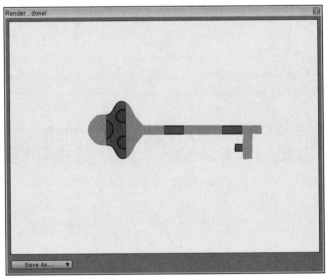

Figure 4.18
Adding to the
Hide All mask.

Using the Clear the Mask option sets the entire mask to black, which is the same as the Hide All option.

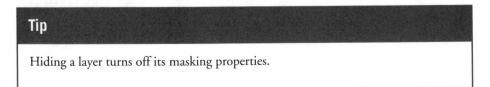

Tip

Hiding a layer turns off its masking properties.

To create a framed picture using masks, follow these steps:

1. Open the Picture frame mask.anme file from the Chapter 04 folder on the included CD. This file includes an image layer with a picture of a flower and three vector layers used to create a frame.

2. Click the New Layer button in the Layers palette and select the Group option in the pop-up menu. Double-click the new group layer and name it *picture*. Then drag and drop the matte layer and the Flower.jpg layer on the picture group layer.

3. Double-click the picture layer and select the Masking panel in the Layer Settings dialog box; then enable the Hide All option. This makes the entire mask black hiding all layers in this group. Double-click the matte sublayer and select the Add to Mask option in the Masking panel. This makes the picture layer visible where the matte rectangle is located.

4. Click the New Layer button in the Layers palette and select the Group option again in the pop-up menu. Double-click the new group layer and name it *frame*. Then drag and drop the circle's layer and the frame mask layer on the frame group layer. Then drag the entire frame group layer below the picture layer.

5. Double-click the frame layer and select the Masking panel in the Layer Settings dialog box; then enable the Reveal All option. This makes the entire mask white and all layers in this group visible. Double-click the circles sub-layer and select the Subtract from Mask option in the Masking panel. This removes the circle objects from the frame mask layer, resulting in a unique frame, as shown in Figure 4.19.

Figure 4.19
Picture frame created using masks.

Using the Layer Tools

The fourth section in the Tools palette includes various tools for working with layers. These tools move, scale, rotate, shear, and flip the selected layer or layers. These tools are especially handy when you are animating objects. For example, if you have a character walking on one layer, you could easily create the illusion of walking by slowly moving the background layer to the side as the character walks.

Figure 4.20 shows the various Layer tools and each tool is described below.

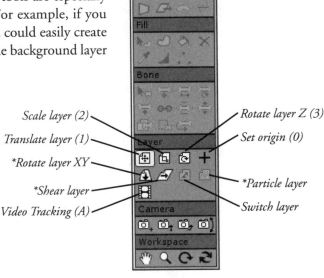

Figure 4.20
Layer tools.

Scale layer (2)

Translate layer (1)

*Rotate layer XY

*Shear layer

Video Tracking (A)

Rotate layer Z (3)

Set origin (0)

*Particle layer

Switch layer

*Anime Studio Pro only

- ■ **Translate Layer (1):** This tool moves the entire layer or layers by simply dragging in the working area.

- ■ **Scale Layer (2):** This tool scales the entire layer or layers using a control that appears in the center of the working area. Drag on the corners to uniformly scale the layer or on one of the edges to scale in a single dimension.

- ■ **Rotate Layer Z (3):** This tool spins the entire layer or layers about the origin point.

- ■ **Set Origin (0):** When this tool is selected, you can select and reposition the origin point located in the center of the working area. The origin point is the point about which the layer is rotated and flipped.

- ■ **Rotate Layer XY:** This tool rotates the layer about the XY plane causing the layer to tilt upward and downward or side to side.

- ■ **Shear Layer:** This tool shears the layer causing all vertical and horizontal lines in the layer to become diagonal.

- **Switch Layer:** This tool is only available when a switch layer is selected in the Layers palette. It places a drop-down list of the available sublayers in the Options bar at the top of the working area.

- **Particle Layer:** This tool is only available when a particle layer is selected in the Layers palette. It places several options in the Options bar at the top of the working area, including a checkbox for disabling particles, a dialog box or particle options, and a Randomize button.

> **Note**
>
> The Rotate Layer XY, Shear Layer, and Particle Layer tools are only available in Anime Studio Pro.

Setting the Origin Point

The layer's origin point is located in the center of the main window by default, and it is marked by two perpendicular arrows. The origin is used by the Scale and Rotation tools to mark the point around which the action occurs. It is also used by the Flip Horizontal and Flip Vertical buttons located in the Options bar to mark the point about which the layer is flipped. Using the Set Origin tool (0), you can change the location of this point. When this tool is selected, you simply need to drag the origin to its new location.

The coordinates of the new origin's location are displayed in the Options bar. Clicking the Reset button causes the origin to return to its original location.

Transforming Layers

The first three layer tools let you transform the layer or layers relative to the other layers. These transforms include translation, scaling, and rotation about the Z axis, which spins the objects around the origin.

Translating Layers

The Translate Layer tool (1) lets you click and drag to move all the objects on the current layer or layers. The layer's position relative to the origin is displayed in the X, Y, and Z fields in the Options bar. Clicking the Reset button causes the layer to return to its original position. You can also enable the Show Path option, which causes a line to be drawn from the origin to the layer's final position. This line is just an indicator of how and where the layer moved, and it is not rendered.

To the right of the Show Path option are buttons to flip the selected layers horizontally and vertically about the origin. Each button takes only a single click to activate and clicking either of these twice in a row causes the layer to right itself. These flip buttons are available on the Options bar for the Translate Layer, Scale Layer, Rotate Layer, and Set Origin tools.

New Feature

The Flip Layer Horizontally and Flip Layer Vertically buttons were layer tools in the previous edition and are now toolbar buttons to simplify the Tools palette. This change is new to Anime Studio 6.

If you hold down the Shift key while dragging a layer, then the layer movements will be constrained to be horizontal or vertical in a straight line. Holding down the Alt/Opt key causes the layer to move along the Z-axis, which is forward and back from the viewer. This makes the object's size appear to change, but only the view is changing, the size remains constant.

You can also nudge the layer by holding down the Ctrl/Cmd key and pressing the arrow keys. This causes the layer to move in the direction of the arrow key using small increments. If you hold down the Ctrl/Cmd and Shift keys, the layer will be nudged using larger increments. Nudging is helpful for positioning a layer precisely after a mouse move gets it close to where it needs to be.

Scaling Layers

The Scale Layer tool (2) places a red box in the center of the main window. This box has handles on each side and corner and by dragging this box's handles, you can change the size of the layer's contents. Dragging a corner handle changes the layer's size equally in both directions, which is helpful in keeping circles looking like circles.

If you drag one of the side handles, then the scaling is constrained to the horizontal or vertical directions, causing the layer objects to be deformed. But, if you hold down the Alt/Opt key while dragging on one of the side handles, the volume of the layer contents is maintained, causing the objects to squash and stretch.

Tip

If you continue to reduce the size of a layer by dragging its corner, the layer will eventually reduce to nothing and then return flipped both vertically and horizontally.

Rotating Layers

The Rotate Layer Z tool (3) spins the entire layer about the origin point regardless of where the origin is located. Holding down the Shift key causes the rotations to be constrained to 45-degree increments.

The Rotate Layer XY tool causes the layer contents to tilt so that one-half of the layer is coming out toward the viewer and the opposite half is receding. Moving the mouse left and right causes the sides of the layer to be distorted and moving the mouse up and down causes the top and bottom of the layer to be tilted. For both directions, the point of tilting occurs at the origin point.

Figure 4.21 shows four image layers. The upper-left image shows the original layer, the lower left has been rotated with the Rotate Layer Z tool, and the upper-right and the lower-right images have been rotated with the Rotate Layer XY tool.

Figure 4.21
Rotated image layers.

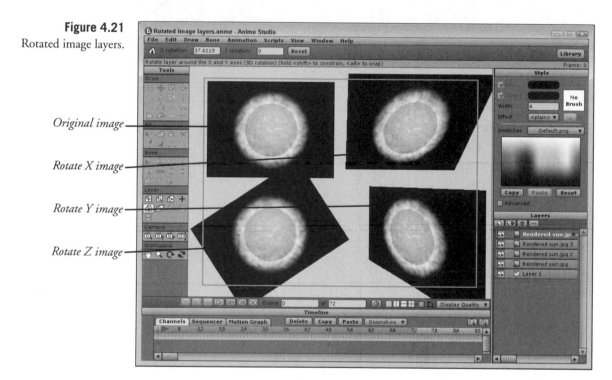

Original image

Rotate X image

Rotate Y image

Rotate Z image

Shearing Layers

The Shear Layer tool lets you shift the layer by moving one edge of the layer in one direction and its opposite side in the opposite direction to create a diagonal movement. Dragging the Shear Layer tool up and down moves the top and bottom edges of the layer and dragging the tool to the side moves the left and right edges of the layer.

Figure 4.22 shows three image layers. The left layer shows the original layer, the middle image has been sheared with the Shear Layer X tool, and the right image has been sheared with the Shear Layer Y tool.

New Feature

The Rotate Layer XY and Shear Layer tools were split into separate tools for each direction in the previous version and have been combined into a single tool for Anime Studio 6.

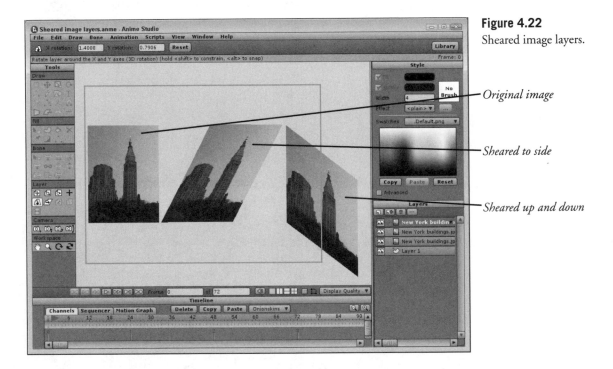

Figure 4.22
Sheared image layers.

— *Original image*

— *Sheared to side*

— *Sheared up and down*

To move, rotate, and scale layers, follow these steps:

1. Open the Variety.anme file from the Chapter 04 folder on the included CD. This file includes several layers, each with a single letter.

2. Select the V layer and click the Translate Layer tool (1); then drag in the working area to move the letter to the left. Click the Scale Layer tool (2) and drag outward on one of the corner handles in the working area to resize the letter.

3. Select the A layer and move it with the Translate Layer tool (1) next to the V letter. Then use the Scale Layer tool (2) and drag inward to decrease the size of the A letter.

4. Continue to select, move, and scale the remaining letters until the word is spelled out using the various letters.

5. Click the New Layer button in the Layers palette and select the Group option from the pop-up menu to create a group layer. Then select and drop each of the letter layers onto the new group layer.

6. Select the group layer and name it *word* in the Layer Settings dialog box. Then click the Duplicate Layer button at the top of the Layers palette and name the new group *word shadow*.

7. With the *word shadow* layer selected, click the Flip Vertically button to flip the shadow text. Then select the Shear Layer X tool and drag to the right in the working area to shear the letters. Then select the Translate Layer tool (1) and move the shadow text to line it up with the lowest point on the original text, as shown in Figure 4.23.

Figure 4.23
Repositioned
layer letters.

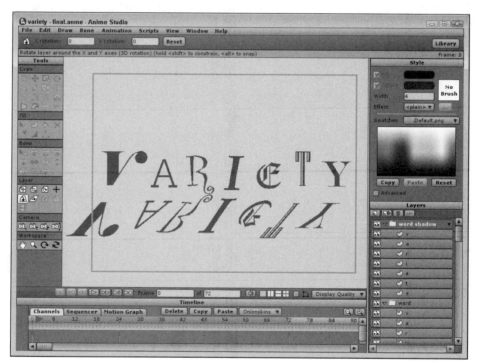

Chapter Summary

This chapter introduced the concept of layers. All content in Anime Studio is placed on layers, but there are several different types of layers and each layer type holds a different type of content. Layers provide a way to organize content and to transform it. All layers are listed in the Layers palette, and this chapter also explained how to work with and access layers using the Layers palette. Within the Layer Settings dialog box are settings for renaming the layer, applying layer parameters, setting its blending mode, and specifying a masking mode. Finally, this chapter showed how the Layer tools are used to manipulate the layers.

The next chapter is a short one providing some insight on where you can go to find more help with Anime Studio because we all need help in one way or another.

5

Getting Help

- Using the Anime Studio docs
- Using the Help status bar
- Getting help from the Web
- Drawing and animation resources

If you need to learn how to use Anime Studio, then you've already taken the most important step—to get this book. I hope this book is helpful, but there are some additional resources that you can access to round out your Anime Studio skills. This chapter takes a close look at using the online documentation and an even closer look at the resources available on the Web and through various forums.

Using the Anime Studio Help File

Under the Help menu is a Help option that opens the Anime Studio User's Manual, as shown in Figure 5.1. This manual is a PDF file and opens in a Web browser or in Adobe Reader if it is installed on your system.

Note

If your Web browser has strict security measures enabled, the Anime Studio User's Manual may be blocked from running in your system's Web browser because it uses scripts.

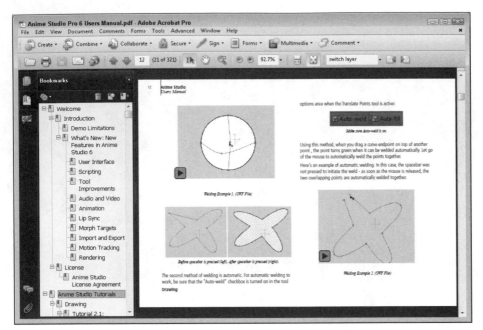

Figure 5.1
The Anime Studio
User's Manual.

The Table of Contents is divided into several categories including a reference of every menu command. The Table of Contents is also linked, so clicking on a topic will take you directly to the corresponding page in the manual. Be aware that the User's Manual has some gaps, but the manual isn't too long, and it is fairly well organized, so it is easy to find specific topics.

Using the Quick Start Guide

If you are brand new to Anime Studio, then you may want to begin with the Quick Start Guide, which is accessed from the Help, Quick Start Guide menu. This guide provides an overview of some of the key features.

Note

You can also access the Anime Studio Quick Start Guide by clicking the Introductory Tutorial button on the Welcome Screen.

Accessing the Manual Tutorials

In addition to the reference materials, the User's Manual also includes a simple set of tutorials. These tutorials are fairly basic and cover only the main features. They are divided into several different topics, including Drawing, Bones, Images, Animation, and Effects.

You can also learn about the various features by examining the content folder on the hard drive. This folder can also be accessed using the Help, Open Content Library menu. More on using the Content Library is covered in Chapter 6, "Working with the Content Library."

Getting Help from the Status Bar

Anime Studio also offers context-sensitive help for the selected tool via the status bar. The status bar is located at the top of the main window under the Options bar, as shown in Figure 5.2. The text displayed in the status bar changes depending on the tool that is selected.

Figure 5.2
Status bar.

Status bar —

The status bar also lists any special keys and their functions. For example, when the Oval tool is selected, the status bar reads "Draw an oval (hold <shift> to constrain, <alt> to center)."

Getting Help on the Web

In addition to the built-in documentation and tutorials, there are several helpful sites online that cover Anime Studio.

Using the Smith Micro Web Site

The first place on the Web to look for Anime Studio help is the Smith Micro Web site. Smith Micro does a great job of supporting all of their products with tutorials, downloads, news, and an inspiring gallery. You can also sign up for a free Anime Studio newsletter that includes tips, tricks, tutorials, and promotional offers.

The Help menu also includes an option to access online tutorials. Choosing this menu command opens your Web browser to the http://my.smithmicro.com/tutorials address. These tutorials are hosted at the Smith Micro Web site and appear side by side with other Smith Micro software products, including Poser, Manga Studio, and Groboto.

The tutorials found here include a random sampling created by various users and new tutorials are added all the time. Check back often to see the new topics.

Checking for Updates

The Help menu also includes an option to Check for Updates. This menu command opens a Web page on the Smith Micro site where any updates to the program are posted. It also offers links for upgrading Anime Studio Debut to the Pro version and upgrading previous versions of the software to version 6. This Web site also offers a link to download the Papagayo software for lip syncing. You can learn more about this free program and lip syncing in Chapter 20, "Using Lip Sync."

Accessing the Anime Studio Forum

A valuable source of news, tips, and tricks is found on the Anime Studio forum located at www.lostmarble.com/forum/, as shown in Figure 5.3. This forum is quite active, with many gurus offering suggestions and happily sharing their experience with users both new and old.

> **Note**
>
> Before it was acquired by Smith Micro, Anime Studio was known as a product called *Moho*, which may come up on some of the older forum posts. Also of note is the Lost Marble Web site, which was founded by the original developers of Moho.

The Anime Studio forum includes several different categories such as a FAQ, a section to post and view artwork completed with Anime Studio, a Tips and Techniques section, a Scripting section, and a section called How Do I ... ? that displays posts on accomplishing specific tasks.

Forum posts can be viewed by anyone, but to participate in the posting process, you'll need to register on the forum site using the Profile link.

Figure 5.3
The Anime Studio forum is available at www.lostmarble.com/forum/.

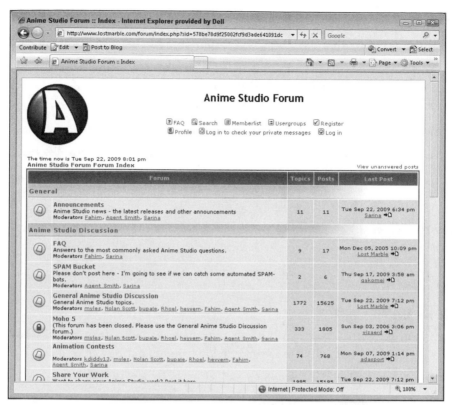

Huge kudos for the success of the forum go to the excellent moderators. These experienced users are quick to provide answers and to share their knowledge and tricks. In particular, look for heyvern, myles, and genete.

Drawing and Animation Resources

Anime Studio enables you to be creative, but it is only a tool. If you need to improve your drawing skills, there are several resources that can help. The listed resources are skewed toward mainly cartooning and animation instead of traditional types of drawing.

Books on Drawing Characters

Drawing characters that have life and personality is an essential skill and the following books can help hone these skills:

- *Creating Characters with Personality: For Film, TV, Animation, Video Games and Graphic Novels* by Tom Bancroft and Glen Keane
- *All About Techniques in Drawing for Animation Production* by Sergi Camara
- *Cartoon Cool: How to Draw New Retro-Style Characters* by Christopher Hart
- *Cartooning: Character Design* by Walter Foster, et al.
- *Exploring Character Design* by Kevin Hedgpeth
- *Better Game Characters by Design: A Psychological Approach* by Katherine Isbister
- *Digital Character Design and Painting* by Don Seegmiller

Books on Animation

Animation skills are uniquely different from drawing and painting skills. The following list of books will help as you develop your animating skills:

- *The Illusion of Life: Disney Animation* by Ollie Johnston and Frank Thomas
- *Acting for Animators* by Ed Hooks
- *Timing for Animation* by Harold Whitaker and John Halas
- *Animation from Pencils to Pixels: Classical Techniques for Digital Animators* by Tony White
- *The Animator's Workbook: Step-by-Step Techniques for Drawn Animation* by Tony White
- *The Animator's Survival Kit: A Manual of Methods, Principles, and Formulas for Classical, Computer, Games, Stop Motion, and Internet Animators* by Richard Williams
- *Digital Character Animation* by George Maestri

Helpful Web Sites

In addition to books, there are a number of helpful Web sites that include online tutorials and lessons:

- **Larry's Toon Institute at AWN:** www.awn.com/tooninstitute/lessonplan/lesson.htm#top

- **Animation Meat:** www.animationmeat.com/

- **Karmatoons:** www.karmatoons.com/drawing/drawing.htm

- **Cartoon Smart:** www.cartoonsmart.com/

- **CG Society: Society of Digital Artists:** www.cgsociety.org/

- **Digital Animators:** http://animators.digitalmedianet.com/

- **Animation Nation:** www.animationnation.com/

These resources are in no way comprehensive and many more excellent books and Web sites are available, but these are provided just as a place to start.

Chapter Summary

This chapter introduced the various methods for getting help such as using the online user's manual and tutorials, tool-specific help in the status bar, and help across the Web, including the Anime Studio pages on the Smith Micro Web site and the Anime Studio forum on the Lost Marble Web site.

The next part shows how to access additional content by using the Library and importing and downloading content.

Part II

Accessing Existing Content

6

Working with the Content Library

- Opening the content library
- Loading content from the library
- Saving content to the library
- Organizing the library

As you work with Anime Studio over time, you'll develop a large set of assets that can be reused in later work. Anime Studio includes a content library that holds a number of props and projects that are helpful as you start, but the content included in the default library is fairly limited.

The library structure, however, is very helpful for making your own content accessible to later projects. It is easy to organize and make your own custom content available from the File menu.

Opening the Content Library

The content library that ships with Anime Studio can be opened using the Library button located at the top right corner of the interface. You can also use the Window, Library menu or the Ctrl/Cmd+Shift+L keyboard shortcut. This opens the Content Library palette, as shown in Figure 6.1.

New Feature

The Content Library palette is new to Anime Studio 6.

The Content Library palette displays folder icons that match the folders on the hard drive located in the Library folder where Anime Studio is installed. You can also access the folders directly in a system window using the Help, Open Content Library menu command. This opens the Library folder (shown for Windows Vista in Figure 6.2).

Caution
Some of the examples included in the content library are governed by the License Agreement. Be sure to read section 6 of the End Use License Agreement before re-using any of the library content.

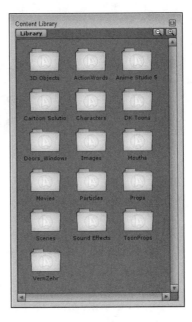

Figure 6.1
The Content
Library palette.

One key benefit of the Content Library palette is that a thumbnail of each asset is displayed within the palette when opened. This can help ensure that you are opening the correct item. As you double-click a folder to open it, its name appears at the top of the palette, providing a way to navigate quickly back to the root level. Figure 6.3 shows the Movies folder open.

You can also use the Zoom In and Zoom Out buttons located at the top right of the palette to increase or decrease the size of the content thumbnails. When a thumbnail is visible, you can double-click it to load it into the current scene.

Figure 6.2
The Library folder
on the hard drive.

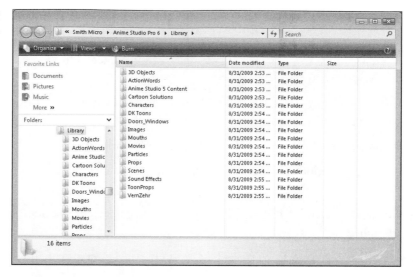

Figure 6.3
The Content
Library palette with
an open folder.

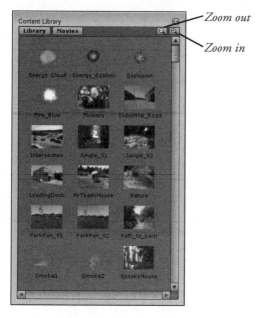

Zoom out

Zoom in

There are many different category folders within the Library folder. The available folders include the following:

- **3D Objects:** A small collection of 3D objects, including OBJ and MTL files.

- **Action Words:** Stylized words in starbursts such as Pow and Bang.

- **Anime Studio 5:** All the content included with the previous version of Anime Studio.

- **Cartoon Solutions:** A variety of different 2D objects and a rigged Rachel character.

- **Characters:** Includes three rigged characters including Jace, Thorn, and Thunder (a rigged horse).

- **DK Toons:** Several cartoon characters and props created by a user with the initials D. K. The folder also includes a number of audio files.

- **Doors Windows:** A collection of animated doors and windows.

- **Images:** A large collection of background photos such as beach, city, and street scenes.

- **Mouths:** Includes several PNG files of a mouth showing different phonemes that are designed for lip syncing.

- **Movies:** A collection of movies to use as backgrounds. The folder also includes several animated explosions and smoke effects.

- **Particles:** Includes several animated particle effects.

- **Props:** A small collection of cartoon objects, including dynamite, hammer, and rocket.

- **Scenes:** Contains a single desert island scene with multiple objects.

- **Sound Effects:** A folder of sound effects divided into several different categories, including cheering, noise, laughter, and whistles.

- **Toon Props:** Another small collection of cartoon objects.

- **Vern Zehr:** Includes a character named Fritz along with the detailed documentation on how to make him work.

New Feature

All the content in the Library folder is new to Anime Studio 6.

Within each folder for each piece of content is a 128 by 128 PNG image file. This image file is named the same as the content file and is used as the thumbnail in the Content Library palette. You can change this thumbnail image file to whatever represents the content, but if the name doesn't match the content file, then the thumbnail will simply load as an image file.

If a matching thumbnail image file isn't found within the same folder, then a default icon is displayed in the Content Library palette.

Note

If you're using a version of Anime Studio prior to version 5.5, then there is a bug for Mac systems that the Help, Content Library doesn't work. If you upgrade to the latest version, this bug is fixed.

Loading Content from the Library

Library content with the .ANME extension can be opened using the File, Open menu command, but the library also includes other files with .OBJ and .MTL extensions. These files are 3D files that can be opened using the File, Import menu command.

Note

The library also includes some older files that have the .MOHO extension. These files can also be opened using the File, Open menu command.

Tip

You can also open the .ANME files by dragging them from the Folder view and dropping them on the Anime Studio main window.

Library content is also instantly accessible from the File, Import menu.

Several content library files include multiple layers of objects, and selecting any of these files from the File, Import menu or from the Content Library palette opens an Insert Object dialog box like the one shown in Figure 6.4.

The Insert Object dialog box lists each of the layers found within the .ANME file. When an object is selected, its preview is shown in the box to the right. After you click the OK button, the selected object is loaded into the current scene without replacing any of the existing layers. This same command can be used on any .ANME file using the File, Import, Anime Studio Object menu.

Figure 6.4
The Insert Object
dialog box.

Saving Content to the Library

To save your own custom content to the Library, simply use the File, Save As menu command and browse to the Library folder where Anime Studio is installed. This folder can hold both .ANME files and folders. Files placed in the Library folder appear under the File, Import menu and folders are listed as submenus.

If you change a folder or file name in the Library folder, then the new name is updated in the File, Import menu the next time Anime Studio is restarted.

Multiple objects can be included in the library in a single .ANME file by separating each object onto its own layer before saving the file.

Organizing Library Content

To organize the library content into folders, simply create a new folder for each different type of content and place all the various files that include that type of content within the respective folder. To delete content, simply select the file or folder and delete or move it outside of the Library folder.

To create and populate a new Library folder, follow these steps:

1. Open the Award.anme file from the Chapter 6 folder on the CD. This file includes an award plaque created in an earlier tutorial.

2. Select the File, Save As menu command and navigate to the Library folder where Anime Studio is installed, such as Program Files, Smith Micro, Anime Studio, Library. Then click the New Folder button to create a new folder and name the new folder *Book Examples*. Save the current file in the new folder.

3. Select the File, Project Settings menu and set the Width and Height values to 128. Then choose the File, Preview menu to render the project.

4. In the Render window that appears, click the Save As button and save the rendered image to the same Book Examples folder as a PNG file. Name the file *Award.png* to match the project file.

5. Exit and restart Anime Studio. Then select the File, Import menu command and notice that Book Examples is a submenu option, as shown in Figure 6.5. Because a matching PNG image file was saved to the same folder, the content library displays a thumbnail of this file, as shown in Figure 6.6.

Tip

Once the new Content Library folder is created, you can select and copy the entire contents of the book's CD into this folder to make all the book examples immediately accessible.

Figure 6.5
New folder added to the content library.

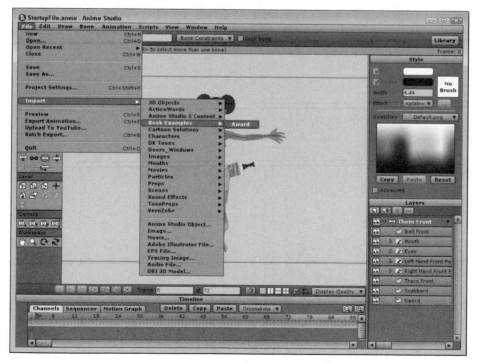

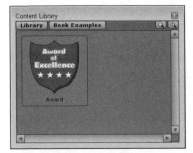

Figure 6.6
Content Library folder displays a thumbnail.

Chapter Summary

This chapter introduced the Content Library palette and showed some of the content that is included within the various library folders. All files and folders included in the Library folder where Anime Studio is installed show up in the File, Import menu. Custom content can also be saved to this folder to make the content easily accessible for reuse.

The next chapter looks at all the various formats that can be imported into Anime Studio. It also shows how new content can be downloaded and used.

7

Importing Content and Downloading New Content

- Loading .ANME files
- Importing images and movies
- Importing Illustrator files
- Importing EPS files
- Converting Photoshop files
- Importing 3D objects
- Accessing Content Paradise
- Browsing for new content

One of the largest submenus in the entire Anime Studio package is found in the File, Import menu. Anime Studio can import a large number of different files, including a diverse collection of prebuilt content. The content included in the library is listed in the top portion of the File, Import menu and is covered in Chapter 6, "Working with the Content Library"; the bottom half of the menu is reserved for loading custom content using a variety of different formats.

Another valuable source for obtaining new content is Content Paradise, an online store that is supplied by multiple third-party vendors. For a fee, new content can be downloaded for use in Anime Studio. Content Paradise also offers content for other Smith Micro packages, such as Poser.

Loading .ANME Files

If you select the File, Import, Anime Studio Object menu command, a file dialog box opens from which you can choose the .ANME (or .MOHO) file you want to open. This menu command works exactly like the File, Open command, except that after the file is selected, another dialog box appears from which you can choose the specific layers to import. Within the Insert Object dialog box, shown in Figure 7.1, you can see a preview pane that shows what the selected layer looks like.

> **Note**
>
> .ANME files can also be opened by dropping them on the working space from the Finder on a Mac or from Windows Explorer.

Figure 7.1
Insert Object dialog box.

The other key difference between File, Import and File, Open is that the content accessed using the File, Import command is added to the existing scene without closing the current project or deleting any content.

Importing Images and Movies

The File, Import, Image and File, Import, Movie menu commands instantly open the File dialog box, which lets you browse for specific images and movie files that you can import. These files are added to an image layer in the Layers palette. (You can learn more about using image layers in Chapter 22, "Adding Image Layers.")

The Image Import command imports several different formats including the following:

- **JPEG:** The most common format for photorealistic images on the Web. JPEG images can be compressed to reduce their file size so they can be transmitted quicker over the Web.

- **BMP:** The image format used by the Windows operating system.

- **PNG:** This format is also used on the Web, but it isn't as common as JPEG or GIF images because it is newer. PNG files support an alpha channel for holding transparent information, which allows a nonrectangular image to be created using this format.

- **Targa:** Another common image format that allows compression and alpha transparency.

- **GIF:** Another common Web format for displaying 256-color, palette-ordered graphics.

> **Tip**
>
> Anime Studio cannot import Photoshop PSD files, but within the Extra Files folder where Anime Studio is installed is a script that runs in Photoshop that saves the document as an .ANME file. This script is covered later in the chapter.

In addition to the common image formats mentioned above, Anime Studio also allows movies to be imported using the following formats:

- **AVI:** The AVI format is used on Windows-based systems, but is not available on Macintosh systems.

- **MPG:** The MPEG format is another cross-platform video format.

- **QuickTime (MOV):** The QuickTime (MOV) format is available for both Windows and Macintosh systems.

After a movie file is loaded into a project, you can view the loaded movie using the Play button (Spacebar) located in the lower-left corner of the main interface. Figure 7.2 shows a movie loaded into Anime Studio.

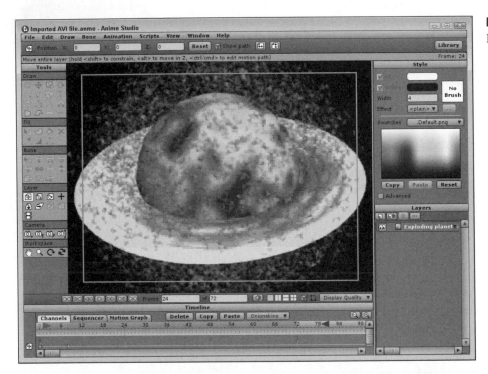

Figure 7.2
Imported movie.

> **Note**
>
> Imported movies can also be used for video tracking, which is covered in Chapter 28, "Using Video Tracking."

Importing Illustrator Files

Because Anime Studio is vector-based, it can import and work with files saved using the Adobe Illustrator (.AI) file format. Not all objects created in Illustrator can be imported, but Anime Studio can work with any Bezier curves and points that are exported.

> **Note**
>
> You can only import Adobe Illustrator files in Anime Studio Pro.

New Feature

Anime Studio doesn't use Bezier curves the same way Adobe Illustrator does, so the imported curves can be a little off. Anime Studio 6 has improved how it places points to make the imported curves cleaner.

Most of the advanced features found in Illustrator cannot be exported to Anime Studio, including text (unless converted to outlines), blends, patterns, effects, gradient fills, and layers. Anime Studio also cannot deal with any CMYK or spot colors. All Illustrator content that will be imported into Anime Studio needs to use the RGB color mode. Be aware also that Anime Studio will often change the colors of the imported vectors and add many extra points that will need to be cleaned up. Also, make sure that you flatten all artwork before importing it into Anime Studio.

> **Note**
>
> Before exporting any Illustrator text for use in Anime Studio, the text should be converted to outlines.

Although many different versions of Adobe Illustrator exist, for best compatibility, you should save your Illustrator file using the Illustrator 8 version or any earlier version. Figure 7.3 shows an imported logo created in Illustrator and saved using the .AI format.

> **Note**
>
> Illustrator files saved using the CS1, CS2, CS3, or CS4 formats cannot be opened within Anime Studio.

To import an Illustrator file into Anime Studio, follow these steps:

1. Open the Box It Up Co logo.ai file from the Chapter 07 folder on the CD into Illustrator. Use the Convert to Outlines feature to convert the text into paths. Make sure the color mode is RGB and flatten all layers to a single layer.

2. Use Illustrator's File, Save As command to save the file as an Illustrator 8 (or earlier) file. This will clear out many of the recent complex features that are common in the newer Illustrator versions.

3. Open Anime Studio and use the File, Import, Adobe Illustrator File menu command to locate and import the saved AI file. The file appears within the center of the working area, as shown in Figure 7.3.

Figure 7.3
Imported Illustrator file.

Tip

If you have Photoshop, you can use the Export Paths to Illustrator command to export any Photoshop paths to a format that can be imported into Anime Studio using the Illustrator import feature.

Importing EPS Files

Another option for importing vector-based graphics is to use the Encapsulated PostScript (EPS) format. Illustrator and other vector-based packages, including CorelDRAW, can export graphics to this format. When preparing an EPS file for being imported into Anime Studio, try to remove all but the most basic curve features, just as you would for an AI file, and save the file using an older, more stable version.

> **Note**
>
> The ability to import EPS files is only available in Anime Studio Pro.

> **Caution**
>
> If Anime Studio has any problems with the AI or EPS file that you are trying to import, then you'll get a warning dialog box and the program will try to import what it can.

Converting Photoshop files to .ANME

If you work with Photoshop, then you'll be happy to know the Anime Studio installation includes a Photoshop script that converts Photoshop PSD files with layers into an Anime Studio file. The script even keeps the Photoshop layers intact.

The Photoshop script is named Export Layers to Anime Studio.jsx, and it is located in the Extra Files folder where Anime Studio is installed. To make the script appear within Photoshop, simply copy the script file and place it in the Photoshop/Presets/Scripts folder, restart Photoshop, and you'll be able to access the script using the File, Scripts, Export Layers to Anime Studio menu command, or you can use the File, Run Script, Browse feature.

> **Note**
>
> This script is compatible with all versions of Photoshop since version 7.

> **Note**
>
> Executing this script converts all PSD layers to PNG image files and places them in a PNG folder in the same folder as the .ANME file.

Importing 3D Objects and Texture Maps

Three-dimensional objects saved in the .OBJ format can be imported into Anime Studio. Any associated texture files saved with the .MTL format are also imported automatically. Figure 7.4 shows a set of 3D daisies imported into Anime Studio using the .OBJ format. Imported 3D objects can be manipulated in the working area. Chapter 29, "Using 3D Layers," has more information on using 3D layers.

> **Note**
>
> The ability to import OBJ files is only available in Anime Studio Pro.

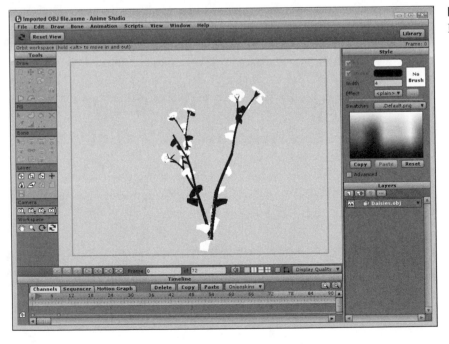

Figure 7.4
Imported 3D objects.

Accessing Content Paradise

Content Paradise can be accessed directly from the Anime Studio's Welcome Page by clicking the www.contentparadise.com link. This link is convenient because it takes you directly to the Anime Studio pages on the Content Paradise Web site. Another way to get to the Anime Studio pages on Content Paradise is with the Help, Buy Content menu.

Note

The Welcome Screen can be reopened at any time with the Help, Welcome Screen menu.

You can also get to these pages by typing www.contentparadise.com in a Web browser and selecting Anime Studio from the Software drop-down list in the search field. Figure 7.5 shows the Anime Studio content available on the Content Paradise Web site.

Figure 7.5
Anime Studio pages on the Content Paradise Web site.

Signing Up

Although you can begin immediately to search and browse for new content, you can only take full advantage of the Content Paradise Web site by signing up for a new account. Signing up doesn't cost anything, but you do have to pay to download content.

To sign up for a new account, click the Sign Up link on the home page. New accounts require a name, street address, phone number, and email address. You also need to provide a unique name and password that you will use to log in to the site in the future.

Note

When you sign up for a new account, you can elect to receive a free email newsletter along with promotional emails. There is also an option to show or hide nudity. Many of the custom characters for Poser are nude models. If you disable the Show Nudity option, then all such models will be hidden from your view.

Browsing for Content

After you log in, you can browse the product categories by selecting a category from the list at the left or by drilling down into the various categories.

Each product has a thumbnail of the item along with its price, as shown in Figure 7.6. To purchase an item, simply click the Add to Cart button to add the item to a shopping cart. When you're ready to check out, click the Checkout link, and you'll be taken to a page where you can enter your credit card information.

Tip

Occasionally, some items are available for download for free.

Figure 7.6
Product items
have thumbnails.

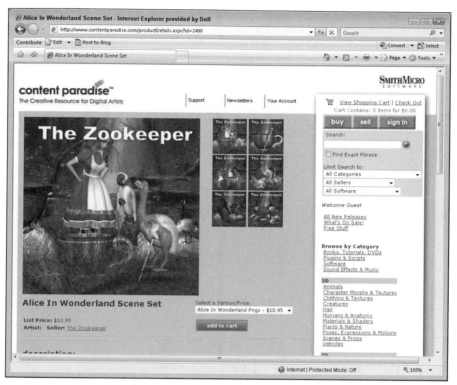

Loading Downloaded Content into Anime Studio

When a purchased file is downloaded from the Content Paradise site, the file is usually archived in a compressed file in order to speed the downloading process. After the file is unzipped, you can open the file from within Anime Studio using the File, Open menu command.

If you place the unzipped downloaded content in the Library folder, you can access the content from within Anime Studio using the File, Import menu.

Chapter Summary

This chapter covered the various options for importing content into Anime Studio. Using the File, Import menu, you can import a variety of files, including images, movies, Illustrator files, and 3D objects. There is also a script for converting Photoshop files (including layers) into .ANME files. The File, Import, Image option can import several different formats, including JPEG, BMP, PNG, Targa, and GIF, and movie import options include AVI and QuickTime (MOV).

This chapter also introduced the Content Paradise Web site as a new source for browsing, purchasing, and downloading content. Once unzipped, the downloaded content can be used directly within Anime Studio using the File, Open menu command.

This chapter concludes Part II covering how to get a handle on the ready-to-use content. In Part III, we'll dive into the drawing tools and vector layers and actually get some content in the main window to play with.

Part III

Drawing in Anime Studio

8

Using Vector Layers

- The benefits of vectors
- Vectors in Anime Studio
- Using vector layer settings

Any drawing that you do within Anime Studio is done on what is called a *vector layer*. That makes vector layers pretty important, and learning to work with them will enable you to master the crucial drawing aspects of this program.

The Benefits of Vectors

When it comes to drawing shapes on a computer, there are essentially two ways to represent drawn lines. The first method works by dividing the screen into pixels; if the line passes through a pixel, it is colored and if the line misses a pixel, it remains white. The computer then remembers in a large array of memory which pixels are colored and which remain white.

This pixel-based method works well, but it has some drawbacks. One drawback is that diagonal lines can appear jagged due to pixilation that occurs when some pixels are fully colored and others are not, as shown in Figure 8.1. This can be reduced by filtering the pixels using a process called *anti-aliasing*, so that the pixels on the edge of a line are a lighter color. Aliasing (or jaggies) can also be eliminated by making the pixel array large, but this introduces another problem with pixel-based drawings, which is that they can take up a large amount of memory.

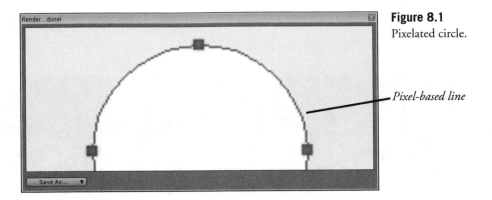

Figure 8.1
Pixelated circle.

Pixel-based line

The memory problem with pixel-based drawings is compounded when you animate them. If a single pixel-based image takes up 1MB of memory, an animation sequence at 24 frames per second would require a whopping 24MB for one second of animation.

An alternative to the pixel-based approach is to have the computer simply remember the mathematical formula used to create the shape. This formula is then recalled and executed every time the shape needs to be drawn, based on the size and position of the shape. This is known as *vector-based drawing*. The benefit of this method is that the drawing is scale independent, which results in smooth lines regardless of the size, as shown in Figure 8.2. It also dramatically reduces the amount of memory required.

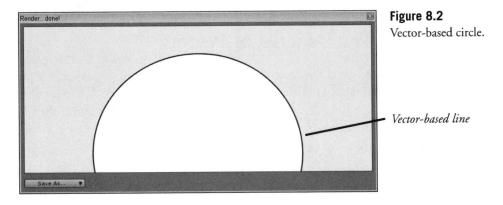

Figure 8.2
Vector-based circle.

Vector-based line

Because vector-based graphics have such a small memory footprint, they are particularly useful for displaying images on the Web, which requires that all graphics be downloaded before they can be displayed.

> **Note**
>
> Flash is another vector-based format, which explains its popularity on the Web.

Vector-based graphics are also very handy for animation because they can be edited easily over time by simply dragging handles and objects. Pixel-based graphics are animated by having to redraw every frame of the animation. The memory required for producing an animated vector-based sequence is also very small when compared with pixel-based movies.

Even though Anime Studio is a vector-based package, it can still deal with pixel-based images using image layers. More on image layers is covered in Chapter 22, "Adding Image Layers." The rendering process converts the vector-based drawings to a pixel-based format when the AVI or QuickTime formats are used. Rendering and exporting topics are presented in Part IX, "Rendering and Exporting."

Anime Studio's Vector Implementation

Anime Studio isn't the first software package to enable vector-based graphics. Other popular vector-based software packages include Adobe Illustrator, Adobe Flash, and CorelDRAW. But, unlike these popular drawing packages, Anime Studio includes some unique features that make it especially easy to use for animating.

> **Note**
>
> If you're comfortable with any of these other vector-based programs, you'll be happy to know that Anime Studio can import Illustrator's AI and EPS formats. More on importing these formats is presented in Chapter 7, "Importing Content and Downloading New Content."

Curves and Points and That's All!

One of the key differences between the other vector-based drawing packages and Anime Studio is in its simplicity. The other packages deal with many different types of objects, but Anime Studio deals only with simple curves and points; all the various shapes are boiled down to these simple elements. This makes animating with Anime Studio incredibly easy, and it also gives you the ability to edit all shapes, whether it's a simple line or a fragment of text, in the same consistent manner.

Points are designated by simple hollow squares, as shown in Figure 8.3. When selected, these hollow squares become solid red squares. Curves are simple lines that run between two points. Points can exist by themselves, but curves always have a point at either end.

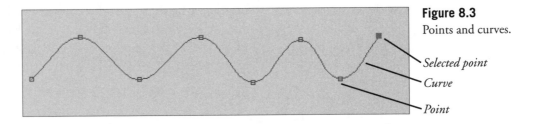

Figure 8.3
Points and curves.

Selected point

Curve

Point

Anime Studio includes an assortment of tools and features for drawing and editing points and curves. These various tools and features are covered in the rest of the chapters in this part.

Welding Points

The simplicity of dealing with only curves and points is helped by another great feature—welding. Any point can be welded instantly to another point or anywhere on a curve within the same layer. By welding points and curves together, you can link the two so that moving one will move the welded curve with it. This not only makes it easy to keep objects secure, but it also helps as you deform the objects during an animation.

For example, Figure 8.4 shows a simple face. The eyeballs and pupils are connected with hidden lines that aren't rendered, but they connect the two eyes together, making it easy to select and move both eyes together. This keeps the relative distance between the eyes constant.

Figure 8.4
Face with connected eyes.

Combined Fill and Stroke Tools

All curves in Anime Studio are referred to as *strokes,* and these strokes have several different properties that you can change, including width, color, and style. When a stroke creates a complete loop so that the beginning and end points coincide, the object becomes a closed curve or a shape.

Shapes are unique because they can hold a fill. A *fill* is a color or pattern that appears inside of the shape, and fills have their own properties that can be set. The properties of strokes and fills are presented in greater detail in Chapter 13, "Filling Shapes and Using Strokes." Default shapes are created using the Draw Shape (E) tool, or you can create a custom shape using one of the other drawing tools by welding the beginning point to ending points to close the shape.

Figure 8.5 shows three raindrops. The left raindrop shows only the paths and points. These lines are not rendered. The middle raindrop shows a raindrop with only strokes, and the right raindrop has a stroke and a fill.

Figure 8.6 shows these raindrops when rendered. The right raindrop includes a shade effect that is only visible when the file is rendered. Notice that the leftmost raindrop isn't rendered since it didn't include a stroke color.

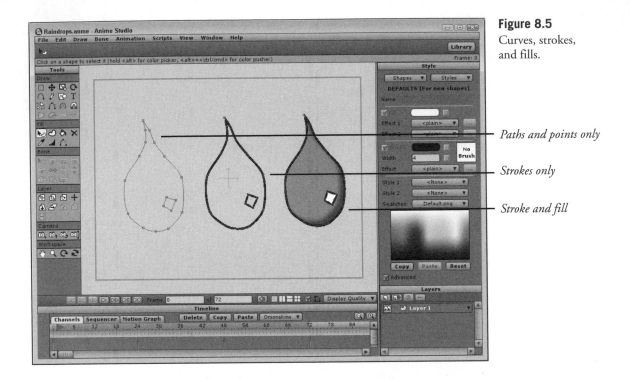

Figure 8.5
Curves, strokes, and fills.

Paths and points only

Strokes only

Stroke and fill

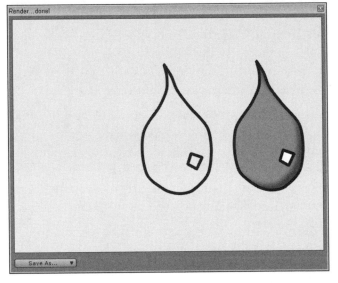

Figure 8.6
Rendered results.

Moving Groups of Points with Bones

Another huge feature in Anime Studio that distinguishes it from other vector-based packages is the ability to bind layers and groups of points to a nonrendered bone object. Once bound, you can move all the bound points quickly by moving the bone object. Bones can be used to animate characters quickly and easily. You can learn more about using bones in Chapter 26, "Creating and Binding Bones," and animating with bones in Chapter 27, "Animating with Bones."

Using the Vector Layer Settings

When a vector layer is selected in the Layers palette, an additional panel is added to the Layer Settings dialog box, as shown in Figure 8.7. You can access the Layer Settings dialog box by double-clicking the layer or by clicking the Layer Settings button at the top of the Layers palette.

Figure 8.7
Vectors panel of the Layer Settings dialog box.

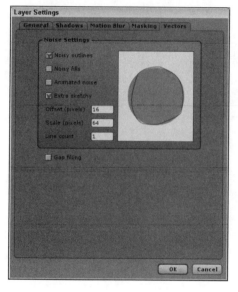

Within the Vectors panel are several settings for giving the stroke or fill of the objects on the current vector layer a hand-drawn look. The Noisy Outlines setting enables this randomness for the object's strokes, and the Noise Fills option does the same for the object's fill. If you enable Animated Noise, the randomness changes within bounds over time. The blue circle in the Vectors panel provides an instant preview of the given settings to give you an idea of what the current settings will produce.

Tip

Enabling the Animated Noise option gives the vector objects a jiggling look when animated.

Caution

The Animated Noise option will be lost to the Flash SWF format during exporting. To keep the animated noise results, export to AVI, QuickTime, or to a sequential image format like PNG.

The Offset, Scale, and Extra Lines options control the variety of randomness applied to the vector layer objects. The Offset value determines the average distance that the stroke or fill strays from its drawn path. Figure 8.8 shows the results of changing the Offset value from left to right to 0, 5, 10, 20, and 50, respectively.

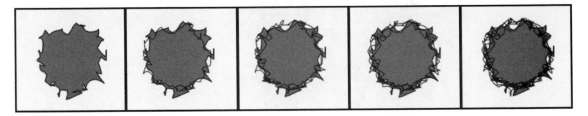

Figure 8.8
Results of changing the Offset value.

The Scale value determines the area within which adjacent sections of the stroke or the fill can be moved. Larger scale values result in gradual changes and smaller scale values yield sharper changes with more details. Figure 8.9 shows the results of changing the Scale value from left to right to 50, 25, 10, 5, and 2.

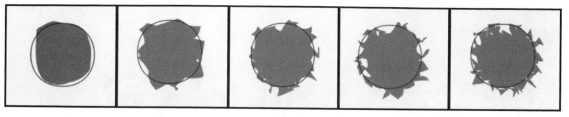

Figure 8.9
Results of changing the Scale value.

Tip

If both the Noisy Outlines and the Noise Fills options are selected, then the fill will match the altered stroke.

The Extra Lines value is only available when the Noisy Outlines option is enabled. This value duplicates the stroke using the same settings to create a new random stroke. The results can create a controlled scribble. Figure 8.10 shows the results by incrementing the Extra Lines value from 0 to 4 from left to right.

Figure 8.10
Results of changing the Extra Lines value.

The Gap Filling option helps fix anti-aliased lines that don't blend together correctly. Enabling this option will help to fix this problem.

Once any of these settings are enabled, the vector layer is updated automatically to show the resulting noisy lines and fills. Using these settings, you can create a kid's-style drawing quickly, such as the one in Figure 8.11. These settings are also good for achieving a hand-drawn look.

Figure 8.11
Random strokes and
fills make a kid's-style
drawing.

Chapter Summary

This chapter introduced the concept of vector layers by explaining the benefits of working with vector-based graphics and showing how they differ from pixel-based graphics. It also explained how Anime Studio's implementation is built for animation and covered the Vectors panel in the Layer Settings dialog box used to create random curves.

In the next chapter, we'll start dissecting the Tools palette. The first section of tools is the Draw section. These are the tools that you'll use to create and edit curves and shapes.

9

Using the Drawing Tools

- Introducing the drawing tools
- Drawing freehand curves
- Using the Add Points tool
- Creating rectangles, ovals, and arrowed lines
- Using the draw scripts

When a vector layer is selected in the Layers palette, the Draw tools become enabled in the Tools palette. These tools are the first and perhaps most used tools in the entire Tools palette. With these tools you can create and edit points and curves. This chapter will introduce the various Draw tools, but only the tools to create curves and shapes will be covered in this chapter, including the tools to draw freehand curves, precise controlled curves, regular shapes, and even arrowed lines. Finally, a number of draw scripts exist for quickly creating and working with curves and shapes. The remaining Draw tools will be covered in subsequent chapters. So don't just sit there—click a tool and dirty up that blank main window.

Introducing the Tools

The tools in the Draw and Fill sections of the Tools palette become available when a vector layer is selected in the Layers palette. The tools in the Draw section let you create and manipulate new points, curves, and shapes, and the tools in the Fill section enable you to change and manipulate the fill and stroke that is applied to an object.

Whenever a tool is selected, it is highlighted yellow and its icon appears in the top-left corner of the Options bar. The available options change depending on the tool that is selected. For example, when the Select Points tool (G) is selected, the Options bar includes a field where you can name the current selection, but when the Translate Points tool (T) is selected, the Options bar includes text fields showing the X and Y position of the selected point relative to the origin point. You can also find information about how to use the selected tool in the status bar located directly underneath the Options bar.

The available tools also depend on what is selected. For example, when no points or only one point is selected, the Scale Points, Rotate Points, Shear, Perspective, Bend, and Noise tools are disabled. When disabled, the tool icons are dimmed.

> **Note**
>
> The tools contained in the default Tools palette can be replaced with custom scripted tools. To learn how to customize the Tools palette, see Chapter 36, "Customizing the Interface."

Using the Draw Tools

It is no coincidence that the Draw section of the Tools palette is the largest section. With these tools, you can create just about any type of shape. Figure 9.1 lists each of the tools available in the Draw section, and the list that follows defines its purpose.

> **Note**
>
> Some of the tools in the Draw section of the Tools palette are only available in Anime Studio Pro as noted in Figure 9.1.

Figure 9.1
The Draw tools are highlighted here.

*Anime Studio
Pro only*

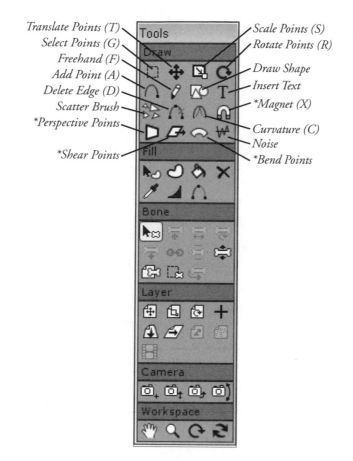

Translate Points (T)
Select Points (G)
Freehand (F)
Add Point (A)
Delete Edge (D)
Scatter Brush
*Perspective Points
*Shear Points

Scale Points (S)
Rotate Points (R)
Draw Shape
Insert Text
*Magnet (X)
Curvature (C)
Noise
*Bend Points

■ **Select Points (G):** This tool selects individual points, a group of points, or all the points on a curve or in a shape.

■ **Translate Points (T):** This tool moves the selected points.

■ **Scale Points (S):** This tool places a scaling tool that is used to scale the selected points by dragging its handles.

■ **Rotate Points (R):** This tool rotates the selected points about their center.

■ **Add Point (A):** This tool draws lines by clicking and dragging in the working area. It also adds points to an existing curve.

■ **Freehand (F):** This tool draws freehand curves by simply dragging in the working area, like using a pencil.

■ **Draw Shape (E):** This tool creates a variety of shapes, including rectangles, ovals, triangles, stars, arrows, and spirals by specifying the shape's upper-left and lower-right corners.

- **Insert Text:** This tool opens the Insert Text dialog box where you enter a text string and select a font to add to the project.
- **Scatter Brush:** This tool paints a selected shape that is randomly oriented and colored to follow a path.
- **Delete Edge (D):** This tool deletes a curve between two adjacent points.
- **Curvature (C):** This tool changes the curvature of the selected points by dragging in the working area.
- **Magnet (X):** This tool moves all points within a specified circular area. The amount that the points move depends on how close they are to the center of the defined magnet area.
- **Perspective Points:** This tool changes the perspective of the selected points by stretching out the points on one side and scrunching the points on the opposite side, as if the selected points were tilted.
- **Shear Points:** This tool slants the selected points by moving the points on one side of the shape in one direction and the points on the opposite side in the opposite direction.
- **Bend Points:** This tool causes the selected points to bend about their center point.
- **Noise:** This tool distorts the selected points by randomly moving them in different directions.

New Feature

The Draw section of the Tools palette has been simplified in Anime Studio 6 by combining several tools into one. For example, the Rectangle, Oval, and Arrow tools are now all part of the Draw Shape tool and the Bend Points H and Bend Points V tools are combined into a single Bend Points tool. The Scatter Brush and Insert Text tools are also new to this section in Anime Studio 6.

Drawing Freehand Curves

If you are tired of all these various buttons and you just want to doodle, then click the Freehand tool (F) (which looks like pencil) and you can draw curves by dragging in the working area, as shown in Figure 9.2. The drawn line and its points appear as you draw if the Show Paths checkbox at the bottom edge of the working area is enabled. If the Show Paths checkbox is disabled, then nothing appears as you draw, but when you release the mouse button, the line appears. The number of points that are created depends on the Freehand options you have selected. The available options for this and all tools are shown in the Options bar located beneath the menus.

Figure 9.2
The Freehand tool
lets you doodle.

In the Options bar are several options that apply to freehand-drawn curves. The Auto-Weld option causes the endpoint of a drawn curve to be welded automatically to a curve or to a point that is within the tolerance area surrounding the endpoint. The tolerance area is highlighted as a light red circle, as shown in Figure 9.3. Holding down the Alt/Opt key when releasing the mouse button causes the Auto-Weld option to be ignored.

When Auto-Fill is enabled, the closed shape is automatically filled using the color and style defined in the Style palette. This only occurs when a closed shape is drawn. You can create a closed shape by enabling the Auto-Weld option and connecting the endpoint to the start point or by enabling the Auto-Close option.

The Auto-Stroke option automatically applies current stroke settings of color, width, and effect to the drawn curve. If this option is disabled, the new curve is drawn with a single pixel-width black line. The default lines are called *paths*. They can be made into a shape and rendered if you apply an stroke to them, but paths by themselves are not rendered.

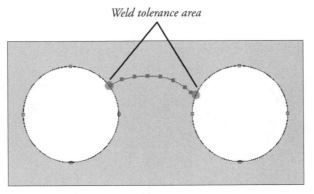

Figure 9.3
The weld tolerance area.

The Auto-Close option automatically connects the last point to the first using a straight line to create a closed shape. The Auto-Weld option is disabled when the Auto-Close option is enabled.

Simplifying Freehand Curves

In addition to the checkbox options, the Freehand tool also includes a pop-up palette of options that you can access. The Freehand Options palette, shown in Figure 9.4, appears when you click the Freehand Options button in the Options bar.

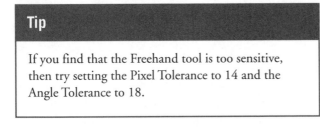

Tip

If you find that the Freehand tool is too sensitive, then try setting the Pixel Tolerance to 14 and the Angle Tolerance to 18.

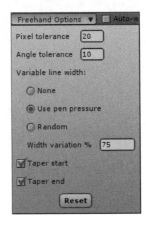

Figure 9.4
Freehand options are shown here.

The Pixel Tolerance is used to determine how close together adjacent points are to each other, which means the minimum distance in pixels between points. Higher pixel tolerance values result in curves that lose all their details, but lower values yield many points that run together. A value between 12 and 15 is a good place to start. If you need more detail, then lower the value, and if you are still getting too many points, then increase the value. The minimum Pixel Tolerance value is 2.

Note

The Freehand options are only applied to curves that are drawn after the settings are made and cannot be applied to existing paths.

Figure 9.5 shows three freehand lightning bolts. The left bolt was drawn with a Pixel Tolerance value of 2. Notice how the points are stacked on top of one another. The middle bolt has a Pixel Tolerance value of 10, which simplifies the points almost too much, and the right bolt has a Pixel Tolerance value of 20, making the bolt lose almost all its details.

Note

Since the Pixel Tolerance value is based on pixels, you'll get a different density of points if you zoom way in on the working area rather than if you zoomed out.

Figure 9.5
Changing Pixel Tolerance.

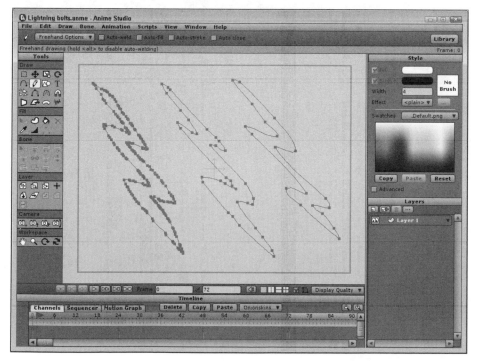

The Angle Tolerance value simplifies curves by removing points that deviate from the drawn curve by less than the designated angle. Setting the Angle Tolerance value to 0 results in no points being removed. This captures every subtle point, but a high Angle Tolerance value will remove all details from a drawn curve. The maximum allowed Angle Tolerance value is 30. Figure 9.6 shows three freehand stars. The left star has an Angle Tolerance of 0, which makes a large number of points visible. The middle star has an Angle Tolerance of 10, allowing a fair number of points, and the right star has an Angle Tolerance of 30, making the resulting curve very round and smooth with few points.

Tip

Keep in mind as you draw that more points means more memory, which is compounded as the object is animated frame over frame. Using the fewest number of points to create an object is a good practice.

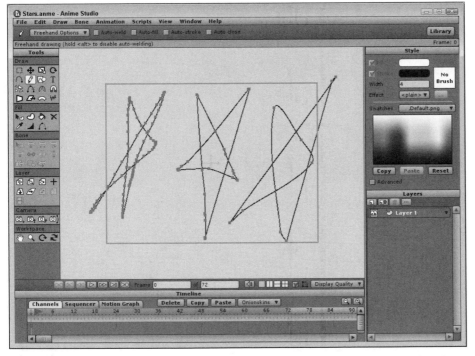

Figure 9.6
Changing Angle Tolerance.

The Variable Line Width settings include options to have the line thickness vary with the pen pressure of a graphics tablet or to randomly vary up to the designated Width Variation percentage. Figure 9.7 shows a simple arrow drawn with the Freehand tool (F) with the Random Variable Line Width option enabled.

Note

If you draw a curve with the Variable Line Width options enabled, the line width will only appear in the working area if the Auto-Stroke option is enabled. If the Auto-Stroke option is disabled, the variable line width is still retained, but it only appears when a stroke is added to the curve. Strokes are also only visible in the working area if the Strokes option in the Display Quality pop-up menu is enabled.

Figure 9.7
Random variable line width.

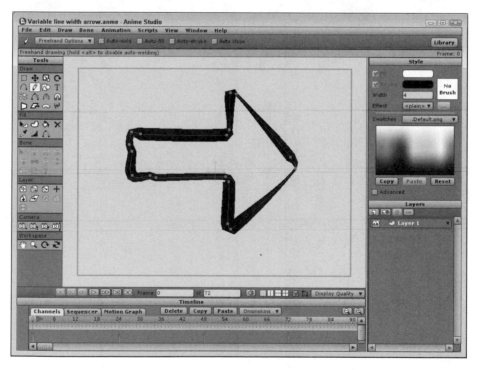

The Taper options set the beginning or end of a line to taper gradually. These options can be used with or without the Variable Line Width options. If the variable line width is set to None and the Taper options are enabled, then the line thickness will gradually increase to the maximum Line Width value, as set in the Style palette, and then gradually taper back to 0 at the end of the curve, as shown in Figure 9.8.

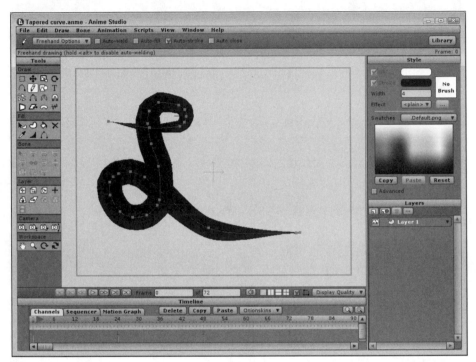

Figure 9.8
Tapering line width.

The Reset button at the bottom of the Freehand Options palette sets all the options to their default values.

Randomizing Line Width

When drawing a line using the Freehand tool, the settings specified in the Options pop-up palette are used. If these settings are incorrect, then you'll need to redraw the line. But the Draw menu includes a couple of commands that you can use to reset the line thickness or randomize the line width.

New Feature

The Random Line Width and Reset Line Width menu commands are new in Anime Studio 6.

You can make the line width for the selected line random using the Draw, Random Line Width (Ctrl/Cmd+D) menu. This opens a simple dialog box where you can set the Minimum and Maximum Width values. This is applied immediately to only the selected points.

To remove the random line width, simply select the Draw, Reset Line Width (Ctrl/Cmd+L) menu. This command resets the selected points to the Width setting that was set when the line was drawn. It also removes any taper effect on the curve.

> **Note**
>
> The Random Line Width and Reset Line Width menu commands are only available in Anime Studio Pro.

Drawing with a Graphics Tablet

Anime Studio supports drawing with a graphics tablet using the Freehand tool. Several different types of graphic tablets are available, but the most common type are tablets that use a pen stylus. Wacom makes several different size graphic tablets ranging from the budget-conscious 4-inch-by-9-inch version to the professional level 12-by-19 version. Most can connect directly using the USB port and others are wireless, allowing you to draw from across the room. You can find more information about Wacom graphic tablets at www.wacom.com.

One of the benefits of using a graphics tablet is that the pen can sense the amount of pressure you are applying to the tablet. This pressure can be used to alter the line width of the freehand curve simulating the result of drawing with an actual pen or pencil.

Using the Add Points Tool

The Freehand tool is great for drawing curves, but sometimes you want to create a curve by placing specific points in specific locations. For this task, the Add Points tool (A) is what you want to use. With the Add Points tool, you can click in the working area to place points, and the curve that is created runs smoothly through these various points.

To create a curve with the Add Points tool, click at the location of the first point and then drag to the location of the second point and release the mouse button.

If you click again after releasing the mouse button, you can drag to place another point that will be attached to the curve. If you move the mouse cursor after creating a point, then a new curve is started.

The Add Points tool can also be used to connect any two existing points with a curve by clicking on one point and dragging to another one. When you connect two end points together, the curve will automatically change so that there is a smooth transition between the two points. You can also press the Spacebar to initiate a weld between the new point you're dragging and the point you're dragging over.

The Add Points tool can also be used to add points to an existing curve. This is helpful if you need to edit an existing curve. To add a new point, simply click on the curve where you want the new point to be. If you hold the mouse button down after creating a new point, you can drag the point and the curve will follow. This allows you to add a new point and edit the curve in one move.

If the welding of points creates a new closed curve, then the shape is automatically filled if the Auto-Fill option is enabled. Fills and strokes are only visible in the working area if their respective options are enabled in the Display Quality dialog box.

If the Sharp Corners option is enabled, the new curves aren't smoothed between adjacent points. This results in a sharp zig-zag shaped line. Figure 9.9 shows a set of curves drawn with the Add Points tool. The one on the left has the Sharp Corners option disabled so that all the lines are smoothed, but the one on the right has the Sharp Corners option enabled so that each line segment is straight.

If you want to prevent new points created with the Add Points tool from being welded to any existing curves, you can hold down the Alt/Opt key while clicking. This forces each new click to begin a new curve instead of attaching them together.

Although grid snapping doesn't apply to the Freehand tool, it does affect any curves created with the Add Points tool (A). If the grid is turned on and the View, Disable Grid Snapping option is disabled, then all points created with the Add Points tool are automatically snapped to the grid points. This makes it easy to quickly create regularly spaced shapes, like those in Figure 9.10.

To draw shapes using the Add Points tool, follow these steps:

1. Select the File, New menu command to open a new blank project.

2. Enable the Grid option at the bottom of the working area and make sure the View, Disable Grid Snapping option is disabled.

Figure 9.9
Smooth versus
sharp corners.

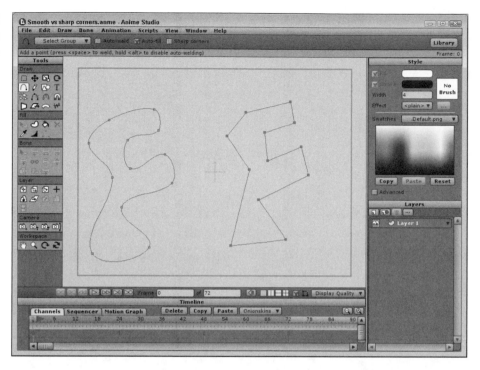

Figure 9.10
Grid snapped curves.

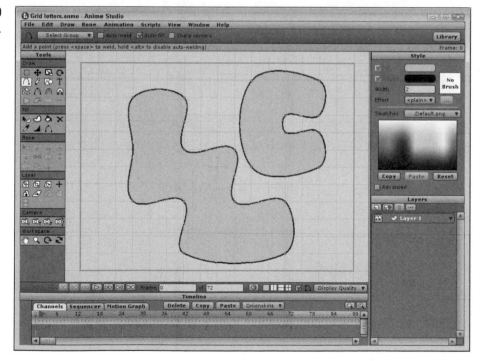

3. Select the Add Points tool or press the A key. Enable the Auto-Weld and the Auto-Fill options in the Options bar at the top of the working area. Then click in the working area on the grid intersections and drag to create a line. Release the mouse button to create a line. Then click on the second point and drag to create a new line. Continue to click and drag to create a letter A shape. When you click on the first point again, the letter is automatically filled and closed.

4. Next to the letter A, create a letter S using the same process. Then draw in a triangle within the letter A.

5. With the Add Points tool still selected, click on one point in the triangle and drag to one of the points in the letter A. Then click and drag to create a line connecting the two closest points between the two letters. Figure 9.11 shows the resulting letters.

6. Choose the Select Points tool (G) and click on one of the points to select it. Then press the Tab key to select all connected points. Click the Translate Points tool (T) and drag the selected points; all the points in both shapes move together since they are connected.

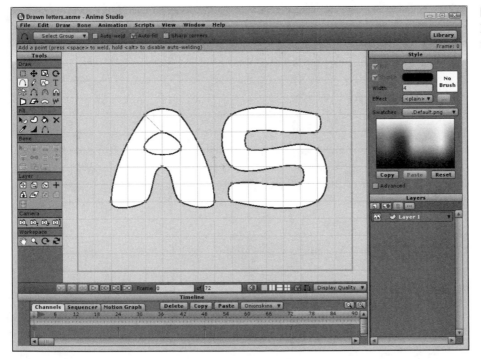

Figure 9.11
Letters drawn with the Add Points tool.

Shapes

The Tools palette includes a single tool for drawing multiple simple shapes. The Draw Shape (E) tool offers the ability to draw rectangles (and squares), ovals (and circles), triangles, stars, arrows, and spirals. Each type of shape is available for selection on the Options bar.

New Feature

Although the ability to draw each of the various shapes was available in the previous version of Anime Studio, combining all these shapes into a single tool is new to Anime Studio 6.

Drawing Rectangles and Ovals

Dragging with the Draw Shape tool with either the Rectangle or the Oval options selected create shapes with four points and connected curves in the working area, as shown in Figure 9.12. If you hold down the Shift key, the Rectangle tool makes a perfect square and the Oval tool makes a perfect circle. You can also hold down the Alt/Opt key to have the shape be created from the center point outward. This is especially helpful if you need to create a circle from a center point, such as when you draw eyeballs.

Figure 9.12
Rectangles
and Ovals.

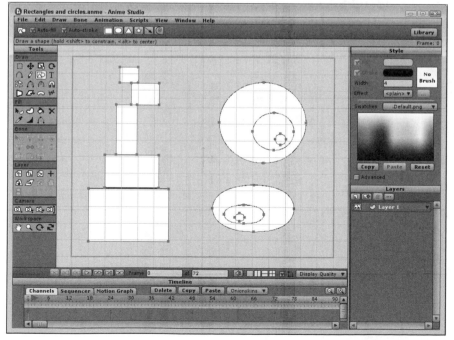

Since both of these tools create completed shapes, you can select the Auto-Fill option to automatically have the Fill options applied to the shape once it is complete. The Auto-Stroke option applies the stroke settings to the shape.

These tools will also work when grid snapping is enabled.

Drawing Triangles and Five-Pointed Stars

Selecting this Triangle option for the Draw Shape tool creates a simple triangle. If you hold down the Shift key while dragging, then the triangle is a perfect equilateral triangle with equal angles at each corner.

The Star option creates a five-pointed star. Holding down the shift key creates a uniform star without any distortion. You can also drag both the triangle and the star from the center outward by holding down the Alt/Opt key.

Note

Using the Scripts, Draw, Stars menu, you can create stars with a different number of points. This script is covered in the next section.

Creating Arrowed Lines and Spirals

The Arrow option for the Draw Shape tool is used to create straight lines with an arrowhead at the end of the line. When an arrowhead is created, as shown in Figure 9.13, it adds a triangle on the tips of the arrowhead that you can alter to change the look of the arrows. Holding down the Shift key constrains the arrow line to a straight vertical or horizontal line.

The Spiral option for the Draw Shape tool is used to create clockwise or counterclockwise spirals, depending on the direction that you drag with the mouse. When you drag with the mouse, the spiral starts as a simple curve, but the farther you drag from the center, the more revolutions are created. Holding down the Alt/Opt key starts the spiral winding in the opposite direction. Figure 9.14 shows a number of simple spirals created with this option.

New Feature

The Spiral option for the Draw Shape tool is new in Anime Studio 6.

Figure 9.13
Arrows.

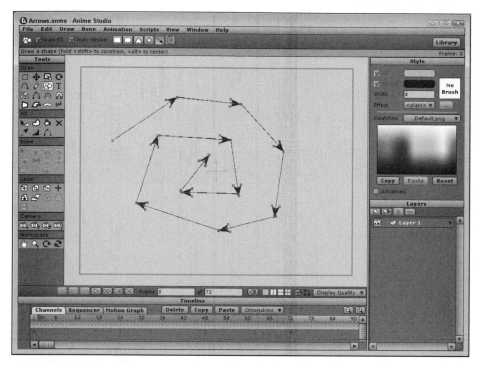

Figure 9.14
Spirals.

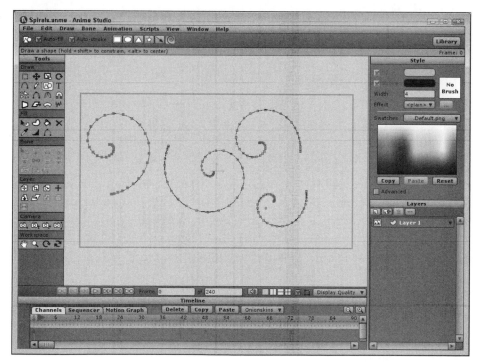

Using Draw Scripts

In the Scripts, Draw menu are several scripts that you can use to apply a sketchy effect, auto weld shapes, quickly create different shapes, and automatically split selected curves into equal segments. The available draw scripts are Apply Sketchy Effect, Auto Weld, Polygon, Split Curve, and Star.

Note

The Scripts menu is only available in Anime Studio Pro.

Creating a Sketchy Effect

The Scripts, Draw, Apply Sketchy Effect randomly changes all paths on all layers to create a sketchy look. The script does this by automatically enabling the Noisy Outlines, Animated Noise, and Extra Sketchy options in the Vectors panel of the Layer Settings dialog box. It also sets the Offset and Line Count values to 6 and the Scale value to 48. You can learn more about these settings in Chapter 8, "Using Vector Layers."

The convenience of this script is that it quickly enables these options for all paths on all layers. Figure 9.15 shows this script applied to the default character.

Auto-Welding Paths

The Freehand tool has an Auto-Weld option on the Options bar that will cause endpoints that end on a point or on a line to be automatically welded. You can also weld points that are moved with the Translate Points tool to a point or a line by holding down the Spacebar while releasing the mouse button.

If you've drawn several lines that you wanted welded without the Auto-Weld option enabled, then it can take some time to weld each point individually. The quicker alternative is to use the Scripts, Draw, Auto Weld menu. This will auto weld any endpoint that is positioned over another point in the selected group of points. It will not weld any points to lines, though.

New Feature

The Sketchy Effect and Auto Weld scripts are both new to Anime Studio 6.

Figure 9.15
Sketchy effect.

Drawing Polygons, and Stars

The Scripts, Draw, Polygon script opens a dialog box when it is selected, as shown in Figure 9.16. Using the Polygon dialog box, you can set the number of points in the polygon. The dialog box also shows a preview of the polygon before it is drawn. If you enable the Create Polygon in New Layer option, the new polygon is drawn in a new layer. If this option isn't enabled, then the polygon is drawn on the current vector layer.

The Star script also opens a dialog box when selected, as shown in Figure 9.17. Using the Star dialog box, you can set the number of points that appear on the outside and inside of the star. You can also set the Inner Radius value for the star shape. The dialog box also shows a preview of the star before it is drawn. This preview is helpful for giving you an idea of what the final star will look like. If you enable the Create Star in New Layer option, the new star is drawn in a new layer. If this option isn't enabled, then the polygon is drawn on the current vector layer.

Splitting Curves

The Split Curve script automatically divides the selected curves into equal segments by adding in the number of points along each curve that is indicated in the Split Curve dialog box, as shown in Figure 9.18. The Split Curve script doesn't actually split the curve into separate segments. The added points are still part of the existing curve.

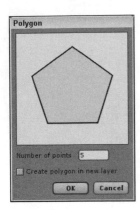

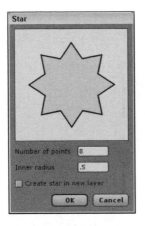

Figure 9.16
Polygon dialog box.

Figure 9.17
Star dialog box.

Figure 9.18
Split Curve dialog box.

Tip

Adding points using the Add Points tool will change the curvature of the object, but using the Split Curves script will add points to the curve without changing its curvature.

Chapter Summary

This chapter introduced the Draw section of tools in the Tools palette. Several of these tools are used to create curves and shapes on the currently selected vector layer. Whether you're creating exact, precise curves with the Add Points tool or doodling with the Freehand tool, each of these tools lets you draw and manipulate curves and shapes to fill out the vector layer. The Scripts, Draw menu also includes some features for creating some unique shapes.

Now that you know how to draw on vector layers, we'll next cover another important type of shape that forms letters. The Insert Text tool lets you add text to a vector layer. You can even select a font to use.

10

Working with Text

- Inserting text
- Changing the font and sizing the text
- Dealing with foreign characters
- Adding credits

While a large number of the tools found in the Draw section of the Tools palette are used to add and edit paths and shapes to the selected vector layer, the Insert Text tool can also be used to add content to the current vector layer.

The Insert Text dialog box lets you add a line of text to the project; the added text is instantly converted to paths and points just like the other vector layer objects. The Insert Text dialog box also includes settings to change the font, center the text, and to create a single fill for the text.

The Scripts, Other, Credits menu command is another way to add text to the project. The Credits script can display multiple lines of text. It also includes settings for controlling how long the text is displayed, the delay between credit screens, and over how many frames the credit text fades.

Inserting Text

To add text to the current project, select the Insert Text tool in the Tools palette or choose the Draw, Insert Text menu command. This opens the Insert Text dialog box shown in Figure 10.1. Simply type the text that you want to add to the scene into the Text field and choose the font from the available system fonts displayed in the list to the right.

> **Note**
>
> The Insert Text tool and the Draw, Insert Text menu command is only available if a vector layer is selected in the Layers palette.

Figure 10.1
Insert Text dialog box.

—Font list

—Text preview

A preview of the text you entered is displayed in the selected font in the middle of the dialog box. This preview text is updated whenever you change the text or select a new font.

> **Note**
>
> When converting text to paths, Anime Studio automatically uses enough points to accurately create the text in the current font. Complex fonts will result in more points than using simple fonts.

When text is created, it is automatically filled using the current fill settings and stroked using the current stroke settings, as shown in Figure 10.2. If the Create One Fill option is enabled, then you can select all letters in the text selection by clicking the fill of just one of the letters. If this option is disabled, then each letter is independent of the others.

Tip

As long as the Insert Text dialog box is open, you can change the fill and stroke properties in the Style palette, but once the OK button is clicked, the style properties are used on the new text.

Figure 10.2
The new text is selected.

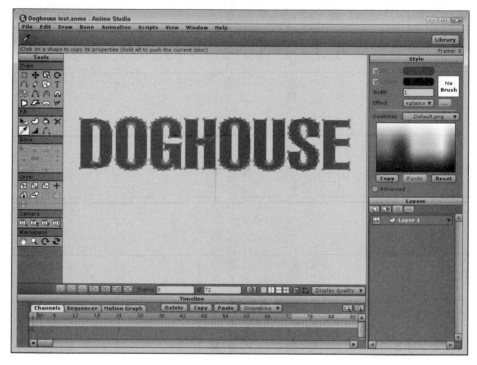

When text is created, it is aligned with the first letter at the main window's origin, but if the Center Text Horizontally option is enabled, then the center of the text is aligned to the window's origin.

> **Note**
>
> When text is created, it is converted automatically to points and paths, which means if you misspell a word, you'll need to insert the missing letter manually.

To create and edit text, follow these steps:

1. Choose a vector layer in the Layer palette and select the Draw, Insert Text menu command or click the Insert Text tool. The Insert Text dialog box appears.

2. Enter the words *Welcome to* in the Text field, select a font from the font list such as Courier New Bold Italic, enable the Create One Fill and the Center Text Horizontally options, and click the OK button. The text is added to the vector layer, and the text is selected.

3. With the text selected, scale the text down to fit within the working area using the Scale Points tool (S). The text remains centered as it is scaled.

4. Choose the Draw, Insert Text menu command again and enter the word *Heaven* in the text field. Then disable the Create One Fill option and click the OK button. The text is added to the working area on top of the existing text.

5. With the new text selected, move the text below the existing text with the Translate Points tool (T).

6. Choose the Select Shape tool (Q) and click one of the letters in the first line of text and then change the fill color in the Style palette. Since the text was created as one fill, all the letters were selected and filled when you clicked on just a single letter.

7. With the Select Shape (Q) tool still selected, click the first letter of the second line of text and change the fill color in the Style palette. Since the second line of text was created with the Create One Fill option disabled, each letter is selected independently of the others. Figure 10.3 shows the resulting text with only the first letter colored differently.

Figure 10.3
Text can be one fill or individually filled by letter.

Copying and Pasting Existing Text

In addition to typing text into the Text field of the Insert Text dialog box, you can also copy text from another application and paste it directly into the Text field.

Caution

There isn't a published limit on the size of the text string that can be entered into the Text field, but keep in mind that letters can create a large number of points and a long string of text can easily become a memory burden that can choke the program.

Converting Text to Paths

If you look for a converting to text feature, you won't find it. Text in Anime Studio is automatically converted to paths when it is added to a vector layer. This gives you an easy way to edit the text as individual characters, but it makes it hard to edit the text and correct any typos. Once the text is added to the vector layer, it loses its text nature and simply becomes a bunch of points and paths.

Changing Font and Text Size

Since the text is automatically converted to points and paths, you can quickly change its size using the Scale Points tool (S), so the Insert Text dialog box doesn't include any Font Size value. When scaling a selection of text, dragging with a corner handle maintains the text's proportions.

Caution

The Insert Text dialog box populates its list of fonts from the Library/fonts folder. If you use a font-handling tool like Suitcase, then your fonts might be located in a different folder where Anime Studio can't find them. If this happens, the Font list in the Insert Text dialog box will be empty. To have the fonts appear, make sure they are located in the Library/fonts folder.

If you select a graphic font such as Wingdings, you can easily create a number of unique shapes, such as those displayed in Figure 10.4.

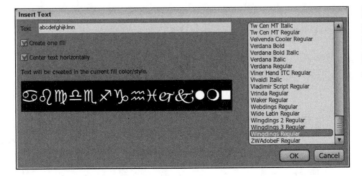

Figure 10.4
Special characters can be copied and pasted in the Insert Text dialog box.

Dealing with Foreign Characters

Some foreign characters such as diacritical accents like the tilde (~)can be added to the Insert Text dialog box, but you need to know the keystrokes that make these special characters. One easy way to do this is to locate the exact characters you want in a word processor and then simply copy and paste them into the Text field, as shown in Figure 10.5.

> **Note**
>
> As of version 6, Anime Studio supports Unicode, so you will be able to include some foreign characters in the Insert Text dialog box such as Asian, Russian, or Arabic characters.

Figure 10.5
Special characters can be copied and pasted in the Insert Text dialog box.

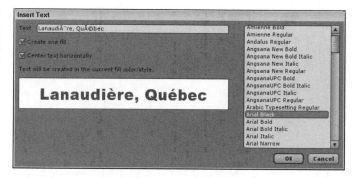

Adding Credits to Your Project

The Scripts, Other, Credits menu command runs a script that opens a file dialog box where you can select a simple text file that includes the credits for the current project. Before the file dialog box opens, the Credits dialog box, shown in Figure 10.6, appears and lets you choose the style for the credits text, including its font, duration, delay, and fade.

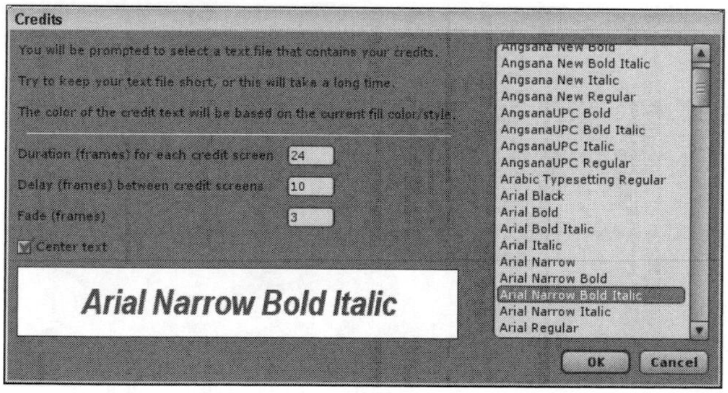

Figure 10.6
The Credits dialog box.

The text file that is added to the Credits script can include several lines of text. Each separate line of text gets its own slide and can fade in and out for the given duration. To create a separate slide of text, you need to add a blank line to the text file. For example, if you have a text file with one line of text followed by a blank line and then two lines of text, and if the duration is set to 24 frames and the Delay is set to 10, then the first line of text will appear from frames 1 to 24, the text will disappear for 10 frames, and then the second two lines of text will appear for another 24 frames.

Tip

The Credits script can be used to insert multiple lines of text into the current project.

Caution

The Credits script won't work with standard word processor files like Microsoft Word unless they are saved as text files.

When text is entered into the scene using the Credits script, each separate slide of text is placed on a vector layer and all the slides together are grouped under a group layer named *Credits*, as shown in Figure 10.7. Selecting an individual vector layer causes the text to appear in the main window and the text's animation keys to appear in the Timeline palette.

Tip

Even though the Credits script lets you insert multiple lines of text, if you include a large text file, it can really slow down your system because all letters are converted to points and paths.

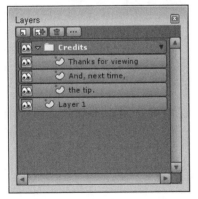

Figure 10.7
Credits in Layers palette.

To use the Credits script, follow these steps:

1. Open a text file and enter the following text. Be sure to include the blank lines and save the file as a text file when finished.

```
Thanks for viewing
this twisted display

And, next time,
try not to forget

the tip.
```

2. Choose a vector layer in the Layer palette and select the Scripts, Other, Credits menu command. The Credits dialog box appears.

3. Set the Duration to 10, the Delay value to 5, and the Fade value to 2. Before closing the Credits dialog box, change the Fill color in the Style palette to black. Choose a font in the Credits dialog box and then click the OK button. A file dialog box appears.

4. In the file dialog box, select the saved text file and click the Open button. The first two lines of text appear in the center of the working area, as shown in Figure 10.8.

Tip

If the text appears jagged in the main window, click the Display Quality pop-up menu in the lower-right corner of the main window and enable the Anti-aliasing option to smooth the text.

5. Drag the current frame bar in the Timeline palette forward to see the first slides of text disappear and the next slide of text appear, as shown in Figure 10.9. Since the text entered in the text file has blank lines, the text is split into several slides.

Note

A third way to add text to a project is with the Note layer that is specified to be rendered. Note text isn't as versatile as normal text. More on using note text is covered in Chapter 24, "Using Switch and Note Layers."

Figure 10.8
The Credits script can be used to enter multi-line text.

Figure 10.9
Dragging the current frame bar in the Timeline palette makes the other slides of text appear.

Chapter Summary

This chapter showed you how to add text to the current project. Added text lies on a vector layer along with the other paths and points and is simply a set of curves and shapes. When inserting text, you also have access to the available system fonts to change the look of the text. The Credits script can also be used to add text to the current project. It works just like the Insert Text feature but includes additional features for controlling the duration and fading of the credit text.

Now that the vector layers are populated with all kinds of curves, shapes, and text, you need to learn how to manipulate the various vector elements. The next two chapters cover all the various modifying features by first working with points and then by presenting a chapter about editing paths.

11

Editing Points

- Selecting points, curves, and shapes
- Deleting points and edges
- Changing curvature
- Transforming points
- Snapping points to a grid

Now that you've been playing around with the Draw tools, take a look at your main window. It probably is a mess with freehand curves splattered across the main window and rectangles and circles littered around the screen. But don't fret. The purpose of this chapter is to help straighten out this mess by showing you how to edit the individual points.

Before you can edit any of the objects strewn across the vector layer, you first need to be able to select the exact points that you want to work with. The Tools palette and the Edit menu include several tools and commands to help you select exactly the right points. After the right points are selected, you can delete the selected points and curves, change the curvature leading into and out of a point, and transform the various points.

Transforming points is more than just moving the points around; it also involves scaling and rotating a group of points around a specific point. This can be really handy if you need to reduce the size of a circle quickly. Simply scaling all four corner points will accomplish the task instead of moving each point individually.

Another handy way to move points around is to use the Snap to Grid feature. This feature causes the moved points or newly created points to align on the grid intersections, resulting in perfectly straight lines and right angles. Glancing again at your main window, it is obvious that you need some help, so let's get this editing points thing figured out.

Selecting Points, Curves, and Shapes

Before you can modify an existing object, you need to select the object that you want to change first. This can be accomplished by using several different tools.

Using the Select Points Tool

The Select Points tool (G) is used to select individual points, but it can also be used to select all the points on a curve or in a shape. To select a single point, simply click it. The selected point turns red. If you click a curve, then all points in the clicked curve or in the clicked shape are selected, and if you click in the middle of a shape, then all points in the shape are selected, as shown in Figure 11.1.

Figure 11.1
Selected points.

Selecting Multiple Points

To select multiple points, you can click and drag out a rectangular section, as shown in Figure 11.2. All points that are within the dragged area are selected, as shown in Figure 11.3. If you need more control over the points that are selected, you can enable Lasso mode using the Lasso Mode checkbox in the Options bar at the top of the main window. This changes the tool so that you can define the selection area by dragging the cursor around the points you want to select. When you release the mouse button, a straight line is drawn back to the beginning of the lasso line to complete the area. You can also access Lasso mode directly by holding down the Ctrl/Cmd key before you begin dragging.

Figure 11.2
Dragging with the Select Points tool.

Rectangular selection area

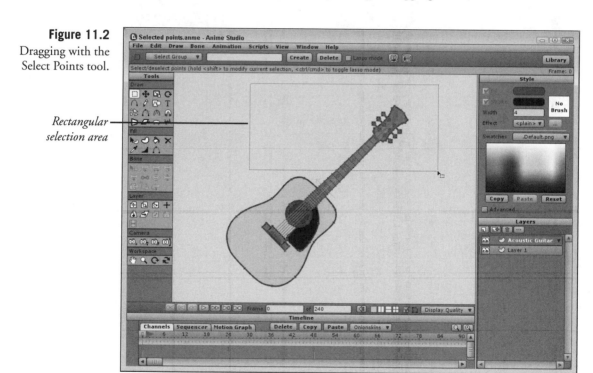

Every time you drag with the Select Points tool, you create a new selection set, but you can maintain the current selection by holding down the Shift key when selecting more points. When you hold down the Shift key, any new points that you select are added to the current selection set, and any points that are already selected will be deselected.

Figure 11.3
Selected points.

Defining a Selection Group

When a group of points is selected with the Select Points tool (G), you can name the selection set using the text field in the Options bar at the top of the main window and the Create button, as shown in Figure 11.4. New selection sets can then be recalled using the Select Group drop-down list (also in the Options bar). The Select Group drop-down list is available on the Options bar for most of the Draw and Fill tools. When a selection set is chosen, it can also be deleted using the Delete button.

> **Tip**
>
> Any time you select a set of points that you'll need to revisit, make a selection set so that you can recall the selected points instantly.

Figure 11.4
Create a selection set.

Selection set name

Selecting Points with the Edit Menu

The Edit menu also includes several commands for selecting points. These commands work regardless of which tool is selected. The Edit, Select All (Ctrl/Cmd+A) menu command selects all points on the current layer. The Edit, Select None command deselects all selected points so that none are selected. The Edit, Select Inverse (Ctrl/Cmd+I) command selects all points that are not currently selected and deselects all points that are currently selected. This is especially handy if you want to select all but a few points.

The Edit, Select Connected command causes the remaining unselected points in a curve or shape to be selected. For example, if one point of a wavy line with seven total points was selected, then the Select Connected command automatically selects all points in the curve.

Tip

It isn't listed in the Edit menu, but the keyboard shortcut for the Select Connected command is the Tab key. This is another valuable shortcut to remember.

Deleting Points

Selected points are easy to delete. Simply press the Delete key, and they are deleted. If an endpoint is deleted, then the curve attached to the endpoint is also deleted. If points on a shape are deleted, then the shape is rearranged to make up for the missing points, as shown in Figure 11.5. Selected points can also be deleted using the Edit, Clear menu.

Figure 11.5
Deleted points.

To practice selecting and deleting points, follow these steps:

1. Open the Checkerboard.anme file from the Chapter 11 folder on the included CD. This file includes two layers creating a checkerboard, but the checkerboard is wider than its length, so you'll need to delete the last column of squares.

2. Choose the black squares layer in the Layers palette; then click the Select Points tool (G) in the Tools palette and click the top black square in the last column. All the points that make up the square are selected. Press the Delete key to delete the square.

3. With the Select Points tool (G) still selected, click the upper-right corner point on the lower black square in the last column. Clicking a single point selects only that point. Choose the Edit, Select Connected menu command (Tab). This selects all points in the square. Press the Delete key to delete this shape also.

4. Select the background layer in the Layers palette and drag with the Select Points tool over the right half of the checkerboard. This selects the two right-most points in the background rectangle. Click the Translate Points tool (S) in the Tools palette and drag the two selected points to the left until they align with the black squares, as shown in Figure 11.6.

Figure 11.6
Shortened
checkerboard.

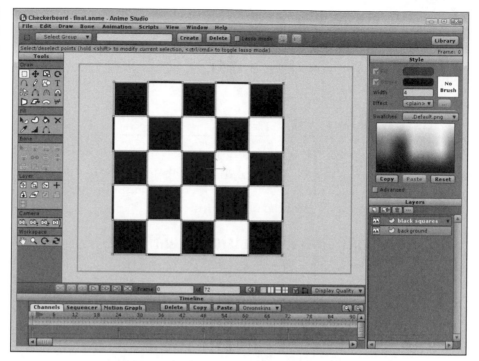

Cutting, Copying, and Pasting Points

When two or more points are selected, you can use the Cut (Ctrl/Cmd+X), Copy (Ctrl/Cmd+C), and Paste (Ctrl/Cmd+V) menu commands in the Edit menu to copy the selected points to a buffer where they can be pasted back into the project. When a curve is pasted, it appears in its original location. If the original object still remains because you did a Copy command, the pasted curve won't be visible, but if you move one of the selected sets of points, the pasted copy will be visible.

> **Note**
>
> Whenever a curve is pasted in the working area, the Translate Points tool is automatically selected regardless of the selected tool when the paste is done.

Moving Points Between Layers

When curves are pasted back into a project, they are pasted into the current layer. This provides a way to move objects between layers using the Cut, Copy, and Paste commands.

Transforming Points

The Tools palette includes three transformation tools located at the very top of the Tools palette. When a set of points is selected, you can use the Translate Points (T), Scale Points (S), or the Rotate Points (R) tools to transform their position, size, and orientation with respect to one another.

Selecting Points with the Transformation Tools

The Point Transformation tools can also be used to select points. If the Shape Select option in the Options bar is enabled, then you can select points with the Translate, Scale, or Rotate Points tools without having to select and use the Select Points tool.

With the Shape Select option set for these tools, you can click a single point to select it, or you can click a line segment between points to select all points on the curve, or you can click the center fill of a shape to select all points that make up the shape. If the Shape Select option is not enabled, then clicking and holding down the mouse will select a single point that is closest to the cursor.

> **Note**
>
> The Translate Points tool lets you make point, line, and shape selections regardless of whether the Shape Select option is enabled.

New Feature

The ability to select points, paths, and shapes with the Transform tools is new to Anime Studio 6.

When any of the Transformation tools are selected, defined selection sets can be chosen from the Select Group drop-down list.

Resetting Points

When a selection of points is moved using any of the transformation tools for any frame besides frame 0, a key is automatically set and the points will move from their default location to the new location over the range of frames between frame 0 and the frame where the key is set. The Reset button on the Options bar that appears when one of the transformation tools is selected is used to move the selected points back to the same position as defined in frame 0. More on setting keys is covered in Chapter 16, "Understanding Keyframes and Tweening."

Flipping Points

At the right end of the Options bar when the Select Points tool or one of the transformation tools is selected are two buttons used to flip the selected points horizontally or vertically. When the points are flipped, they are flipped about the center of the selection, so the flipped object is typically not moved from its current location, but you can use the Translate Points tool to move the flipped object. Figure 11.7 shows a caterpillar that has been copied and flipped both horizontally and vertically.

> **Tip**
>
> The Edit, Copy and Edit, Paste commands can be used to create a copy of the object before flipping if you want to keep the original object.

New Feature

In the previous versions, the Flip features were buttons in the Tools palette, but moving these features to the Options bar was done to simplify the Tools palette, which is new to Anime Studio 6.

Using the Translate Points Tool

The Translate Points tool (T) is used to move a single point or a set of selected points around the working area, as shown in Figure 11.8. For precise positioning, the X and Y coordinate values for the center of the selected points is displayed in the Options bar. These coordinates are absolute coordinates in reference to the working area origin. You can also enter the translation values manually in the text fields located in the Options bar.

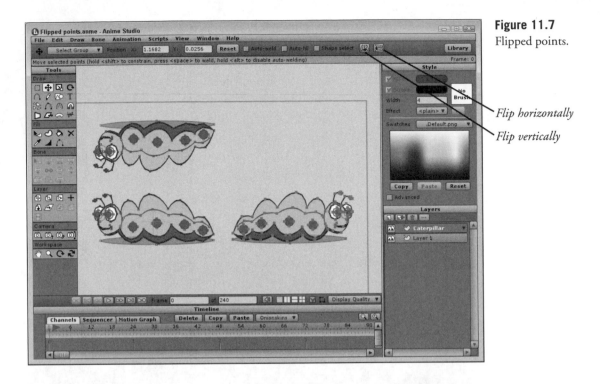

Figure 11.7
Flipped points.

Flip horizontally

Flip vertically

Figure 11.8
Translated points.

Holding down the Shift key while dragging the points causes the movement to be constrained to only horizontal or vertical movement.

Nudging Points

Holding down the Ctrl/Cmd key and pressing the arrow keys lets you nudge the selected points in the direction of the pressed arrow key. Holding down both the Ctrl/Cmd and Shift keys nudges the selected points a greater amount.

> **Note**
>
> The normal nudge with the Ctrl/Cmd key moves the selected points 1 pixel for every arrow press and the greater nudge with the Ctrl/Cmd and Shift keys moves the points 10 pixels. There isn't a preference to change these nudge amounts.

Auto-Welding Points

When a single endpoint is selected and the Auto-Weld option in the Options bar is enabled, you can weld the endpoint of a curve to any other point or line in the layer by dropping the point on another point. A small green circle will appear when the endpoint is positioned over a point and a small red circle appears when the endpoint is over a portion of the curve where it will be welded. A tone will sound when the welding is complete. If the selected point isn't an endpoint, then you can still weld it to another point or directly to a curve segment that the cursor is over by pressing the Spacebar.

If the Auto-Weld option is enabled, you can disable the welding of points by holding down the Alt/Opt key when releasing the mouse.

If two endpoints of a curve are welded together to form a closed shape and the Auto-Fill option is enabled, then the new shape is created and filled with the set fill color.

> **Note**
>
> If you have a bunch of overlaying points that need to be welded, you can select to the points and use the Scripts, Draw, Auto-Weld command to weld them all at once. More on this script is covered in Chapter 9, "Using the Drawing Tools."

Using the Scale Points Tool

The Scale Points tool (S) is only available when two or more points are selected. If a single point is selected, the tool is dimmed. When this tool is selected, a red bounding box with handles at each corner and edge appears, as shown in Figure 11.9. Dragging these handles causes the selected points to be scaled relative to each other. Dragging a side handle scales the points along a single axis, but dragging a corner scales along two axes.

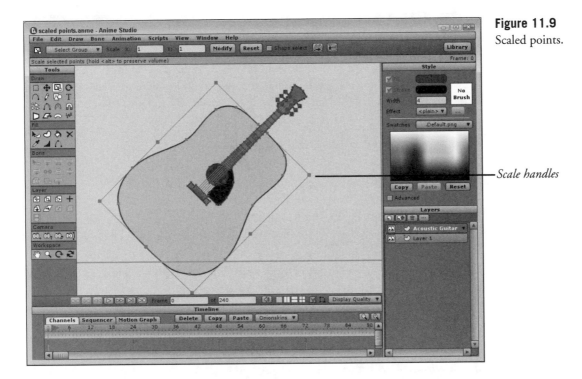

Figure 11.9
Scaled points.

Scale handles

Dragging a corner handle maintains the aspect ratio of the object, and holding down the Alt/Opt key while dragging a side handle maintains the volume of the filled object.

Tip

Using the Scale Points tool with the Alt/Opt key simulates the squash and stretch effects common for exaggerated animations.

For more precise scaling, you can use the Scale X and Scale Y values in the Options bar. Click the Modify button to apply the designated values. You can click the Modify button multiple times. Values of 1 result in no change. Scale values less than 1 reduce the scale of the selected points; values greater than 1 increase the scale of the points. The Scale values can accept negative values to move the points past one another.

Using the Rotate Points Tool

The Rotate Points tool (R) lets you spin the selected set of points around its local center, as shown in Figure 11.10. The center point around which the rotation takes place is marked with a red plus sign that appears when the tool is selected. This tool is only available when two or more points are selected. It wouldn't make any sense to rotate a single point around itself.

Figure 11.10
Rotated points.

Rotation center

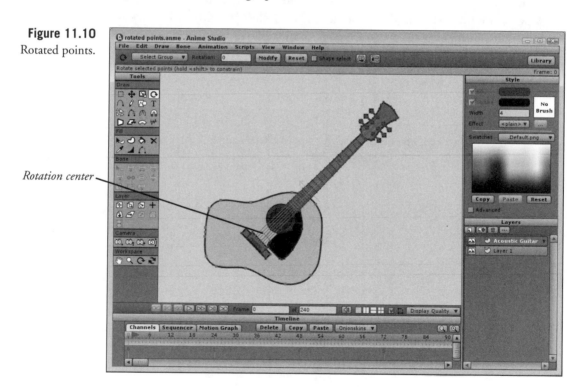

The Options bar lets you choose a selection set, enter a rotation value, and apply the rotated value with the Modify button. Holding down the Shift key rotates the selected points at 45 degree increments.

Tip

All point rotations with the Rotate Points tool are done about the center of the selected points, and currently there is no way to change this rotation center, although some modified tool scripts are available that make this possible. You can learn more about these modified tool scripts in Chapter 37, "Using Scripts and Lua."

To create a ninja star, follow these steps:

1. Use the File, New menu command to create a new project.

2. Select the Scripts, Draw, Star menu command and in the Star dialog box that opens, enter 8 as the number of points and click the OK button. This creates an eight-pointed star in the center of the working area.

3. With all points selected, select the Scripts, Draw, Split Curve menu command. This opens the Split Curve dialog box. Enter a Point Count value of 1 and click the OK button. This adds a midpoint to each line segment.

4. Click the Select Points tool (G), enable the Lasso Mode option in the Options bar, and drag around the star points closest to the center to select them.

5. Select the Rotate Points tool (R) and drag in the working area to rotate the selected points about their center point.

6. Choose the Select Points tool (G) again and drag around all the points except for the points on the outer tips on the star with the lasso. Then select the Edit, Select Inverse menu command (Ctrl/Cmd+I) to invert the selection so that only the outer tip points are selected.

7. Select and drag with the Rotate Points tool (R) in the opposite direction from the first drag. Then choose the Scale Points tool (S) and drag the corner handle to pull the tip points in tighter to the star center.

8. Complete the star by selecting the Oval tool (L) and dragging in the center of the star to create a circle. The completed star is shown in Figure 11.11.

Figure 11.11
Star created by
rotating and
scaling points.

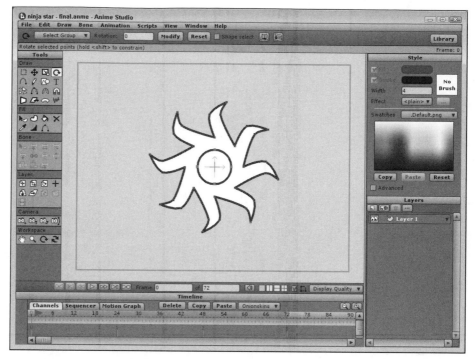

Snapping Points to the Grid

When the background grid is enabled, the Draw, Snap to Grid (Ctrl/Cmd+G) menu command becomes active. When the Snap to Grid command is selected, all selected points are automatically moved to the nearest grid intersection, as shown in Figure 11.12, and all new points drawn with the Draw tools from that point onward, except for the Freehand tool, are automatically snapped to the nearest grid point.

> **Note**
>
> The grid snapping feature is only available in Anime Studio Pro.

This behavior continues until the grid is turned off or until the View, Disable Grid Snapping option is selected. When grid snapping is disabled, a checkmark appears to the right of the Disable Grid Snapping menu command in the View menu.

Controlling Moving Grids

You may notice when you move a layer that the grid is tied to the layer. If you find that this is causing you problems when trying to line up points and objects, you can take a snapshot of the grid and import it onto an image layer or load it as a tracing paper. By doing this, the grid remains stationary on a lower layer. The drawback to this approach is that you can no longer snap to the grid points.

Changing Curvature at a Point

If you've created a sharp corner with the Add Points tool and later realize you want a smooth corner instead, you can use the Curvature tool (C) to smooth the curves leading to and away from a single point. Simply drag the mouse to the left to increase the curvature or to the right to reduce it to a sharp point. This tool also works on multiple selected points, and the Options bar lets you select a selection set. Figure 11.13 shows a shape whose curvature has been reduced to straight lines, and Figure 11.14 shows the same shape with an exaggerated curvature.

Figure 11.13
Reduced curvature.

Figure 11.14
Extreme curvature.

Peak button

Smooth button

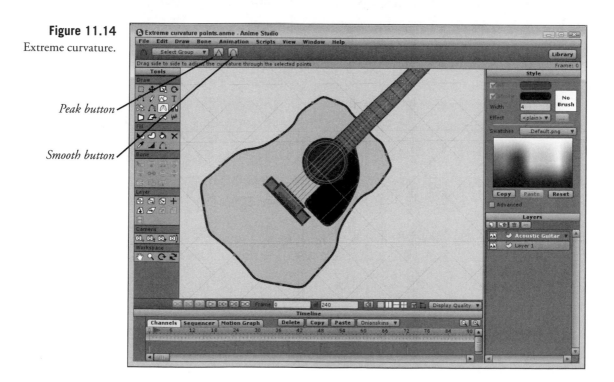

The Curvature tool (C) lets you change the amount of curvature that is applied to a point variably, but if you want to jump immediately to no curvature, you can use the Peak button (Ctrl/Cmd+P), or to a smooth setting with the Smooth button (Ctrl/Cmd+M). These buttons are both located on the Options bar. These features are also available in the Draw menu.

New Feature

In the previous versions, the Peak and Smooth commands were buttons in the Tools palette, but moving these features to the Options bar was done to simplify the Tools palette, which is new to Anime Studio 6. The keyboard shortcuts have also changed.

Changing the curvature at a point also impacts the curves on either side of the point, so more on curvature is presented in Chapter 12, "Editing Paths."

Using the Magnet Tool

After drawing an object, you may find that you spend a lot of time tweaking the placement of multiple individual points. This can be time consuming, so if you need to move a lot of points at once, you'll want to consider using the Magnet tool.

The Magnet tool (X) selects and moves all points within a defined radius, but the points nearest the center of the defined radius will move the greatest degree and points farther from the center move to a lesser extent, based on their distance from the center. The result is a smooth shifting of the selected points.

Using the Options bar, you can change the radius of the Magnet tool. Figure 11.15 shows the Magnet tool being used to modify the base of a guitar.

Note

The Magnet tool is only available in Anime Studio Pro.

Figure 11.15
The Magnet tool.

Magnet radius

To use the Magnet tool, follow these steps:

1. Open the Tree.anme file from the Chapter 11 folder on the included CD. This file includes a single tree, but if you want to add multiple trees to the current project, then it is a good idea to alter this original tree so it doesn't look exactly like its duplicate.

2. Select the Tree 3 layer and click the Duplicate Layer button in the Layers palette to create a clone of the original tree. Select the Translate Layer tool (1) and move the tree to the right of the original.

3. Select the Magnet tool (X) and change the Magnet Radius value in the Options bar to 0.2. Then drag on the various tree limbs to reorient them to be different from the original tree, as shown in Figure 11.16. With the variation added to the new tree, the tree object can be added to the same project without looking like the same tree.

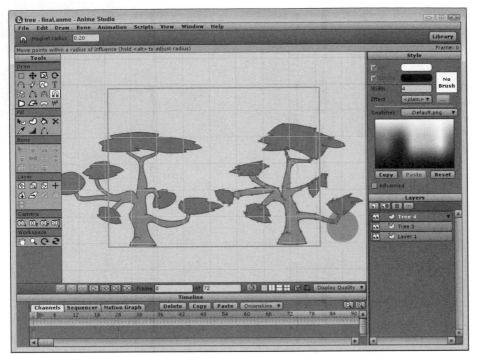

Figure 11.16
Unique trees with
the Magnet tool.

Adding Noise

When a group of points is selected, you can use the Noise (N) tool to move all the selected points randomly, as shown in Figure 11.17. This is helpful if you need to add a little bit of randomness to a curve. This tool works by dragging in the main window. The farther you drag the mouse, the greater the change to the points. This tool can be applied multiple times.

Chapter Summary

This chapter covered a lot of ground on manipulating points. With the ability to select, delete, change the curvature of, transform, and snap points, you're ready to manipulate any shape we throw your way. Being able to work with points will allow you to create anything you can imagine.

Although being able to move points around is all you really need to know, there are some situations where knowing how to edit the curve segments themselves will really save you a lot of time. It's all about efficiency, and the faster you can work, the more you can get done. Editing paths is the topic of the next chapter and knowing how to do that will let you work at light speed.

Figure 11.17
Random point
movement.

12

Editing Paths

- Selecting paths
- Deleting and hiding edges
- Closing paths
- Changing curvature
- Shearing, perspective, bend, and noise effects

When it comes to editing paths, you can simply just move an individual point, which causes the connected paths to move, but it is much easier to select a path along with its points on either end and move the entire path as one object. Anime Studio includes tools that make it easy to delete and hide edges, close an existing path to make a shape, and change the curvature of a path.

There are also effects for altering a path's perspective, shear, bend, and noise effect, and learning to use these tools will let you deform paths quickly and easily.

Selecting Paths

Paths are selected with the Select Points tool (G) by clicking the path away from any points. This works by automatically selecting all the points on the path. If the path makes a shape, then all points of the shape are selected. Holding down the Shift key lets you select multiple paths at once, and holding down the Ctrl/Cmd key switches to Lasso mode so that you can drag over the points you want to select.

> **Note**
>
> Previous versions of Anime Studio referred to vector lines as construction curves, but as of Anime Studio 6, construction curves are now called paths.

When a path is clicked on, all the points that make up the selected path are highlighted red, as shown in Figure 12.1. This object includes only two paths, the lion's stroke and an interior path to define the mane.

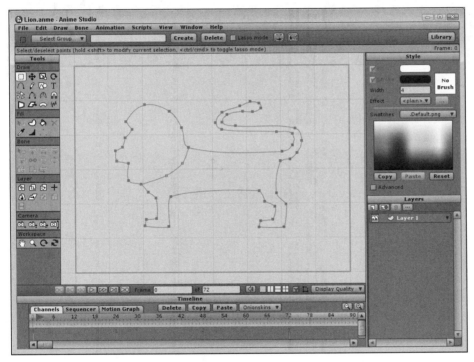

Figure 12.1
Selected path.

You can also select all points in the active layer using the Edit, Select All (Ctrl/Cmd+A) menu command. The Edit, Select None menu command deselects all points, or you can click in the working area away from all other objects and points. The Edit, Select Inverse (Ctrl/Cmd+I) menu command deselects all the currently selected points and selects all the points that weren't selected.

The Edit, Select Connected (Tab) selects all points that are part of the same object. This doesn't select just the current path, it selects all paths that are attached to the current selection.

> **Note**
>
> All of the menu commands in the Edit menu and the Lasso tool will only select points and not paths.

Deleting Edges

Selected points are easy to delete. Simply press the Delete key or use the Edit, Clear menu and they are deleted. Edges, however, work differently. To delete a path between two points without deleting the points, you can use the Delete Edges tool (D). Figure 12.2 shows an example of this. By clicking the edge forming the lion's back with the Delete Edges tool, only the edge between the two points is deleted.

Figure 12.2
Deleted edge.

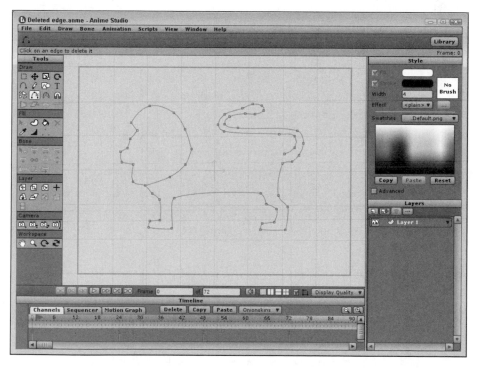

If the edge you click on is connected to an endpoint, then the endpoint is also deleted, and if you click on the edge of a shape, then the shape's fill is deleted and the path is changed to an open path.

An alternative to deleting the edge is to hide the edge with the Hide Edge tool (H). This tool is located in the Fill section of the Tools palette. It simply removes the stroke from the edge so it isn't rendered. Shapes with hidden edges keep their fill color. Hiding edges is covered later in this chapter.

Closing a Path

Although there isn't an automatic way to close a path, if you drag the endpoint of a path with the Add Points tool and press the Spacebar when positioned over the first point, the path will be closed and a new shape is created. Once a shape is created, you can fill it with a color.

Paths drawn with the Freehand tool (F) can be automatically closed by enabling the Auto Close option in the Options bar.

Changing the Curvature of a Path

When the points on a path are selected, you can use the Curvature tool (C) to change how curvy the path is as it enters and leaves each point by dragging in the scene. Dragging all the way to the left causes the path points to be sharp, and dragging to the right smoothes out the path on either side of the selected points. You can also use the Peak button (Ctrl/Cmd+P) on the Options bar or the Draw, Peak menu to instantly make all selected points sharp, or you can use the Smooth button (Ctrl/Cmd+M) on the Options bar or the Draw, Smooth menu to smooth all lines paths around the selected points.

Figure 12.3 shows a good example of this. A simple tree shape has had its curvature reduced to sharp corners on the left tree and to maximum curvature on the tree on the right. Notice the topmost point, the way the curvature moves from none on the left tree to smooth on the middle tree and to extreme on the right tree.

Hiding Edges

All paths that are drawn actually don't show up on the rendered image unless a stroke is added to them. Strokes are covered in Chapter 13, "Filling Shapes and Using Strokes," but there are times when you'll want to hide an edge or include an extra edge so that you have more control over the curvature at the end of a pointed object.

Figure 12.3
Trees with
varying
curvature.

> **Tip**
>
> Hidden edges can also be used to connect objects together so they can be moved by dragging one part of the object. For example, it is often helpful to have the eyes of a character connected so they can move as a single unit.

To hide an edge, select the Hide Edge tool (H), which is actually found in the Fill section of the Tools palette, and click on the path to hide. This removes any stroke from the selected path between its adjacent points.

To control the curvature at the tip of an object using hidden edges, follow these steps:

1. Open the Twin lizards.anme file from the Chapter 12 folder on the CD.

   This file includes two simple lizard shapes side by side. Each path has a simple stroke with a Line Width of 1 applied to it. The lizard's tail is pointed using the Peak modifier.

2. Select the Delete Edges tool (D) and click on the two edges making up the end of the left lizard's tail.

3. Select the Add Points tool (A) and drag from each end point to create two overlapping paths with three points each.

4. Use the Translate Points tool (T) to select the first new point on one of the lines and drag it over the top of the first new point on the other line and press the Spacebar while the mouse button is still held down to weld the two points together.

5. Select the last two points and move them to define the curvature of the tail.

6. Select the Hide Edges tool (H) and click on the extending paths to make them hidden from the shape.

The two paths that extend beyond the end of the tail are used to control the curvature of the tail, as you can see in Figure 12.4. The lizard on the right uses the Peak command, but the lizard's tail on the left has more curvature at its tip.

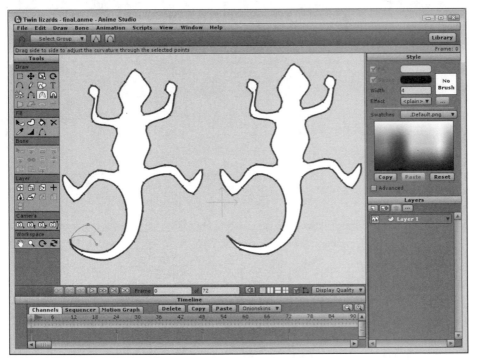

Figure 12.4
Curved tip with hidden edges.

> **Tip**
>
> This same technique of adding an extra edge at the end of a path can also be used with a variable width path.

Adding Perspective and Shear Effects

The Perspective Points tool is used to simulate the effect of having items reduce in size as they recede into the distance. If you imagine looking at a billboard sign running parallel to a street, the letters on the far end of the sign appear smaller than the letters on the sign closest to you.

For the selected set of points, these tools cause one end of the selection to increase while the opposite end decreases in size. Dragging with the Perspective Points tool to the side causes the left and right sides of the selection set to change size depending on the direction that you drag the mouse, and dragging the Perspective Points tool up and down causes the top and bottom sides of the selection set to change size. Figure 12.5 shows the resulting effect of using this tool.

> **Note**
>
> The Shear Points and Perspective Points tools are only available in Anime Studio Pro.

The Shear Points tool let you slant the selected set of points, causing circles to become ovals and squares to become parallelograms. Dragging to the left and right with the Shear Points tool causes the top and bottom edges of the selected points to move in opposite directions based on the direction that you drag the mouse. Dragging up and down with the Shear Points tool causes the left and right edges of the selected points to move in opposite directions. Figure 12.6 shows the results of this tool.

The Shear and Perspective Points tools work in a similar manner to the Shear and Perspective Layer tools covered in Chapter 4, "Working with Layers."

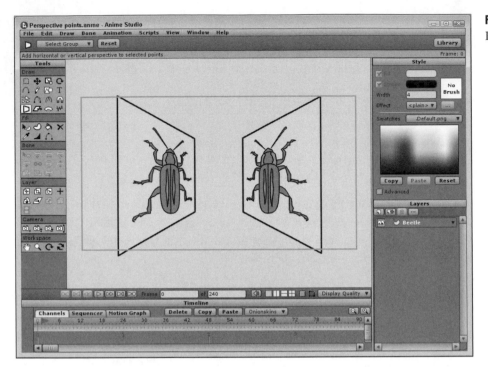

Figure 12.5
Perspective points.

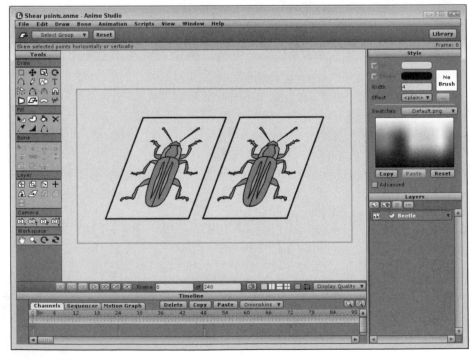

Figure 12.6
Sheared points.

> **Note**
>
> The Shear Points and Perspective Points tools are unavailable if only a single point is selected.

To create a simple cube, follow these steps:

1. Select and drag in the working area with the Rectangle tool (E) while holding down the Shift key to create a square. Then add a couple of circles with the Oval (L) tool to the center of the square.

2. Choose the Edit, Select All (Ctrl/Cmd+A) menu command to select all the points in the project. Then create a copy using the Edit, Copy (Ctrl/Cmd+C) and the Edit, Paste (Ctrl/Cmd+V) commands.

   The pasted copy is placed exactly on top of the original so it doesn't appear that anything has happened. If you move the pasted copy, the original is still there. The pasted copy is selected after you paste it.

3. With the pasted objects still selected, click the Shear Points X tool and drag to shear the pasted copy.

4. Click the Scale Points tool (S) and drag the top edge handle down to reduce the size of the pasted copy while maintaining the width of the lower edge. Select the Translate Points tool (T) and move the pasted copy so that its bottom edge aligns with the top edge of the square.

5. With the Select Points tool (G), select the original square's points by dragging over the lower half of the square object and choose the Edit, Select Connected menu (Tab).

6. Repeat step 2 to create another copy of the original square. Then use the Translate Points tool (T) to move the new copy so that its left edge aligns with the right edge of the original square. If you hold down the Shift key while moving it, the object will stay horizontally aligned.

7. Select the Shear Points Y tool and drag upward until the diagonal lines of the two copied squares are parallel. Then drag the right edge handle using the Scale Points tool (S) to size the newest square copy to fit with the other square copy object. Then move the newest copy into place.

   Figure 12.7 shows the final cube object created using the Shear tools.

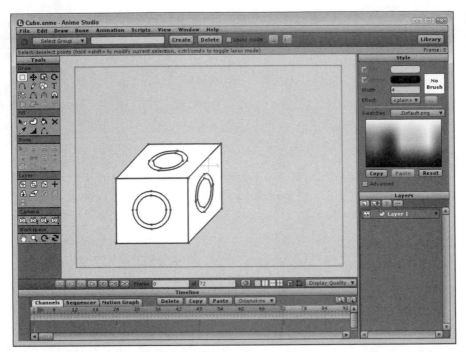

Figure 12.7
A cube created with the Shear tools.

Note

Although the created cube appears 3D, it really isn't. However, Anime Studio can import and view 3D objects. More on this feature is covered in Chapter 29, "Using 3D Layers."

Adding Bend and Noise Effects

The Bend Points tool lets you bend the selected points around the midpoint of one of the edges of the selected set of points. If you bend the points far enough, they'll form a circle. Bending a square forms a trapezoid shape. Figure 12.8 shows three shapes in various stages of being bent.

Dragging up and down with the Bend Points tool causes all vertically aligned points along the midline to remain still while the rest of the points bend outward and down or up from the center depending on how you drag with the mouse. Dragging to the side with the Bend Points tool causes all horizontally aligned points along the midline to remain still while the rest of the points bend upward and downward from the center depending on how you drag with the mouse.

Figure 12.8
Bending shapes.

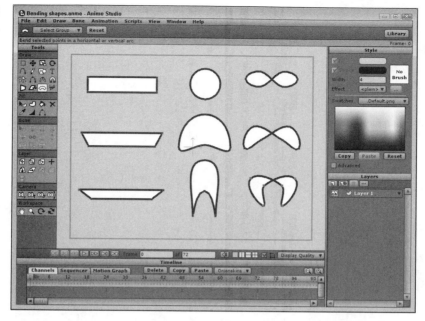

Figure 12.9 shows a simple example of dragging down with the Bend Points tool. Notice how the text with its many points bends nicely about a center point, but the rectangles don't bend at all since they only have four points. The bend causes the rectangles' points to move outward.

Figure 12.9
Logo created with the Bend tool.

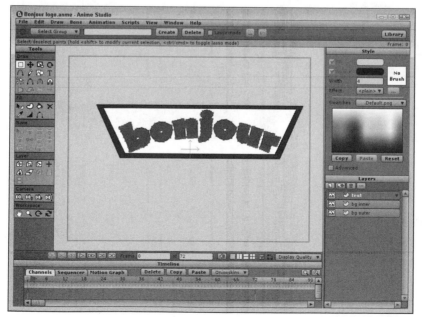

The Noise tool causes the selected points to move randomly in different directions; the end result will be slightly different from the original. If you drag with the Noise tool continuously, the points continue to move consistently in the same direction as long as you drag. If you drag and release the mouse button and drag again, the points are moved repeatedly in different directions each time you drag. Figure 12.10 shows the text from the previous figure dragged once with the Noise tool.

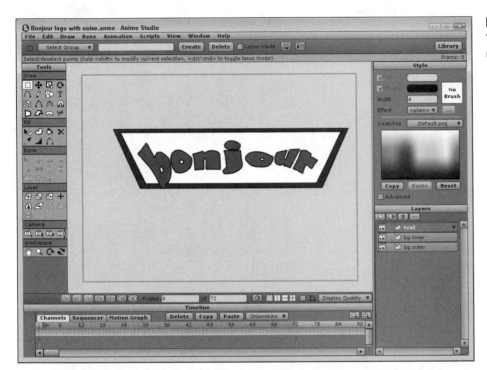

Figure 12.10
Text altered with the Noise tool.

Note

The Bend Points tool is only available in Anime Studio Pro.

Caution

If you use the Noise tool on the same set of points over and over, the points eventually start to group together.

Chapter Summary

This chapter covered all the ways you can edit paths in a project, including selecting, deleting, hiding, closing, changing the curvature, shearing, bending, and adding noise and perspective effects. Your editing skills for working with points and paths are now complete. Be sure to practice these skills to improve them.

In the next chapter, we'll look at how shapes can be filled and how paths can be stroked using solid colors or specialized styles, so hurry over to the next chapter before the paint bucket starts to dry out.

13

Filling Shapes and Using Strokes

- Introducing the Fill tools
- Selecting a shape
- Defining a fill region
- Selecting and transferring colors
- Adding a stroke
- Changing stacking order

Lines created on a vector layer aren't rendered unless they have a fill and a stroke. If a line is drawn without any stroke, then the line won't appear when the project is rendered. A *fill* is a colored area that is applied to a closed shape. When a fill is selected, it is highlighted with a checkerboard pattern. Selected shapes can be filled with a color and effects as defined in the Style palette.

Independent of a shape's fill, the curves that make up the shape can also be colored and styled. When a color, line width, or effect is applied to a curve, it is called a *stroke*. Strokes can be applied to an entire curve or to only a portion of a curve.

When fills and strokes overlap, the fill and stroke that are visible are determined by the object's stacking order. The stacking order can be adjusted as needed.

Introducing the Fill Tools

When a vector layer is selected, the tools in the Draw and Fill sections of the Tools palette become available. The tools in the Draw section let you create and manipulate new points, curves, and shapes; the tools in the Fill section let you change and manipulate the fill and stroke applied to an object.

Whenever a tool is selected, it is highlighted yellow, its icon appears in the top left corner of the main window in the Options bar, any tool settings appear in the Options bar, and information on how to use the selected tool appears in the status bar directly underneath the Options bar.

Directly below the Draw tools are the Fill tools, as shown in Figure 13.1.

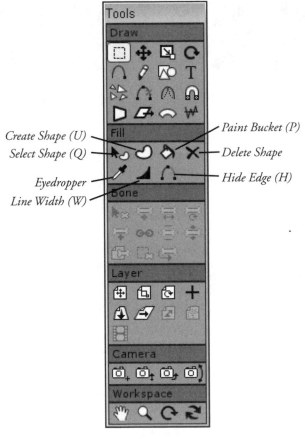

Figure 13.1
The Fill tools.

- **Select Shape (Q):** This tool selects a shape when you click it. The selected fill is highlighted with a checkerboard pattern when selected.

- **Create Shape (U):** This tool also selects a shape or a stroke to be filled. When selected, the shape appears as a checkerboard pattern. Pressing the Spacebar applies the current fill or stroke settings in the Style palette.

- **Paint Bucket (P):** This tool automatically applies the current fill to the shape that is clicked on.

- **Delete Shape:** This tool removes any applied fill from a shape when you click within the shape.

- **Eyedropper:** This tool grabs the fill and stroke from the clicked-on object on any layer.

- **Line Width (W):** This tool changes the line width around the selected points by dragging with the mouse.

- **Hide Edge (H):** This tool removes any applied stroke style from the edge that you click on.

Selecting Shapes

Before you can change the properties of a point, shape, or path, you need to select the element; Anime Studio has several different ways to select each element type. Points and curves are highlighted red when selected and fills are displayed using a crosshatch pattern when selected.

Selecting a Shape

In addition to points that can be selected, you can also select a shape using the Select Shape tool (Q). When a shape is selected, its fill is displayed as a checkerboard pattern using the defined color, as shown in Figure 13.2. If the fill on the object is disabled and if the stroke is thick enough, then the stroke is displayed as a checkerboard pattern. The checkerboard pattern alternates with a light gray and the applied fill or stroke color.

With the Select Shape tool selected, you can alter the shape's fill and stroke properties using the settings in the Style palette. The Style palette is covered in more detail in Chapter 15, "Setting Object Style."

When several shapes are stacked on top of one another, you can use the Ctrl/Cmd key with the up and down arrow keys to navigate up and down the stacked shapes.

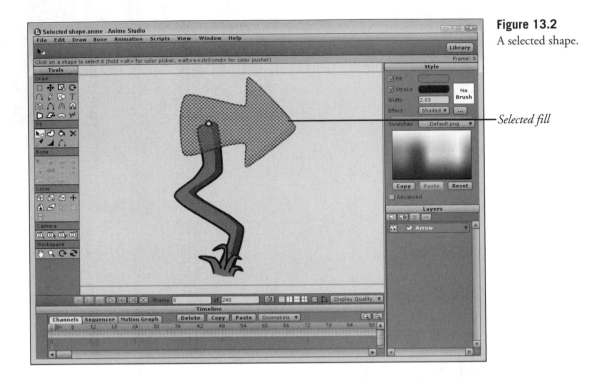

Figure 13.2
A selected shape.

—Selected fill

If you click the area of a fill where several objects are overlapped, the topmost shape is selected, but if you hold down the Ctrl/Cmd key and press the down arrow, the next shape in the stack is selected. If the second shape in a stack is selected, then the Ctrl/Cmd key and the up arrow will move the selection back to the top shape again.

Hiding a Shape

Once a shape is selected, you can choose to hide it with the Draw, Hide Shape (Ctrl/Cmd+Shift+H) menu. This only hides the shape's fill and stroke, but if the Show Paths option at the bottom of the working area is enabled, then you'll still be able to see the shape's paths. Hiding shapes will simplify the workspace, allowing you to focus on a particular shape. To view hidden shapes again, select the Draw, Show All Shapes (Ctrl/Cmd+Shift+S). This makes all hidden shapes visible.

New Feature

The Hide Shape and the Show All Shapes features are new to Anime Studio 6.

> **Tip**
>
> When a file is first opened, all hidden shapes are visible.

Defining a Fill Region

Custom fill regions can be defined using the Create Shape (U) tool. This tool works just like the Select Points tool, allowing you to click on points to select them or click on a curve to select the entire line. If the selected points form a closed curve, you can create a new fill, but if the selected curve is not closed, you can add a stroke style to the selection.

When selecting points and lines that make up a shape, you can enable the Lasso Mode on the Options bar to use the Lasso tool to draw around the specific points that you want to include. You can also access the Lasso tool if the Lasso Mode isn't enabled by holding down the Ctrl/Cmd key.

Once a selection is made, you can apply the fill or stroke style defined in the Style palette by clicking the Create Shape button in the Options bar or by pressing the Spacebar. Figure 13.3 shows an arrow shape that has been divided into two shapes by adding a path that divides the arrowhead from the rest of the arrow. Then the new closed arrowhead shape can be selected and colored differently.

Figure 13.3
A custom-defined fill.

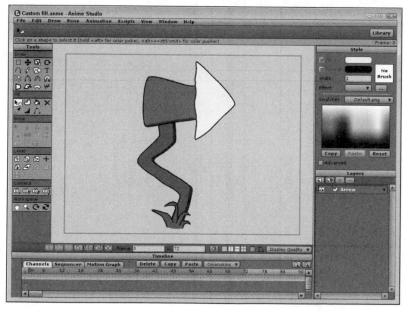

Filling Irregular Strokes

When you use the Create Shape tool (U), simply clicking the stroke often doesn't give you the exact shape that you want to fill. When using this tool, though, you can click a single point and then by holding down the Shift key, you can select other points to define the exact shape you want to fill.

To use the Create Shape tool (U) to define a complex shape, follow these steps:

1. Open the Candy cane.anme file from the Chapter 13 folder on the CD. This file shows a simple candy cane object with lines drawn for shapes. If you click the candy cane's stroke with the Create Shape tool, the entire object is selected, but we want to apply the color red to the stripes.

2. Choose the Create Shape tool (U) from the Tools palette and click one of the corner points of the stripe you want to color red. Hold down the Shift key and then click all the points that surround the red stripe area. When a closed area is selected, the checkered fill pattern is displayed.

3. Change the fill color in the Style palette to red and press the Spacebar to apply the new color.

4. Repeat steps 2 and 3 for the remaining red stripes. Figure 13.4 shows the resulting candy cane after the stripes have been filled.

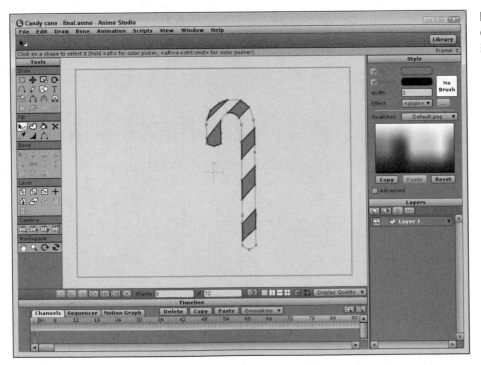

Figure 13.4

Candy cane with irregular fills.

Filling with Solid Colors

Another way to fill a shape with a color is with the Paint Bucket (P) tool. This tool works just like the Create Shape tool except you don't need to select the shape before using the tool. Clicking a closed shape with the Paint Bucket instantly applies the defined fill and stroke to the shape. You can also click on an open path with the Paint Bucket tool to apply only stroke properties.

When the Paint Bucket tool is selected, the Options bar gives options to apply only the Fill, only the Stroke, or Both. You can also hold down the Ctrl/Cmd key to see a preview of the fill before applying it. If you don't want to apply the fill, simply drag the mouse away from the shape before releasing the mouse button.

> **Caution**
>
> If you've zoomed in on the current view so that one of the points of a shape you are trying to fill isn't visible in the main window, then the Paint Bucket tool won't work. Try zooming out so that all points are visible and try the operation again.

If a shape is contained within a shape that you're trying to fill, then the interior shape is considered a hole and is not filled when the outer shape is clicked with the Paint Bucket tool. However, if two shapes are overlapping, then the Paint Bucket tool cannot be used to fill either object.

> **Tip**
>
> If you click and drag the Paint Bucket tool over the main window without releasing the mouse button, each shape that can be filled is highlighted. This provides an easy way to see exactly what area will be filled before it actually does it.

Removing a Fill

If you want to remove a fill from a shape, you can do so with the Delete Shape tool. With the Delete Shape tool selected, any fill that you click will be removed. Fills can also be removed by first selecting the fill with the Select Shape tool (Q). When selected, the checkered pattern will appear. If you choose the Edit, Clear menu command or press the Delete key, the fill will be removed. Figure 13.5 shows the arrow sign with the arrow fills removed.

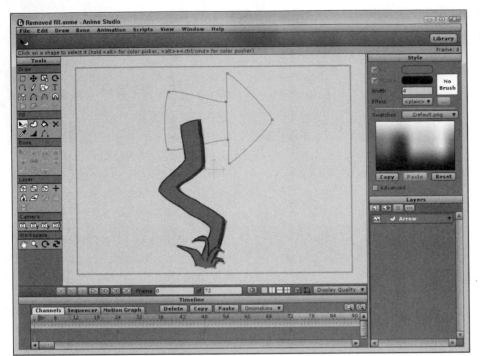

Figure 13.5
Arrow sign with
removed fills.

Selecting Colors

Fill and stroke color is set using the Style palette. If you want to change the color of either, you can simply click the color palette located at the bottom of the Style palette. Left-clicking a color in the color palette changes the Fill color and right-clicking a color in the color palette changes the Stroke color. More on using colors and the Color Picker is covered in Chapter 15, "Setting Object Style."

Once a shape's fill color and style are defined, there are ways to quickly copy and paste the defined fill color and style to other shapes using the Eyedropper tool.

Using the Eyedropper Tool

The Eyedropper tool loads the fill and stroke color for any shape on any layer by simply clicking it. After the colors are loaded into the Style palette, you can apply them using the Paint Bucket tool or by holding down the Alt/Opt key and clicking the shape.

New Feature

The Eyedropper tool is new to Anime Studio 6.

Pulling Colors and Styles from Other Shapes

If a shape is selected, you can pull a fill color and style from another shape by holding down the Alt/Opt key and clicking the fill that you want to borrow. This copies the fill color to the selected shape. The technique is called *pulling the fill color*.

> **Note**
>
> Pushing and pulling only works with fills and cannot be used with strokes by themselves.

Pushing Colors and Styles from Other Shapes

When a shape is selected, you can push the selected shape's fill color and style to another shape by holding down the Alt/Opt and Ctrl/Cmd keys and clicking on the shape that you want to push the fill color and style to. This copies the fill color from the selected shape and pushes its fill color and style to the shape you click on.

> **Tip**
>
> You can quickly apply fill colors to your objects by pushing and pulling colors. One method for speed filling is to keep a small set of squares off to the side that holds the project colors. These squares can then be used to push and pull colors quickly.

Filling Holes

If a shape defined by curves is nested completely within another shape, you can elect to fill the shape without filling the hole by selecting both the outer shape's curves and the hole's curves. With both selected, Anime Studio determines that the interior shape is a hole and won't fill it. If a third shape is within the hole and it is selected also, then the shape in the hole will be filled as well.

To use the Create Shape tool (U) to define a complex shape, follow these steps:

1. Open the Doughnuts.anme file from the Chapter 13 folder on the CD. This file shows two doughnut objects created from two ovals, but neither has a fill applied.

2. Select the doughnut on the left and click the outer oval with the Create Shape tool (U). The entire oval is selected, including the inner oval. Then click a color swatch in the Style palette and press the Spacebar. The selected fill is applied to the entire doughnut.

3. With the Create Shape tool (U) still selected, click the outer oval for the right doughnut; then hold down the Shift key and click the inner oval. Press the Spacebar to apply the same color to the second doughnut. With both ovals selected, the doughnut hole is recognized, as shown in Figure 13.6.

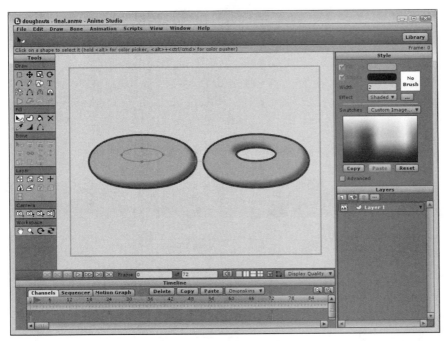

Figure 13.6
Filling doughnut holes.

Creating a Stroke

If you draw a shape or a line with the Auto-Stroke option disabled, you'll see a simple line without any style applied to it. This line will not be visible in the final render, but you can convert this default line into a line with a style applied or a default shape into a shape with a fill using the Create Shape tool (U).

To convert a default line or shape to one with a fill and stroke, simply select the line or shape with the Create Shape tool. The line or shape will turn red when selected, as shown in Figure 13.7. Then press the Spacebar or click the Create Shape button in the Options bar, and the current fill and stroke styles as defined in the Style palette are applied to the selected object.

Figure 13.7
Selecting a curve
for a stroke.

Selected paths ———

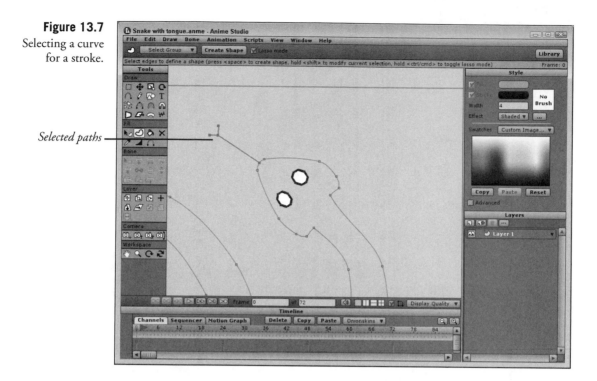

When selecting a shape, you need to select all the curves that make up the shape in order to apply a fill to it. If you click any part of the closed shape's curve, then the entire shape, including its fill, is automatically selected and the fill is shown as a checkerboard pattern. If the curve isn't a closed shape, then the curve is displayed red, and if the curve is thick enough, the checkerboard pattern is displayed on the curve, as shown in Figure 13.8.

When you want to select only a portion of the shape's curve, just drag over a selection area that includes the points on either end of the segment you want to stroke, and they will be selected. If you hold down the Ctrl/Cmd key or enable the Lasso Mode option in the Options bar, the mouse cursor changes to a lasso that you can use to encircle the segments you want to choose.

To create a road using strokes, follow these steps:

1. Select the File, New menu command to open a blank project.

2. In the Style palette, click the black color swatch to change the fill color to black and right-click the white color swatch to change the stroke color to white. Then select the Rectangle tool (E) and drag in the working area to create a black rectangle.

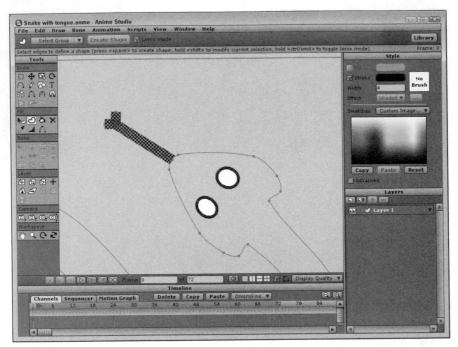

Figure 13.8
Patterned stroke.

3. Select the Add Points tool (A) and draw a dashed line down the center of the black rectangle. When creating this line, create a larger section with two points farther away from each other followed by three points fairly close together before creating another large dashed section. You can enable the grid and use grid snapping to make the dashes consistent.

4. In the Style palette, right-click the bright yellow color swatch to change the stroke color and set the Line Width value to 16. Then select the Create Shape tool (U), click the first point of the large dashed section, hold down the Shift key, and select the points on either side of the large dashed section. When all the dashed sections are selected, press the Spacebar to apply the current stroke color and width. This colors the larger dashed sections yellow and increases their width.

5. Select the Rotate Layer XY tool in the Layers tool section and drag to change the perspective of the road so it recedes into the distance, as shown in Figure 13.9.

Caution

If you look closely at the road example, you'll see that the perspective effect isn't applied to the dashed center line.

Figure 13.9
Perspective road.

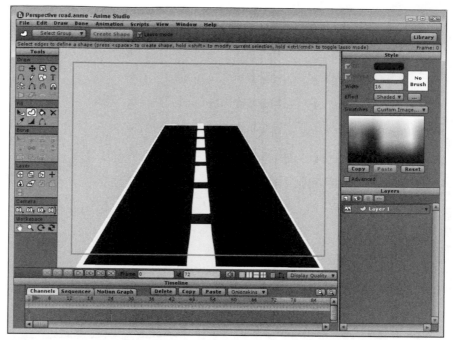

Changing Line Width

By default, line thickness is defined using the Line Width value in the Style palette for new stroked lines. This specified value remains constant for the entire curve, but if you select a specific point, you can use the Line Width tool (W) to change the thickness of the line entering and leaving the selected point by dragging the mouse. You can also set the thickness value using the Width field in the Options bar.

If multiple points are selected, then the line thickness is changed for all selected points. However, if the line has no stroke applied, then the Line Width tool does nothing. Figure 13.10 shows the line width around the front point of the arrow shape being increased. Notice how the width gradually decreases as it gets closer to the adjacent points.

Caution

Once the line width for a point has been adjusted with the Line Width tool, the point will no longer be included when a new stroke width is applied to the entire curve. Adjustments made to line width with the Line Width tool take precedence over the Line Width value in the Style palette.

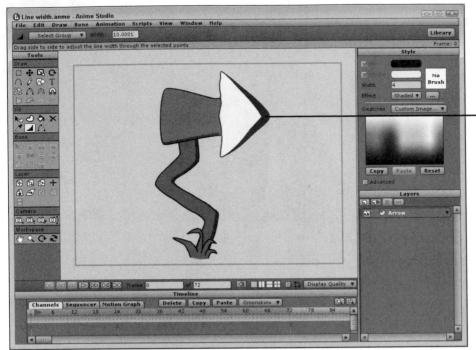

Figure 13.10
Adjusted line width.

Point with thicker width

Note

Another way to alter the line width is with the Reset Line Width and the Random Line Width commands in the Draw menu. These features are covered in Chapter 9, "Using the Drawing Tools."

Applying Multiple Stroke Widths

When playing with line widths, Anime Studio has an interesting ability to apply multiple line widths and colors to a single curve. This technique doesn't work for fills, but it can be applied to open curves that have a stroke. To use this technique, you'll need to apply a stroke with a larger line width value to a curve, alter the color and decrease the line width value in the Style palette, and reapply the stroke. The first larger color will remain and the small line width will also be visible. This technique will also work if you apply a larger semi-transparent color on top of a smaller line width.

To create a rainbow by applying multiple line widths to a curve, follow these steps:

1. Open the Rainbow in the forest.anme file from the Chapter 13 folder on the CD. This file includes the forest background with a single curved line added to a new layer.

2. Right-click the purple swatch in the Style palette to select it as the stroke color. Set the Line Width value to 40 and select the Create Shape tool (U). Then click the rainbow curve and press the Spacebar to apply the stroke.

3. Click away from the curve to deselect the stroke; then right-click the blue swatch in the Style palette to select it as the stroke color. Set the Line Width value to 35 and select the Create Shape tool (U). Click the rainbow curve and press the Spacebar to apply the stroke.

> **Note**
>
> If you don't deselect the stroke each time, the new color will be applied immediately to the curve.

4. Repeat step 3 for cyan, green, yellow, orange, and red while decreasing the line width by 5 each time. The resulting rainbow is shown in Figure 13.11.

> **Note**
>
> To create a more realistic rainbow, you'll want to make the colors semi-transparent, which can be done by adjusting the alpha value for each color. Chapter 15, "Setting Object Style," shows how to do this.

Using the Scale Compensation Setting

When adjusting the thickness of a curve, you should be aware that when the layer that contains variable width lines is rotated or tilted, the line width may change with the rotation. There is a setting in the Layer Settings dialog box for controlling whether the stroke thickness scales with the objects as the layer is rotated. When the Scale Compensation option is enabled in the Layer Settings dialog box, all stroke widths are adjusted with the rotating layer. When this option is disabled, the line width stays consistent despite the rotation.

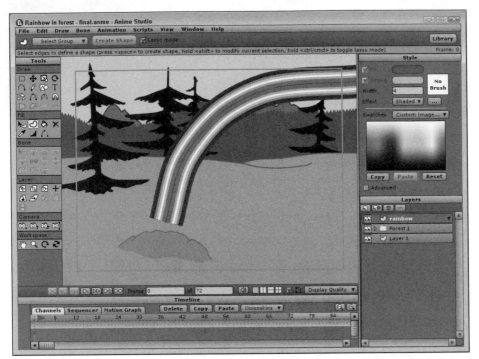

Figure 13.11
Rainbow created with
multiple line widths.

Figure 13.12 shows this effect by revisiting the road example done earlier in this chapter. It shows the road with the Scale Compensation option disabled. Notice how the center dashed line remains the same thickness along the entire road.

> **Note**
>
> The Scale Compensation option has no effect on the Perspective Points tools. Line width is always constant when using these tools.

Hiding Edges with the Hide Edge Tool

Using the Delete Shape tool, you can remove the entire stroke from the selected shape, but if you want to only remove the stroke from a single segment, you can use the Hide Edge (H) tool, located in the Draw section of the Tools palette. This tool selectively removes the stroke from the single segment you click on. Figure 13.13 shows a thick stroke applied to the arrow shape, but the line that separates the arrowhead from the arrow body has been hidden using the Hide Edge tool.

Figure 13.12
Road with Scale
Compensation
option disabled.

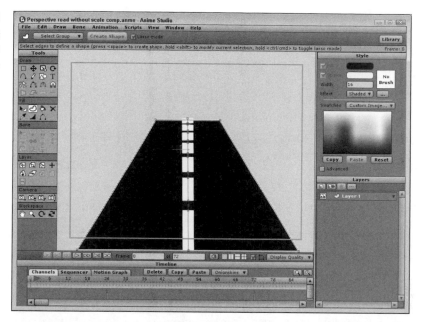

> **Note**
>
> Even if you click an edge that is part of a shape, the shape's fill will remain.

Figure 13.13
Hidden line.

Hidden line —

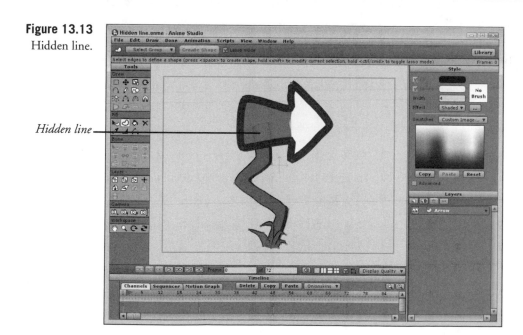

Raise or Lower a Shape's Stacking Order

Shapes are stacked on top of one another in the order they are created, so the first object created becomes the bottom object and is obscured by all subsequent objects that overlap it. But you can change the stacking order of objects using the commands found in the Draw menu.

Note

Stacking order only affects objects on the same layer. All objects on a higher layer will appear on top of the objects on a lower layer regardless of their stacking order.

The Lower Shape and Raise Shape commands in the Draw menu are only available when a shape object is selected (and the checkerboard pattern is visible). Selecting either of these commands changes the current object's order in the stack even if there isn't an overlapping object. You can also use the Raise to Front or the Lower to Back commands to move the current shape to the very front or the very back of the stacking order.

Tip

If you hold the Shift key down and press the down arrow, you can move the current shape to the bottom of the stack; holding the Shift key down and pressing the up arrow moves the current shape to the top of the stack.

Figure 13.14 shows some text added to the sign. Even though the text is on the same layer, it is visible because its stacking level is higher than that of the sign. The sign post, however, is at a lower stacking level so its top end is hidden behind the sign. Using the Draw, Raise Shape and Lower Shape menus, you could move the text in front of the sign or the sign post below the sign.

Note

If the fill or stroke color of an object is semi-transparent, then the objects underneath will be at least partially visible.

Figure 13.14
Text stacked
on a sign.

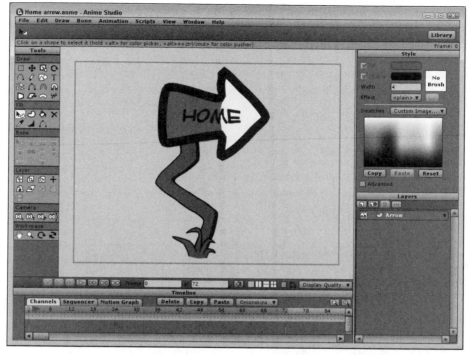

Selecting Obscured Shapes

Once an object's shapes are filled, you can select the shapes with the Select Shape tool (Q) and move their stacking order up or back with the Draw menu. But if a shape is moved to the back of the stacking order and is obscured by another shape, it can be difficult to select with the Select Shape tool if you want to change its fill style. For these situations, you can use the Ctrl/Cmd+down arrow keys to select the obscured shape. When selected, the checkered pattern appears on the obscured shape.

To select an obscured shape with the Select Shape tool (Q), follow these steps:

1. Open the Bell.anme file from the Chapter 13 folder on the CD. This file shows a simple bell object with filled shapes and a ringer located inside it.

2. Choose the Create Shape tool (U) from the Tools palette and click one of the corner points of the interior ringer. Then hold down the Shift key and click all the points that surround the ringer. When a closed area is selected, the checkered fill pattern is displayed.

3. Change the fill color in the Style palette to black and press the Spacebar to apply the new color. The ringer appears on the outside of the bell since it was created after the bell.

4. Select the filled ringer with the Select Shape tool (Q) and click the Lower Shape button in the Tools palette several times until the ringer moves behind the bell shape.

5. Click the ringer again with the Select Shape tool (Q). The bell shape is selected. Hold down the Ctrl/Cmd key and press the down arrow key. This selects the next shape just under where you clicked, which is the ringer.

6. Select a reddish-brown fill color and press the Spacebar to apply it to the selected ringer shape.

7. With the Select Points tool (G), click the points that make up the ringer and then move the ringer down with the Translate Points tool (T) so that it is just visible below the bottom of the bell, as shown in Figure 13.15.

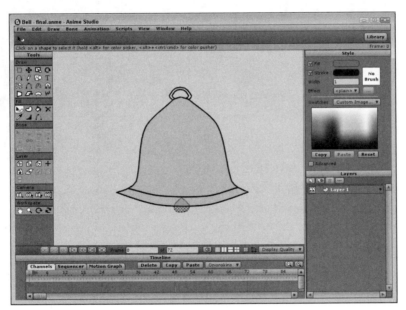

Figure 13.15
Bell with filled ringer.

Chapter Summary

This chapter introduced fills and strokes and showed how the Fill tools are used to select and apply fills and strokes. The chapter also showed how you can use the Create Shape tool to fill a specific region and how to select, push, and pull existing colors and hide stroked lines. Finally, the chapter covered the menu commands used to adjust the stacking order of shapes.

Now that you've mastered drawing straight, precise lines, the next chapter covers the Scatter Brush and shows you how to spread your straight lines all over the place.

14

Using the Scatter Brush

- Using the Scatter Brush tool
- Randomizing the Scatter Brush
- Creating a custom Scatter Brush with the Clipboard
- Creating a unique Scatter Brush

Many scenes in nature are composed of multiple occurrences of a single object. Think of a tree. In addition to the trunk and limbs, it has thousands of leaves, but each leaf, although similar to the others, is positioned and oriented in a different direction. Placing each leaf on a tree would be a tiresome task, but with the Scatter Brush tool, you can apply multiple leaves in a random pattern easily.

The Scatter Brush lets you select a single object from a drop-down list and paint with that object placing random clones of the selected object around the scene. The objects will roughly follow the strokes that you paint and randomly position and orient the objects. You can even change the size, spacing between objects, and color variations.

The Scatter Brush also lets you create new sets of objects that you can select from the list or pick up from those saved to the clipboard.

> **Note**
>
> If you want to animate the movement of multiple objects, then check out the Particle layer feature covered in Chapter 31, "Using Particle Layers."

Using the Scatter Brush

The Scatter Brush tool is available in the Draw section of the Tools palette. Once it is selected, you can choose from several default scatter sets from a drop-down list located in the Options bar. The default scatter sets include Bubbles, Leaves, Letters, Smoke, and Stars. Figure 14.1 shows a simple tree populated with leaves using the Scatter Brush.

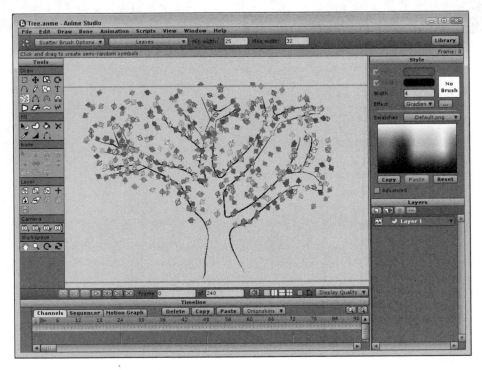

Figure 14.1
Tree with leaves.

New Feature

The Scatter Brush tool is new to Anime Studio 6.

> **Caution**
>
> The Scatter Brush tool can add a huge number of points to a scene very quickly making it complex. The Scatter Brush tool should be used with caution.

After an object is selected from the drop-down list, you can simply drag the mouse in the working area and objects are placed automatically to follow the stroke.

Setting the Object Size

The size of the Scatter Brush objects is determined by the Min Width and Max Width values found in the Options bar. Each of these values measures the square width in pixels of the randomly placed objects. The difference between these two values sets the range of sizes. If the Min and Max Width values are equal, then all objects will be the same size. Figure 14.2 shows a range of bubbles created by setting the Min Width value to 10 and the Max Width value to 100. Notice the vast different in the size of the different bubbles.

Figure 14.2
Bubbles of different sizes.

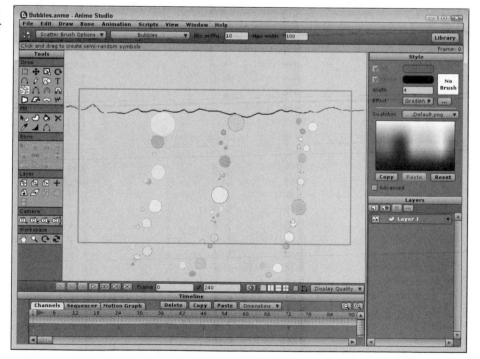

Changing the Scatter Brush Options

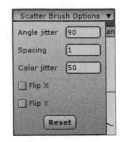

Figure 14.3
Scatter Brush Options.

When the Scatter Brush tool is selected, a pop-up dialog box of options becomes available on the Options bar, as shown in Figure 14.3. Using these options, you can alter the randomness of the object's orientation, its spacing between objects, and even its color. There are also options to enable the object to randomly flip horizontally and vertically.

Setting the Angle Jitter

The Angle Jitter setting sets the maximum value that the object can rotate from the direction that the mouse is moving. An Angle Jitter value of 0 will make all objects line up in the direction that the mouse is moving and a value of 360 will let the object be rotated randomly to any angle. Figure 14.4 shows a series of arrows with progressively greater Angle Jitter values. The top line is set to 0 and each line downward is set to 45, 90, 180, and 360. Notice how the arrows in the second to the last line still all point to the right but that the last line has arrows pointing any direction.

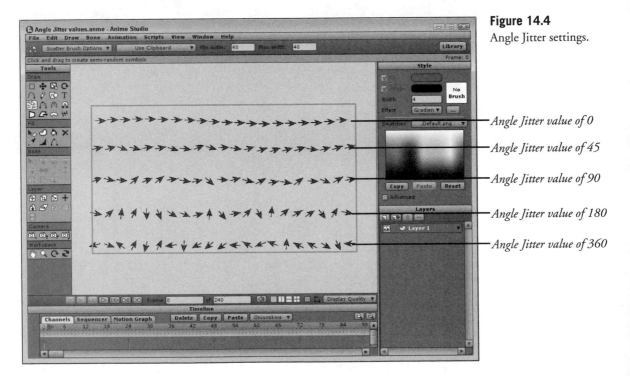

Figure 14.4
Angle Jitter settings.

Angle Jitter value of 0

Angle Jitter value of 45

Angle Jitter value of 90

Angle Jitter value of 180

Angle Jitter value of 360

Controlling Object Spacing

The Spacing setting sets the required space that must appear between each object. This value is measured using object size, so if the Min Width value is set to 40, then for a Spacing value of 1, the mouse must move at least 40 pixels before a second object is drawn and if the Spacing value is 2, then the mouse must move at least 80 pixels before a second object is drawn.

If this value is set to less than 1, objects can be drawn on top of one another. If the Min and Max Width values are quite different, the spacing will also be altered. For example, if the Min Width value is set to 10, the Max Width value is set to 100, and the Spacing value is set to 1, then an object that is 10 pixels wide would only require the mouse to move 10 pixels before drawing another object, but an object that is 80 would require a movement of 80 pixels. Figure 14.5 shows a set of stars with different Spacing values.

> **Note**
>
> The Spacing value represents only a minimum required spacing. If you move the mouse fast enough, the spacing between objects could be much greater.

Figure 14.5
Spacing settings.

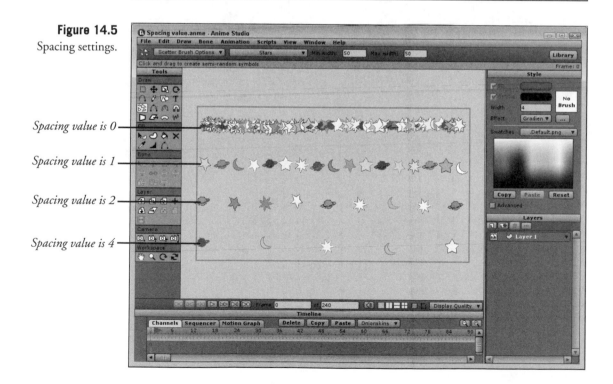

Spacing value is 0

Spacing value is 1

Spacing value is 2

Spacing value is 4

Changing Colors

The Color Jitter value can be set between 0 and 100. At a value of 0, the objects are drawn without any change in their color, but greater values will cause a random slight color change between different objects. These changes are still within the same hue, so a yellow star set to 100 would change from white to light yellow to dark yellow, but that is all.

Flipping Objects

The Flip X and Flip Y options allow the objects to be flipped horizontally or vertically or both. When enabled, the objects are not consistently flipped, but enabling these options allows them to sometimes be flipped. Figure 14.6 shows a string of letters with the Flip X option enabled. Notice that some letters are vertically flipped and some are not.

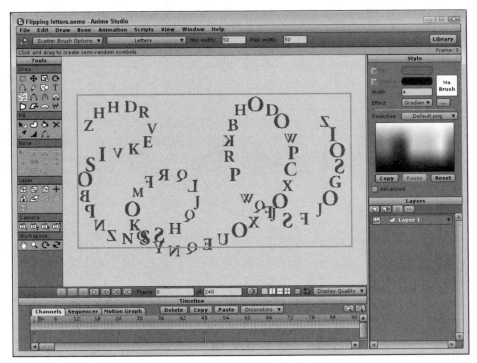

Figure 14.6
Flipping objects.

Customizing the Scatter Brush

The available Scatter Brush presets are a good place to start, but they quickly get tiresome. There are a couple of ways to customize the objects that are used by the Scatter Brush. You can use an object saved to the clipboard as a new Scatter Brush object, or you can create your own set of objects and place the saved file in the Scatter Brushes folder where Anime Studio is installed.

> **Tip**
>
> When creating objects that will be used with the Scatter Brush tool, keep the total number of points in the Scatter Brush object to a minimum.

Using the Clipboard

Any object drawn on a Vector layer can be used as a Scatter Brush object. To do so, simply select the object's points with the Select Points tool and copy the selected object to the clipboard with the Edit, Cut (Ctrl/Cmd+X) or Edit, Copy (Ctrl/Cmd+C) menu. Then select the Use Clipboard preset option from the drop-down list in the Options bar when the Scatter Brush tool is selected. You'll be able to paint with the copied object.

To use a custom Scatter Brush, follow these steps:

1. Open the Raindrops.anme file from the Chapter 14 folder on the CD. This file has three raindrops.

2. Choose the Select Points tool (G) and click the shaded raindrop; then select the Edit, Copy (Ctrl/Cmd+C) command to copy the object to the clipboard.

3. Select the File, New menu to create a new file.

4. Select the Scatter Brush tool and set the Min and Max Width values to 50. Then click the Scatter Brush options on the Options bar and set the Angle Jitter to 15, the Spacing to 2, the Color Jitter to 100, and enable the Flip X option. Drag in the working area to create a series of raindrops, as shown in Figure 14.7.

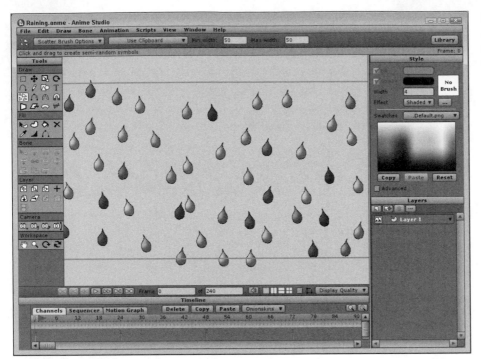

Figure 14.7
A Custom Scatter set created with the clipboard.

Creating a Custom Scatter Preset

If you look closely where Anime Studio is installed, you'll find a folder called Scatter Brushes. Within this folder are several Anime Studio files. Each file in this folder matches one of the preset Scatter Brush options. If you copy an Anime Studio file into this folder, then the objects included within the file are used as a scatter set and the file will be included in the list of presets after you restart Anime Studio.

To include multiple different objects in the Scatter Brush preset, simply include each different object on its own layer. Figure 14.8 shows a custom scatter set created by simply copying the Dynamite file from the Library folder and pasting it in the Scatter Brushes folder. After you restart, the Dynamite option appears with the other presets in the Options bar.

Figure 14.8
Dynamite added
to the presets.

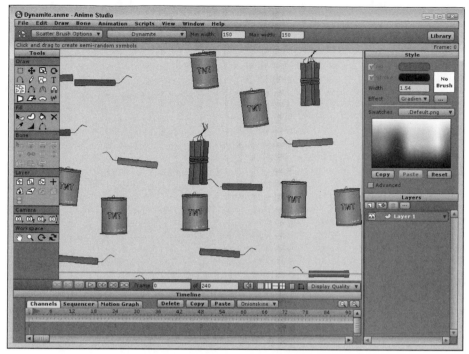

Chapter Summary

This chapter covered the Scatter Brush tool and showed how this tool is used to spread object clones randomly around the project. The Scatter Brush also includes options for changing the size, spacing, orientation, and color of the object. Using the clipboard and Anime Studio files added to the Scatter Brushes folder will enable you to create custom scatter set presets.

The next chapter covers the Style palette and shows how you can create a custom fill.

15

Setting Object Style

- Using the Style palette
- Selecting colors
- Using fill effects
- Using strokes
- Working with brushes
- Copying and pasting styles
- Using color swatches

Once you've figured out how to apply fills and strokes to shapes, you can use the Style palette to create all kinds of effects. Although the Style palette is a relatively simple palette, it includes many settings that control the look and style of fills and strokes.

The Style palette can add a lot more than just fill and stroke colors. Fills and strokes can have a wide variety of effects applied, which can include shaded effects, halos, gradients, and even bitmap textures. The Style palette also lets you specify a specific brush to use when drawing strokes. Finally, the Style palette lets you save and apply defined styles making it easy to reuse consistent designs.

Using the Style Palette

The Style palette, shown in Figure 15.1, provides a group of settings that define the look, color, and style of an object's fill or stroke.

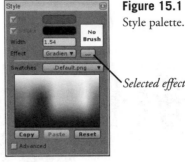

Figure 15.1
Style palette.

Selected effect options

The Style palette is opened and docked by default when you start Anime Studio, but you can close it by selecting it from the Window menu to make it a floating palette and then clicking the X icon in its upper-right corner. If you accidentally close the Style palette, you can reopen it using the Window, Style menu command (Ctrl/Cmd+]). You can also reposition the Style palette when it is floating by dragging its title bar. To re-dock the floating style palette, just select the Window, Style menu again.

> **Note**
>
> The Style palette cannot be resized when it is floating.

Only the simplest settings are visible by default, but you can expand the Style palette by clicking the Advanced checkbox at the bottom of the palette. This makes all the style settings available, as shown in Figure 15.2.

New Feature

The ability to toggle the Style between simple and advanced is new to Anime Studio 6.

Figure 15.2
Expanded Style palette.

Naming a Shape

When a shape is selected using the Shape Select tool, its fill color or stroke is displayed in the working area as a checkered pattern. Another change is that the Name field in the Style palette becomes enabled. When enabled, you can give the selected shape a name by typing it into the Name field in the Style palette.

All named shapes appear in the Shapes drop-down list at the top of the Style palette. Selecting a named shape from this list recalls all the settings for this shape, including its fill and stroke color, and automatically selects the shape. It also displays the word "Shape" above the Name field. This is to indicate that any changes to the Style palette are automatically applied to the named shape.

Auto-Naming a Shape

The Preferences dialog box, which is opened using the Edit, Preferences menu command, includes an option to Auto-Name Bones and Shapes. If this option is enabled, then each new shape that is created is automatically given a sequential number as its name, which is automatically added to the Shapes drop-down list.

Caution

The Shapes list can hold a maximum of 100 names. Any names created after this are simply not added to the list.

Auto-Naming works for new shapes created with the Create Shape tool (U), as well as for shapes and stroked curves created when the Auto-Fill or Auto-Stroke options for the Freehand tool are enabled.

Tip

Although using numbers for a shape name isn't especially helpful, they can be changed easily by typing a new name in the Style palette. Keeping this preference option enabled is a time-saver for selecting shapes and altering their style.

Turning Off Fill and Stroke

When a shape is filled, it automatically gets the color that is shown in the Fill color swatch if the Fill option is enabled. If this option is disabled, the shape won't have a fill, it will only have a stroke. You can also turn off a shape's stroke by disabling the Stroke option in the Style palette.

Note

It is possible to turn off both the fill and stroke for a shape. If this happens, the shape is displayed in the working area using the default line if the Show Paths option is enabled, but nothing is rendered.

Caution

If you're sure that a fill or a stroke has been applied but it is not visible in the working area, check the Display Quality pop-up menu in the lower-right corner of the main window and make sure that the Strokes and Fills options are enabled. You can also check for strokes by rendering the project with the Ctrl/Cmd+R command.

To turn off the fills and strokes in a project, follow these steps:

1. Open the Glass of juice.anme file from the Chapter 15 folder on the CD. This file has three glasses of juice. Each glass has four fills.

2. Choose the Select Shape tool (Q) and click the lowest fill for the middle glass; then disable the Fill option in the Style palette. This disables the fill and leaves only the stroke. Repeat this step for the other three fills in the middle glass.

Note

Only one shape can be selected at a time with the Select Shape tool (Q).

3. With the Select Shape tool (Q) still selected, click the lowest fill in the right glass and disable the Stroke option. This disables the stroke for the fill. Continue to remove all the strokes for the right glass. Figure 15.3 shows the results.

Figure 15.3
Objects with disabled fills and strokes.

Defining a Style

In addition to naming shapes, you can also create and define styles that can be applied to multiple shapes. To create a new style, select the New option from the Styles drop-down list. This adds the label *Style 1* to the Name field; you can change this name if you want. The name then appears at the bottom of the Styles drop-down list. The text *Style* is also listed above the Name field to show that any changes to the Style palette will affect the named style.

The Styles drop-down list also includes a command to delete the current style and an option to Delete Unused, which deletes any listed style that isn't currently being used in the project.

Once a custom style is defined, you can apply it to a selected shape using the Style 1 drop-down list, located in the Style palette.

Caution

The Style palette limits the number of named styles to 100.

Applying Multiple Styles

As you create styles, you'll use some styles for strokes and others just for fills. Using the Style 1 and Style 2 drop-down lists, located under the Stroke settings, you can apply up to two styles to a single shape. The available styles listed in the drop-down list are any styles defined in the Styles button at the top of the Style palette.

> **Note**
>
> The Style 1 and Style 2 drop-down lists are only available in Anime Studio Pro.

To apply the same styles to multiple shapes, follow these steps:

1. Open the Forest.anme file from the Chapter 15 folder on the CD. This file includes the forest background file.

2. Click the Styles button in the Style palette and select the New option. Name the new style *tree*. Set the Fill color to a light green and the stroke color to black with a Line Width of 1.

3. Click the Styles button again and create a new style named *mountain*. Change the Fill color to blue and the stroke color to black with a Line Width value of 1.

4. Select the Select Shape tool (Q) and click the foreground tree; then select the tree style from the Style 1 drop-down list. Select the Trees layer and repeat this step for the available trees on that layer. All the trees should now be a dark green color.

5. Select the Mountains layer and click the mountain objects with the Select Shape tool (Q); then select the mountain style in the top Style 1 drop-down list. The mountains will now all be blue.

6. Select the tree style from the Styles list at the top of the Style palette. Change the fill color from light green to dark green. Notice how all the trees with that style applied are automatically changed to the new fill color, as shown in Figure 15.4.

Figure 15.4

Forest scene with applied styles.

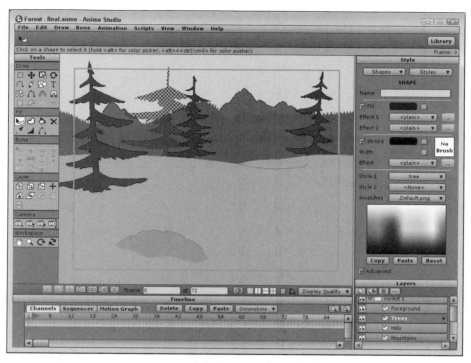

Overriding a Style

When a defined style is selected in the Style 1 or Style 2 list, the fill color, line color, and Line Width values are retrieved from the applied style, but if you click the checkbox to the left of the fill color, line color, or Line Width swatches and values, the specified setting will override the current style setting.

To override an existing style, follow these steps:

1. Open the Sun.anme file from the Chapter 15 folder on the CD. This file includes a simple sun object with an orange center and a yellow outer ring.

2. Click the Styles button in the Style palette and select the New option. Name the new style *sun*. Set the Fill color to a bright yellow and the stroke color to black with a Line Width of 1.

3. Select the Select Shape tool (Q) and click the sun's center; then select the sun style from the first Applied Style drop-down list. Then select the sun's outer ring and apply the sun style again. The entire sun is now yellow with a black stroke.

4. Select the sun's center again and enable the Fill Color checkbox to the right of the orange color. The center of the sun is now orange, but the stroke is still taken from the sun style.

5. Select the sun's outer ring and disable the Stroke option. This removes the outer border on the sun's ring.

6. Select the File, Project Settings command to open the Project Settings dialog box; then set the Background Color to light blue and render the project. The results are shown in Figure 15.5.

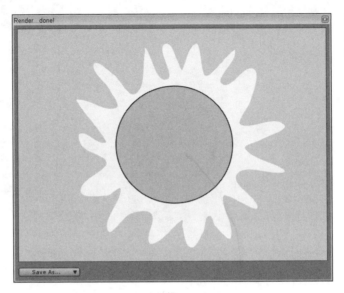

Figure 15.5
Sun object with overridden styles.

Copying and Pasting Styles

If you have a specific style that you want to apply to another shape, simply select the style that you want to copy and click the Copy button in the Style palette. Then select the shape or stroke of the object that you want to receive the copied style and press the Paste button. This copies the style to the new selection. The Copy and Paste buttons are located under the Style 1 and Style 2 lists in the Style palette.

> **Note**
>
> Don't confuse the Copy and Paste style buttons with the Copy and Paste commands located in the Edit menu. The Copy and Paste menu commands are used to clone the selected points.

> **Tip**
>
> An alternative to using the Copy and Paste buttons is to hold down the Alt/Opt key while clicking a shape with a style you want to copy using the Select Shape tool. Then hold down the Ctrl/Cmd and Alt/Opt keys and click the shape you want to paste the style to. This is called pushing and pulling the style and was presented in Chapter 13, "Filling Shapes and Using Strokes."

Whenever a style is applied to a shape, it is typically applied using the Applied Styles drop-down list. This applied style overrides the current style settings. If you want to apply the style at the base level instead of as an applied style, you can use the Copy and Paste buttons to transfer the style. However, if you copy and paste a style, the new style is independent of the original style and will not be updated if the original style is changed.

Defining the Default Style

When Anime Studio is first opened, the settings in the Style palette are set to define the default fill and stroke colors. You can see this when you look at the text just under the Shapes and Styles button. It reads *Defaults (for new shapes)*. These settings are used for all new shapes that have the Auto-Fill or Auto-Stroke options enabled.

The factory defaults include a white fill and a black stroke with a Line Width of 1, but you can change the default settings in the Style palette, and the new settings will be used on all new shapes that are created. Once the default style is changed, it remains when you open a new project, but if you restart the application, then the original black-and-white style returns.

> **Tip**
>
> If you want to change the startup default style, then save a file that has the default style you want to use to the Startup folder where Anime Studio is installed and name the file *StartupFile.anme*. This file with its custom default style will be loaded whenever Anime Studio is started.

Whenever a shape is selected with the Select Shape tool (Q), you can recall the default style by clicking the Reset button in the Style palette. This automatically applies the default fill and stroke.

Using the Color Picker

Whenever either the fill or stroke color is clicked, the default Color Picker shown in Figure 15.6 opens. Using this Color Picker, you can choose a new color and set the transparency for the color. The Color Picker also includes text fields for the Red, Green, Blue, and Alpha channels.

Selected new color

Current color

Hue color bar

Alpha transparency color bar

Hexadecimal color value

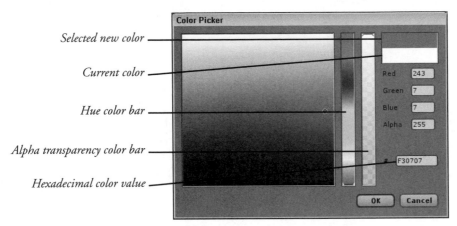

Figure 15.6
The Color Picker.

Beneath the Red, Green, and Blue values is the hexadecimal value for the selected color. This hexadecimal value can be used to specify the color on a Web page. Hexadecimal values use a number system with 16 digits instead of 10 like our common counting system. The numbers 10–15 are represented by the letters A–F. By using these numbers, the computer can use six digits to represent the color value instead of nine if the 10 digit number system were used. This may not seem like much at first glance, but when you multiply this over 300,000 for the number of pixels in a simple 640×480 image, you can see the amount of savings.

To apply a semi-transparent stroke, follow these steps:

1. Open the Freehand turtle.anme file from the Chapter 15 folder on the CD. This file has a simple turtle shape with the default black-and-white fill applied.

2. In the Style palette, click a blue color from the swatches to set the fill color and right-click the red color to set the stroke color.

3. Click the Line color swatch and drag the Alpha bar down about halfway to make the new color a semi-transparent red. Then click the OK button to exit the Color Picker.

4. Set the Line Width value to 10 and press the Enter key to accept this value.

Caution

If the current color is white or black, then dragging the Hue slider won't change the current color because all colors have white along the top and black along the bottom. To change to a new color, click in the center of the large color area before closing the Color Picker. The new color is always displayed above the current color in the upper-right corner of the Color Picker.

5. Choose the Create Shape tool (U) and click the turtle's stroke away from any points to define the turtle's shape; then press the Spacebar to apply the defined style. The fill and stroke styles are applied to the turtle shape. With the Line Width set to 10, the stroke shows 5 pixels outside of the shape and 5 within. The pixels within the shape are mixed with the fill color to create a purple stroke, as shown in Figure 15.7.

Figure 15.7
Applying a semi-transparent stroke.

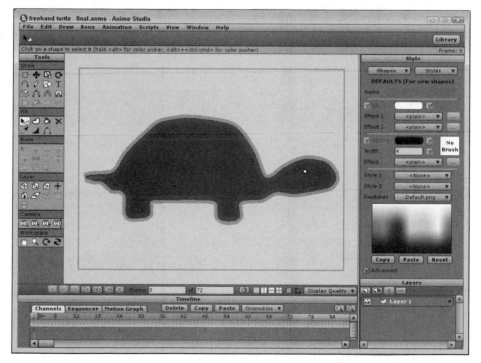

Using Fill Effects

Directly beneath the Fill color swatch on the Style palette are two effects that you can select. The available effects include the following:

- **Shaded:** This effect adds a gradient along one edge of the object to make it appear to be raised.

- **Soft Edge:** This effect blurs the edges of the shape.

- **Halo:** This effect adds a colored glow that surrounds the stroke of the shape.

- **Gradient:** This effect adds a two-color gradient across the surface of the shape.

- **Image Texture:** This effect fills the shape with a selected texture.

When a fill effect is selected, a dialog box of options automatically opens. After the dialog box is closed, you can reopen it at any time by clicking the button with three dots on it to the right of the Effect list. The Options dialog box includes a preview pane that displays a circle showing the new effect with the current settings.

You can apply two effects channels to the current fill. When two effects are applied, they are stacked with Effect 2 on top of Effect 1. However, if you place a solid effect such as a gradient without any transparency in Effect 2, it will obscure any effect placed in Effect 1.

Note

Although the preview pane in the Effect Options dialog box shows what the effect looks like, when the effect is applied to a shape, the effect isn't visible in the working area. The actual effect won't be displayed until the scene is rendered.

Tip

Anime Studio only allows two effects to be applied at one time, but if you use the Style 1 and Style 2 drop-down lists, each applied style could have an additional two effects for a total of six effects in a single style.

Using a Shaded Effect

The Shaded effect is used to add some highlight shading to the selected shape. It is useful, for example, when you want to make buttons that appear raised. The options for the Shaded effect, shown in Figure 15.8, include a Light Angle, which controls where the shading appears. You can change the angle by dragging within the Light Angle control.

Figure 15.8
Shaded effect options.

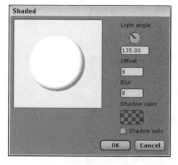

The Offset value sets the size of the shadow. Figure 15.9 shows a preview of a circle with an offset value that changes from left to right to 0, 8, 24, 56, and 96.

The Blur value determines how sharp the line between the shape color and the shaded color is. Figure 15.10 shows the preview circle with a blur value that changes from left to right to 0, 8, 24, 56, and 96.

Figure 15.9
Changing offset values.

Figure 15.10
Changing blur values.

Figure 15.11
Enabling shadow only.

The Shadow color swatch opens the Color Picker where you can choose a new color for the shaded portion. The default color is black with a 128 alpha value. This color is a light gray color that is half transparent, thus allowing the fill color to show through.

If you enable the Shadow Only option as shown in Figure 15.11, then only the shaded portion is visible.

Using a Soft Edge Effect

The Soft Edge effect is used to feather the edges of the selected shape by blurring its edges. The options for the Soft Edge effect, shown in Figure 15.12, include a Blur Radius, which defines the number of pixels that are used to blur the edge.

Using a Halo Effect

The Halo effect is used to add a glow around the shape. The options for the Halo effect, shown in Figure 15.13, let you set the halo color and its size.

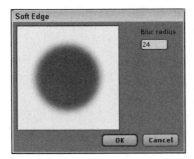

Figure 15.12
Soft Edge effect options.

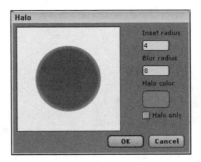

Figure 15.13
Halo effect options.

The Inset Radius value can range between 1 and 30, depending on the size of the shape. This value sets the number of pixels from the shape's edge that are solid shaded with the halo color. The Blur Radius value defines where the blur starts. Figure 15.14 shows the preview circle with inset radius values of 2 and 8 and blur radius values of 1, 16, and 64.

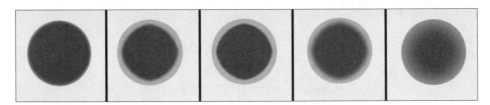

Figure 15.14
Changing inset and blur radius values.

Figure 15.15
Enabling halo only.

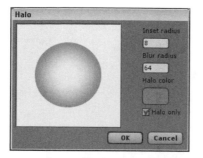

The Halo Only option removes the fill color and displays only the halo color, as shown in Figure 15.15.

Using a Gradient Effect

The Gradient effect is used to fill the shape with a gradient that transitions gradually among a range of colors. The options for the Gradient effect, shown in Figure 15.16, let you choose the Gradient Type and set the gradient in a color bar. The available Gradient Types include Linear, Radial, Reflected, and Angle.

New Feature

The Gradient features have been improved in Anime Studio 6 to include Reflected and Angle gradient types along with a color bar for adding multiple gradient stops and colors. Gradient effects can be animated.

Figure 15.16
Gradient effect
options.

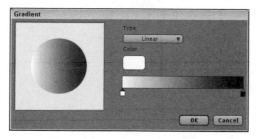

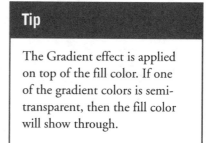

Tip

The Gradient effect is applied on top of the fill color. If one of the gradient colors is semi-transparent, then the fill color will show through.

The Linear gradient type runs by default from left to right, causing a gradual change in color from one side of the shape to the other. Using the interactive control, you can change the direction of the linear gradient. The Radial gradient type starts with one color at a center location and gradually changes in concentric circles as the distance from the center is increased. The Reflected gradient type transitions from the end color to the start color at a center location and back to the end color in a linear direction. The Angle gradient type sweeps about a center point from one color to another. Figure 15.17 shows an example of each of the gradient types.

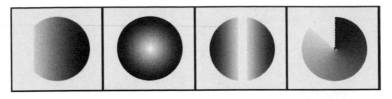

Figure 15.17
Linear, Radial,
Reflected, and Angle
Gradient types.

The color swatch sets the color for the selected color stop. The selected color stop
has a black arrow above it. The gradient color bar starts with two color stops at
either end of the bar, but you can add more color stops by clicking below the
gradient color bar. Clicking an existing color stop makes it the selected color stop
and displays its color in the color swatch. Double-clicking a color stop opens the
Color Picker for the selected color stop. You can also move the color stops to
the left or right by dragging them. Figure 15.18 shows a gradient with multiple
gradient stops.

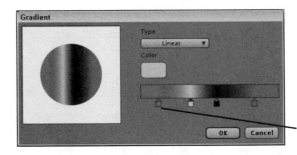

Figure 15.18
Gradient with
multiple color stops.

Gradient color stop

Using an Image Texture Effect

The Image Texture effect is used to fill the shape with a bitmap texture. The
options for the Image Texture effect, as shown in Figure 15.19, let you select the
bitmap texture to use from a File dialog box and also choose from two fill modes.
The Tile fill mode tiles the bitmap by placing it end to end until it fills the entire
fill area. The Don't Repeat fill mode fits the bitmap within the shape by aligning
its edges to the edges of the shape.

Figure 15.19
Texture effect in
Tile fill mode.

Positioning and Rotating Gradients and Images

If either the Gradient or Image Texture effects are added to a shape, then an interactive control line with circles at either end appear when the Select Shape tool is selected. This interactive control, shown in Figure 15.20, lets you position and rotate the gradient or image.

New Feature

The interactive control that lets you move and rotate gradients and images is new to Anime Studio 6.

Figure 15.20
Interactive position control.

Interactive texture control

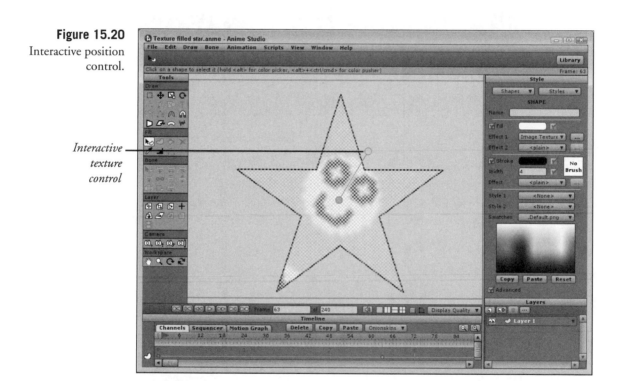

One end of the interactive control is a solid circle. This marks the center of the gradient or image. Moving this end of the control repositions the gradient or image. The opposite end has an open circle. Dragging this end will rotate the gradient or image about the circle at the opposite end. Figure 15.21 shows the repositioned image. By moving the solid circle down, the center of the image has been repositioned and by dragging the open circle to the side, the entire image has been rotated.

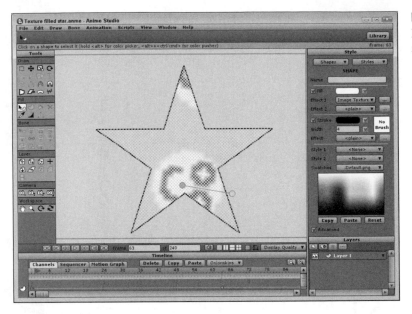

Figure 15.21
Repositioned and rotated image.

The distance between the two ends represents the scale of the image. By moving the two circles closer together, you can reduce the image's scale or tighten the length of the gradient. Moving the two circles farther apart will increase the image's scale or stretch out the gradient. Figure 15.22 shows a change in the image's scale. With the Tile option set for the texture image, the image is repeated end to end both horizontally and vertically.

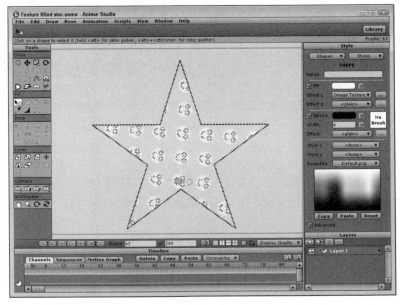

Figure 15.22
Scaled image.

Removing an Effect

To remove an effect from a style, you simply need to select the Plain option from the Effect drop-down list.

Adding Line Effects

When the Stroke option is enabled, the shape stroke is colored using the designated color and its thickness is determined by the Line Width value. A stroke can also include a single effect applied using the Effect drop-down list. The available line effects include the following:

- **Shaded:** This effect adds a gradient along one edge of the object to make it appear to be raised.

- **Soft Edge:** This effect blurs the edges of the stroke.

- **Halo:** This effect adds a colored glow that surrounds the stroke.

- **Gradient:** This effect adds a two-color gradient across the surface of the stroke.

- **Image Texture:** This effect fills the stroke with a selected texture.

These available line effects that can be applied to a stroke are the same as those for fills, as shown in Figure 15.23. For strokes, there are two new effects that only apply to strokes.

> **Caution**
>
> The Soft Edge and Halo stroke effects are only visible when rendered.

Selecting and Using Brushes

By default a stroke is drawn with a consistent width all the way around the shape. This thickness can be changed by applying an effect or by changing the brush that is used to draw the stroke. Anime Studio includes several preset brushes that can give a stroke a unique look. To change the brush used to draw the stroke, click the Brush button next to the Line color swatch. This opens the Brush Settings dialog box shown in Figure 15.24.

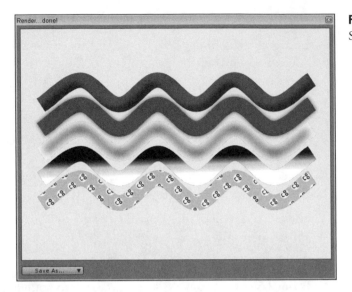

Figure 15.23
Stroke effects.

Caution

If the Stroke Width value is kept at its default value of 4, then most brushes will be too small to be seen. When using a Brush effect, increase the Stroke Width to see the effect.

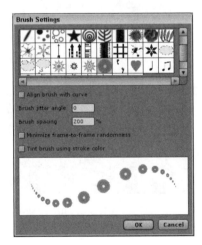

Figure 15.24
Brush Settings dialog box.

Creating a New Brush

All available brush presets are located within the Brushes folder where Anime Studio is installed. Each of these brushes is simply a square PNG file. If you add a new brush to this folder and then restart Anime Studio, the new brush is available when you return to the Brush Settings dialog box.

New Feature

Brushes in the previous version had to be grayscale and could only be 128 pixels wide, but support for color brushes that are 512 pixels wide is new to Anime Studio 6.

To create a new custom brush, follow these steps:

1. Open the Brushes folder at the location where Anime Studio is installed. Select and open one of the default brush presets in an image editor such as Photoshop.

2. Create a new brush that fits within the existing artboard using a grayscale or color scheme. Brush presets can use colors.

   Use the File, Save As menu command to save the new custom brush preset as a new file.

   Close and restart Anime Studio and then click the Brush button in the Style palette.

   The new custom brush preset appears within the Brush Settings dialog box, as shown in Figure 15.25.

Figure 15.25
New custom brush.

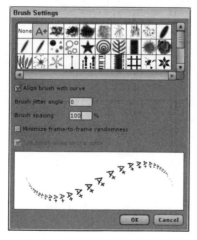

Aligning the Brush to the Curve

Within the Brush Settings dialog box is an option to Align Brush to Curve. If this option is disabled, the curve is drawn by positioning the brush preset end to end, but if this option is enabled, it causes the brush preset to be oriented to run parallel to the curve. Figure 15.26 shows the results of enabling this option. The left two strokes have the Align Brush to Curve option disabled and the right two strokes have it enabled.

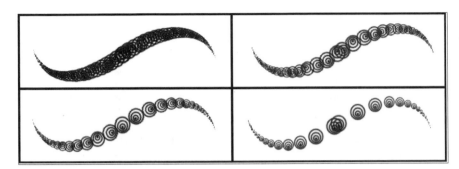

Figure 15.26
Aligning brush to curve.

Setting the Brush Jitter

Some brushes work best when the brush is aligned to the curve, but other times making the brush random fits better. The Brush Jitter Angle value in the Brush Settings dialog box lets you set the angular range that the brush can rotate every time it is drawn. A Brush Jitter Angle of 0 results in no rotation, a value of 30 lets each brush stroke be rotated randomly up to 30 degrees, and a value of 360 lets each brush stroke be rotated to any angle. Figure 15.27 shows a preview of a stroke using Brush Jitter Angle values of 0, 30, 60, and 90.

When randomness is added to the vectors, it can cause the brush strokes to be altered dramatically while an animation progresses. If you enable the Minimize Frame-to-Frame Randomness option in the Brush Settings dialog box, the jitter of a stroke during animation will be kept in check.

Changing the Brush Spacing

The Brush Spacing value in the Brush Settings dialog box controls how far apart each brush stroke is from its neighbor. A value of 100% spaces the brush strokes so that the full width of the brush preset is presented next to each other, but values less than 100% cause each stroke to be overlapped with its adjacent strokes and values greater than 100% add some space between each stroke. Figure 15.28 shows a stroke with Brush Spacing values of 40, 80, 100, and 140.

Figure 15.27
Changing Brush
Jitter Angle.

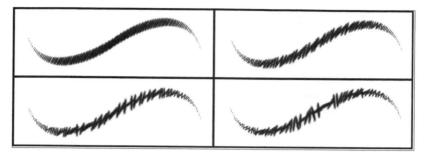

Figure 15.28
Changing Brush
Spacing.

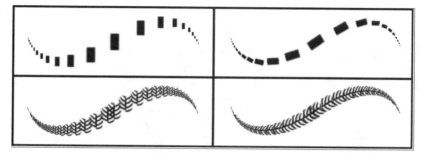

Tinting Stroke Color

The Tint Brush using Stroke Color option causes the brush stroke to assume the stroke color when enabled. For grayscale brushes, this option simply colors the stroke to match the stroke color, but if the brush is colored, then the various colors are replaced by the stroke color based on their saturation.

Using the Color Swatches

You can quickly select a color for the current fill and stroke colors by clicking one of the colors in the color palette at the bottom of the Style palette. You can select a stroke color by holding down the Alt/Opt key while clicking or by right-clicking the color palette. You can also switch between the different Swatch palettes available in the drop-down list above the color palette. This drop-down list can hold custom color palettes, color swatches, or even images, such as the face image shown in Figure 15.29.

Loading a Custom Palette Image

If you have an image that holds all the colors you want to use in a scene, you can load the image into the Style palette using the Custom Image option, which is found in the Swatches drop-down list. This option opens a File dialog box where you can locate an image to load, such as the image shown in Figure 15.30. When a custom image is loaded, any of the colors within the image can be selected by simply clicking the color in the image.

Figure 15.29
Face palette colors.

Figure 15.30
Custom image palette colors.

All of the images available in the Swatches drop-down list are found in the Swatches folder where Anime Studio is installed. If you want a custom image to appear in the drop-down list, simply add the image file to the Swatches folder and the next time you restart Anime Studio the image will be listed in the Swatches drop-down list.

Chapter Summary

This chapter covered the Style palette, which is used to define the properties of the fill and stroke that are applied to shapes. It also covered the available effects that can enhance fill and strokes. Various brushes can also be selected from within the Style palette as well as custom color palettes.

The next chapter covers the basics of animation in Anime Studio using keyframing and tweening.

Part IV

Animating in Anime Studio

16

Understanding Keyframes and Tweening

- Understanding keyframes
- Changing numbers of frames and frame rates
- Enabling frame skipping
- Using playback buttons
- Using animation scripts
- Clearing animation keys

There are several different ways to animate content in Anime Studio, and this chapter serves as an introduction to each of them. Regardless of the animation method you use, all animation is accomplished by setting *keyframes*, or *keys* for short. Keyframes define a state in time, whether it is a Fill color, the position of a point, or the orientation of a layer.

All keyframes are saved in the Timeline palette, where they can be moved, copied, and altered as needed. These keyframes look like small round dots. This chapter serves as an introduction to animating with keyframes, and Chapter 17, "Working with the Timeline," gets into more details on animating using the Timeline palette.

Understanding Keyframes

A keyframe captures the state of the scene at the current frame. Keyframes will only work if two or more keyframes exist and if there is a difference between the two states. For example, suppose a key is set for a circle shape at frame 1, where the shape is located near the left edge of the working area, and then at frame 11 another key is set for the same circle that has the shape positioned over near the right edge of the working area. When the scene is animated, the circle will gradually move from its starting position in frame 1 to its ending position in frame 11. At frame 2, the circle will move 1/10 of the way toward the end position at frame 11, which is where the second key is located. With each successive frame, the circle will move closer to its end position.

In addition to the shape's position, you can also set keys for the shape's rotation and scale transformations. Keys can also be set for properties such as a shape's line width, and even changing colors and the movement of bones can be animated over time.

The speed of an object's movement or the rate that an object's property changes depends on the distance between the adjacent keys. If an object moves across the working area over 20 frames with keys set at frame 1 and frame 21, then the same object will move twice as fast if the same keys are positioned at frame 1 and frame 11.

All animated actions can be broken down into a series of keyframes. The trick is to divide the motion into a series of small key positions. For example, consider a wheel rolling across the scene. If you create two position keys, the wheel will move the correct distance, but to improve the animation, you should also create keys that make the wheel rotate as it is moving across the scene. By combining different transformations, you can create complex motions.

All keys created in Anime Studio appear in the Timeline palette. From there, you can move, scale, copy, and paste them between frames. (More detailed information on using the Timeline palette is covered in Chapter 17.)

There are several different types of objects that can be animated in Anime Studio and the software distinguishes between these different types. Anime Studio classifies animated objects into the following groups:

- **Point Motion:** Allows individual points to be moved. It gives you the most flexibility and is the simplest type of motion, but it can be time consuming if you need to move a lot of points.

- **Bone Animation:** Allows multiple points to be animated at once using a bone construct.

- **Morphing:** Defines several different morph targets and blends between these morph targets to move between the different states.

- **Layer Animation:** Transforms the entire layer.

Using Point Motion

Perhaps the simplest animation method is to move individual points. This type of animation is good for making small tweaks to an existing animation, but if an animation requires a lot of points to move, this method may not be the most efficient.

Point motion also makes it possible to convert one shape into another. For example, if you take a standard circle and gradually move the points on the circle to create a star, the shape of the object has changed, with a start shape and an end shape, as shown in Figure 16.1. The process of changing a shape is accomplished by using keys, but the entire process is called *tweening* because all the intermediate steps are automatically computed as "in-between" steps.

> **Note**
>
> Creating tweens in Anime Studio is automatic—you simply need to move the object's points. This is quite different from creating tweens in other packages like Flash, which requires that you select two keyframes and choose a Tween command.

Figure 16.1
Tweening example.

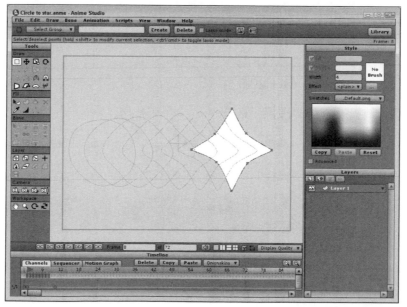

Using Bone Animation

Another common animation method is to animate objects by moving their bones. Bones are underlying linked structures that have influence over the surrounding points. By moving the bones, the points move along with them. Bones are an efficient way to move multiple points. Setting up bones and working with them is covered in Chapter 26, "Creating and Binding Bones."

Morph Animation

Anime Studio Pro lets you define morph targets and once several morph targets are defined, you can blend between these targets to create a range of new motions. Morphing is often used to create subtle changes, such as facial animations. Morphing is covered in Chapter 21, "Morphing Objects and Using Actions."

Using Layer Animation

More generalized animations can be accomplished by moving layers between frames. This method moves every object on the current layer and is much more efficient than moving all the individual points contained on a layer. For example, if you use bones to create an animation of a character walking down the sidewalk, you could use layer animation to slowly move the background layer to the side to emphasize the movement of the walking character.

Changing the Number of Frames and the Frame Rate

The current frame range is shown as a blue highlight that runs along the top of the Timeline palette. This range is the default range that is exported when the File, Export Animation command is used. Keys can be placed before and after the current frame range, but if they fall outside of this range, they won't be exported.

The *frame rate* is the number of frames that are displayed per second. Common frame rates include 24 frames per second (or fps) for film, 30 frames per second in television, and 12 fps for the Web. Anime Studio projects can have a maximum frame rate of 120 fps.

> **Note**
>
> Many real-time console games run at 60 fps.

You can alter the frame range and the frame rate values using the File, Project Settings dialog box, as shown in Figure 16.2. The Start Frame doesn't have to start at 1 and the End Frame can be as high as your machine has memory for.

Figure 16.2
Project Settings
dialog box.

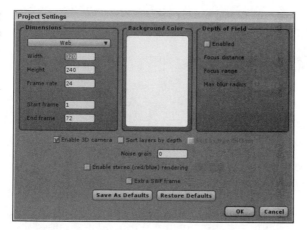

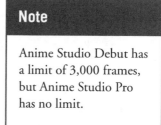

Note

Anime Studio Debut has a limit of 3,000 frames, but Anime Studio Pro has no limit.

Enabling Frame Skipping

When you click the Play button, the defined animation will play back as closely as it can to the specified frame rate, but if the scene is complex—particularly if it has a lot of particles—then the real-time display in the main window may take more computing power than it has time to display. If this happens, the timing of the animation will fail as the computer struggles to display the scene as created.

To solve this problem, the Animation menu includes an option to Allow Frame Skipping. With this menu option enabled, the display will automatically drop any frames that it can't render in time to keep a consistent frame rate. This affects the display quality, but it maintains the timing of the animation.

Tip

If the frame skipping is too much, then try exporting the animation with the Render at Half Dimensions, Render at Half Frame Rate, or Reduced Particles options enabled.

To enable frame skipping, follow these steps:

1. Open the American flag.anme file from the Chapter 16 folder on the CD. This file includes a vector layer of the American flag. With all the stars, this layer has a lot of points and animating it will cause the playback to slow down. The flag has been animated moving and rotating about the working area, as shown in Figure 16.3.

2. Use the File, Project Settings command to open the Project Settings dialog box and set the frame rate to 12 and close the dialog box. Then click the Play button in the lower-left corner of the main window to see the resulting animation. With a low frame rate, the animation plays back slowly and the display has no trouble keeping up.

3. Open the Project Settings dialog box again and change the frame rate to 120. Then click the Play button again. This time the animation plays faster, but it's more jumpy and erratic, and the stars seem to be falling behind.

4. Select the Animation, Allow Frame Skipping menu command and notice the change. The animation plays back without the jumpy, erratic motion because some of the frames are being skipped. At this high frame rate, the skipped frames won't even be noticed.

Figure 16.3
Animated American flag.

Using the Playback Buttons

You use the playback buttons, shown in Figure 16.4, to view the current animation. They are located in the lower-left corner of the main window. The playback buttons include the following:

- **Previous Keyframe:** This button moves to the frame where the previous keyfame is located.

- **Rewind:** This button rewinds the animation back to the first frame.

- **Step Back (left arrow):** This button moves the animation back one frame.

- **Play/Stop (Spacebar):** This button starts the animation at the specified frame rate. The button changes to a Stop button when an animation is playing.

- **Step Forward (right arrow):** This button moves the animation forward one frame.

- **Jump to End:** This button jumps the animation to the last frame in its range.

- **Next Keyframe:** This button moves to the frame where the next keyframe is located.

> **Tip**
>
> The Spacebar is used to start and stop an animation. You can also use the left and right arrows to move back and forward one frame.

> **Tip**
>
> The playback buttons will work whether you right- or left-click them.

New Feature

The Previous and Next Keyframe buttons are new to Anime Studio 6.

Figure 16.4
Playback buttons.

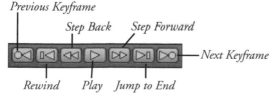

Previous Keyframe
Step Back *Step Forward*
Next Keyframe
Rewind *Play* *Jump to End*

Understanding Channels

One of the great benefits of using keys in Anime Studio is that they are automatically created when a change is made to the project, but if every change to the project were recorded for the given frame, then locating a specific change later to make an adjustment would be difficult. Anime Studio's answer to this dilemma is to use channels.

Channels keep track of the changes for a specific parameter such as a layer translation independent from the other parameters. This allows you to revisit and alter just the layer translation key for a given frame without changing the layer scale or layer rotation at that same frame. Each of the available channels shows up as a separate row in the Timeline palette.

Each channel keeps track of its parameter's state for each frame, but only one state is allowed for each frame. For example, if you set a key to scale a layer to 200% at frame 10 and later you change the scale layer value at frame 10 to 50%, the key only remembers the latest change, which would be 50%. The 200% value would be overwritten for this frame.

One other tricky aspect of working with channels is that the interpolation between channel keys is also independent of all other channels. For example, if you want to create an animation where a logo flies in from the left, stops and spins around once, and then flies off to the right, you'll need to set keys for each channel independently, including when a motion starts and stops. The next example demonstrates this effect.

When creating this simple animation, you might proceed like this:

1. Select the vector layer and move it to the left of the working area at frame 0 with the Layer Translate tool (T).

2. Move the Time Slider to frame 20 and with the Layer Translate tool (T) move the layer from the left to the middle of the working area.

3. Move the Time Slider to frame 40, select the Rotate Layer tool (R), and spin the layer one revolution.

4. Move the Time Slider to frame 60, select the Layer Translate tool (T), and move the object off to the right of the working area.

5. Press the Play button (Spacebar) and notice how the logo moves, as shown in Figure 16.5.

Figure 16.5

Spinning logo, take 1.

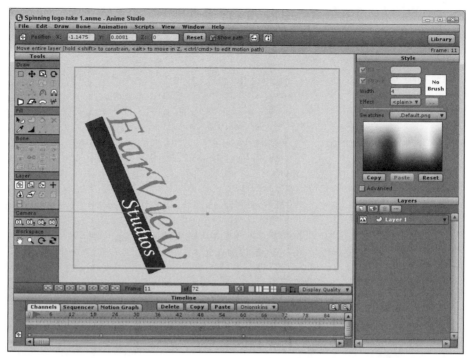

The resulting animation has the movement of the logo combined with the rotation, which is probably not what you expected. If you look at the Timeline, you'll see a whole column of keys at frame 0 and three other keys on two different rows or channels.

What is happening is that the motion between keys is automatically interpolating between the adjacent keys, so since there is only a single Layer Rotation key at frame 40, the rotation is interpolating between its default rotation value at frame 0 and its new state at frame 40, causing the rotation to be extended across 40 frames.

The same condition happens for the Translate Layer channel. The logo's motion is caused by the interpolation between the adjacent keys and since the states at frame 20 and frame 60 are different, the layer simply moves slowly between the two states.

The *gotcha* is that we didn't create the appropriate start and stop keys for each channel because we assumed that they would be created automatically when a key in another channel was added. When setting keys, you need to be explicit about each state and create a key to stop a motion if you want that behavior.

To correct the spinning logo animation so each motion is independent, follow these steps:

1. Open the Spinning logo-take 1.anme file from the Chapter 16 folder on the CD. This file includes the spinning logo along with the keys created in the above example.

2. We'll start by addressing the layer translation motion. We want the logo to fly in from the left and stop at frame 20 and then start again at frame 40. The key at frame 20 works fine for flying the layer in, but we need to address its motion that happens while the logo spins. Drag the Time Slider to frame 40, which is the end of the spin cycle, and drag the logo with the Layer Translate tool (T) back to where it stopped at frame 20.

3. Click the Play button (Spacebar) and notice how the motion has changed. The logo now stands still between frames 20 and 40.

4. Next, we'll deal with the logo's rotation. The key at frame 40 tells the logo to spin a complete revolution, which it does, but it does it over the first 40 frames. We want it to spin between frame 20 and frame 40, so we'll need to add a key at frame 20 that is the same as the key at frame 0, which is the state at the start of the rotation. Click the layer rotation key at frame 0 to select it. It turns red when selected. Then click the Copy button at the top of the Timeline palette. Drag the Time Slider to frame 20 and click the Paste button. This pastes a copy of the frame 0 key to frame 20.

5. Click the Play button (Spacebar) and notice how the logo enters, stops and spins, and then flies off to the right just like we wanted, as shown in Figure 16.6.

Using Visibility and Warp Scripts

Scripts are a great way to automate specific animation techniques. When any of the animation scripts are used, the keys are automatically created and added to the Timeline. Several of the categories in the Scripts menu include scripts that create animation keys. The Camera category includes a script to animate the camera so that it has a jiggle added to it (the Handheld Camera script) and another script to automatically rotate the camera about the current object (the Orbit Camera script). Both of these scripts are covered in Chapter 25, "Changing the View with Cameras."

The Particle Effects category also includes a number of scripts for animating particles. These are covered in Chapter 31, "Using Particle Layers." The Visibility and Warp script categories also include some fun animation scripts that let you fade and warp objects.

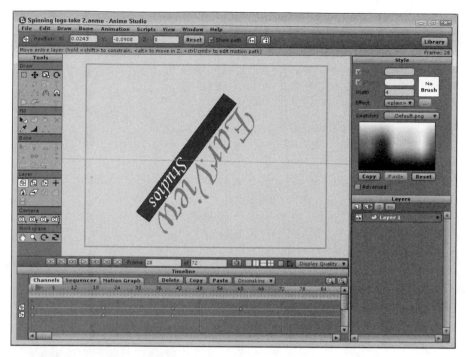

Figure 16.6
Spinning logo,
take 2.

Caution

Keep in mind that some of the animation scripts create a large number of keys, which can make it hard to edit any changes.

Note

These scripts are only designed to work with vector layers.

Fading Objects

The Scripts, Visibility menu includes two excellent examples of animation techniques: Fade and Wavy Fade. The Fade script causes the selected layer to fade away over a given number of frames. You can set the number of frames the effect takes place over (the duration), the Blur Radius, and whether the selected object fades in or out by using the Fade dialog box that opens when you select the script command (see Figure 16.7).

Figure 16.7
Fade script dialog box.

Caution

If no points are selected, then the Wavy script is disabled. The Fade script can be applied to all layer types, but it only works when applied to a vector layer.

The Wavy Fade is a little more complex; it allows the object to undulate as it fades away. For this script, you can set the frequency and the amplitude, as shown in Figure 16.8. The Frequency value sets how often the object waves up and down and the Amplitude value measures how high each wave is.

Tip

The Duration of the animation is measured from the current frame, so you can set this effect to begin in the middle of a sequence by choosing a frame before accessing the script.

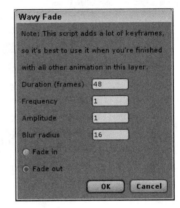

Figure 16.8
Wavy Fade script dialog box.

To create a wavy fade effect for a desert scene, follow these steps:

1. Open the Desert.anme file from the Chapter 16 folder on the CD. This file includes the default desert background.

2. Select the Cactus layer in the Layers palette and choose the Edit, Select All command (Ctrl/Cmd+A) to select all the points on this layer.

3. Select the Scripts, Visibility, Wavy Fade menu command to open the Wavy Fade dialog box. Set the Duration to 72, the Frequency to 1, the Amplitude to 0.1, and the Blur Radius to 16. Then click the OK button to close the dialog box. All the keys are automatically added to the Timeline palette.

4. Click the Play button (Spacebar) and notice how the cacti are waving as the animation progresses. Also notice how the Fill color fades, as shown in Figure 16.9.

Figure 16.9
Desert waving
effect.

Warping Objects

The Scripts, Warp menu includes two more examples that automate animation techniques. The Black Hole script causes an object to spiral toward the center of the layer as it slowly disappears. It works especially well with a particle layer. The Black Hole dialog box, shown in Figure 16.10, sets the number of frames that the effect happens over (the duration). You can also set the Angle, which is the amount of rotation that the object takes as it moves toward the center of the working area. There is also an option to Run Backwards that makes the points spiral outward from the center when enabled.

Figure 16.10
Black Hole script
dialog box.

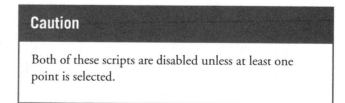

Caution

Both of these scripts are disabled unless at least one point is selected.

Figure 16.11 shows an example of the Black Hole script: five stars rotating toward the center of the working area.

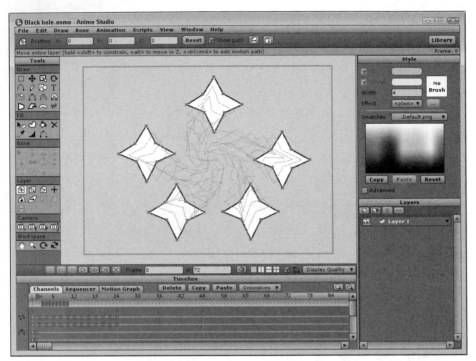

Figure 16.11
Results of the Black Hole script.

The Wavy script causes the layer to undulate over a given number of frames. Using the Wavy dialog box, as shown in Figure 16.12, you can set the number of frames, the frequency, and the amplitude.

There are also options to have the object wave using a constant amplitude or a temporary wave. The Constant Amplitude option keeps the distance that each point moves constant from wave to wave, which results in an animation that repeats the same way as the waves progress. The Temporary Wave option starts out gradually and gets progressively larger as the animation progresses, resulting in wild fluctuations at the end of the animation.

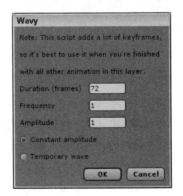

Figure 16.12
Wavy script dialog box.

Figure 16.13 shows a simple star waving over several frames.

Figure 16.13
Results of the
Wavy script.

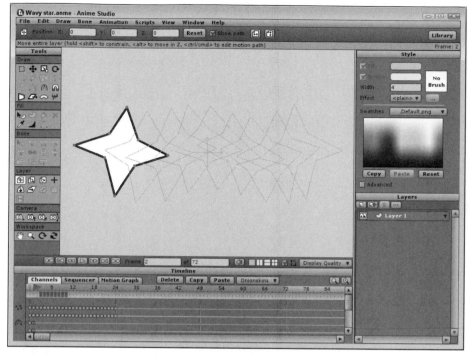

Figure 16.13
Results of the
Wavy script.

Clearing Animation Keys

If you create a number of keys on several layers and then determine that you've made a mistake, the task of selecting and removing the correct keys can be a difficult one. The Animation menu includes two commands that help resolve this issue. The Animation, Clear Animation from Layer menu command will remove all the animation keys from the current layer. You can also remove all animation keys for the current project with the Animation, Clear Animation from Document.

Chapter Summary

This chapter introduced the concept of keyframing, which enables you to animate objects. It also covered setting the frame rate and the total number of frames in the animation. In addition, this chapter also discussed frame skipping, the playback buttons, and several available animation scripts.

The next chapter dives into the Timeline palette and shows how it is used to help you with your animating tasks.

17

Working with the Timeline

- Introducing the Timeline palette
- Working with animation channels
- Creating and manipulating keys
- Understanding interpolation types
- Using onion skinning

The Timeline palette holds all the animation data for an animated sequence, including all keyframes. It lets you place and manipulate keys and control the interpolation method used between adjacent keyframes. Understanding the Timeline palette is the key to being able to animate in Anime Studio.

The Timeline palette also includes a feature called *onion skinning* that lets you see the position of objects for other frames. This is helpful for seeing how objects move through the project.

Introducing the Timeline Palette

The Timeline palette, shown in Figure 17.1, appears at the bottom of the interface by default, but you can move it anywhere in the open screen by making it into a floating palette with the Windows, Timeline menu. If the Timeline palette isn't visible, you can open it using the Window, Timeline (Ctrl/Cmd+[ )menu command. You can also resize the Timeline palette by dragging its edges or corners.

Time slider   *Selected key*   *Onionskin bar*   *Frame range*

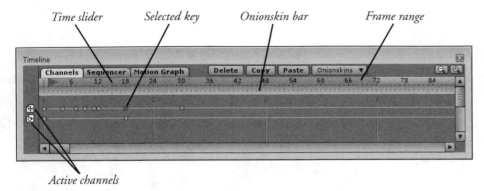

Figure 17.1
Timeline palette.

Active channels

Along the top of the Timeline palette are several tabs, control buttons, and a drop-down menu. The available tabs include Channels, Sequencer, and Motion Graph. Each of these tabs changes the Timeline palette's display. The Channels tab is the default mode showing all the keys for the active channels. The Sequencer tab lets you load and work with audio and video files. This mode is covered in Chapter 19, "Working with Sound," and the Motion Graph mode is covered in Chapter 18, "Manipulating Animation Graphs."

> **Note**
>
> The Motion Graph tab is only available in Anime Studio Pro.

Next to the tabs are buttons for deleting, copying, and pasting keys. The Onionskins drop-down list is covered later in this chapter. Directly above the Timeline palette, located along the bottom edge of the main window are fields for displaying the current frame number and the total number of frames. You can change the current frame number and the ending frame number by entering a new value in the Frame and adjacent field. You can also change the current frame number by dragging the time slider or by pressing on the animation control buttons at the bottom left of the working area.

Setting the Frame Range

Any frame value can be entered into the Frame field, but only those frames within the designated frame range will be rendered or exported. The frame range is indicated by the blue area in the Timeline palette directly under the tabs and buttons.

You can alter the frame range using the File, Project Settings dialog box. You can also change the beginning frame of the animation by holding down the Alt/Opt key and clicking the frame in the Timeline palette where you want the animation to start. The end frame can be changed by holding down the Alt/Opt key and clicking with the right mouse button where you want the animation range to end.

Note

On Mac systems with a single-button mouse, the end frame is set by clicking with Ctrl and Option keys held down instead of a right-click.

Playing a Partial Range

Whenever you click the Play button in the animation controls, the entire frame range is played, but if you hold down the Ctrl/Cmd key and click the frame range bar in the Timeline palette, a green marker is placed on the frame range to mark the starting frame of a partial range. You can also hold down the Ctrl/Cmd key and click with the right mouse button to mark an end frame for the partial range.

Note

Again, on Mac systems with a single-button mouse, the partial range end frame is set by clicking with Ctrl and Option keys held down.

Once a partial range is marked, the Play button will only play the partial range instead of the entire range. You can remove the partial range markers by holding down the Ctrl/Cmd key and clicking the markers again.

Note

If you have a Video or Audio layer selected, then the start and end frames of the selected video or audio file is marked with a right-pointing green arrow icon and a left-pointing red arrow icon on the range bar.

Viewing Time Markers

Directly beneath the Onionskin bar is a set of numbers that are spread out farther than the frame numbers. These values represent the time in seconds for the current animation. The positions of these time values change as the frame rate changes. Figure 17.2 shows the time markers for a setting of 24 frames per second, so each second aligns with a multiple of 24 frames. The frame rate is set in the Project Settings dialog box.

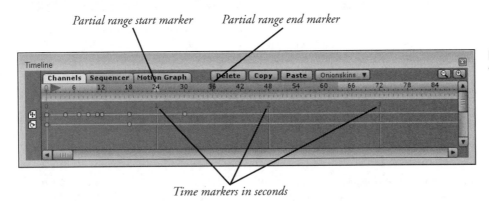

Figure 17.2
Time markers.

If you're working with broadcast video, then time is designated using a timecode that consists of four double-digit numbers for the hours, minutes, seconds, and tenths of seconds. To change the time values in the Timeline palette to reflect these standard timecodes, simply enable the Use SMPTE timecode option in the Preferences dialog box.

Zooming the Timeline

At the top right of the Timeline palette are two buttons marked with a minus sign and a plus sign. These buttons are used to zoom out and zoom in on the current frame settings. By zooming out, you'll be able to see a wider range of frames, but zooming in makes it easier to work with individual keys.

Figure 17.3 shows the Timeline after it has been zoomed out using the minus sign button.

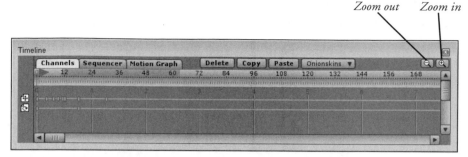

Figure 17.3
Zoomed out
Timeline.

Working with Animation Channels

Any time a parameter or layer is altered when a frame other than 0 is selected, a key is created. These keys are added to the Timeline palette for the channel that matches the change. By separating the changes to different channels, you can quickly identify the keys that control the animated changes. Keys in the Timeline are only displayed for the currently selected layer. If keys for an object on another layer are created, then those keys aren't visible until the layer is selected. Even if multiple layers are selected in the Layers palette, only the keys for the currently active layer are displayed in the Timeline palette.

The Timeline palette only shows those channels that have keys. Each channel is indicated by a graphical icon located at the far left side of the Timeline palette. If you move the mouse over the top of the channel icon, then the name of the channel is displayed in a tooltip.

New Feature

Showing only those Timeline channels that have keys is a new feature in Anime Studio 6.

The Preference dialog box, opened with the Edit, Preferences menu, includes an option to Consolidate Timeline Channels. This option shows all active animation channels as a single channel.

New Feature

The Consolidate Timeline Channels option in the Preferences dialog box is new to Anime Studio 6.

The available channels found in the Timeline palette depend on the type of layer that is selected. The first category of channels affects entire layers. The layer motion channel's parameters are changed using the various Layer tools.

The channels in this category include the following:

Layer Translation: This channel enables keys to be set when a layer is moved.

Layer Scale: This channel enables keys to be set when a layer changes size.

Layer Z Rotation: This channel enables keys to be set when a layer spins around its center.

Layer Y Rotation: This channel enables keys to be set when a layer is tilted to the left or right.

Layer X Rotation: This channel enables keys to be set when a layer is tilted up or down.

Layer Horizontal Flip: This channel enables keys to be set when a layer is flipped horizontally.

Layer Vertical Flip: This channel enables keys to be set when a layer is flipped vertically.

Layer Shear: This channel enables keys to be set when a layer is sheared either horizontally or vertically.

Note

The Layer Y Rotation, Layer X Rotation, and Layer Shear channels are only available in Anime Studio Pro.

The layer effect channel's parameters are altered using the settings in the Layer Settings dialog box. The channels in this category include the following:

Layer Visibility: This channel enables keys to be set when a layer is hidden and made visible again.

Layer Blur: This channel enables keys to be set when a layer's blur parameter is changed.

Layer Opacity: This channel enables keys to be set when a layer's opacity parameter is changed.

Layer Auto Shading: This channel enables keys to be set when a layer's auto shading parameter is changed.

Layer Shadow: This channel enables keys to be set when a layer's shadows are changed.

Layer Shading: This channel enables keys to be set when a layer's shading parameters are changed.

Layer Motion Blur: This channel enables keys to be set when a layer's motion blur parameters are changed.

The camera motion channel's parameters are changed using the various Camera tools. The channels in this category include the following:

Camera Tracking: This channel enables keys to be set when a camera is moved.

Camera Zoom: This channel enables keys to be set when a camera is zoomed in and out of the scene.

Camera Roll: This channel enables keys to be set when a camera spins around its center.

Camera Pan/Tilt: This channel enables keys to be set when a camera view is changed by panning or tilting the camera.

When a vector layer is selected in the Layers palette, you can choose to alter these parameters found in the Draw tools and in the Style palette. The channels in this category include the following vector channels:

Point Motion: This channel enables keys to be set when any points in the vector layer are moved.

Selected Point Motion: This channel enables keys to be set when any of the selected points in the vector layer are moved.

Point Curvature: This channel enables keys to be set when the curvature of any points in the vector layer is changed.

Selected Point Curvature: This channel enables keys to be set when the curvature of the selected points in the vector layer is changed.

Fill Color: This channel enables keys to be set when the fill color of any of the vector layer shapes is changed.

Selected Fill Color: This channel enables keys to be set when the fill color of the selected shapes is changed.

Line Color: This channel enables keys to be set when the stroke color of any of the vector layer lines is changed.

Selected Line Color: This channel enables keys to be set when the stroke color of the selected vector layer lines is changed.

Line Width: This channel enables keys to be set when the stroke line width of any of the vector layer lines is changed.

Selected Line Width: This channel enables keys to be set when the selected stroke line width of the vector layer lines is changed.

Shape Effect: This channel enables keys to be set when a shape effect is applied or when a shape effect parameter is changed.

Selected Shape Effect: This channel enables keys to be set when a shape effect for the selected shape is applied or when its shape effect parameter is changed.

Shape Effect Transform: This channel enables keys to be set when a gradient's or image texture's transform is changed using the interactive control.

Selected Shape Effect Transform: This channel enables keys to be set when a gradient's or image texture's transform for the selected shape is changed using the interactive control.

New Feature

The capability to set keys for layer auto shading, shape effects, and shape effect transforms is new to Anime Studio 6.

When a bone layer is selected in the Layers palette, you can alter its parameters using the various Bone tools, which will set a key for one of these available bone channels:

Bone Angle: This channel enables keys to be set when any of the bones are rotated.

Selected Bone Angle: This channel enables keys to be set when the selected bones are rotated.

Bone Translation: This channel enables keys to be set when any of the bones are moved to a new location.

Selected Bone Translation: This channel enables keys to be set when the selected bones are moved to a new location.

Bone Scale: This channel enables keys to be set when any of the bones are scaled to a new size.

Selected Bone Scale: This channel enables keys to be set when the selected bones are scaled to a new size.

Bone Lock: This channel enables keys to be set when any of the bones are locked.

Selected Bone Lock: This channel enables keys to be set when the selected bones are locked.

Bone Dynamics: This channel enables keys to be set when bone dynamics are enabled.

Selected Bone Dynamics: This channel enables keys to be set when bone dynamics are enabled for the selected bones.

When a switch layer is selected in the Layers palette, you can choose a switch channel:

Switch Layer: This channel enables keys to be set when the visible sub-layer in the switch layer is changed.

When a particle layer is selected in the Layers palette, you can choose a particles on/off channel, found in the Particles panel of the Layer Settings dialog box:

Particles On/Off: This channel enables keys to be set when particles are turned on or off.

When a tracking point is added to a video layer, then its motion is saved as keys in the Motion Tracking channel:

Motion Tracking: This channel enables keys to be set when a tracking point moves.

If the Consolidate Timeline Channels option in the Preferences dialog box is enabled, then all channels are represented by a single channel icon:

All Channels: This channel holds keys for all channels.

Creating Keys

When Anime Studio is first opened, the Timeline is set to frame 0. At frame 0, you can set the default state for all objects on the current layer. If you want to set a key for the current selection, you first need to move the time slider to a frame other than frame 0. Once a new frame is selected, you simply need to change the current state and a key for the corresponding channel is automatically set.

> **Note**
>
> The Timeline palette only shows the keys for the current layer. If another layer is selected, a different set of keys will be visible.

Another way to set a keyframe is to right-click in the Timeline palette at the intersection of the channel and frame where you want to place a key and then select Add Keyframe from the pop-up menu.

Because frame 0 is a special mode where you can set up and test bones and edit objects without any keys being recorded, it is important to know if you are at frame 0. In the Options panel of the Preferences dialog box is an option to Highlight Frame 0. By enabling this option, the working area is surrounded with a red border to remind you that you are set to frame 0.

By default, frame 0 represents the default starting frame for all layer channels, but you can reset the starting frame to be any frame with the Animation, Set Layer Start Time. The Start Frame is indicated in the Timeline palette by a small green arrow located on the frame range. Note that this location isn't necessarily the beginning of the range or where the Play button starts, but represents the frame where all objects are at their default value. If the Animation, Reset All Layer Channels menu is used, then the designated layer start time is copied to the current frame.

Another useful option in the Preferences dialog box is the Enable Drawing Tools Only on Frame 0 option. When this option is enabled, the drawing tools for creating new shapes are disabled if the Timeline is set to anywhere but frame 0.

This prevents you from creating new shapes outside of frame 0. If this option is disabled and a shape is created at a non-zero frame, then the shape will be hidden until the specific frame is reached.

To animate the solution to a maze, follow these steps:

1. Open the Maze.anme file from the Chapter 17 folder on the CD. This file includes a maze created using the Add Point tool (A) and the snapping grid feature.

2. With the arrow layer selected, select the Set Origin tool (0) and drag the origin crosshairs to the center of the arrow.

3. Drag the Time Slider to frame 5 and move the arrow down the first hall with the Layer Translate tool (1).

4. Drag the Time Slider to frame 10 and move the arrow down the next hall. The keys are added automatically to the Timeline palette whenever you move the layer. Continue to create new keys for the arrow moving through the maze setting keys every five frames.

5. Click the Play button (Spacebar) to see the arrow move through the maze, as shown in Figure 17.4.

Figure 17.4
Arrow moving through a maze.

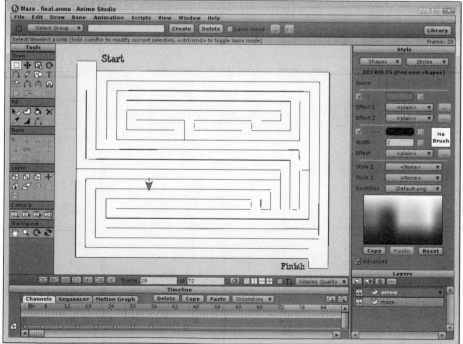

Rotating to Follow Translation Path

Although most keys need to be set manually by changing a parameter or using a tool when the frame is not set to 0, there is one motion that you can get automatically. Within the Layer Settings dialog box is an option to Rotate to Follow Path. When this option is enabled, the layer is rotated automatically to follow the path.

Figure 17.5 shows two rockets, each on a different layer. Both rockets are animated following similar paths that move the rockets up into the air and then turns and returns toward them to the ground. The left rocket maintains its default orientation, but the rocket on the right has the Rotate to Follow Path option enabled causing it to rotate to stay parallel to the path.

> **Note**
>
> When the Rotate to Follow Path option is enabled, no rotation keys are added to the Timeline.

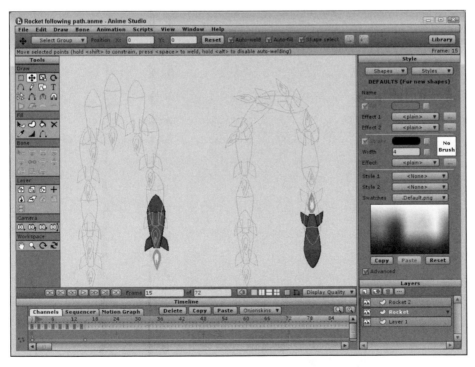

Figure 17.5

Rockets without and with the Rotate to Follow Path option enabled.

Caution

The layer rotation for the layer that is following its translation takes place about the layer's origin. If a single object is moving along a path, then you should position the origin in the center of the object or the rotation will be misaligned.

To make the layer rotate to follow the translation path, follow these steps:

1. Open the Maze with path rotate.anme file from the Chapter 17 folder on the CD. This file includes the animated arrow moving through a maze from the last example.

2. Double-click the arrow layer and enable the Rotate to Follow Path option. Then close the Layer Settings dialog box.

3. Click the Play button (Spacebar) and notice how the arrow moves through the maze. With the Rotate to Follow Path option enabled, the arrow rotates at each turn, but the arrow is pointing backward.

4. Drag the Time Slider to frame 0 and rotate the arrow so it is pointing down the maze hallway with the Rotate Layer tool (3).

5. Click the Play button (Spacebar) again and notice how the arrow is correctly pointing the way through the maze, as shown in Figure 17.6.

Figure 17.6
Arrow moving and rotating through a maze.

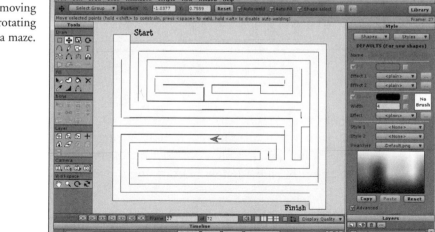

Manipulating Keys

Once keys are set, they appear on the Timeline palette. These keys can be selected and moved by first selecting the keys and then dragging them to a new location in the Timeline palette. You select keys in the Timeline palette by simply clicking them, and they turn red when they are selected. You can also select multiple keys by dragging over them in the Timeline palette.

If you want to select all keyframes at once, you can use the Animation, Select All Keyframes menu command. When a key or a group of keys is selected, you can move them to a new frame by dragging them to the left or right. You can also use the Edit, Cut, Copy, and Paste menu commands to move keys. This feature is covered below.

Once a keyframe or a group of keyframes is selected, you can delete the selected keyframes by simply pressing the Delete button at the top of the Timeline palette or by holding down the Alt/Opt key and pressing the Backspace key.

If you want to remove all keyframes from the selected layer, you can use the Animation, Clear Animation from Layer; if you want to remove all keyframes from the entire document, you can use the Animation, Clear Animation from Document menu command. This last command is pretty heavy and will remove all keys, so a warning dialog box appears before this command is completed, warning you that this action cannot be undone.

Tip
Keys cannot be moved or copied between channels.

Rescaling Keyframes

Although it is easy to move selected keyframes between frames, sometimes you want to keep the relative distance between adjacent keys without having to move each individual key. Using the Animation, Rescale Keyframes menu command, you can extend or reduce a section of animation without having to move each keyframe.

Scaling keyframes is an easy way to adjust the timing of your animation. If your objects are moving way too fast, then scaling to a larger number of frames will slow them down, and if your objects move too slowly, then try scaling the keys to a smaller range.

You can also rescale the selected keys by holding down the Alt/Opt key and dragging in the Timeline palette.

New Feature

The ability to rescale selected keys by dragging with the Alt/Opt key held down is new to Anime Studio 6.

Selecting the Animation, Rescale Keyframes menu command opens the Rescale Keyframes dialog box shown in Figure 17.7. When the dialog box is first opened, the Start and End Frame values are automatically set to 1 and the frame of the last key is on the current layer.

> **Note**
>
> The Rescale Keyframes dialog box affects those keys within the designated range regardless of which keys are selected in the Timeline palette.

Figure 17.7
Rescale Keyframes
dialog box.

Using the channel checkboxes, you can select precisely which channels on the current layer get scaled. However, if the Rescale Entire Document option is selected, all channels on all layers are scaled. This option also causes the End Frame to be automatically set to coincide with the frame of the last key from all layers. It also disables all the individual channels located at the bottom of the dialog box. This provides a way to scale all the keys across multiple layers at once.

> **Note**
>
> If Rescale Entire Document is disabled and no channels are selected in the Rescale Keyframes dialog box, it will also have no effect.

The Rescale Keyframes dialog box can be used to scale ranges of keys, but it also can be used to shift a range of keys. If you specify a range of keys, such as 20 to 30, and then enter the New Start Frame and New End Frame as 40 and 50, then the keys within that range will be moved to the new location.

Note

The Rescale Keyframes dialog box will not let you enter a keyframe value of 0.

Caution

When scaling keys to a smaller range of frames, be aware that if two adjacent keys are close together, they will be squashed together rather than being deleted. This could impact your timing.

Caution

The Rescale Keyframes feature occasionally behaves erratically depending on the keys you select and the type of scaling you're trying to do, so be sure to save your project before attempting to rescale any keys, especially since you can't undo the command.

Copying and Pasting Keys

At the top of the Timeline palette are buttons you can use to copy and paste selected keyframes to another frame. Clicking the Copy button or pressing the Alt/Opt+C keyboard shortcut copies the current selection of keys into a temporary buffer. If you then move to another frame and click the Paste button or press the Alt/Opt+V keyboard shortcut, the copied keyframes are pasted in the current frame.

Looping Animations

An easy way to create a looping animation is to copy the beginning keyframe of an object to the ending frame. This causes the object to return to the exact position where it first started.

The Animation menu also includes a command to set the key values for all layer channels to match the value set at frame 0. The command is Reset All Layer Channels. This command provides a great way to create an animation that has all objects returning to their initial state. By setting the end locations for all objects to match the start, the animation will start looping without any jumps. To rescale keyframes to speed up an animation and to copy keys to create a loop, follow these steps:

1. Open the Rolling tire.anme file from the Chapter 17 folder on the CD. This file includes an animated sequence of a tire rolling down a hill. It includes layer translation and rotation keys, but if you play the sequence, it moves too slowly.

2. Select the Animation, Rescale Keyframes menu command to open the Rescale Keyframes dialog box. The Start Frame is automatically set to 1 and the End Frame is set to 60. Leave the New Start Frame at 1 and change the New End Frame to 18; then select the Layer Translate and Layer Rotation channels in the dialog box and click the OK button. The keys in the Timeline palette are scaled.

3. In the Timeline palette, hold down the Shift key and click the key at frame 0 for the Layer Translate channel; then click the Copy button at the top of the Timeline palette.

4. Drag the Time Slider to frame 30 and click the Paste button at the top of the Timeline palette. The copied key is added to frame 30.

5. Click the Play button (Spacebar) to see the resulting animation. The tire now rotates quickly down the hill and bounces back to the start point, as shown in Figure 17.8.

Figure 17.8
Rescaled and
looping keys.

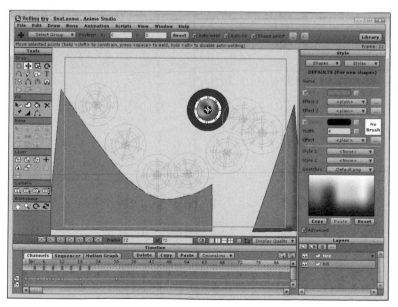

Understanding Interpolation Types

The object motion between adjacent keyframes can be controlled by altering the interpolation type. To understand interpolation types, think of a baseball player circling the bases. Although the shortest route between the bases is to run at right angles when viewed from above, base runners rarely run the bases in this manner. Instead, a runner circles around each base because his momentum carries him past the base. The resulting motion is rounded at each corner instead of a perfect square.

The same motion can be simulated by changing the interpolation type, which is found in the Timeline Settings dialog box. The selected interpolation type is then used for all new keys. The surface of each key has a marking that identifies the interpolation type. The available interpolation types in the Timeline Settings dialog box include the following:

- **Smooth:** Causes the interpolated motions between adjacent keys to be smooth to produce a gradual transition.

- **Linear:** Causes the interpolated motions between adjacent keys to be constant to produce a straight line.

- **Ease In/Out:** Gradually slows the motion as the key is approached and, likewise, gradually leaves the key as it moves to the next one.

- **Ease In:** Causes the interpolated motion between adjacent keys to be slowed as it approaches a new key.

- **Ease Out:** Causes the interpolated motion between adjacent keys to gradually increase as it moves away from a key.

- **Step:** Causes the position of the current key to remain until a new key is encountered and then the position of the new key is immediately jumped to.

- **Noisy:** Causes the interpolated motion between adjacent keys to be jittered like it is controlled by a noise function.

The default interpolation type that is used for all new keys is set using the Default Interpolation setting in the Preferences dialog box. You can change this default to be any of the available interpolation types, but the default is the Smooth option.

Note

Some layers are limited in the interpolation types they can use. For example, Switch and Particle layers only have the Step and Cycle interpolation types available.

Once keys are added to the Timeline palette, you can change the interpolation type for the selected key or keys by right-clicking on the key and selecting the interpolation type from the pop-up menu. If multiple keys are selected, then the new interpolation type is used for all the selected keys.

When the Noisy interpolation type is selected from the pop-up menu, the Noisy Interpolation dialog box shown in Figure 17.9 appears. Using this dialog box, you can set the amplitude of the jittering noise. This amplitude value defines how far from center the object can move. The Scale value multiplies the effect.

Figure 17.9
Noisy Interpolation dialog box.

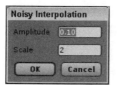

If you accidentally enable an interpolation type that you don't want, such as the Noisy interpolation type, you can remove its effects by right-clicking the keys that have the noise applied and selecting a new interpolation type. Any keys with the Noisy interpolation type applied can be easily identified by looking at the pattern that is on the key.

To use the Step interpolation type to change a stoplight, follow these steps:

1. Open the Stoplight.anme file from the Chapter 17 folder on the CD. This file includes a simple stoplight with red, yellow, and green lights. Each light is set to change color after twenty frames. The problem is that between frames 1 and 20, the red light slowly dims to gray while the yellow light slowly turns yellow and then dims to gray by frame 40, and the green light slowly becomes green at frame 40. This would not be a very effective stoplight, but we can fix it with the correct interpolation type.

2. Click the Settings button in the Timeline palette and enable the Fill Color and Selected Fill Color channels. Then close the Timeline Settings dialog box. This makes the keys for these channels visible in the Timeline palette.

3. Right-click each of the keys for the Fill Color channel and change its interpolation type to Step.

4. Click the Play button (Spacebar) and notice how each color stays the same until the frame where the key is located. Then it instantly changes to the new color, just as a stoplight should, as shown in Figure 17.10.

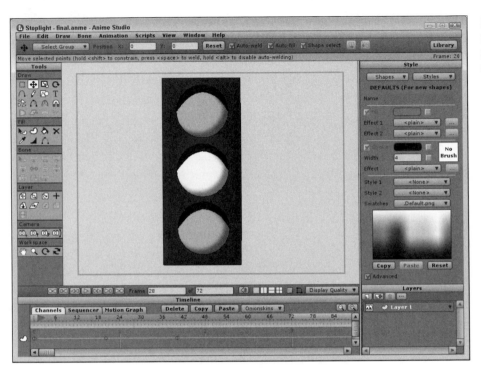

Figure 17.10
Stoplight with the Step interpolation type.

Channel Cycling

The key right-click pop-up menu also includes an option to Cycle. When this interpolation method is used, the animated section that is cycled repeats indefinitely. Choosing this option opens the Cycle Interpolation dialog box shown in Figure 17.11. The Absolute option lets you specify a frame number (in the Value field), and the cycling section will run from the current key to the designated frame. The Relative option defines a section by counting backward from the current frame the value you specify.

Figure 17.11
Cycle Interpolation
dialog box.

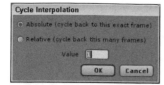

The cycling section in the Timeline palette is indicated by changing the key to an arrow and attaching a red line back to the cycled section, as shown in Figure 17.12.

Figure 17.12
Cycling section
in the Timeline.

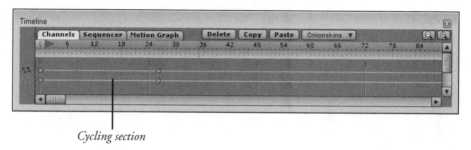

Cycling section

To use the Cycle interpolation method to repeat a set of walking legs, follow these steps:

1. Open the Walking legs.anme file from the Chapter 17 folder on the CD. This file is the same file created in Chapter 26, "Creating and Binding Bones," where a set of legs is controlled with some bones. The legs have been animated with keys that complete one walk cycle.

2. Select the left leg bone layer in the Layers palette and right-click on the last bone at frame 24. From the pop-up menu, select the Cycle option. In the Cycle Interpolation dialog box that appears, select the Absolute option with a Value of 1. This will create a cycle from frame 24 back to frame 1.

3. Repeat step 2 for the right leg bone.

4. Press the Play button (Spacebar) to see the resulting animation. The walk cycle works fine until it gets to the end of the frame range, where it shudders as the animation starts over. To fix this problem, hold down the Alt/Opt key and click the frame range at frame 69. This sets the frame range to repeat over exactly where the legs begin their cycle, resulting in a smooth repeating walk cycle, as shown in Figure 17.13.

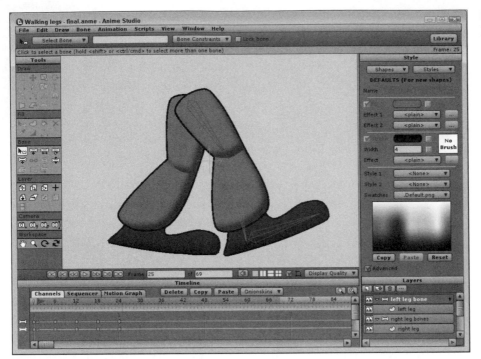

Figure 17.13
Looping walk cycle.

Using Onion Skinning

Onion skinning is a feature that shows the paths of the adjacent frames next to the actual frame. This is helpful when you're trying to line up objects during an animation. Any frame can be specified as an onion skin frame using the row of slots located directly under the frame range in the Timeline palette.

Before you can click the Onionskin bar to specify an onion skin frame, you'll first need to enable onion skinning using the Onionskins drop-down list located at the top of the Timeline palette, as shown in Figure 17.14.

Figure 17.14
Onionskins
pop-up menu.

The Enable onion skins option turns on the onion skin feature. If this option is disabled, then you will not be able to click the Onionskin bar. The Relative Frames option causes all the designated onion skin frames to move along with the time slider so that the offset between them is maintained. If this option is disabled, then the specified onion skin frames remain constant as the animation plays. The Selected Layer Only Option shows onion skinning only for objects on the current layer. If disabled, then all objects on all layers are onion skinned. The Clear All button removes all onion skin markers from the Onionskin bar.

New Feature

The Onionskins pop-up menu along with the ability to turn onion skinning on and off is new to Anime Studio 6.

Once onion skinning is enabled, simply click the Onionskin bar for the frame that you want to mark. A dark gray marker appears for the marked frame, as shown in Figure 17.15. All content for the marked frames are displayed as paths. Up to eight frames can be onion skinned at a time. To turn off a specific onion skin frame, simply click its marker in the Onionskin bar.

Figure 17.15
Onion skinned frames for a cannonball.

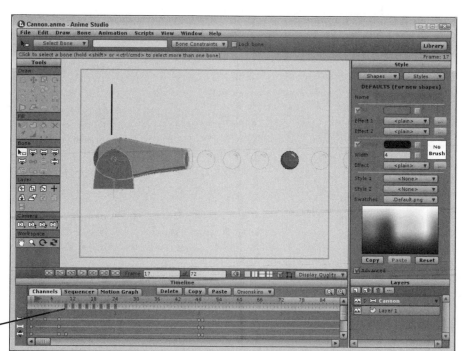

Onion skin markers

Note

Parameter changes such as a fill color aren't visible using onion skinning.

Viewing Layer Visibility

When a toggle key, such as the Visible option in the Layer Settings dialog box, is used to toggle the visibility of a layer on and off, the portion of the Timeline palette where the layer is hidden is shaded red, as shown in Figure 17.16. This is to provide a visual reference to the area where the layer objects will not be visible.

Note

Keys can still be added to the shaded area where the layer contents are hidden, but the changes aren't visible.

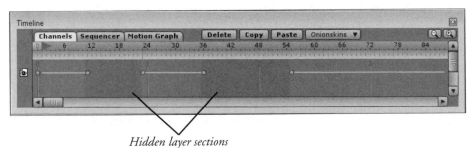

Hidden layer sections

Figure 17.16
Hidden layer sections are highlighted in red.

Chapter Summary

This chapter introduced the Timeline palette and showed how to work with channels and keys. It also showed how keys can be manipulated, copied, and pasted to new locations and rescaled. This chapter also explained the various interpolation types, including the ability to cycle sections of animation. Finally, the onion skinning feature was shown.

The next chapter explains the animation graphs and shows how they can be used to fine-tune an animation sequence.

18

Manipulating Animation Graphs

- Accessing graph mode
- Displaying channel graphs
- Editing a graph
- Viewing interpolation types in graph mode
- Zooming in on edit keys

The Timeline palette includes a motion graph mode that you can use to visually see the animated value as a function of frames. This mode provides a way to change the scale of the value axis and to zoom in on the keys being edited. Each channel is color coded to match its graph line. In editing mode, you can move keys, add new keys, and change the keys' interpolation type. Graph mode is especially helpful for understanding the various interpolation types.

Accessing Graph Mode

Graph mode is accessed in the Timeline palette by clicking the Motion Graph tab at the top of the Timeline palette, as shown in Figure 18.1. Each channel that has keys is displayed to the left of the graph. Each channel is highlighted with a color that matches the color of its graph line.

Note

Motion graphs are only available in Anime Studio Pro.

Channel icons

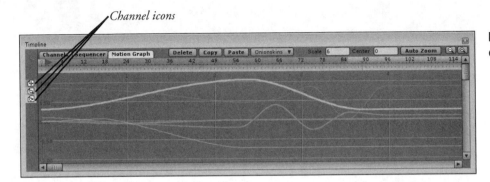

Figure 18.1
Graph mode options.

Changing the Graph Scale

While in graph mode, the vertical axis displays the various channel values. You can change the range of values using the Scale field at the top of the Timeline palette. This scale value defines the total range of values displayed on the vertical axis. For example, if the scale value is set to 2, then the top of the vertical axis will show 1.0 and the bottom of the vertical axis will show -1.0 for a total range of 2.

You set the center point of the vertical axis using the Center field, also located at the top of the Timeline palette. A center value of 0 will spread the range from 1.0 to -1.0. If the scale is set to 4 and the center value is set to 1, then the upper value on the vertical axis will be 3.0 and the lower value will be -1 with the graph centered on 1, as shown in Figure 18.2.

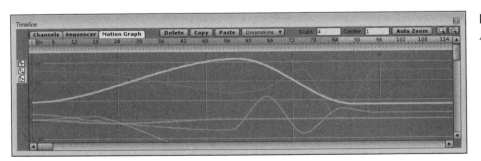

Figure 18.2
Altered value range.

The scale can also be changed using the Page Up and Page Down keys. These keys will increase or decrease the vertical value range, which in turn will scale any displayed graphs. Holding down the Shift key while pressing the Page Up and Page Down keys will alter the center value, thereby causing the entire graph to be shifted up or down.

Displaying Channel Graphs

When graph mode is first enabled, you'll see graphs for all the available channels. To hide a channel's graph, simply click the channel icon on the left in the Timeline palette. When a channel is enabled, its icon is highlighted with a color. Figure 18.3 shows the Timeline palette with multiple channels enabled; as you can see, the graph for each particular channel is displayed using a color that corresponds to its channel icon. For example, if four channels are enabled, then graph mode will show four graphs in the Timeline palette using four colors that match their icons.

> **Note**
>
> Some channel graphs have multiple lines. For example, the Layer Translation channel has separate lines for the X, Y, and Z values, each with a different value. You can tell these apart by looking at the thickness of each line. The X value line is the thinnest, the Y value line has a medium thickness, and the Z value line is the thickest.

Figure 18.3
Enabled channels.

Enabled channel
Disabled channel

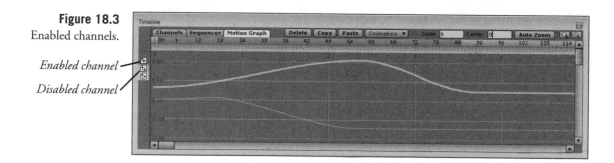

Clicking again on an enabled channel icon will disable it. By disabling channels, you can focus on one or two channels without the clutter of the other graphs.

> **Note**
>
> The Selected Point Motion channel only displays a line (actually two lines, one for the X axis and one for the Y axis) when a single point in the working area is selected. If two or more points are selected, then no lines appear.

Editing a Graph

Among the enabled channels, you can double-click one of the channel icons to make its curve editable. When a curve is editable, its keys are displayed along the graph, as shown in Figure 18.4, and its channel icon is surrounded with a border.

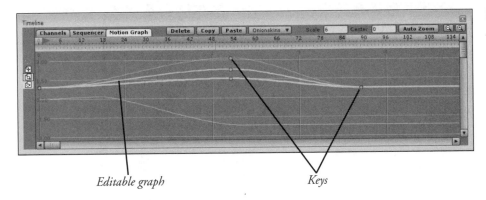

Editable graph   *Keys*

Figure 18.4
An editable graph.

Moving and Adding Keys

When a curve is editable, you can select and drag its keys to change the curvature of the graph. Holding down the Alt/Opt key while dragging a key in the Timeline palette restricts the movement of the key to a vertical direction only; holding down the Ctrl/Cmd key lets you move the key only horizontally. You can also right-click on the graph and select the Add Keyframe option from the pop-up menu to add a new key to the graph.

To edit and manipulate keys in graph mode, follow these steps:

1. Open the Dune buggy.anme file from the Chapter 18 folder on the CD. This file includes a simple little car that is moving across a landscape, but the animation keys are rough, and we'll use graph mode to adjust the car's position.

2. Click the Graph Mode button at the top of the Timeline palette and select the Motion Graph tab. This makes several colored curves appear in the Timeline palette.

3. Click the channel icons to the left of the curves to disable all except the Layer Translation channel. This displays three lines, only one of which is curved. The other two are perfectly horizontal.

4. Double-click the Layer Translate channel icon to enter edit mode. This makes the keys appear along the curve.

5. Right-click on the curve at frames 24, 39, and 58 and select the Add Keyframes option from the pop-up menu. New keys are added to the curve at these frames.

Tip

If you float and resize the Timeline palette, then the keys are easier to work with. Using the Zoom feature is also helpful.

---

6. Drag the Time slider to frame 39 and select the key at frame 39 that is on the middle thick line, which represents the Y axis, and drag it until the car is aligned with the background hill. Then do the same for the other new keys. Continue to add and edit the keys to match the car's vertical position to the hill.

7. After the keys for the vertical position are completed, click the Layer Translate channel and double-click the Layer Z Rotation channel icon. Drag the Time slider to frame 25 and add a new key. Then drag the key upward until the rotation matches the hill. Continue to add and edit keys to match the motion of the car along the hill, as shown in Figure 18.5.

8. Click the Auto Zoom button to scale the Timeline palette so that the current keys are maximized in the palette. Figure 18.6 shows the resulting Timeline palette.

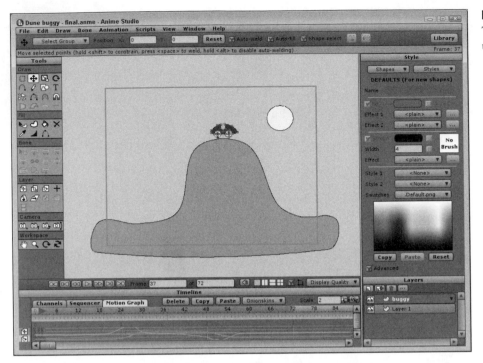

Figure 18.5
The car conforms to the hill.

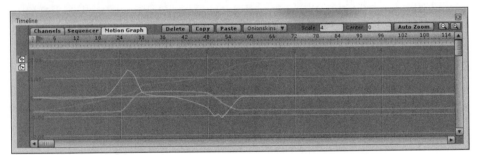

Figure 18.6
Edited Timeline keys.

Changing Interpolation Type

The default interpolation type that is used on all new keys is set in the Options panel of the Preferences dialog box. You can open this dialog box using the Edit, Preferences menu.

New Feature

The ability to change the default interpolation type in the Preference dialog box is new to Anime Studio 6.

The right-click pop-up menu can also be used to change the interpolation type of the selected key. You need to right-click on a key to cause the interpolation options to appear in the pop-up menu. The various interpolation types are easy to see in graph mode. If multiple keys are selected, then selecting a new interpolation type will apply the option to all selected keys. For example, Figure 18.7 shows the graph using the Linear interpolation type.

Figure 18.7
Linear
interpolation
type.

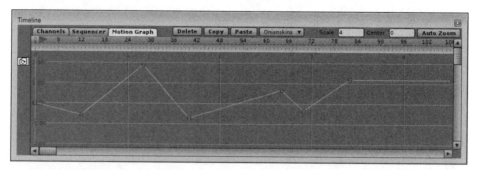

Figure 18.8 shows the Ease In/Out interpolation type. Notice how the graph is altered to be almost a straight line as the graph approaches and leaves each key.

Figure 18.8
Ease In/Out
interpolation
type.

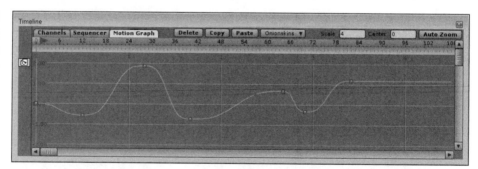

Figure 18.9 shows the Step interpolation type. This interpolation type keeps the current value until the next key is reached and then quickly changes to the new value, resulting in mostly straight lines.

Figure 18.10 shows the Noisy interpolation type. This interpolation type jitters the animation value between keys, which results in some random motion.

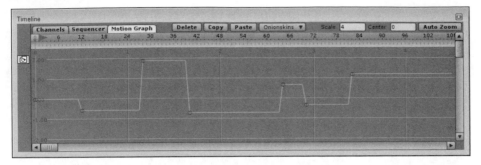

Figure 18.9
Step interpolation type.

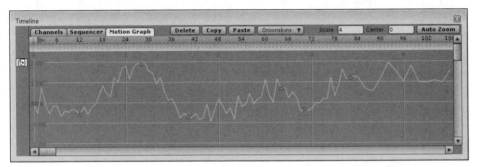

Figure 18.10
Noisy interpolation type.

Figure 18.11 shows the Cycle interpolation type. The entire motion has been scaled to the first 18 frames and then the final key has been set to cycle to frame 1. This causes the scaled keys to be repeated for the rest of the animation.

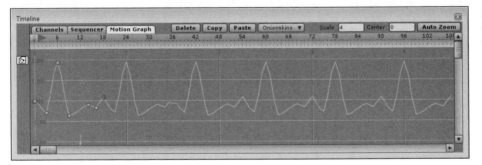

Figure 18.11
Cycle interpolation type.

To edit and manipulate keys in graph mode, follow these steps:

1. Open the Dancing fruit.anme file from the Chapter 18 folder on the CD. This file includes several fruit characters on different layers.

2. Click the Motion Graph tab at the top of the Timeline palette and click the Enable Graph Mode option.

3. Select the cherry layer in the Layers palette; then double-click the Layer Translation channel in the Timeline palette. This makes the curves and the keys for this channel visible. The only key for this channel is at frame 0. Right-click this key and select the Noisy interpolation type. In the Noisy Interpolation dialog box that appears, set the Amplitude to 0.1 and the Scale to 2.

4. Select the banana layer in the Layers palette and double-click the Layer Z Rotation channel in the Timeline palette. Right-click the key at frame 0 and select the Noisy option. Click the OK button to accept the default values.

5. Select the orange layer in the Layers palette and double-click the Layer Scale channel in the Timeline palette. Right-click the key at frame 0 and select the Noisy option. Click the OK button to accept the default values.

6. Select the apple layer in the Layers palette, click the Settings button at the top of the Timeline palette, and enable the Layer Shear channel. Then close the Timeline Settings dialog box and double-click the Layer Shear channel in the Timeline palette. Right-click the key at frame 0 and select the Noisy option. Click the OK button to accept the default values. Figure 18.12 shows the dancing fruit.

Figure 18.12
Dancing fruit.

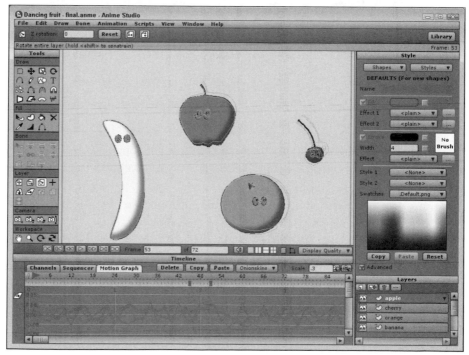

Zooming in on the Edited Keys

When a curve is in edit mode, you can use the Auto Zoom button at the top of the Timeline palette to zoom in on the curve that you are editing. This expands the value scale so that the lowest value is positioned at the bottom of the Timeline palette and the highest key is positioned at the top of the Timeline palette, as shown in Figure 18.13.

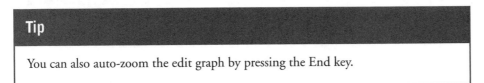

Tip

You can also auto-zoom the edit graph by pressing the End key.

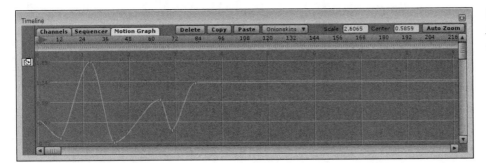

Figure 18.13
Auto-zoom
on edit curve.

Chapter Summary

This chapter introduced motion graph mode in the Timeline palette. Using this mode, you can see the animation graphs as a function of value over frames. You can view the resulting graphs of multiple channels and even edit the graphs by moving keys, adding keys, or changing the interpolation type. We also took a close look at the various interpolation types using graph mode.

Chapter 19 covers working with sound and shows how adding audio to your animation can enhance it.

Working with Sound

■ Preparing audio files

■ Adding audio

■ Working with the Sequencer

■ Syncing sound to animation

■ Using sound scripts

The presentation of animation files without sound makes the animation feel incomplete. By adding and synchronizing simple sound effects, the animation will take on a whole new life. Animations can also benefit from a soundtrack that sets the mood of the animation. Learning to work with sound pays big dividends for the audience.

Audio files are loaded into a project using the File, Import, Audio File menu. Anime Studio allows multiple audio files to be loaded into a single project. Once audio files are loaded, you can manipulate them by dragging them in the Sequencer interface. The Sequencer interface is located within the Timeline palette. Audio files can also be loaded from the Library.

Preparing Audio Files

Anime Studio allows multiple sound files to be added to an animated sequence including separate sounds for sound effects, dialogue, and a background music track.

Several sound-editing software packages are available that can help you record and create the needed sound files. Two good options are Cool Edit and Sound Forge. When recording and mixing the soundtrack for the animation, be sure to check the starting and ending of the audio file because the ability to edit sounds in Anime Studio is limited.

Tip

Another popular software package for preparing audio files is Audacity. It is free from http://audacity.sourceforge.net and works on Windows, Mac, and Linux.

Another aspect of the audio file to keep track of is where the final animation will be viewed. If the animation is intended for the Web, you'll want to keep the size of the audio file down without losing any of its quality. The audio settings you use really depend on the type of sound you are using. Consider the following options:

- **CD-Quality Music:** To get CD-quality music, use a sampling rate of 44.1 KHz with 16-bit resolution and stereo. This will result in large files, about 10.3 MB for a minute.

- **Standard Music:** If you drop the sampling rate to 22.5 KHz with 16-bit resolution and a single mono channel, you can drop the file size to 2.5 MB for a minute.

- **Sound Effects:** For sound effects, you can keep the sampling rate at 22.5 KHz with 8-bit resolution in a mono channel to get the size down to 1.25 MB per minute.

- **Voice:** If you are dealing with only voice and quality is less important than size, then using a sampling rate of 11.25 KHz with 8-bit resolution in a mono channel results in a file size of 630 KB per minute.

> **Tip**
>
> When preparing your audio file, be sure to use a sampling rate that is a multiple of 11.025 KHz (11.025, 22.050, or 44.1 KHz). If you use any other sampling rate, Anime Studio will have trouble when you try to export the animation to SWF.

If you have a video-editing package at your disposal such as Final Cut Pro or Adobe Premiere, then you can select to simply export the Anime Studio animation without sound and use the video editor to add a soundtrack. Video editors offer more flexibility than Anime Studio for working with sound.

Adding an Audio File

Once you've got all the sound files created for the animated sequence, you can add them to the project using the File, Import, Audio File menu command. This command automatically opens a file dialog box where you can choose the sound file to include. The supported sound file formats include .WAV files for Windows machines and .AIFF files for Macintosh machines. Anime Studio also lets you load and use MP3 files.

> **Note**
>
> Anime Studio Debut 6 allows two audio files and one video track to be added to the Sequencer, and Anime Studio Pro 6 allows an unlimited number of tracks.

The Library palette also includes a folder of sound effects. You can add audio files to your project by double-clicking an audio file in the Library palette. The loaded audio file will be set to start at the current frame.

> **Tip**
>
> If you select an audio file in the Library with a single click, the audio file will play through once. This helps to identify and select the correct audio file before importing it.

A third way to add an audio file to a project is by creating a new Audio layer using the Layers palette. When this option is selected from the New Layer button at the top of the Layers palette, a File dialog box opens where you can select an audio file. Each audio layer can only hold a single audio file.

When an audio file is added to a project, its file name appears in the Layers palette. When its layer is selected, you can see a waveform of the audio file displayed as a background in the Timeline palette, as shown in Figure 19.1. All audio files are identified in the Timeline and Layers palette with a small speaker icon.

Note

All audio files are set to start playing at the current frame when loaded. So, if the current frame is frame 20, then loading an audio file will cause the sound to begin at this frame. The Sequencer is an interface that lets you change the audio file's start time.

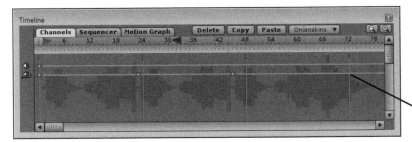

Figure 19.1
Sound waveform on the Timeline.

Sound waveform

Removing an Audio File

To delete an audio file from the project, simply select and delete its layer in the Layers palette.

Caution

Audio files cannot be deleted from the Sequencer panel in the Timeline palette. Selecting an audio file and clicking the Delete button at the top of the Timeline palette has no effect.

Muting Audio

When an audio file is added to a project, it plays whenever the animation is played. This can be bothersome if you're working with the content, so the Animation, Mute Audio menu command may be used to quiet all sound files. The file is still attached to the project, but it just doesn't play when the animation is played.

Clicking the Visibility icon (the googly eyes) next to an audio layer in the Layers palette lets you mute a single audio file without having to remove it from the project. Click again on the Visibility icon to make the audio file active again.

Caution

You may notice the Disable Audio Feedback option in the Options panel of the Preferences dialog box. This option has no impact on the scene's audio files. When two points are welded, a click is heard; this option disables that click feedback instead.

Adding Video

Video clips are another way to add audio to your project. Video clips are loaded into a project using the File, Import, Movie menu command or by double-clicking them in the Library palette. Although movies appear on an image layer in the Layers palette, they are dealt with in the Sequencer panel of the Timeline palette exactly like audio files. You can learn more about working with image layers in Chapter 22, "Adding Image Layers."

Using the Sequencer

Loaded audio files appear in the Layers palette and in the Timeline palette when the audio file layer is selected. You can also view all loaded audio files together by clicking the Sequencer tab in the Timeline palette. Within the Sequencer panel, each audio and video file is displayed on a separate row, as shown in Figure 19.2. Audio files are easy to identify in the Sequencer because their waveform is displayed on their bar.

New Feature

The Audio Sequencer and its ability to load and work with multiple sound tracks is new to Anime Studio 6.

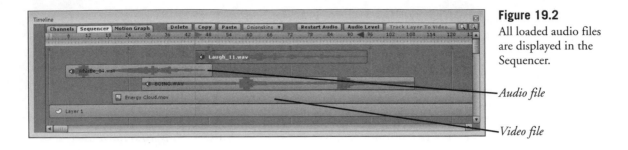

Figure 19.2
All loaded audio files are displayed in the Sequencer.

Audio file

Video file

Setting the Audio Start Time

The length of each bar is the length of the audio file. By dragging the bars in the Sequencer to the left or right, you can change the starting frame for the audio file.

Repeating Audio

If you want to cause a loaded audio file to repeat a second or third time, you can position the frame at the place where you want the repeat to start and click the Restart Audio button at the top of the Timeline palette when the Sequencer panel is open. You can also access this command using the Animation, Restart Audio Track menu. This places a duplicate bar at the desired location, as shown in Figure 19.3.

> **Caution**
>
> Repeated audio files can overlap one another, but you cannot place a repeated audio instance in front of the first instance.

> **Caution**
>
> Be aware when creating repeats that moving one instance will move all instances together and that you cannot delete an instance without deleting the entire layer.

> **Note**
>
> Although multiple instances of an audio file may appear in the Sequencer, only the first instance displays the waveform on its audio bar.

Figure 19.3
Audio files can be repeated multiple times.

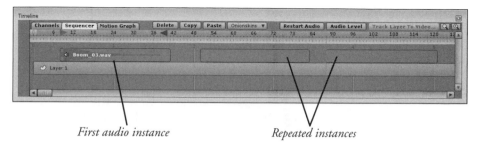

First audio instance   *Repeated instances*

Every copy of an audio file that is created with the Restart Audio command automatically creates a key in the Timeline palette. You can view these keys by switching back to the Channels panel and selecting the audio layer. The channel for these keys is called *Audio Jump*.

Changing Audio Level

Loaded audio files will play at the level they were recorded, which can cause an abrupt change in the sound, but within Anime Studio is a command to set a key to adjust the audio level. By using this command, you can have sounds fade in and out.

To change the level for an audio file, select the frame where you want the key to be set, choose the audio layer, and click the Audio Level button at the top of the Sequencer panel in the Timeline palette or choose the Animation, Audio Level menu. This causes the Audio Level dialog box, shown in Figure 19.4, to appear where you can set the value. A value of 0 will cause the sound to be silent.

Figure 19.4
By changing the audio level you can fade a sound in or out.

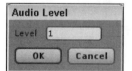

Changes to an audio layer's level value create a key in the Audio Level channel. They also impact the waveforms displayed in the Channels panel of the Timeline palette, as shown in Figure 19.5. This provides visual feedback for seeing the audio level changes.

Figure 19.5
Reduced audio levels.

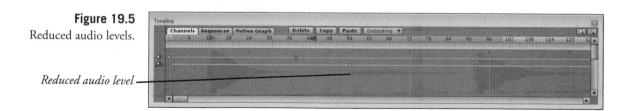

Reduced audio level

Enabling Spatial Positioning

Using the Spatial Positioning option in the Audio panel of the Layer Settings dialog box, you can control the left and right balance of the audio being played. This is a great feature if you want create a sound that moves from left to right as an object moves.

Enabling the Spatial Positioning option allows the audio file to be played back in the left or right speaker based on the left and right movement of the audio layer. When an audio file is loaded, a small speaker icon appears at the center of the working area when the audio layer is selected. Using the Translate Layer tool, you can set keys to move the audio icon across the working area, as shown in Figure 19.6. This will cause the audio to move as it plays back from the left speaker gradually to the right speaker.

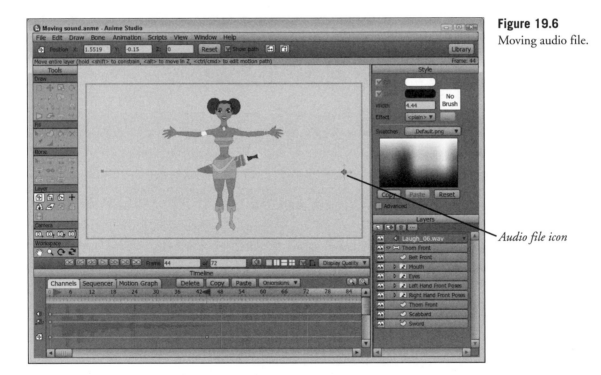

Figure 19.6
Moving audio file.

Audio file icon

Syncing Animation to Sound

Using the displayed waveform in the Timeline palette, you can begin to synchronize the keyframes to the waveform's sound. It is accomplished by simply selecting and moving those keys that are associated with the various sounds and aligning them to the waveform that is displayed in the Timeline palette or dragging the audio bars in the Sequencer to align with the Timeline keys. If you're trying to synchronize your animation to a vocal track, then you'll want to look into the lip-syncing methods, which are covered in Chapter 20, "Using Lip-Sync."

If you're dealing with a complex animation scene with lots of moving points, then the audio track may be slowed down as the computer struggles to display the animation and the sound. This problem only exists when playing back the animation in the working area. When the project is exported, the computer takes all the time it needs to export all the frames in sync with the audio.

Tip

To reduce the drain on the computer while playing back an animation in the working area, you can enable the Animation, Allow Frame Skipping menu command. This allows the system to skip some animation frames in order to speed the playback. You can also enable the Fast Buffer option in the Display Quality dialog box to speed playback.

To synchronize keys with a soundtrack, follow these steps:

1. Open the Pogo stick.anme file from the Chapter 19 folder on the CD. This file includes a simple character on a pogo stick. The stick has been animated bobbing up and down using point motion to compress the spring and layer translation to move the remainder of the layer.

2. Select the File, Import, Audio File menu command and in the File dialog box that opens, select the Boing.wav file from the Chapter 19 folder on the CD. This sound file has two boing sounds over a couple of seconds. Once added to the project, the sound file's waveform is shown in the Timeline palette.

3. In the Timeline palette, select the keys at frame 30 that are near the first boing sound as seen in the waveform and move them to just before the sound to frame 28.

4. Select the keys at frame 36 and move them to frame 32 where the boing sound is the loudest on the waveform. Then repeat steps 3 and 4 for the keys at frames 54 and 60 where the second boing sound happens.

5. Click the Motion Graph button at the top of the Timeline palette. Set the Scale value to 0.5 and the Center to 0. Click all the channels to the left to disable them except for the Layer Translation channel, which you need to double-click to access edit mode.

6. Notice the keys near the area of the sound waveform where the sound is the loudest. The key should be on the top part of the undulation wave. Select the key at frame 32 and drag it upward to increase the amount of bounce for this frame. This high bounce coincides with the boing sound shown in the waveform. Repeat this key movement for the second boing sound at frame 60. The resulting curve graph in the Timeline palette is shown in Figure 19.7.

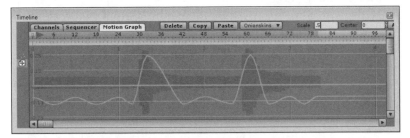

Figure 19.7
The keys are moved to match the sound's waveform.

7. Click the Play button (Spacebar) to see the resulting motion and hear the synchronized sound. Figure 19.8 shows the pogo stick dude.

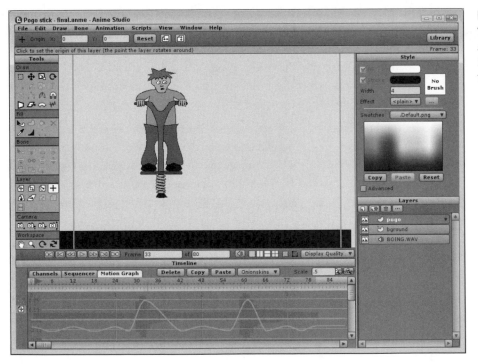

Figure 19.8
The pogo stick's motion is synchronized with the sound.

Using Sound Scripts

The Scripts, Sound menu includes a couple of scripts for working with sound. The Bone Audio Wiggle script causes the attached bones to wiggle around as the sound plays and the Layer Audio Wiggle script causes the entire layer to wiggle around as the sound plays. This is a great way to make a character or layer dance and randomly move around along with the music.

> **Note**
>
> The Scripts menu and all its contents are only available in Anime Studio Pro.

To use the Bone Audio Wiggle script, you need to have a bone layer defined and at least one bone selected. You also need to have an audio file added to the project. The script is disabled until these conditions are met. When the script is executed, the Bone Audio Wiggle dialog box appears, as shown in Figure 19.9. Using the settings in this dialog box, you can control maximum amount of rotation that the bone can move along with the frequency of the keys added to the Timeline palette. You can also choose from the available audio files that are loaded if there are several.

Figure 19.9
Bone Audio Wiggle dialog box.

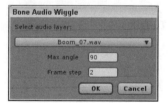

The keys that are added to the selected bones are only added from the current frame to the end of the audio file. If you have a frame in the middle of your animation selected, then the wiggle keys are only added from the selected frame on, but the sound will start at frame 1.

The Layer Audio Wiggle script works exactly like the Bone Audio Wiggle script, except it lets you specify a Max Offset value that determines the extent to which the layer can move.

To make a flower dance in time with an audio file, follow these steps:

1. Open the Dancing flower.anme file from the Chapter 19 folder on the CD. This file includes a simple flower that has bones added to it.

2. Select the File, Import, Audio File menu; then locate and load the Tutdrum.wav file from the Chapter 19 folder on the CD.

3. Select the bone layer in the Layers palette and click the Select Bone tool (B). Then hold down the Shift key and select each of the flower bones.

4. Select the Scripts, Sound, Bone Audio Wiggle menu command. In the Bone Audio Wiggle dialog box that appears, enter 90 as the Maximum Angle value and 2 and the Frame Step; then click the OK button. The keys to make the flower dance with the music are automatically added to the Timeline palette.

5. Click the Play button (Spacebar) and watch the flower jump around with the music, as shown in Figure 19.10.

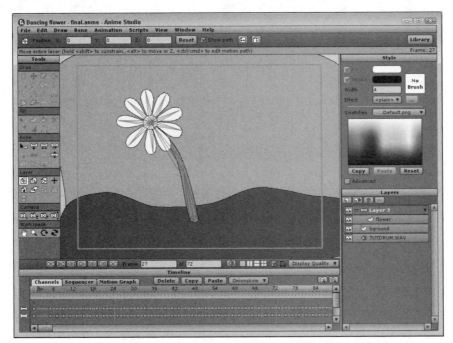

Figure 19.10
Dancing flower.

Working with System Audio

The audio capabilities of Anime Studio are highly dependent on the system that the software is loaded on. Below are some tips for working with audio on each of the different systems.

Using Audio in Windows

For Windows-based systems, you can select and use the WAV format. This format stores uncompressed audio and is generally audio CD quality, although WAV files can be downgraded to use a lower bit rate and sampling. WAV files work great and are generally good quality, but their downside is that they are huge.

For compressed audio, the MP3 format is the format of choice. It is popular, and most sound editing software can easily convert various sound files to the MP3 format. Anime Studio also supports loading or playing back MP3 files. You can also use them when exporting your animation to the Flash or QuickTime formats. To learn more on using MP3 files, see Chapter 34, "Exporting to the Web."

New Feature

The ability to load and use MP3 audio files is new to Anime Studio 6.

> **Caution**
>
> If exporting the project to the Flash (SWF) format, make sure you only use a single MP3 audio file. Anime Studio cannot encode multiple MP3 files when exporting to Flash.

Using Audio in Macintosh

Mac-based systems use the AIFF audio format. This format is the default audio format for Macs, and these files can be loaded and used within Anime Studio without any trouble.

> **Caution**
>
> Sometimes audio files have trouble when loaded into Anime Studio. If you are trying to use a sound file that has an odd sampling rate, then the sound file will not work. To fix problem sound files, load and export the sound files using a standard sampling rate.

Using Audio in Linux

If you're running Anime Studio on Linux, you'll need to do some additional configuration to make the audio work correctly. If you've added an audio file to the animation that isn't being played back when you run the animation, try entering the following in the terminal window:

```
> ls /dev/dsp*
```

This lists the devices available on your system. From this list of devices, make sure that an audio device is available. If an audio device is available and other applications can play audio, then another process probably has exclusive access to the audio device. To free the audio device, enter the following into the terminal window:

```
> fuser /dev/dsp
```

This command returns the number of the process that has control over the audio device. Once you've determined that another application has control over the audio device, you can try to manually disable the application that has control, but if this doesn't work, you can issue the following command to the end of the process:

```
> kill -9 fuser /dev/dsp
```

> **Tip**
>
> If the audio only works when the controlling process is killed, you can add this command to a startup script that is executed automatically when Anime Studio is started.

Chapter Summary

This chapter introduced adding sound to an Anime Studio project. Anime Studio can load and manipulate multiple audio files using the Sequencer. The Sequencer interface also includes commands to repeat a sound and control its audio level. When imported, the waveform of the audio file appears in the Timeline palette where it can be synced with the animation keys.

Sound can be used for sound effects, for ambient background sounds, and for music tracks, but it can also be used for dialogue as your actors speak. The next chapter looks at the specific case of lip-syncing sound to the facial motions.

20

Using Lip-Sync

- Using Automatic Lip-Sync
- Using Phoneme Lip-Sync
- Enabling lip-syncing with a Switch layer
- Using external lip-sync packages

Lip-sync is the process of synchronizing the animated mouth movements of a character to match the spoken dialogue. Although it can be a tricky process, Anime Studio includes some features that make it easy to accomplish. Anime Studio makes lip-syncing possible by using Switch layers. Switch layers let you display one of many available sublayers using an external source. You can learn more about Switch layers in Chapter 24, "Using Switch and Note Layers."

There are actually two different ways to do lip-syncing in Anime Studio. One method is to switch between several different sublayer graphics using the amplitude of a linked audio file. A second lip-sync method is to create a graphic for each possible sound. Anime Studio then computes the correct graphic to show based on the sound file.

Anime Studio can also use an external lip-sync program such as Papagayo to prepare data files for syncing.

> **Note**
>
> Within the Library palette is a Mouths folder that includes several sample mouth graphics that can be lip-synced.

Using Automatic Lip-Sync

The simplest lip-sync solution switches between the available sublayers in a Switch layer based on the amplitude level of the associated audio file. This method is called *Automatic Lip-Sync*. For example, if you create three mouth graphics showing the mouth closed, half-open, and fully open, then the Switch layer will switch between these graphics showing the mouth closed graphic when the audio is silent, half-open when the volume is mid-level, and fully open when the audio is at its loudest. This isn't an exact match, but for some characters it is close enough to show the character speaking.

> **Note**
>
> Automatic lip-sync is available in both Anime Studio Debut and Anime Studio Pro.

Ordering Graphics

To use the Automatic Lip-Sync solution, first create a Switch layer by clicking the New Layer button at the top of the Layers palette and selecting the Switch option from the pop-up menu. Then create several mouth graphics showing the mouth at different stages between open and closed. Each graphic should be located in the same location, and each should be on its own layer.

Drop these layers onto the Switch layer in order from closed to fully open. The order of the mouth graphics is important with the closed layer at the bottom of the open layer at the top, as shown in Figure 20.1.

Figure 20.1
Mouth graphic sublayers are ordered from closed to open.

Linking to an Audio Source

Once the Switch layer is correctly configured, you'll need to import the dialogue audio file using the File, Import, Audio File menu command. The audio file needs to be either a WAV or an AIFF file. You can learn more about loading and working with audio files in Chapter 19, "Working with Sound."

Note

The Library palette includes several short dialogue phrases in the DK Toons Audio Boy and Audio Man folders.

Figure 20.2
The Switch panel lets you specify the audio source.

After an audio file is loaded into the project, you can make it the source file for the Switch layer using the Layer Settings dialog box. Simply double-click the Switch layer and choose the Switch panel in the Layer Settings dialog box. Then select the audio file from the Audio Sync Source drop-down list, as shown in Figure 20.2.

Interpolating Sublayers

The mouth graphics aren't limited to a specific layer type. They could be image layers, vector layers, or even particle layers. But if all the mouth graphic sublayers are vector layers and if each sublayer has an equal number of points, then you can enable the Interpolate Sublayers option in the Switch layer panel to make the layers smoothly move between the adjacent sublayers as the audio level is increased or decreased.

To lip-sync audio using the automatic method, follow these steps:

1. Open the Glasses face.anme file from the Chapter 20 folder on the CD. This file includes a simple face minus the mouth.

2. Click the New Layer button in the Layers palette and select the Switch option from the pop-up menu to create a new Switch layer.

3. Use the New Layer button in the Layers palette to create a new vector layer. Name the new layers *Closed*. Select a black Fill color and with the Draw Shape tool, draw a thin, horizontally aligned oval to represent the closed mouth.

4. With the Closed layer selected, click the Duplicate Layer button in the Layers palette. Name this new layer *Mid*, and with the Translate Points tool, select the top point and drag it upward to widen the mouth. Then repeat this for the lower point.

5. Repeat step #4 to create a third mouth layer that is named *Open* and has a wide-open mouth.

6. Drag and drop the mouth layers into the Switch layer starting with the Closed, Mid, and then Open layers.

7. Open the Library palette and locate and double-click the Areyousure audio file in the DK Toons, Audio Man folder to add the audio file to the project. The waveform for the audio file appears in the Timeline palette when loaded.

8. Double-click the Switch layer in the Layers palette and choose the Switch panel. Select the Areyousure.wav file as the source file, enable the Interpolate Sublayers option, and close the Layer Settings dialog box.

9. Click the Play button located at the bottom left corner of the working area to see the resulting animation, as shown in Figure 20.3.

Using Phoneme Lip-Sync

Phonemes are the basic mouth shapes used to create all the various sounds. The best way to learn the basic phonemes is to get a mirror and look at your facial expressions while making different sounds. For example, when making an O sound, your mouth is open and round, and when making the TH sound, the lips are almost closed and the tongue sticks out just a little.

Each bit of spoken dialogue can be broken down into its phoneme components, and combining several phonemes together, you can create words and sentences.

Figure 20.3
Automatic lip-sync.

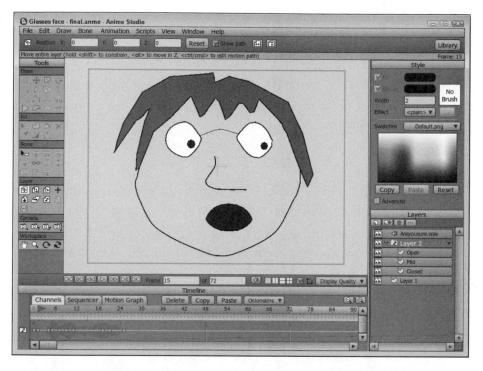

Note

Phoneme lip-sync is only available within Anime Studio Pro.

For example, the word *poor* consists of three phonemes, the first one pulls the lips together to make the P sound, the second one curves the lips into a round shape to make the O sound, and the final one draws the lips back to make the R sound.

There are a lot of different phonemes that make up the English language and even more if you consider other languages, but luckily for animators, many sounds look the same on the outside, even though the sound is different based on the position of the tongue. For example, the M, B, and P sounds all look the same.

Although including a larger number of phonemes in your animation will make your lip-syncing more detailed, for most animations, you can get away with using only 10 distinct phonemes.

These phonemes are labeled the following and matching examples of each phoneme are available in the File, Import, Mouths menu:

- **AI:** The vowel A as in the word, *may*, which leaves the mouth open and the tongue visible.

- **O:** The vowel O as in the word, *go*, which curls the sides of the mouth in to form an O shape.

- **E:** The vowel E as in the word, *squeek*, which pulls the sides of the mouth back and leaves the mouth open.

- **U:** The vowel U as in the word, *up*, which pulls the sides of the mouth in like the O sound, but the mouth doesn't open as wide. The lips also pucker for this sound.

- **Etc:** A miscellaneous phoneme with the teeth clenched like a smile. This is used for the T sound and for intermediate positions between sounds.

- **L:** The sound L as in the word, *love*, which opens the mouth but places the tongue higher as it touches the back of the top teeth.

- **WQ:** The sound W or Q as in the word, *word*, which pulls the lips in real tight with a pucker that is tighter than the U sound.

- **MBP:** The sound M, B, or P as in the word, *map*, which closes the lips tight.

- **FV:** The sound F or V as in the word, *four*, which curls the bottom lip under the top teeth.

- **Rest:** The lip positions when no sound is being made with the lips relaxed and together.

The File, Import, Mouths menu command includes several sets of mouths. Each of these sets has the above listed 10 layers contained within a Switch layer. Figure 20.4 shows each of these layers for one of these sets.

If you create a graphic for each of the 10 phonemes listed previously, then you'll be able to match any English spoken dialogue. Each graphic should be on its own layer and added to a Switch layer. Remember to name each layer using the name presented in the list above.

Note

The above list of phonemes are intended for the English language. Other languages will require their own set of phonemes.

Figure 20.4
Mouth phonemes.

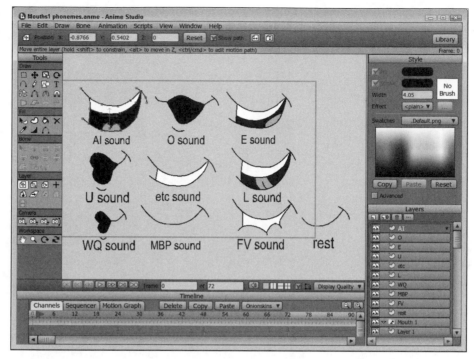

Loading an Audio File

After the graphics for the mouth phonemes are created and added to a Switch layer, you will need to load in the audio file that has the dialogue that you are trying to match. This is done using the File, Import, Audio File menu command. Loaded audio files appear as waveforms in the Timeline palette, and you can adjust their starting time using the Sequencer panel. More on working with audio files is covered in Chapter 19, "Working with Sound."

Tip

Try to avoid audio dialogue files with background music and sounds as they could throw off the syncing.

Entering Audio Text

If you double-click the Audio layer and select the Audio panel in the Layer Settings dialog box, shown in Figure 20.5, then you can type in the text that matches the spoken dialogue. If you forget to enter the spoken dialogue, Anime Studio will still do its best to align the phonemes to the dialogue track, but entering the text will often help make the lip-sync more accurate.

Figure 20.5
Audio panel.

Linking to an Audio Sync Source

Once the phoneme graphics are in place and the audio file has been added to the project, you can link the Switch layer with the audio file using the Switch panel in the Layer Settings dialog box. Within the Select Audio Sync Source drop-down list are all the loaded audio files. Simply select the audio file for the dialogue that you want to sync too and the keys are automatically added to the Timeline palette. Click the Play button to see the results.

If the phonemes are off, you can edit the keys to match better.

> **Tip**
>
> It generally looks better if the phoneme precedes the sound rather than coming after the sound. It is also a good habit to end a sentence with the mouth closed.

To lip-sync audio using the phoneme method, follow these steps:

1. Open the Apple face.anme file from the Chapter 20 folder on the CD. This file includes a simple apple face minus the mouth.

2. Open the Library palette and within the Mouths folder, double-click Mouth 2 to add it to the project. Move the mouth layer into place with the Translate Layer tool.

3. Select the File, Import, Audio File menu and load the Wowdidyouseethat.wav file from the Chapter 20 folder on the CD.

4. Double-click the audio layer in the Layers palette and open the Audio panel. In the text field, type in the dialogue, "Wow! Did you see that?" Then close the dialog box.

5. Double-click the Switch layer that holds the mouth graphics, and in the Switch panel, select the Wowdidyouseethat.wav file from the Select Audio Sync Source drop-down list. Then close the dialog box.

6. Click the Play button located at the bottom left corner of the working area to see the resulting animation, as shown in Figure 20.6.

Figure 20.6
Automatic lip-sync.

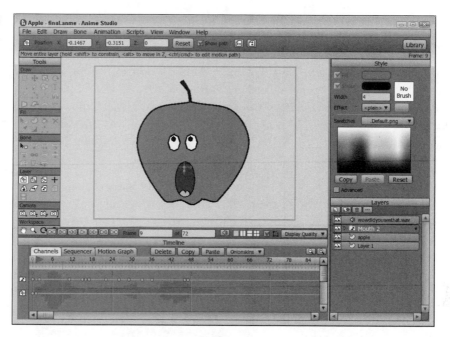

Using External Lip-Sync Packages

Anime Studio also works with several different lip-syncing packages. Some are companion add-ons like Papagayo and others are scripted plug-ins. Some of these packages automate the creation of the Switch Data File for you. The available lip-syncing add-ons to Anime Studio include the following:

■ **Papagayo:** An add-on package with a surprising array of features. This package can be downloaded from the Smith Micro Web site.

■ **Myna:** A scripted solution created by an Anime Studio user. It converts output from Microsoft's lip-sync tool to a format that Anime Studio can read. Information on this script can be found at the Lost Marble forum. This tool is only available for Windows users.

- **Magpie Pro:** A commercially available tool for handling lip-syncing. Information on this tool is available at www.thirdwishsoftware.com/.

- **JLipSync:** This tool is similar to Magpie, but it is written in Java, which makes it accessible on all platforms. Information on this tool is available at http://sourceforge.net/projects/jlipsync/.

- **Poser:** e frontier's Poser 8 includes a Talk Designer module that can be used to automate the lip-syncing process. The files can then be exported to Anime Studio. More information on Poser can be found at the Smith Micro Web site at www.smithmicro.com/.

Using Source Data Files

The default method for doing lip-syncing in Anime Studio is to link the audio file to the Switch layer, but previous versions of Anime Studio used a simple text file (with the .DAT extension) that told the program which Switch sublayer to use and at which frame to use it. This feature is still supported by Anime Studio and is selected as an option in the Select Audio Sync Source drop-down list in the Switch panel.

The DAT file includes a list that tells the program which sublayer to display at which frame. You can learn more about generating these DAT files in Chapter 24, "Using Switch and Note Layers." Remember to use the correct sublayer names within the DAT file.

After you've created a DAT file, you can link it to the Switch layer using the Switch panel in the Layer Settings dialog box. Click the Select Audio Sync Source button and select the Switch Data File option from the pop-up menu, as shown in Figure 20.7; then choose the DAT file from the File dialog box.

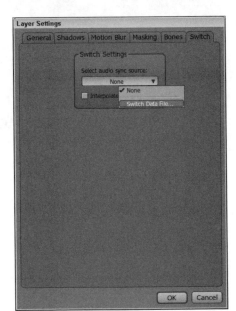

Figure 20.7
Switch Data File option.

Using Papagayo

Papagayo is a lip-syncing program that creates DAT source files that work with Anime Studio. It can be downloaded for free from the Smith Micro Web site. Versions are available for Windows, Mac, and Linux. Papagayo is licensed under the GNU license. The source code is even available for you to review and make changes if you want.

> **Note**
>
> Although Papagayo is freely available, it is being phased out now that the new phoneme features are available within Anime Studio.

Once installed, Papagayo loads as a separate program. Figure 20.8 shows the Papagayo interface. You can load an audio file, and it automatically breaks it down into phonemes that you can match with mouth keyframes. The software even supports audio in English, Spanish, and Italian.

To get the software to work, you first need to load an audio file. You can then type in the dialogue of the spoken audio and press the English button to get a phonetic breakdown of the spoken audio. The audio may need some tweaking. You can adjust the sentences, individual words, and finally the phonemes by dragging on either end of their bars in the interface. After the various phonemes are identified and aligned, you can export the results to a switch data file with the .DAT extension using the Export Voice button.

Figure 20.8
Papagayo interface.

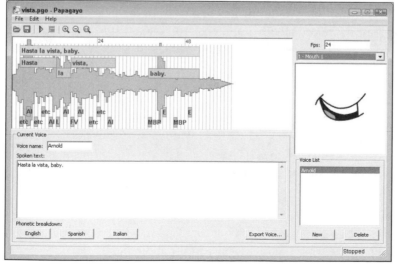

Note

Before adjusting the audio file in the Papagayo interface, make sure the frames per second are set to a value equal to your animation file.

Figure 20.9 shows what the DAT file looks like. This file can be loaded into Anime Studio using the Source Data button in the Switch panel of the Layer Settings dialog box. Notice how the DAT file is looking for several layers named O, AI, L, E, and so on. These layer names match the various sounds, or phonemes, that make up the spoken sentences.

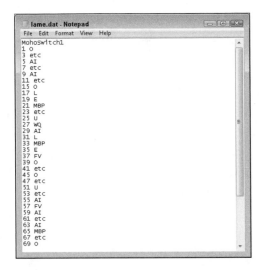

Figure 20.9
DAT file from Papagayo.

To lip-sync audio using Papagayo, follow these steps:

1. Open the Lip Sync.anme file from the Chapter 20 folder on the CD. This file includes a simple girl's face minus the mouth.

2. Select the File, Import, Mouths menu command. In the Insert Object dialog box that appears, select Mouth 1 and click the OK button. This places the mouth object in the center of the working area.

3. With the Mouth 1 Switch layer selected, resize the mouth on the face with the Scale Layer tool (2).

4. Open the Papagayo program and select the File, Open menu command. In the File dialog box that opens, select the GoHome.wav file in the Chapter 20 folder on the CD and click the Open button. The waveform for the audio file is displayed in the interface. Then click the Zoom In button to expand the waveform to fill the top pane.

5. In the Spoken Text pane, type in the words for this audio file, "Time to go home now." Then click the English button. Papagayo makes its best guess at the position of the words and phonemes in the audio file.

6. Move to the end of the audio file and notice how the green sentence bar doesn't go all the way to the end of the waveform. Select and drag the right end of the sentence bar to align with the end of the waveform. Next adjust the orange word bars to coincide with the waveform bumps for each word. Notice how the last word, *now,* is drawn out much longer than the rest. Finally, adjust the pink phoneme bars at the bottom of the waveforms. The resulting adjustment should look like the one in Figure 20.10.

Figure 20.10
Adjusted Papagayo
audio file.

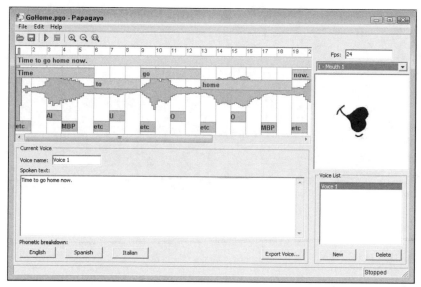

7. After the audio file is adjusted, click the Export Voice button at the bottom of the Papagayo interface and name the file GoHome.dat. Then save the Papagayo file in case you need to adjust the file some again.

8. Back in Anime Studio, select and double-click the Mouth 1 Switch layer to open the Layer Settings dialog box. In the Switch panel, click the Source Data button and choose the GoHome.dat file from the Chapter 20 folder on the CD. This is the same file that Papagayo exported. Then close the Layer Settings dialog box.

9 Select the File, Import, Audio File menu and load the GoHome.wav file into the Anime Studio project. Then click the Play button (Spacebar) to see the resulting character speak, as shown in Figure 20.11.

Figure 20.11
Final lip-synced character.

Chapter Summary

This chapter showed the various lip-sync methods that are available in Anime Studio, including Automatic and Phoneme Lip-Sync. Both methods accomplish lip-syncing using Switch layers, which are especially useful for creating lip-syncing for a character. Several lip-syncing packages are available for Anime Studio, including Papagayo.

The next chapter covers morphing objects from one state to another.

21

Morphing Objects and Using Actions

- Accessing the Actions palette
- Creating morph targets
- Blending morphs
- Creating animation clips
- Editing an existing clip
- Reusing clips

Objects outside of the working area are not exported with the project. This area provides a place where you can place objects that you aren't ready to use just yet. But Anime Studio includes another place where you can keep animation and object states in limbo.

The Actions palette provides a simple interface for defining different object states and for holding animation clips called *actions*. Once an action is created within the Actions palette, you can select and edit it without changing the current project. With several actions created, you can also morph between the different defined states to create new results. The Actions palette also allows animated objects to be saved.

As you create small animation clips that you want to reuse, you can use the Actions palette to insert these animation clips into the current project. New clips can be edited in the Timeline palette and inserted into the main animation.

The Actions palette is used to keep track of all the reusable animation clips. Each layer can have its own set of action clips, and these clips can be inserted easily throughout the animation as a reference or as a copy. Using referenced actions has the advantage of being updated automatically when the action clip changes.

New Feature

The morphing features are new to Anime Studio 6.

Note

The full set of morphing features are only available in Anime Studio Pro. Anime Studio Debut can blend morph targets, but cannot create them.

Accessing the Actions Palette

The Actions palette is opened by selecting the Window, Actions menu command or by pressing the Ctrl/Cmd+K menu command. The Actions palette, shown in Figure 21.1, is simply a list that can hold several morph targets or animation clips. The Actions palette is not open when Anime Studio starts. It also cannot be docked to the main interface.

Caution

When editing an action in the Timeline, do not access any menus or use any keyboard shortcuts. Doing so will cause an error to appear.

New Action

Insert Reference

Insert Copy

Delete Action

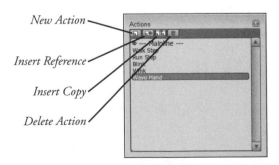

Figure 21.1
Actions palette.

Creating Morph Targets

At the top of the Actions palette is a New Action button. Clicking this button opens a simple dialog box where you can name the new action. Once created, the new action is selected and made active. When an action is active, its current layer is available for editing. You can tell when an object is ready to be edited because the background of the Timeline palette is white and a red arrow points to the active action in the Actions palette, as shown in Figure 21.2.

Figure 21.2
Timeline in clip editing mode.

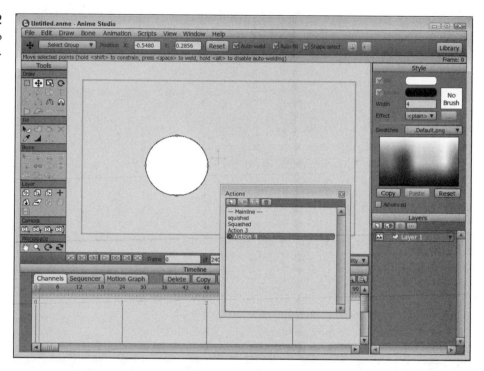

When an action is active, you can create a new state by editing the existing layer. The edits are remembered as a specific state called a *morph target*. You can make another action (or the Mainline) active by double-clicking the action in the Actions palette. You can also rename an action by right-clicking it and selecting the Rename option from the pop-up menu.

When the Mainline option in the Actions palette is made active, you can insert any of the available actions by selecting an action and clicking on either the Insert Reference or the Insert Copy buttons. The Insert Reference maintains a link to the original action, so that if the action is edited, the instance is also updated.

Deleting an action with the Delete Action button will also delete any referenced instances.

The Insert Copy button places a copy of the action at the current frame. This copy remains unchanged if the original action is edited or deleted.

Adding an action to the current project creates a key at the frame where it is inserted. This key represents an edited state for the layer, and the points in the object will move from the positions in their previous key to their new keyed location over the number of frames separating the two keys. For example, if your default layer is a circle and an action named *Square* is created where the circle has been edited to be a square, then if the Square action is inserted as a copy at frame 10, the circle points will gradually move to form a square over the first 10 frames of the project.

Using actions, you can morph between different shapes over a designated number of frames. Keep in mind that when creating morph targets, you can only edit the existing points and not add new points to the existing layer. If you want to add new points or objects, you can keep them outside of the working area and then move them within the object for the new morph target.

Blending Morphs

If several morph target actions are included within the Actions palette, then you can use the Animation, Blend Morphs (Ctrl/Cmd+Shift+B) menu to access the Blend Morphs dialog box, shown in Figure 21.3. Using the sliders in the Blend Morphs dialog box, you can blend between the default shape and any defined morph targets to create an entirely new morph target.

> **Tip**
>
> If you want to return any morph target to its original default shape, you can do so using the Default slider in the Blend Morphs dialog box or you can simply use the Draw, Reset All Points menu.

When blending morphs together, it is best to create a new action and make this new action active before blending. The blended morph will then be placed in the new active action.

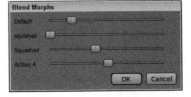

Figure 21.3
Blend Morphs dialog box.

To add an action to an animation, follow these steps:

1. Open the Glasses face.anme file from the Chapter 21 folder on the CD. This file includes a single vector layer of a kid's face.

2. Select the Window, Actions menu command (Ctrl/Cmd+K) to open the Actions palette. Then select the New Action from the top of the Actions palette and name the new action *Frown*.

3. With the Frown action made active in the Actions palette, drag the points of the mouth and eyes to make a frowning face, as shown in Figure 21.4.

Figure 21.4
Frown expression.

4. Repeat Step #3 to create another action named Surprise with a surprised look, like the one shown in Figure 21.5.

5. Click the New Action button in the Actions palette and create another action named *Grimace*. Then choose the Animation, Blend Morphs menu command. In the Blend Morphs dialog box, drag the Frown slider all the way to the right and the Surprise slider about halfway. Figure 21.6 shows the resulting expression.

Figure 21.5
Surprised expression.

Figure 21.6
Blended expression.

Working with Animated Actions

In addition to morph targets, the Actions palette can also be used to hold animation clips. The difference between morph targets and animated actions is that the latter has key set.

Caution

Animated actions will not appear in the Blend Morphs dialog box and cannot be blended.

At the top of the list of Actions is an entry labeled *Mainline*. This entry isn't an action but represents the project's main animation. A red arrow marks the current action that is open, and its keys are displayed in the Timeline palette. When the Mainline option is open, the project's default animation keys are visible in the Timeline palette.

Creating Animation Clips

To create an animation clip, click the New Action button at the top of the Actions palette. This command opens a dialog box where you can give the new action a name. The clip is then added to the Actions palette list.

Caution

When a new action is created, the timeline automatically snaps to frame 0. If you drag the timeline to a frame other than 0 thinking on making a morph target, then you'll be working with an animation and the morph blend option will not be available.

Editing an Existing Clip

If you double-click an animation clip in the Actions palette, the clip is loaded into the Timeline palette where you can edit it. The clip being edited is identified by a red arrow pointing to it in the Actions palette. Once it's loaded, you can create animation keys for the loaded action using the various tools. The keys will appear on the Timeline as normal.

The background color of the Timeline palette also changes to white, as shown in Figure 21.7. This is to remind you that you are in clip editing mode. To switch back to the main timeline editing mode, double-click the Mainline option in the Actions palette.

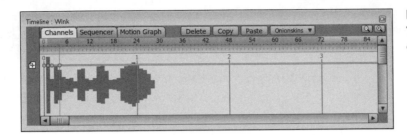

Figure 21.7
Timeline in clip editing mode.

Reusing Clips

Once a clip is defined and ready to use in the Actions palette, you can add it to the main animation by selecting the clip in the Actions palette, choosing a frame where you want to insert the clip in the Timeline palette, and clicking on either the Insert Reference or the Insert Copy buttons.

The Insert Reference option maintains a link to the clip that is inserted. If the clip ever gets changed, the referenced clip that is inserted into the main animation will also be updated with the clip changes. If a clip is inserted as a copy, then any changes to the clip in the future are not propagated to the inserted animation.

To add an action to an animation, follow these steps:

1. Open the Lip-Sync with blinking.anme file from the Chapter 21 folder on the CD. This file includes the woman lip-syncing to an audio file completed in an earlier tutorial.

2. Select the Window, Actions menu command (Ctrl/Cmd+K) to open the Actions palette. Then select the New Action from the top of the Actions palette to create a new action named *Action 1*.

3. With the Action 1 action selected in the Actions palette, select the face layer in the Layers palette. Then drag the Time Slider to frame 1 and edit the eyes so they pull together as if blinking. Three keys are added to the Timeline palette for the Point Motion channel.

4. Select the same three keys in frame 0 as the newly created keys and click the Copy button at the top of the Timeline palette. Then drag the Time slider to frame 3 and click the Paste button to copy the keys with the eyes wide open to frame 3.

5. Double-click the Mainline option in the Actions palette to return to the main animation. Then drag the Time slider to frame 10 and click only once on Action 1 and click the Insert Reference button at the top of the Actions palette. This adds the action keys to the main timeline.

6. Drag the Time slider to frame 30 and click the Insert Reference button again.

7. Click the Play button (Spacebar) to see the resulting animation with blinking, as shown in Figure 21.8.

Figure 21.8
Random blinking added as an action.

Chapter Summary

This chapter introduced the Actions palette and showed how it can be used to hold morph targets and animation clips. The chapter also showed how the Blend Morphs command is used to blend two or more morph targets together. Animated actions can be reused within an animation as a reference or as a copy.

The next chapter covers working with image layers.

Part V

Working with Image, Group, Switch, and Note Layers

22

Adding Image Layers

- Importing images
- Using tracing paper
- Moving and resizing image layers
- Importing movies
- Using the HSV modifier

Although Anime Studio is a vector-based software package, it still has the capability to work with pixel-based images by using image layers. These images need to be imported into the image layer. In fact, when you create a new image layer, a File dialog box opens so that you can import a pixel-based image. Imported video clips are also placed on image layers.

Image layers can be moved, scaled, and rotated, but Anime Studio doesn't include any pixel-editing tools. Any image editing will need to be accomplished in an external program.

Importing Images and Videos

When you create an image layer by selecting it from the New Layer pop-up list in the Layers palette, a File dialog box opens from which you can locate an image or video clip to place within the layer. If you click the Cancel button in the File dialog box, then no new layer is created. Once a picture is selected, the name of the image layer in the Layers palette is automatically changed to be the image's name, as shown in Figure 22.1.

> **Note**
>
> Even though the layer name is changed to match the image file's name, you can still change the image layer's name in the Layer Settings dialog box.

You can also create a new image layer by selecting the File, Import, Image or the File, Import, Movie menu command. This menu also opens a File dialog box where you can select an image or video to import. Each image layer can only hold a single image or video file.

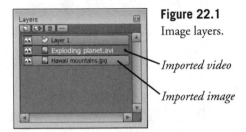

Figure 22.1
Image layers.

Imported video

Imported image

Supported Image Formats

Anime Studio can import several different image formats, including the following:

- **BMP:** This format is common on Windows-based computers.
- **GIF:** This format is used on the Web and supports 256-colors.
- **JPEG:** Another common Web format that supports 16.7 million colors. JPEG images can also be compressed to reduce their size, but severe compression can destroy the image.
- **PNG:** The PNG format is a newer Web format. It offers compression and full alpha channel support.
- **Targa:** This format allows lossless compression.

> **Caution**
>
> Although the supported image formats are filtered in the File dialog box, the File Type drop-down list doesn't list the supported image formats.

The supported movie formats that can be imported include the following:

- **AVI:** A Windows-based video format.
- **QuickTime:** A video format available for Windows and Macs.

New Feature

The ability to import HD Video is new to Anime Studio 6. This feature is only available in Anime Studio Pro. Note that the output will not be HD.

> ### Caution
>
> Imported movies import both the video images and sound, but you cannot edit video and audio separately.

> ### Note
>
> Anime Studio will allow you to import an MPEG video file, but only the first frame of the loaded video will appear and be exported.

Updating an Image Layer

If you ever need to update or change the image used in an existing image layer, you can use the Source Image button in the Image panel of the Layer Settings dialog box, shown in Figure 22.2. Clicking this button opens a File dialog box where you can select a new image file to replace the current one.

Figure 22.2
Image panel in the Layer Settings dialog box.

Loading an Alpha Channel Movie

If the video file that you are loading into an image layer contains an alpha channel, Anime Studio will detect the alpha channel and use it to composite the movie with the other layers. QuickTime movies are automatically detected, but the Image panel of the Layer Settings dialog box has an option to explicitly tell Anime Studio that AVI movie has an alpha channel.

Note

You can check to see if your QuickTime movie has an alpha channel by opening the movie file in the QuickTime player and selecting the Window, Show Movie Info menu. If the movie info states that the movie has Millions of Colors+, then the + sign indicates that it has an alpha channel.

Organizing Images with Projects

When image files are used within a project, Anime Studio doesn't embed the image files into the .ANME file but instead only keeps track of the link to the image file. This helps to keep the project files small, but it can result in missing image files if the linked images get moved. For this reason, it is best to keep the image file located with the project file. If image files are placed within a subfolder, then a relative link to the subfolder is remembered by the project.

Tip

One way to keep all the pieces of the project together is to create a project folder within the Library folder where Anime Studio is installed. Then all content included in the project including subfolders will be visible for review in the Library palette.

Caution

Losing files applies to all external files, not just to images, so 3D object, movie, and sound files can get lost also.

If the image files that are used in a project are moved to a location different from what the link is, or if the image file is renamed, then a missing file icon appears within the project, as shown in Figure 22.3. The missing icon is the size of the missing image.

> **Tip**
>
> Keeping all the files together in a single folder also helps when you get ready to upload the project to the Web. If the image files used by the project aren't uploaded with the project, then they will appear as missing.

Figure 22.3
Missing image icons.

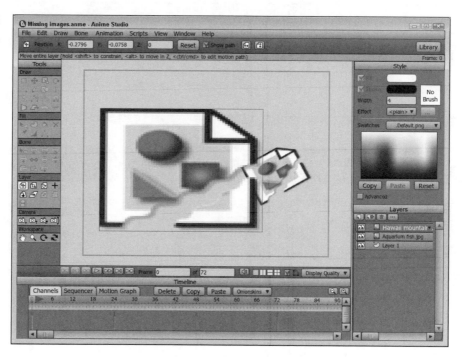

Using Tracing Paper

One helpful way to use image layers is to load in a reference image that you can use to guide you as you create vector objects. The problem with using an image layer is that the details are typically too bright to see the vector lines. Anime Studio includes a tracing paper feature that can be used to hold a reference image you want to trace.

To load an image as a tracing image, use the View, Select Tracing Image (Ctrl/Cmd+Y) menu command. You can also use the File, Import, Tracing Image menu. This opens a File dialog box where you can locate the image to load. Once loaded, the image is automatically sized to fit within the working area. It also appears dimmed in the background of the working area. You can use the View, Show Tracing Image (Ctrl/Cmd+U) menu command to hide or restore the tracing image. Figure 22.4 shows the working area with a tracing image enabled.

Caution
AVI and QuickTime video files cannot be loaded as a tracing image.

Note
The tracing image feature is only available in Anime Studio Pro.

Note
The tracing image is independent of the Layers palette and does not exist on a layer. The tracing image is also never rendered.

One drawback of working with a tracing image is that the image is not saved with the project and will need to be reloaded after the project is reopened. You also cannot change the amount of dimming that is applied to the tracing image.

Using an Image Layer to Trace

Although the Tracing Image feature automatically dims an image, the same effect can be accomplished using an image layer. If you create an image layer and load in an image that you want to trace, you can adjust the transparency of the image using the Opacity setting in the Layer Settings dialog box, but this will only display the transparency when the image is rendered. Instead, add a vector layer in front of the tracing image and cover the image with a large white rectangle.

Figure 22.4
Tracing image.

You can then set the Opacity value of the vector layer to 60 or 70 depending on how dark the image layer underneath is. Transparency for a vector layer is displayed in the working area if the Transparency option in the Display Quality dialog box is enabled.

By using an image layer as a tracing image, you can adjust the amount of dimming, load AVI or MOV video files to trace and move, rotate, and scale the image layer as needed.

To create a tracing image using an image layer, follow these steps:

1. Select the File, New menu command (Ctrl/Cmd+N) to create a new blank project.

2. Click the New Layer button in the Layers palette and select the Image option from the pop-up menu. In the File dialog box that opens, select the Dog Show.jpg file from the Chapter 22 folder on the CD.

3. Select the Layer Scale tool (2) and drag in the working area to reduce the size of the layer until it fills the working area.

4. Click the New Layer button in the Layers palette again and select the Vector option to create a new vector layer.

5. In the Style palette, click the white color swatch to make the fill color white. With the Rectangle tool (E), drag over the top of the image to create a new rectangle box that covers the image.

6. Double-click the new vector layer and change the Opacity setting to 60 in the Layer Settings dialog box.

7. Select and drag the image layer to the bottom of the Layers palette so it's beneath all other layers. Then drag the new vector layer so it is just above the image layer.

8. In the Display Quality dialog box, make sure the Transparency option is enabled. The image should now look semi-transparent, as shown in Figure 22.5.

Figure 22.5
Tracing image made with an image layer.

Locating Reference Images

The Internet is full of reference images that can give you a jumpstart on drawing specific characters and objects.

Drawing human characters with realistic proportions can be tricky, but using a reference image will help keep your character proportions in check. The site at www.3d.sk includes a wealth of photographs of human characters. Be aware that the site contains some nudity, though. If you're looking to get information on the movement of characters that you can use for reference, try the Carnegie Mellon University Graphics Lab Motion Capture Database at http://mocap.cs.cmu.edu.

Caution

Most images on the Web are copyrighted, so before you use a tracing image of your favorite cartoon or movie, be sure that you abide by the copyright laws. For example, if you use a reference image from a Star Wars film to create a ship that resembles a Tie Fighter for your latest game, don't be surprised if a team of lawyers calls you.

Tip

In addition to Anime Studio, Smith Micro also distributes a software package named *Poser* that is great for creating human reference images. You can learn more about Poser at the Smith Micro Web site at www.smithmicro.com.

Moving and Resizing Image Layers

If an image layer is selected in the Layers palette, you can use the Layer tools to move, scale, and rotate the image in the scene.

Rotating Image Layers

When rotating an image layer using the Rotate Layer Z (3) tool, the image spins around its origin point. The origin point can be relocated using the Set Origin (0) tool. For example, if you want to rotate the image around one of its corners, you can click the Set Origin tool, click the corner, and then use the Rotate Layer Z tool to rotate the entire image around the new origin point.

Using the Rotate Layer XY tool, you can rotate the flat 2D image about the X- and Y-axes. This provides a way to make the image recede toward the center to give it perspective. Imagine a billboard with a flat image applied to it. By rotating the image with the Rotate Layer XY tool, you can make the image so the end closest to the camera is larger and the opposite end recedes into the distance.

You can also use the Shear Layer tool to skew the image.

> **Note**
>
> The Rotate Layer XY and Shear Layer tools are only available in Anime Studio Pro.

Understanding Stacking Order

Images are also displayed in the scene according to their order in the Layers palette. Image layers at the top of the Layers palette appear on top of any overlapping image layers that are located below them in the Layers palette. For example, in Figure 22.6, the dog image layer is located underneath the aquarium image layer because the dog image layer in the Layers palette is located below the aquarium image layer.

> **Tip**
>
> Stacking order of the various layers can be animated if the layers are contained within the same Group layer. More on this technique is presented in Chapter 23, "Organizing Layers into Groups."

Figure 22.6
Stacked image layers.

Importing Movies

Movie files are loaded into an image layer the same way images are, except that from the File, Import menu, you need to choose the Movies option instead of the Images option. The File dialog box that opens limits the files to AVI and MOV files.

Once loaded, the frames for the imported movie are shown in the Timeline, and if you press the Play button, the movie will play forward through the loaded frames. Loaded movies will start playing on the frame that is selected when the movie is loaded. For example, if the current frame is frame 20 and the movie clip runs from 30 frames, then the loaded movie will begin at frame 20 and end at frame 50.

Using the Sequencer panel in the Timeline palette, you can change the beginning frame of any loaded movie. More on the Sequencer panel is covered in Chapter 19, "Working with Sound."

Exporting and Importing an Image Sequence

Movie formats like AVI and QuickTime are great for combining and compressing many frames of images together to make a complete animation, but animated images can also be exported using standard image formats including JPEG, BMP, Targa, and PNG. When an animation sequence is exported to one of these image formats, each frame is given a number that is added to the end of the name. So the first frame is exported as image001.jpg, the second frame is named image002.jpg, and so on.

There are benefits to exporting an animation as an image sequence. First, they are uncompressed, so none of the rendered image quality is lost. Second, the image files are easy to edit; and third, they can still be loaded back into Anime Studio.

To load an image sequence into Anime Studio, simply select the Scripts, Image, Import Image Sequence menu command. This accesses a script that lets you choose the images to load.

> **Caution**
>
> In earlier versions of Anime Studio, this script didn't work on Mac systems, but it has been fixed in later versions.

> **Note**
>
> The ability to export and import sequenced images is only available in Anime Studio Pro.

Using HSV Modifiers

In the General panel of the Layer Settings dialog box is an option to use an HSV modifier image. If this option is enabled, you can select an image to use as a filter that is applied to the layer. The selected HSV image is blended with the selected layer, resulting in a layer that has some interesting variety.

When the blend happens, the red channel on the HSV modifier image affects the hue of the layer, the green channel affects the saturation of the layer, and the blue channel in the image affects the luminosity of the layer. The effect is greatest when the red, green, and blue colors are near 0 or 255. Less effect happens when the image has a gray color with a value around 128.

> **Note**
>
> The HSV modifier can be applied to any layer type.

The Samples/HSV Modifier Images folder where Anime Studio is installed includes several sample HSV images that you can apply to different layers. These samples are mainly gray clouds that result in subtle differences to the layer.

> **Note**
>
> The results of the HSV modifier are only visible when the scene is rendered.

Figure 22.7 shows a simple rocket vector layer with a flower applied as an HSV modifier.

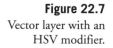

Figure 22.7
Vector layer with an
HSV modifier.

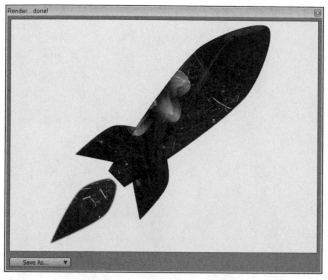

Controlling Images with Bones

In Chapter 26, "Creating and Binding Bones," we'll show you how you can use bones to control the objects on a vector layer, but bones can also be used to control image layers. There are two distinct ways to use bones with images.

Making a Bone Control an Image Layer

The first way to use bones with image layers is to bind the bones to the entire image layer so that the movement and rotation of the bone works to move and rotate the layer. This method works when creating a character from various drawn and scanned body parts. If you locate the layer's origin at the rotation point of the body part, then you can use the Layer Rotate tool to rotate the body part, such as an arm, relative to the rest of the body.

The Winsor character that was the default in Anime Studio 5 is a good example of this. If you drag the Time Slider to frame 0, then you can see several of the bone-controlled body parts separated from one another, as shown in Figure 22.8. Notice in the Layers palette how the various body parts are all image layers.

> **Note**
>
> The Winsor character is still available in the Anime Studio 5 Content folder in the Library.

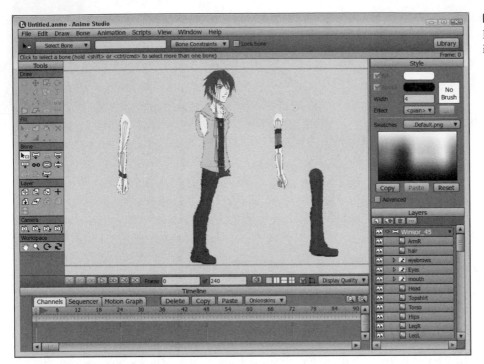

Figure 22.8
Bone-controlled
image layers.

Using Bones to Warp Images

If bones cross the middle of the image layer, then the resulting image can be distorted as the bones are moved. The key to getting this distortion is to enable the Warp Using Bones option in the Image panel of the Layer Settings dialog box. When this option is enabled, the image will warp to match the movement of the controlling bones.

One type of animation that has become popular on the Web using this method is the Jib-Jab style of animation. To animate in this style, you simply need to split the desired image into separate files that can be loaded and animated independently.

Tip

If you save the foreground images as PNG files, then you can save the image with the option of making the background color transparent. This allows the background to be visible.

To create a Jib-Jab style of animation, follow these steps:

1. Select the File, New menu command (Ctrl/Cmd+N) to create a new blank project.

2. Click the New Layer button in the Layers palette and select the Image option from the pop-up menu. In the File dialog box that opens, select the Background.jpg file from the Chapter 22 folder on the CD. Add two more image layers and load the Head.png and the Trunk.png files into these new layers. Make sure the head image layer is the top layer in the Layers palette.

3. Select each of the image layers and scale its size to match the other image layers with the Scale Layer tool (2) and then move them into position with the Translate Layer tool (1).

4. Select the Set Origin tool (0) and move the origin for the head image layer to the base of the elephant's neck. Move the origin of the elephant's trunk to the base of its trunk.

5. Click the New Layer button in the Layers palette and select the Bone option from the pop-up menu. Then drag and drop the Trunk.png and the Head.png image layers onto the new bone layer. Select the bone layer and with the Add Bone tool (A), create a single bone for the elephant's head that runs from the elephant's neck to its tusks. Then create three additional bones that run the length of the elephant's trunk. If the bones are created in succession, the trunk bones will be parented automatically to the head bone, causing the trunk to move with the head.

6. Select the Trunk.png layer in the Layers palette and open the Layer Settings dialog box. In the Image panel, enable the Warp Using Bones option and close the dialog box.

7. With the bone layer selected, drag the Time Slider in the Timeline palette to frame 6 and select the Manipulate Bones tool (Z); then drag the tips of the head bone upward. Then drag the tip of the last trunk bone forward.

8. Drag the Time slider to frame 12 and move the elephant's bones again. Repeat for frames 18, 24, and 30. Notice how the elephant's trunk warps as the bones are moved but the elephant's head remains undistorted.

9. Click the Play button (Spacebar) to see the resulting motion, as shown in Figure 22.9.

Figure 22.9
Elephant body parts
animated using bones.

Chapter Summary

This chapter covered image layers and showed how they can be used to hold images and movies. It also showed how images can be used as tracing paper and it presented the unique HSV modifier images for adding variety to layers and using image layers with bones.

The next chapter covers another layer type, the group layer, for organizing several layers together.

23

Organizing Layers into Groups

- Working with group layers
- Moving a group layer
- Hiding groups
- Applying effects to a group
- Working with masks
- Animating layer order

A *group layer* is simply a folder that can hold sublayers. A group layer can also hold other group layers so that nesting layers are supported. All sublayers within a group layer inherit the actions applied to the group layer, so if a group layer is moved, all of its sublayers are moved also.

One key place where group layers are used is when working with masks. Masks require that layers be contained within the same group layer.

Creating a Group Layer

Group layers can be created in the Layers palette by clicking the New Layer button in the Layers palette and selecting the Group option from the pop-up list. The icon for group layers looks like a folder. The new layer is added to the Layers palette directly above the selected layer and given the name of *Layer* followed by a sequential number.

> **Note**
>
> Group layers are only available in Anime Studio Pro.

Group layers are initially empty when they are created, but you can add sublayers to the group layer by dragging and dropping any existing layers onto the group layer icon. When you drag a layer or multiple selected layers over the top of a group layer, the group layer is highlighted in red. If you drop a layer when the group layer is highlighted like this, the dropped layer or layers are added to the group. You can also add layers to the group by selecting a layer within the group layer and creating a new layer. The new layer is added to the layer list automatically directly above the selected layer.

> **Tip**
>
> Although group layers are only available in Anime Studio Pro, if you need a group layer in Anime Studio Debut, you can use a bone layer to accomplish the same results.

Group layers can be renamed by double-clicking the layer's name to access the Layer Settings dialog box. In this dialog box, you can enter a new name for the layer. All layer settings made to a group layer are automatically applied to all the group's sublayers.

> **Note**
>
> In addition to group layers, bone, switch, and particle layers can also hold sublayers just like group layers.

Nesting Group Layers

If a group layer that contains multiple sublayers is dropped onto another group layer, the group is added to the group, making a nested group. Figure 23.1 shows a nested set of group layers in the Layers palette.

Figure 23.1
Nested group layers.

Caution

If a group layer is contained within a bone layer, then the bone can control the group layer, but the bone cannot be bound to the points in the group's sublayer. This will work if you have a nested set of bone layers.

Deleting a Group Layer

If you want to delete a group layer, simply select the layer and click the Delete Layer button in the Layers palette. When a group layer is deleted, all its sublayers are also deleted.

Note

If the group layer is the topmost layer in the Layers palette, the Delete Layer button is disabled because Anime Studio requires that at least one layer is always available.

Working with Groups

When a group layer is selected in the Layers palette, you can work with it just like any of the other layers, except that any changes you make to the group layer are automatically applied to the sublayers also.

Moving a Group Layer

When a group layer is selected in the Layers palette, you can use the Layer tools to move, scale, and rotate the layer. (All of the Layer tools are covered in Chapter 4, "Working with Layers.") All transformations that are applied to a group layer are also applied to all the sublayers.

Making a layer a sublayer of a group adds a new level of control to the layer where the group layer becomes the parent of the sublayer. For example, if you have a layer that is animated that you want to move to a new location, that layer would need to be repositioned at every frame where there is a key, which could be a large task if there are lots of keys. However, if you add the layer to a group layer, you can simply move the group and the sublayer, and all its keys are moved relative to the parent without altering any of the keys.

To relocate an animated object without changing its keys, follow these steps:

1. Open the Cannon.anme file from the Chapter 23 folder on the CD. This file includes a cannon object that is animated shooting a cannonball. It was taken from an earlier tutorial. The cannon is located at the center of the working area. If you use the Translate Layer tool (1) to move the cannon at frame 0 to the bottom of the working area, then the cannon simply moves from this new location back to the center of the working area when you play the project.

2. To move the entire animation with all its keys to the bottom of the working area, you'll need to add a group layer. Select the New Layer button at the top of the Layers palette and choose the Group option in the pop-up menu to create a new group layer.

3. Drag the Cannon layer and drop it on the group layer to add it as a sublayer.

4. With the group layer selected in the Layers palette, select and drag the cannon at frame 0 to the bottom of the working area with the Translate Layer tool (1).

5. Click the Play button (Spacebar) to see the resulting animation. The entire cannon animation is now relocated to the bottom of the working area, as shown in Figure 23.2.

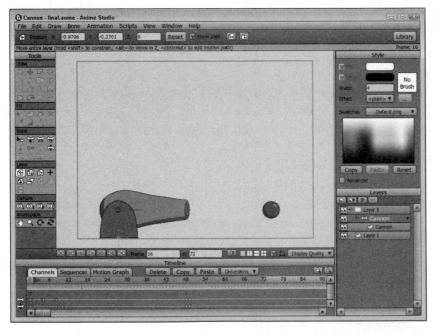

Figure 23.2
Relocated animation.

> **Caution**
>
> Group sublayers inherit specific attributes from their group parents. If you move a sublayer out of a group, it will lose these inherited attributes. For example, if you add several layers to a group and then scale the group and then remove one of the sublayers from the group, it will revert to its original scaling value.

Hiding Group Layers

Group layers and all their sublayers can be hidden from the current scene by disabling the Visible option in the Layer Settings dialog box. You can also hide a group layer and all its sublayers by deselecting the googly eyes icon to the left of the layer name in the Layers palette. Both of these options make the layers invisible in the working area but do not delete the layer from the scene.

Applying Effects to a Group

Finally, any layer effects that are applied to a group layer are applied equally to all sublayers. The various layer effects are located in the Layer Settings dialog box.

Working with Masks

The options for specifying a layer mask are contained in the Masking panel of the Layer Settings dialog box, as shown in Figure 23.3. Masking will only work across layers that are contained within the same group layer. To make a layer a sublayer of the group layer, simply drag and drop the layer onto the group layer in the Layers palette. You can learn more about the various masking options in Chapter 4.

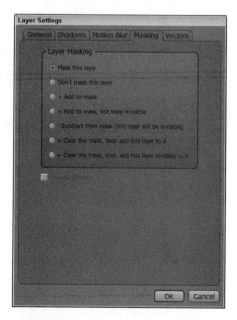

Figure 23.3
Masking panel.

Masks are useful if you want to confine the display of a layer's object to a specific region. The classic example of masking is to use masks to create a set of eyeballs. If you have separate sublayers for the eyeballs and the pupils, you can easily make the eyeball layers a mask. This causes the pupils to only be visible when they are within the eyeball layer; if the pupils move to the side of the eyeball, then only the portion that is within the eyeball is visible.

> **Tip**
>
> Masking can also be used to make a cloth texture appear within the limits of a shirt or some other clothed area.

To use layer masks to create a set of eyes, follow these steps:

1. In the Layers palette, click the New Layer button and select the Group option from the pop-up menu. Open the Layer Settings dialog box and name the group layer *Eyes*.

2. Select and drag the default vector layer onto the Eyes layer. Name this layer *Whites* and draw two circles in the working area. Make sure that the circles have a white fill.

> **Tip**
>
> If you draw one circle and then copy and paste the first circle, you can hold down the Shift key while moving the second circle to the side to constrain its vertical movement. This results in eyes that are exactly the same size and horizontally aligned.

3. With the Whites layer selected, click the New Layer button and create a new vector layer. The new layer will appear directly above the Whites layer within the group layer. Name this new layer *Pupils*.

4. Change the fill color to black and draw two pupils within the eyeball circles.

5. Select the group layer and open the Masking panel in the Layer Settings dialog box and enable the Hide All option for the group. This makes the white portions of the mask show where the visible sections are.

6. Select the Whites layer, and then in the Masking panel, enable the Add to Mask option. This makes the whites visible.

7. Select and move the Pupils layer to the edge of the eyeballs. Notice how the portion outside of the whites is masked, as shown in Figure 23.4.

Figure 23.4
Eyes with masked whites.

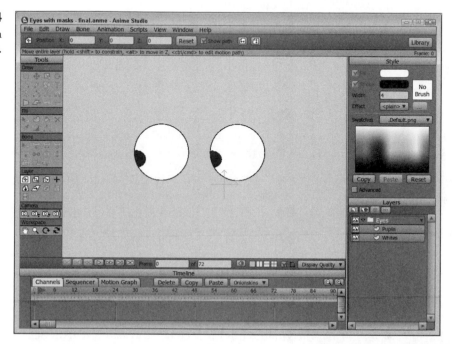

Animating Layer Order

When a group layer is created, you can access the Depth Sort panel in the Layer Settings dialog box by double-clicking the layer in the Layers palette. The Depth Sort panel, shown in Figure 23.5, includes options for specifying how the sublayers within the group are sorted. The options of sorting layers by depth and sorting layers by distance are described in Chapter 25, "Changing the View with Cameras."

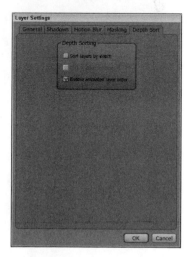

Figure 23.5
Depth Sort panel.

The third option, Enable Animated Layer Order, lets you change the layer order of the group's sublayers as the animation progresses. The default layer behavior is that the layer at the top of the Layers palette obscures all overlapping layers beneath it, but when the Enable Animated Layer Order option is enabled in the Depth Sort panel of the group layer, you can set a key for changing layer order by dragging a group sublayer above or below another layer.

For example, imagine a character that is standing with its arms in front of it. If the arms are on a different layer, then having the character move its arms so they are positioned behind the character would be possible by changing the layer order as the arms move.

To animate the change in layer order, follow these steps:

1. Open the Satellite orbiting Earth.anme file from the Chapter 23 folder on the CD. This file includes a large Earth object on one layer and a satellite object on another layer.

2. In the Layers palette, click the New Layer button and select the Group option from the pop-up menu. Open the Layer Settings dialog box and select the Depth Sort panel. Then enable the Enable Animated Layer Order option and close the Layer Settings dialog box.

3. Select and drag both layers onto the group layer. Position the Satellite layer so it is initially above the Earth layer.

4. Set the current frame in the Timeline palette to frame 5; then use the Translate Layer (1) tool to drag the satellite until it is centered over the Earth. Select the Scale Layer (2) tool and drag slightly to increase the size of the satellite.

5. Set the current frame in the Timeline palette to frame 10 and drag the satellite with the Translate Layer tool to the right of the Earth. Select the Scale Layer key located at frame 0 and copy the key and paste it to frame 10 using the Copy and Paste button at the top of the Timeline palette.

6. With the satellite located to the right of the Earth, select and drag the Satellite sublayer in the Layers palette below the Earth layer to change the layer order.

7. Set the current frame to frame 20 and then copy the Translate Layer key at frame 0 to frame 20.

8. Set the end frame in the frame range to frame 20 and click the Play button to see the satellite orbiting the Earth, as shown in Figure 23.6.

Figure 23.6
Satellite orbiting
the Earth.

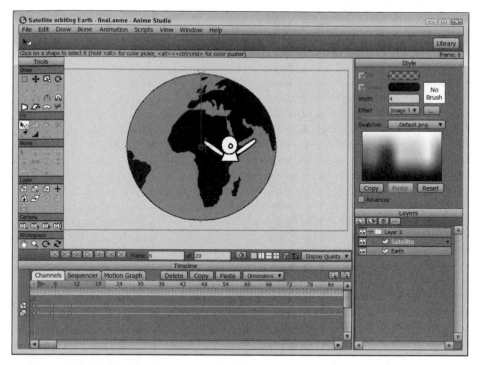

Chapter Summary

This chapter covered the basics of creating and working with group layers. The key to remember is that all changes applied to the group layer are also applied to all sublayers. Group layers are also used to combine layers that are masked and to animate changes in the order layer.

The next chapter covers another type of grouping layer, that of switch layers. The next chapter also covers note layers for commenting on your work.

24

Using Switch Layers and Note Layers

- ▓ Creating a Switch layer
- ▓ Working with a Switch layer
- ▓ Documenting with notes
- ▓ Rendering notes
- ▓ Disabling notes

Switch layers are similar to group layers in that they can hold several sublayers, but the key difference is that only one of the switch sublayers is visible at a time. This is helpful for creating certain effects. For example, if you want to highlight the letters on a sign, you could create one sublayer with all the letters filled with black and another sublayer with all the letters filled in yellow. You could then switch between the two sublayers to make the sign letters appear highlighted, or you could switch back and forth to make the letters blink.

To control which sublayer is visible, simply right-click the sublayer and choose the Visible option from the pop-up menu. This option can be animated. You can also control which sublayer is displayed using a switch data file.

Note layers document your work as you create it. These notes don't appear in the final rendering file; instead they appear only in the loaded Anime Studio project.

In addition, note layers are remembered along with the frame to which they are applied, so a note layer added to frame 10 will only show up when that frame is accessed. They provide a great way to document your project while it is being completed or when working with a team.

Creating a Switch Layer

To create a Switch layer, simply click the New Layer button in the Layers palette and choose the Switch option from the pop-up menu. The new Switch layer is created directly above the current selected layer and is named *Layer* followed by a consecutive number.

The Switch layer icon is a folder with a small black diagonal arrow on it, as shown in Figure 24.1. Switch folders can hold multiple sublayers. To add a layer or multiple selected layers to the Switch layer, simply drag-and-drop the layer or layers onto the Switch layer in the Layers palette. The Switch layer will be highlighted red when the dragged layer or layers can be dropped.

Figure 24.1
Switch layer.

Working with Switch Layers

Once a Switch layer is created, you can manually select which sublayer is visible. You can also create a switch data file that tells which sublayer to view at which frame using an external text file.

Making a Sublayer Visible

Only one of the sublayers in the Switch layer is visible at a time. If you right-click the Switch layer, a pop-up menu shows each of the available sublayers. If you select one from the list, then the selected layer becomes visible and remains visible until another sublayer is selected.

Tip

The visible sublayer can be animated, so if you select another sublayer at frame 10, then that sublayer will be visible from frame 10 onward.

Creating a Switch Data File

Another way to control which sublayer is visible is to use an external data file. A switch data file is used to determine which sublayer is visible at each frame. To create a switch data file, you need to give each sublayer a name. The switch data file then includes a list of frame numbers and sublayer names so that at the specified frame, the listed sublayer is displayed. For any frames that aren't listed, the current sublayer remains displayed.

The switch data file is a simple text file created using Notepad or another text editor. It needs to include MohoSwitch1 at the start of the text file to identify it as a switch data file. Then each new line needs to contain a frame number followed by a space and then a sublayer name. For example, the following switch data file would display Layer1 at frame 1, Layer2 at frame 10, Layer3 at frame 20, and then switch back to Layer1 at frame 30.

```
MohoSwitch1
1 Layer1
10 Layer2
20 Layer3
30 Layer1
```

After a switch data file is created, you can attach it to a Switch layer using the Source Data button in the Switch panel of the Layer Settings dialog box. You can open this dialog box by double-clicking the Switch layer. If you click the Select Audio Sync Source button, then you can choose from any loaded audio files or select the Switch Data File option from a pop-up menu, shown in Figure 24.2.

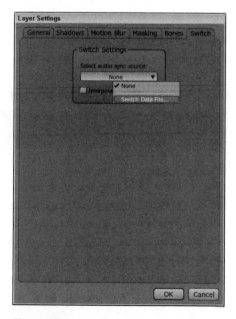

Figure 24.2
Switch panel of the Layer Settings dialog box.

Using an Audio Switch File

In addition to a text file, the Source button in the Switch panel of the Layer Settings dialog box can also open and use an audio file. This audio file needs to be either a WAV or an AIFF file. When an audio file is loaded as the source switch, then the quiet portions of the audio will display the lowest sublayer in the Switch layer and the noisy portions of the audio file will switch to the highest sublayer. All intermediate sounds will cause one of the middle sublayers to be displayed.

The main purpose of the audio switch source is to perform a rudimentary lip-syncing. To prepare a project for this type of lip-syncing, you should place the graphic with the lips closed in the lowest sublayer and the graphic with the mouth open in the highest sublayer and all the intermediate positions in between these two extremes. The resulting lip-syncing will sync the opening and closing of the mouth in sync with the audio file. More on lip-syncing in covered in Chapter 20, "Using Lip-Sync."

Tip

Since the audio switch source file responds to the volume level of the audio file, you should keep any background sounds and music out of the audio file used to control the Switch layer. A different audio file that includes the background noises can be used as a soundtrack.

An audio file can be used in different ways to control the Switch layer, such as the opening and closing of a door or the running and stopping of a water faucet.

To control a Switch layer with an audio file, follow these steps:

1. Open the Alarm clock.anme file from the Chapter 24 folder on the CD. This file includes the stroke of a simple alarm clock.

2. Click the Duplicate Layer button in the Layers palette to create a copy of the alarm clock layer. Then move the alarm clock to the side slightly with the Translate Layer tool (1). Draw some short intermediate noise lines surrounding the clock.

3. Create another duplicate layer of the alarm clock and move the clock again with the Translate Layer tool (1) to create the effect of the clock shaking when the alarm goes off. Then extend the noisy lines even farther for this copy.

4. Click the New Layer button in the Layers palette and select the Switch option from the pop-up menu to create a new Switch layer. Then drag and drop each of the clock layers into the Switch layer so that the clock layer is at the bottom, the clock 2 layer is in the middle, and the clock 3 layer is at the top.

5. Select and double-click the Switch layer to open the Layer Settings dialog box. Select the Switch panel and click the Source Data button. In the File dialog box that opens, locate and open the Beeping clock.wav file from the Chapter 24 folder on the CD. Then enable the Automatic Gain option in the Switch panel and close the Layer Settings dialog box.

6. Select the Animation, Select Soundtrack menu command and load the same Beeping clock.wav audio file. The waveform for the audio file appears in the Timeline palette.

7. Click the Play button (Spacebar) to see the resulting animation. The various clock layers are displayed along with the beeping of the alarm clock, as shown in Figure 24.3.

Figure 24.3
Switch layer controlled by an audio file.

The above example uses a syncing method known as *Automatic Lip-Sync,* and it works for both Anime Studio Debut and Anime Studio Pro, but another method is available for Anime Studio Pro called *Phoneme Lip-Sync.* The key difference is that specific sounds are matched to specific named graphics in the Switch layer.

By naming the graphics correctly, you can have specific graphics appear when certain sounds are played.

For example, one user created a project where a hammer was raised when the Ahh sound was heard and the hammer was lowered when the Ohh sound was played. The audio file was a series of dwarfs chanting these sounds, which animated the hammer going up and down. You can learn more about this type of lip-syncing in Chapter 20, "Using Lip-Sync."

Enabling Smooth Switching

If each of the sublayers in the Switch layer is a vector layer, you can enable smooth switching. Smooth switching is turned on by enabling the Interpolate Sublayers option in the Switch panel of the Layer Settings dialog box. This causes each sublayer to transition smoothly between the different sublayers. This is especially helpful when using the Switch layer for doing lip-syncing.

> **Note**
>
> In order for smooth switching to be enabled, each sublayer must have the same number of points.

To interpolate smoothly between two layers using a Switch layer, follow these steps:

1. Open the Pinwheel.anme file from the Chapter 24 folder on the CD. This file includes a simple pinwheel, as shown in Figure 24.4.

2. In the Layers palette, select the Duplicate Layer button to create an identical layer named *Pinwheel 2*. With the new layer selected, choose the four extended points on the pinwheel with the Shift key held down and rotate them with the Rotate Points tool (R) until the crossing lines form a square around the center circle.

3. Select the New Layer button in the Layers palette and select the Switch option from the pop-up menu. Drag and drop both pinwheel layers onto the Switch layer. The layer that is directly under the Switch layer is visible in the working area.

4. Select and double-click the Switch layer to open the Layer Settings dialog box. Open the Switch panel, enable the Interpolate Sublayers option, and then close the Layer Settings dialog box.

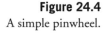

Figure 24.4
A simple pinwheel.

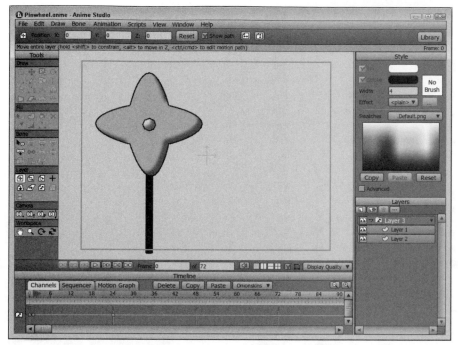

5. Drag the time slider in the Timeline palette to frame 1 and right-click the Switch layer and choose the Pinwheel layer. Then drag the time slider to frame 12 and right-click the Switch layer and choose the Pinwheel 2 layer.

6. Click the key at frame 1 and click the Copy button at the top of the Timeline palette. Then drag the time slider to frame 24 and click the Paste button. This action copies the key at frame 1 to the end frame so that the animation will loop back to its starting position.

7. Click the Play button located at the bottom-left corner of the working area to see the resulting animation. The pinwheel gradually changes to the position in the second layer and back again. Figure 24.5 shows the pinwheel as it makes this change.

Morphing Between Layers with a Different Number of Points

In order for the interpolation between sublayers in a Switch layer to work, the layers must have the same number of points. If two layers have a different number of points, they still can be included together in the Switch layer, but there won't be any interpolation between them. The layer with the different number of points will just appear when it is selected. Anime Studio also supports morphing features covered in Chapter 21, "Morphing Objects and Using Actions."

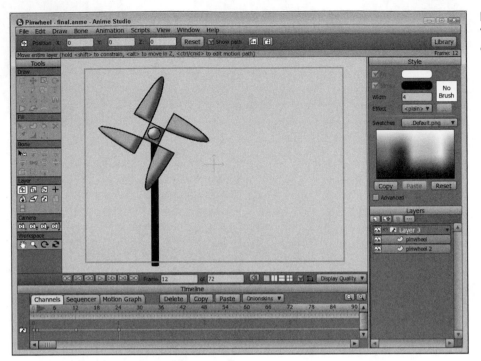

Figure 24.5
The pinwheel changing shape.

However, there is a way to trick the program so that it appears to morph between the two layers. The trick is to create a duplicate of the first layer. The duplicate layer will have the same number of points as the first one. Then edit the new layer so that it aligns with the second layer. Even though the new layer has a different number of points than the second layer, you can still interpolate between the first layer and the new layer and then switch to the second layer.

To morph between layers with a differing number of points, follow these steps:

1. Open the Umbrella to heart.anme file from the Chapter 24 folder on the CD. This file includes a simple umbrella in one layer and a heart shape in another, as shown in Figure 24.6.

2. In the Layers palette, select the umbrella layer and click the Duplicate Layer button to create an identical layer named *umbrella 2*.

3. Select all the points in the umbrella 2 layer with the Edit, Select All command (Ctrl/Cmd+A) and move the umbrella on top of the heart. With the Translate Point tool (T), select and drag each of the points around the umbrella 2 layer and position them on the perimeter of the heart.

Figure 24.6
Umbrella and
heart shapes.

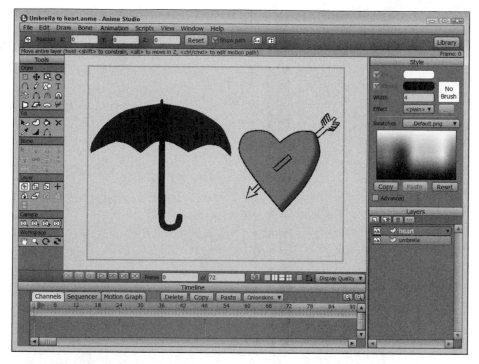

4. Select the New Layer button in the Layers palette and select the Switch option from the pop-up menu. Drag and drop all three layers onto the Switch layer. Drag the umbrella layer until it is directly under the Switch layer.

5. Select and double-click the Switch layer to open the Layer Settings dialog box. Open the Switch panel, enable the Interpolate Sublayers option, and then close the Layer Settings dialog box.

6. Drag the time slider in the Timeline palette to frame 1, right-click the Switch layer, and choose the umbrella layer. Then drag the time slider to frame 24, right-click the Switch layer, and choose the umbrella 2 layer. Finally, drag the time slider in the Timeline palette to frame 25, right-click the Switch layer, and choose the heart layer.

Note

If you set keys to change the color of the umbrella as it morphs into a new shape, the color will change in the umbrella layer but not as the object morphs.

7. Click the Play button located at the bottom-left corner of the working area to see the resulting animation. The umbrella gradually morphs into the heart shape. Figure 24.7 shows the umbrella as it is making this change.

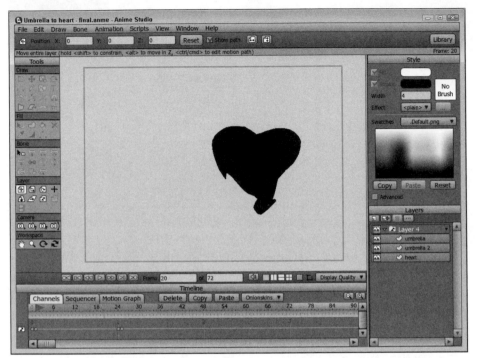

Figure 24.7
The umbrella is morphing into a heart.

Documenting Your Work with Notes

Notes can be used to document your work between team members or just to remind yourself of something. To create a note, simply create a note layer using the New Layer button in the Layers palette and select the Note option from the pop-up menu. This creates a note layer and opens the Layer Settings dialog box with the Note panel selected, as shown in Figure 24.8.

The Note panel includes a simple text field for adding text. After entering some text and clicking the OK button, the note is added to the working area. The note layer can be transformed just like other layers. Figure 24.9 shows a project with a note layer added.

Each layer can hold only a single note. If you need more notes, you must add another layer for each additional note.

Figure 24.8
Note panel of the Layer Settings dialog box.

Note

Note layers are only available in Anime Studio Pro.

Note

Note layers can be moved, but they cannot be rotated or scaled. You also cannot change the note font or size.

Figure 24.9
Notes appear as simple text boxes.

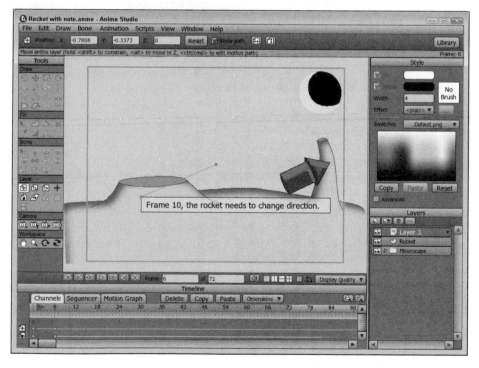

Rendering Notes

By default, notes are set not to be rendered, but if you disable the Don't Render This Layer option in the General panel of the Layer Settings dialog box, the note will be rendered along with the scene. Within the General panel, you can also alter the Visible option and the Blur and Opacity values. Figure 24.10 shows several duplicated layers of notes slowly being blurred.

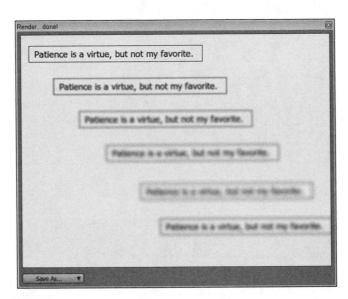

Figure 24.10
Note text can be blurred.

Changing Note Colors

If you open the Shadows panel in the Layer Settings dialog box, you can enable the Layer Shading option to set the text color, but the Offset, Blur, and Contraction values have no effect on the note text. You can also enable the Layer Shadow to give the note text a shadow. If you set the Offset and Blur values to 0 and the Expansion value to 10, you can create a colored background for the note text, as shown with the jumbled color example in Figure 24.11.

> **Note**
>
> Layer colors and shadows only show up when the project is rendered.

Figure 24.11
Note text can be colored and shadowed.

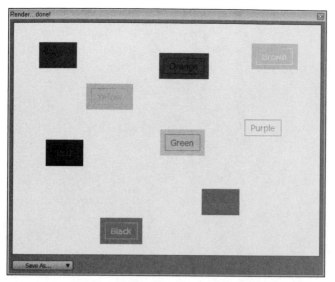

Disabling Notes

If you ever want to hide any note layers, the easiest way is to click the Visibility icon in the Layers palette, or you could disable the Visible option in the Layer Settings dialog box.

Chapter Summary

This chapter introduced the useful Switch layer, which only displays one of its sublayers at a time. The specific sublayer that is visible at any one time can be set manually by right-clicking the Switch layer, or you can create an external data file to control which sublayer appears at which frame of the animation. Audio files can also be used to control which Switch layer is displayed. This chapter also covered note layers and showed how they can be used to add reminder notes to a current project. Note layers are added using the Layers palette and are used to document the project. They can also be rendered with the project.

The next chapter covers changing the camera view of the scene.

Part VI

Using Cameras and Bones

25

Changing the
View with Cameras

- Understanding 3D cameras
- Tracking a camera
- Zooming a camera
- Rolling, panning, and tilting a camera
- Using depth sort
- Using camera scripts

Cameras take pictures that are two-dimensional, but the camera itself is a three-dimensional object that can be positioned in 3D space. Imagine taking a picture of a family gathering. You probably start by taking the picture directly in front of the group, but you could move to the side and take a picture at an angle from the front, or you could move directly behind the group to take the picture. If you were feeling athletic, you could climb a tree and take a picture from above the group looking down on them. Each of these pictures would show the group from a different angle, and the background would be different for each photo, even though the resulting pictures are still 2D.

The same applies for cameras in Anime Studio. You have free control to move around the 2D layers and display them from different positions in the 3D world.

This results not only in a change in the background, but also in the object perspective. This chapter looks at the Camera tools that make it possible to reposition the camera in 3D space, so read on because the family is getting antsy and is ready for lunch.

Understanding 3D Cameras in a 2D World

All layers in Anime Studio are 2D. They do understand the concept of stacking, which essentially makes them 2.5D, but all content is drawn in 2D and placed on 2D layers. But, even though the content is 2D, Anime Studio supports cameras that can manipulate the project in 3D.

Imagine a billboard with a 2D drawing on it. If you have a remote-controlled helicopter, you could fly it around the billboard looking at it from all different directions. This is how the cameras work in Anime Studio.

The various Camera tools work in a similar manner to the Workspace tools, but they actually alter the main window view and can be animated. Figure 25.1 shows the Camera tools available in the Tools palette.

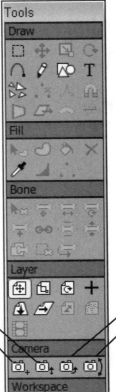

Figure 25.1
Camera tools.

* Anime Studio Pro only

> **Note**
>
> The difference between the Camera and Workspace tools is that the Workspace tools cause the working area (including its border) to move with the tools, but the Camera tools change the scene objects without changing the working area. Another key difference is that changes made with the Camera tools can be undone, but Workspace tool changes cannot.

Zoom Camera (5)
Track Camera (4)
Roll Camera (6)
* Pan/Tilt Camera (7)

Tracking the Camera

A tracking camera is one that moves up, down, and side to side. This is different from simply pointing the camera in a different direction. The tracking move actually changes the camera's position. Holding down the Shift key constrains the tracking to vertical and horizontal movements only and holding down the Alt/Opt key moves the camera closer to or farther away from the scene.

When using the Track Camera tool (4), you'll notice the project objects move, but that the working area border remains motionless. The actual coordinates of the camera in space are shown in the Options bar, and you can enter precise values if you know exactly where the camera needs to be. The Reset button moves the camera to its default location. The Show Path option appears as a line from the origin that shows how the camera has moved. Figure 25.2 shows a scene with a beach ball that has been tracked.

> **Note**
>
> The motion path that is enabled by checking the Show Path option is only visible when the view is at an angle to the camera.

Figure 25.2
Tracked camera scene.

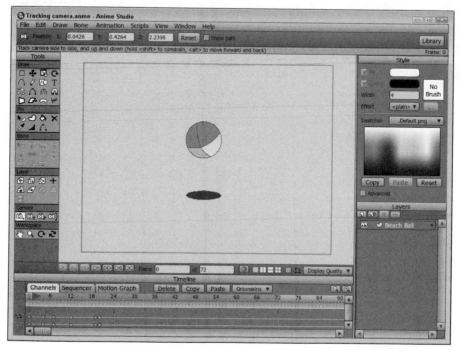

Zooming the Camera

A camera zoom leaves the camera in the same position, but it zooms in on the scene by changing the camera's focal length. The results are that the layer contents increase or decrease in size. The Zoom value is displayed in the Options bar. Figure 25.3 shows the same beach ball scene after the camera has been zoomed.

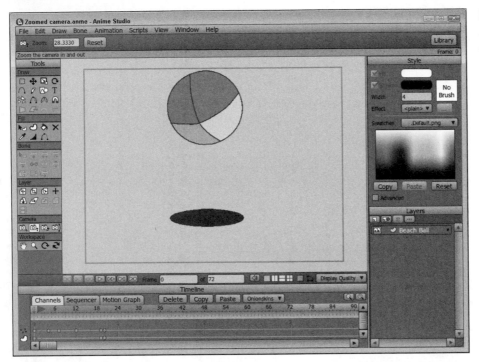

Figure 25.3
Zoomed camera scene.

Rolling the Camera

A camera roll spins the camera around the axis that focuses on the scene. This causes the scene objects to rotate around the center of focus, which is the center of the screen. The roll value is expressed in degrees, with 360 degrees equal to one full revolution in the Options bar. Figure 25.4 shows the beach ball scene rolled about 60 degrees around its center.

Figure 25.4
Rolled camera scene.

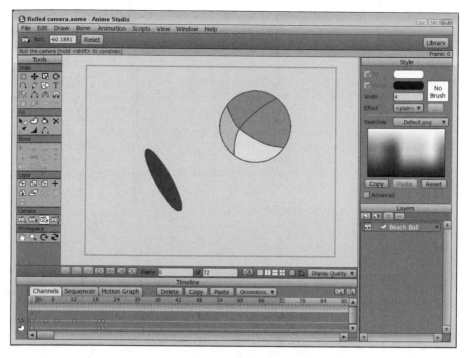

Panning and Tilting the Camera

Panning the camera happens when you rotate the camera to the side like turning your head to the side. A camera tilt works by rotating the camera up and down as if nodding your head. Both of these motions are accomplished without moving the camera's position, only its orientation changes. Figure 25.5 shows the beach ball project tilted. This position was accomplished by tilting the camera and then tracking it back into the scene. Notice how the ball appears skewed and larger than its shadow due to the angle of the camera.

> **Note**
>
> If the Enable 3D Camera option in the Project Settings dialog box is disabled, then you will not be able to use the Pan/Tilt Camera tool.

> **Note**
>
> The Pan/Tilt Camera tool (7) is only available in Anime Studio Pro.

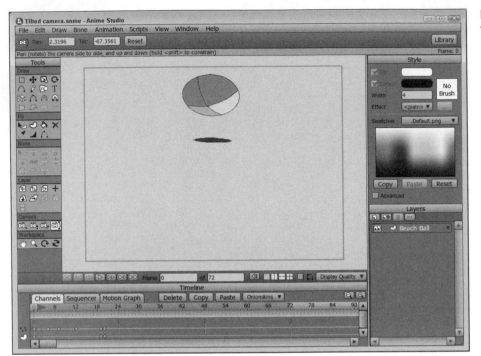

Figure 25.5

Tilted camera scene.

Resetting the View

If at any time you don't like the results of a Camera tool action, you can use the Reset button in the Options bar to return the view to its default state. However, the Reset button will only reset the actions taken with the current Camera tool. For example, if you track the camera and then zoom the camera, the Reset button that is available when the Zoom Camera tool is selected will only reset the zooming action, the tracking action remains.

Tip

Actions done with the Camera tools can also be undone with the Edit, Undo (Ctrl/Cmd+Z) command.

Viewing the Camera Icon

At any time, you can change the view direction of the scene. By default, the scene is viewed using the Camera view, but by using the View, Direction menu options, you can view the scene from the Front, Top, Right, Back, Bottom, and Left views. There is also an option to return the view to the Camera view.

> **Note**
>
> The View, Direction menu options are only available in Anime Studio Pro.

When one of these other views is selected, the camera is shown as a triangle with an arrow projected from it. Figure 25.6 shows the Front view of the scene, making the camera icon visible. When you use the various camera tools while viewing the project from one of the different directions, you'll see the camera icon move.

> **Tip**
>
> You can tell when a different view is being used because the working area border isn't visible.

> **Caution**
>
> If the scene objects haven't been rotated and are viewed from the top, left, right, or bottom, they will appear as a single straight line.

> **Note**
>
> The View, Reset menu command has no effect on camera movements. This command is only used to reset actions done with the Workspace tools.

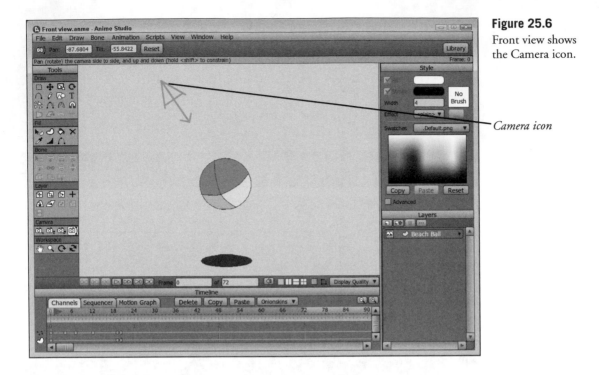

Figure 25.6
Front view shows
the Camera icon.

Camera icon

Using Depth Sort

When a project includes multiple layers, the layers appear in both the working area and in the rendered project based on their position in the Layers palette with layers at the top of the Layers palette appearing above any lower layers that are overlapped. This is the default behavior, but using the Translate Layer tool (1) while holding down the Alt/Opt key causes the layer to move backward along the Z-axis.

The relative position along the Z-axis of the various layers is clearly visible if you change the view to the top or side using the View, Direction, Top menu command. The layers will be a straight line when viewed from this perspective unless the camera has been tilted, but you still will be able to tell that the layers are different distances from the front camera.

If you open the Project Settings dialog box, found in the File menu, you'll see that there is an option to Sort Layers by Depth. If this option is enabled, then the layer content is displayed based on its depth from the camera. Next to the Sort Layers by Depth is another option to Sort Layers by Distance. This option is only available if the Sort Layers by Depth option is enabled, and it determines the layer's stacking order based on the layer's origin from the camera. This is helpful when the layers are rotating.

> **Note**
>
> The Sort Layers by Depth and Sort Layers by Distance options are also available for a group. Check out Chapter 23, "Organizing Layers into Groups," for more information on group layers.

To layer content by depth, follow these steps:

1. Open the Desert scene.anme file from the Chapter 25 folder on the CD. This file includes four layers for the cactus, the rock, the sun, and the background. Notice in Figure 25.7 that the cactus is displayed in front of the rock, the sun, and the background because it is positioned at the top of the Layers palette.

Figure 25.7
The top layer appears in front of the other layers.

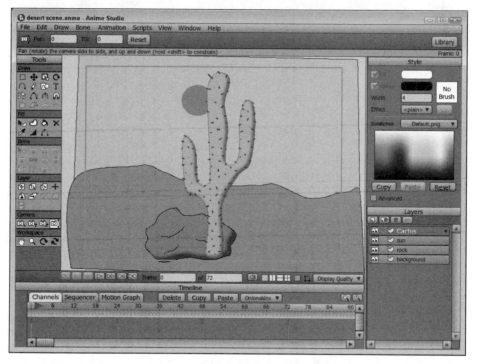

2. Select the background layer in the Layers palette and choose the Translate Layer tool (1). Then hold down the Shift key and drag in the working area to push the background layer content back into the scene. The background will get smaller as it is pushed backward.

3. Select the cactus layer in the Layers palette, and with the Translate Layer tool (1), hold down the Shift key and drag in the working area to pull the cactus layer content forward. The background will get larger as it is pulled forward. Use the Scale Layer tool (2) to resize the cactus layer after moving it forward.

4. Repeat step 3 for the rock layer, but move it farther forward than the cactus layer. Even though the rock layer is closer to the camera than the cactus, the cactus is still on top of the rock.

5. Select each layer and with the Rotate Layer X tool, drag upward in the working area to tilt the layer slightly. Then choose the View, Direction, Top menu command. Notice how each layer is at a different distance from the camera, as shown in Figure 25.8.

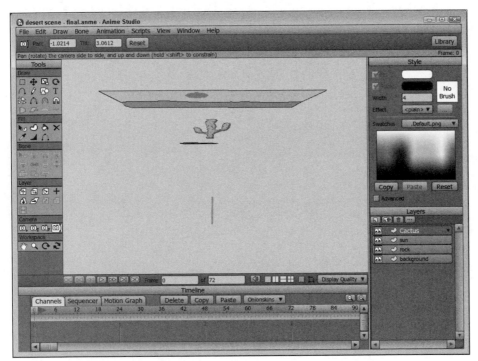

Figure 25.8

The Top view shows the distance of each layer from the camera.

6. Select the File, Project Settings menu command and enable the Sort Layers by Depth option and close the Project Settings dialog box. Select the View, Direction, Camera menu command to switch back to the camera view. Notice that the depth of each layer is controlling its visibility, making the rock appear in front of the cactus now, as shown in Figure 25.9.

Figure 25.9
The distance
from the camera
controls which
layers are visible.

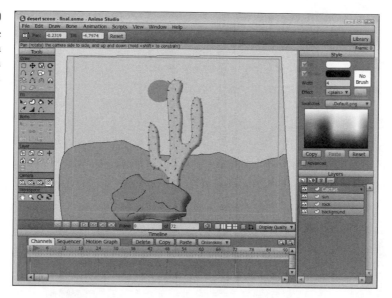

Using Camera Scripts

In the Scripts, Camera menu are two specialized scripts that work with cameras. The Handheld Camera script causes the camera to be animated with a random noise that simulates a shaky handheld camera. This is a special effect that can be used during animation. Selecting this script menu automatically creates all the keys that you need to create this behavior.

Note

The Scripts menu and all its contents are only available in Anime Studio Pro.

The second camera script is the Orbit Camera script. This script spins the camera about its origin. When this menu command is selected, an Orbit Camera dialog box, shown in Figure 25.10, opens with options to set the duration for a single revolution, a radius, and a checkbox for making the camera spin in the clockwise direction. Setting the Duration to a small value will cause the project to spin quickly and larger values will spin the project more slowly. The Radius value controls how far away from the origin the camera is located.

Figure 25.10
Orbit Camera
dialog box.

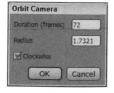

To automate the spinning of a project, follow these steps:

1. Open the Top.anme file from the Chapter 25 folder on the CD. This file includes a single 2D layer of a top.

2. Select the top layer and choose the Scripts, Camera, Orbit Camera menu command. In the Orbit Camera dialog box, set the Duration to 15 and the Radius to 1.5 and close the dialog box. Keys are automatically added to the Timeline palette.

3. Click the Play button in the bottom-left corner of the main interface to see the top spinning about, as shown in Figure 25.11.

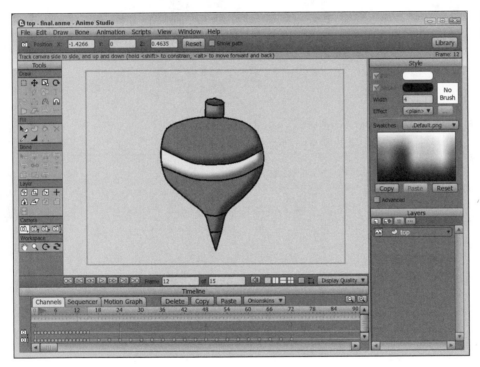

Figure 25.11
Spinning top.

4. If you select the View, Direction, Top menu command to switch to the top view, you'll see that the top layer is actually standing still and the camera is being animated moving about the stationary top.

Rotating a Layer to Face the Camera

One of the benefits of using 3D cameras is that they can be animated. For example, if your scene includes a 3D object, you can animate the camera easily by moving around the 3D object to see it from all sides. When such a motion is performed on a 2D object, however, the 2D object becomes skewed and eventually turns into a line when you look at the object from the side.

You can fix this behavior by enabling the Rotate to Face Camera option in the Layer Settings dialog box. When this option is enabled, the layer is automatically rotated to stay perpendicular to the camera, so as the camera moves, the 2D layer remains flat and visible. A 2D object that faces the camera at all times is often called a *sprite*.

> **Tip**
>
> Enabling the Rotate to Face Camera option for background objects like trees and mountains is a great way to make sure that a 2D background stays consistent as the camera moves.

To make a layer rotate with the camera, follow these steps:

1. Open the Top on table.anme file from the Chapter 25 folder on the CD. This file is the file created at the end of the last tutorial with the top spinning.

2. Click the New Layer button in the Layers palette to create a new layer. Name the new layer "tabletop" and drag the layer below the top layer.

3. Click a brown color in the Style swatches to change the fill color and then select the Rectangle tool (E) and drag in the working area to create a filled rectangle over the bottom portion of the top.

4. Click the Play button in the bottom-left corner of the main interface to see the top and the tabletop spinning around.

5. Double-click the tabletop layer and enable the Rotate to Face Camera option in the Layer Settings dialog box. Then close the Layer Settings dialog box.

6. Click the Play button again and notice how the table doesn't appear to be rotating with the top anymore, as shown in Figure 25.12.

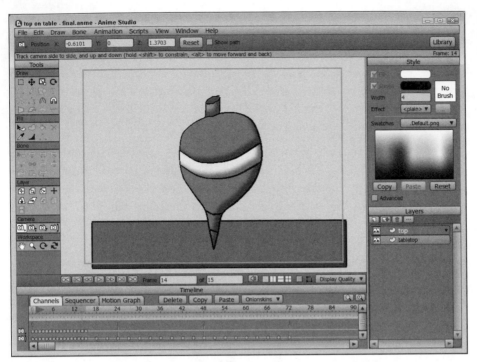

Figure 25.12
Spinning top with stationary table.

7. If you select the View, Direction, Top menu command to switch to the top view, you'll see that the top layer is still standing still and the table is rotating along with the camera.

Making a Layer Immune from Camera Movements

The Layer Settings dialog box also includes an option called Immune to Camera Movements, which makes the current layer ignore any camera movements. When this option is enabled, all objects on the current layer stay in their current position and orientation regardless of how the camera is moved, like a sticker that is placed on the camera lens.

> **Tip**
>
> Enabling the Immune to Camera Movements option in the Layer Settings dialog box is perfect for project names or logos that are placed in the corner of the scene.

Note

Even if you change the view using the View, Direction menu, layers that are immune to Camera Movements are still visible.

Caution

Layers that are grouped within another layer cannot be set to be immune to camera movements. This is common for text. To resolve this, just move the text out of its group layer.

Chapter Summary

This chapter introduced the various 3D camera tools and showed how they can be used to track, zoom, roll, pan, and tilt the camera in 3D space. We also looked at the various options that impact the camera's control over the current layer and the camera scripts that make it possible to simulate a handheld camera and to orbit the camera around a point.

The next chapter is a critical one that introduces working with bones. Bones are common among 3D packages for controlling 3D models, but Anime Studio is unique in how it can use bones to tween 2D vector-based drawings, and just think, it is coming up next.

26

Creating and Binding Bones

- Understanding bones and skeletons
- Working with hierarchies and FK
- Drawing objects to use with bones
- Using the Bone tools
- Binding to bones

Bones are nonrenderable objects that are contained within—and control a specified layer of—a group of points. Using bones lets you control the transformation of a group of points without having to move each individual point separately, thereby providing a way to quickly animate objects in your scene.

Bones are connected to other bones to form a hierarchical skeleton. This skeleton allows children bones to move automatically with their parents, but also allows the children bones to be moved independently of their parents.

Once a skeleton of bones is created, you'll need to bind each bone to a selection of points that the bone controls. This can be done using automatic binding or manual binding. Each method has its advantages.

The Bone tools found in the Tools palette let you create and connect new bones, move and manipulate bones, and bind the selected bone to a layer or to a selection of points. The Timeline palette includes several channels for working with bones. This chapter covers the process of creating and binding bones, and the next chapter covers animating with bones.

Understanding Bones and Skeletons

Bone objects are common in 3D. They are typically used as a method to control the motion and position of a group of 3D points without having to move the points individually. Bones are not rendered; they are only included as guides to manipulate the character. Anime Studio uses bones in a similar manner to 3D packages, but there are some differences.

When many bones are combined together, they form a skeleton, which is hierarchically organized with parent and children bones. All bones are parented under a root bone that controls the entire character. While bones and skeletons are common in the 3D world, they can be scaled to the 2D world and are quite revolutionary.

All bones are included on a separate bone layer, which makes them easy to locate and manipulate. Bone layers, like group layers, can hold several sublayers.

Working with Hierarchies and Forward Kinematics (FK)

One of the key features of bones is their ability to be parented to other bone objects. By creating a hierarchy of bones, you can control all the bones in the skeleton by simply moving the root bone. The *root bone* is the bone that is at the top of the hierarchy, and it is the parent of all the other bones.

A parent bone can have several children attached to it so that moving the parent bone automatically causes the children to move with their parent. Children bones, however, can move without altering their parents. This allows a parent bone located at the shoulder, for example, to control the movement of all the rest of the arm bones, but the forearm bone can still move independently of the shoulder.

The ability of a parent bone to control its children bones is called *forward kinematics*, or FK for short. Using FK, Anime Studio can calculate the movement of children bones when the parent bone moves by using the connection between the two bones.

Drawing Objects to Be Used with Bones

Bones can be used to control layers and points. If a bone controls a layer, the rotation point for the layer is defined by the bone's base point. Having a bone control an entire layer keeps the layer from being deformed as the bone moves.

However, if the bone is bound to a selection of points, then the way the vector object is drawn will determine how the object is distorted when the bones are moved. When drawing objects that will be controlled by bones, try to keep the curves smooth. Any sharp points located near the bone joint will be distorted when the bones are moved, which will cause the fill to overlap on itself.

> **Tip**
>
> If you are using bones to control a layer, the layer could be a vector or an image layer.

Using the Bone Tools

Within the Tools palette is a special section of tools for working with bones. The Bone tools, shown in Figure 26.1, are only activated when a bone layer is selected in the Layers palette. To create a bone layer, click the New Layer button at the top of the Layers palette and select the Bone option from the pop-up menu. Bone layers can hold sublayers. To add a layer to a bone layer, simply drag the layer and drop it on the bone layer in the Layers palette.

Adding Bones

With a bone layer selected, you can begin to add bones to the scene using the Add Bones tool (A). To add a bone, simply click and drag in the working area. Bones are triangular shaped, as shown in Figure 26.2, with a thick portion at one end tapering to a point at the opposite end. The thicker portion represents the jointed end or base of the bone and the pointed end represents the bone's tip.

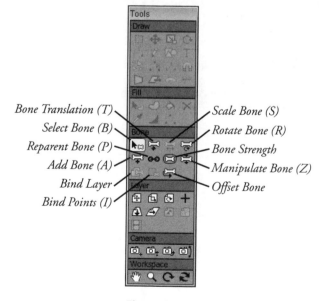

Bone Translation (T)
Select Bone (B)
Reparent Bone (P)
Add Bone (A)
Bind Layer
Bind Points (I)

Scale Bone (S)
Rotate Bone (R)
Bone Strength
Manipulate Bone (Z)
Offset Bone

Figure 26.1
Bone tools.

> **Caution**
>
> Bones are only visible in the main window when the Show Paths button at the bottom of the main window is enabled.

> **Caution**
>
> If the Enable Drawing Tools Only at Frame 0 option in the Preferences dialog box is enabled, then the Add Bone tool will be disabled if a frame other than 0 is selected.

> **Note**
>
> You may note that the Add Bones tool has the same keyboard shortcut as the Add Points tool. Both of these tools can share the same shortcut because the Add Points tool is only available when a vector layer is selected and the Add Bones tool is only available when a bone layer is selected.

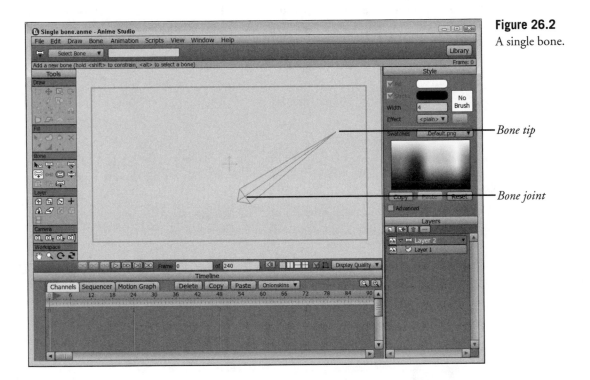

Figure 26.2
A single bone.

Bone tip

Bone joint

If you hold down the Shift key while creating a new bone, the new bone will be created at 45-degree increments.

Selecting Bones

After a group of bones is created, you can select the bone that you want to work with specifically by selecting the bone with the Select Bone tool (B). Bones will only be visible in the working area if the bone layer is selected in the Layers palette or one of the bone layer's sublayers is selected. To select a bone, simply click it. The selected bone turns red. If you hold down the Ctrl/Cmd key while clicking, you can select multiple bones at once.

> **Tip**
>
> When a bone is selected, it turns red and its parent bone turns blue.

Naming Bones

The selected bone can be named using the empty field located in the Options bar at the top of the working area. The bone name can be used when writing scripts to reference the bone.

> **Caution**
>
> Although bones can be selected when a bone sublayer is selected, bones can only be renamed when the bone layer is selected in the Layers palette.

> **Tip**
>
> Named bones can be selected from the Bone Constraints dialog box. To help keep all the bones you create organized, you should name every bone.

Anime Studio includes a preference that will automatically name every bone that is created. If you open the Edit, Preferences dialog box and enable the Auto-Name Bones and Shapes option, then every new bone is given a sequential number as its name. These numbers can be renamed with a more meaningful name if you select the bone layer.

Connecting Bones

If you drag to create another bone with the Add Bones tool (A) when an existing bone is selected, the new bone will be connected automatically to the existing bone as its child. Child bones can move independently of their parent, but when a parent bone is moved, the child moves with it.

By creating several bones in succession in a straight line, you can quickly create a linkage of bones that resembles a spine, as shown in Figure 26.3.

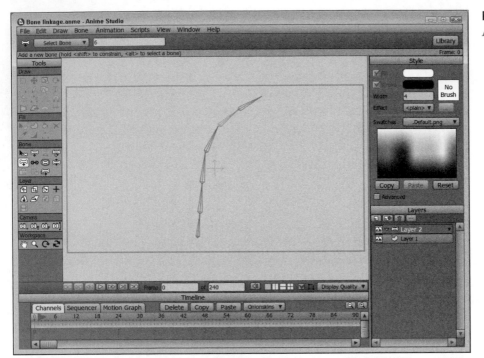

Figure 26.3
A linkage of bones.

Translating and Rotating Bones

Once a bone is created, you can move and rotate it to get it into the correct position using the Translate Bone tool (T). If you click the selected bone at its thick base, then the entire bone will move while maintaining its current orientation, but if you click near the bone's tip, you can drag to change the bone's orientation and even the bone's length.

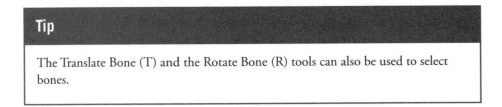

Tip

The Translate Bone (T) and the Rotate Bone (R) tools can also be used to select bones.

If you hold down the Shift key while moving a bone, the bone will be constrained to move only in the vertical or horizontal directions. If you drag a bone tip with the Shift key held down, then the bone's orientation will snap to 45-degree increments.

If you hold down the Shift key while dragging a child bone, the bone's movement will be constrained to the vertical and horizontal axes of the parent bone. This provides an easy way to align children bones at right angles to their parents.

If you want to rotate the selected bone without changing its length, you can use the Rotate Bone tool (R). This tool lets you rotate the bone regardless of where you click on the bone. Holding down the Shift key lets you rotate the bone at 45-degree increments.

Nudging Bones

If the Translate Bone tool (T) is selected, you can hold down the Ctrl/Cmd key and press the arrow keys to nudge the selected bone a small distance in the direction of the pressed arrow. Holding down the Ctrl/Cmd key with the Shift key nudges the bone a larger nudge distance. The actual nudge distance is 1 pixel for a short nudge and 10 pixels for a large nudge.

Reparenting Bones

If you create a parent-child connection that isn't correct, you can fix the linkage with the Reparent Bone tool (P). To use this tool, select a bone and click the tool. All parented bones in the current layer are identified by red arrows that point from the child bone to its parent, as shown in Figure 26.4. If you click a bone other than the one that is selected, the selected bone becomes the new parent to the original selected bone.

> **Note**
>
> You can make the selected bone a root bone without a parent if you click the working area with the Reparent Bone tool (P).

Copying and Pasting Bones

When a bone or multiple bones are selected in a bone layer, you can use the Edit, Cut (Ctrl/Cmd+X) or Edit, Copy (Ctrl/Cmd+C) menus to copy a duplicate of the selected bones. These copied bones can then be pasted onto another bone layer using the Edit, Paste (Ctrl/Cmd+V) command.

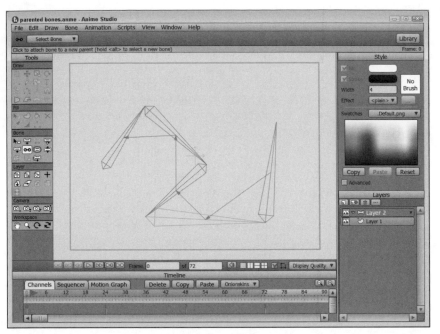

Figure 26.4
Red arrows identify parent bones.

Note

When working on bones, the Edit, Cut command doesn't remove the bones from the original layer but acts just like the Edit, Copy command.

New Feature

The ability to copy and paste bones between layers is new to Anime Studio 6.

Deleting Bones

To delete a selected bone, simply press the Delete key or the Backspace key. If a parent bone is deleted, then all its children are also deleted.

Note

Bones cannot be deleted when the Manipulate Bones tool (Z) is selected, but any tool that can select bones can also delete them.

Creating a Skeleton

Before you create a set of bones, it is helpful to have visible the layer of the objects that the bones will be controlling so that you can line the bones up correctly. Bones can control any type of layer including vectors, images, and 3D layers. To add a layer to a bone group so that it can be controlled by the bones, simply drag the layer and drop it on the bone layer in the Layers palette. By creating a linkage of bones that are parented, you can create a skeleton that will give you control over all the parts of the drawing layer.

To create a skeleton of bones to control a lizard character, follow these steps:

1. Open the Lizard with bones.anme file from the Chapter 26 folder on the CD. This file includes a single vector layer with a lizard stroke.

2. Click the New Layer button at the top of the Layers palette and select the Bone option from the pop-up menu to create a new bone layer.

3. With the bone layer selected in the Layers palette, click the Add Bone tool (A) and click the top of the lizard's head and drag to the lizard's neck to create a bone. Continue the bone chain that runs down the lizard's back and tail by clicking and dragging to create about seven bones.

4. Click the Select Bone tool (B) and select the head bone; then select the Add Bone tool (A) again and click and drag to create two arm bones. The new bone is automatically connected to the tip of the head bone. Repeat this step for the opposite arm.

5. Select the Select Bone tool (B) and choose the second bone, whose tip is located where the legs are connected. Then choose the Add Bone tool (A) again and create three bones that run the length of the leg. Then repeat this step for the opposite leg. Figure 26.5 shows the resulting bone structure over the lizard.

6. Select the vector layer that contains the lizard drawing and drop it on the bone layer in the Layers palette.

7. Select the Manipulate Bone tool (Z) and select and drag the created bones around to deform the lizard.

Note

When creating a skeleton of bones, be aware that children and parent bones do not need to be touching.

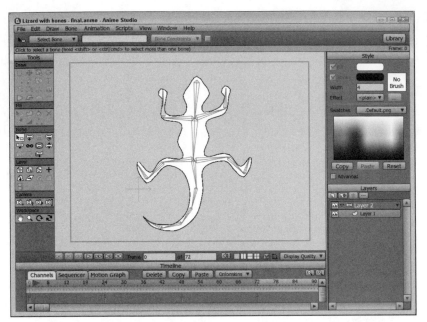

Figure 26.5
A skeleton of bones
for the lizard.

Binding to Bones

After you've created a skeleton that matches the shape of the objects that the bones will control, you need to bind the bones to the object. This can be done by using Anime Studio's automatic binding feature or manually if you want more control. If you elect to manually bind the points to the bone, then you have the option of binding either the layer or the points. Once bound, the selected points or layer will move when the bone is moved.

Using Automatic Flexible Binding

Automatic binding, which is also known as flexible binding, occurs whenever you add bones to a bone layer and place the matching sublayer of content within the bone layer. You can test out the automatic binding by selecting the Manipulate Bones tool (Z) and dragging the bones around. As you move the bones, the bound objects will move with the bones, as shown in Figure 26.6.

> **Note**
>
> When the Manipulate Bones tool (Z) is selected, each bone is surrounded by a shaded area that shows the bone strength.

Tip

The Manipulate Bones tool (Z) impacts all bones within the skeleton. If you want to isolate the movement or rotation of a single bone, use the Translate Bone tool (T) or the Rotate Bone tool (R).

Figure 26.6
A tree with flexible binding.

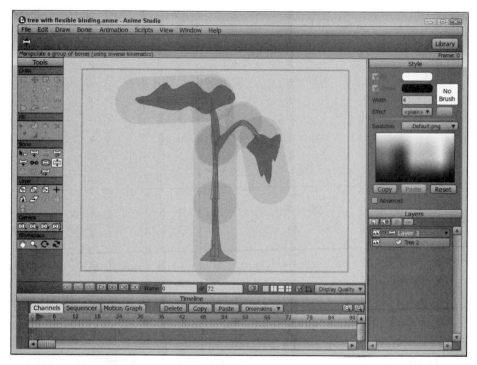

Flexible binding works well as a first start, but it has an effect over all points in the sublayer. The points that are closest to the bone will move the most and the points farther away will move only a small amount if at all. This type of binding works fine if each of the bones moves in a separate direction, but if two bones are fairly close to one another, then moving one bone will pull at the points near it even if they belong to another part of the object. Figure 26.7 shows this problem. Some flexible bound bones were added to the lion's tail, but the tail is close to head, so moving the tail bones also moves the points at the top of the lion's head resulting in some undesirable deformation.

> **Tip**
>
> Flexible binding works best when all the bones point in different directions, and it should be avoided if the bones run parallel to each other or if two bones are fairly close to one another.

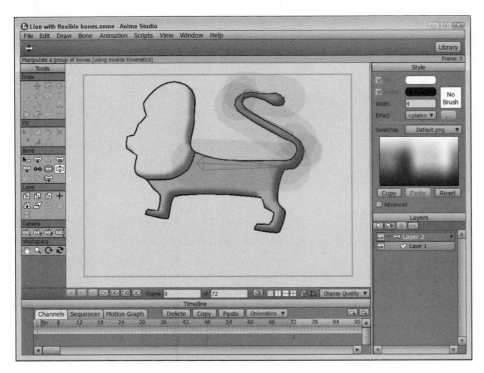

Figure 26.7
Flexible binding moves all points near the moved bone.

Using Automatic Region Binding

Flexible binding is the default option, but if you select the Bones panel in the Layer Settings dialog box, shown in Figure 26.8, you can enable the Region Binding option. The Bones panel is only available when a bone layer is selected in the Layers palette.

When the Region Binding option is selected in the Bones panel of the Layer Settings dialog box, then only those points within the shaded area that surrounds the bone are moved with the bone. This binding option lets you control which points get moved with the bone.

Figure 26.8

The Bones panel.

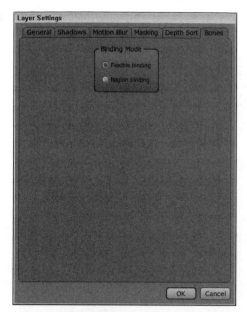

The shaded influence area that surrounds the bone is called the *bone strength*, and it can be altered using the Bone Strength tool. When this tool is selected, you can drag in the working area to increase or decrease the size of the strength area around the bone. Points near the bone's base will be within one or more bone strength areas. These points are influenced by each of the bones that it is within.

Caution

If you adjust the bone strength area, be careful not to make the area too small. If some points get left out of the area, they will be left behind when the bone moves.

To alter the bone strength for the bones of a tree, follow these steps:

1. Open the Tree with region binding.anme file from the Chapter 26 folder on the CD. This file includes a tree object with several bones for controlling its movement.

2. Click the Manipulate Bones tool (Z) and drag the lower limb's bone. Notice how the upper tree branch moves with the lower branch. Select the Edit, Undo menu command (Ctrl/Cmd+Z) to undo the movement.

3. Double-click the bone layer in the Layers palette to open the Layer Settings dialog box. Open the Bones panel and select the Region Binding option; then close the Layer Settings dialog box.

4. Select the Bone Strength tool and click and drag on the upper tree branch's bone. Resize the bone strength area until it just contains the tree branch object, as shown in Figure 26.9. Repeat this step for the other bones.

5. Select the Manipulate Bones tool (Z) again and drag on the lower limb's bone. Notice how the movement is focused to only the limb this time

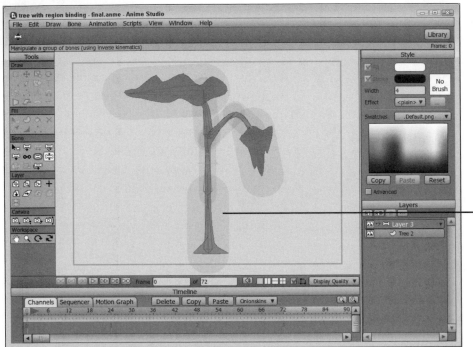

Figure 26.9
Tree with region binding.

—Bone strength area

Manually Binding Layers

All objects in the current layer can be manually bound to a bone using the Bind Layer tool. To use this tool, just select a bone and a layer that is a sublayer of the bone layer and click the Bind Layer tool. Once bound, the entire layer and all its contents will move and rotate along with the bone. Figure 26.10 shows a clock on which each hand is controlled by a bone. Because each clock hand doesn't need to be parented to the other, the clock actually includes two bone layers with a layer for each hand. This lets the hands move independently around the center of the clock.

> **Note**
>
> Each layer can only be bound to a single bone at a time.

> **Caution**
>
> Binding layers to a bone works well if you are controlling an image layer with a bone, because they are less likely to distort when the entire layer is moving and rotating together.

Figure 26.10
Clock hands controlled with bones.

Manually Binding Points

If the vector layer includes multiple points, you can use the Bind Points tool (I) to select and bind specific points to a specific bone. To use this tool, first select a bone, and then within the vector layer, choose the points that you want to be bound to the selected bone with the Bind Points tool. If you hold down the Ctrl/Cmd key, you can access the Lasso tool to select points.

> **Caution**
>
> The Bind Points tool will only be available when the vector sublayer is selected.

After all the points you want to bind are selected, you need to press the Spacebar or click the Bind Points button in the Options bar at the top of the working area to complete the binding.

To manually bind points to a gingerbread man character, follow these steps:

1. Open the Gingerbread man.anme file from the Chapter 26 folder on the CD. This file includes a simple gingerbread man character with several bones added to it.

2. Choose the Select Bone tool (B) and click the head bone to select it. Then choose the vector sublayer in the Layers panel and drag over all the head and face points with the Select Points tool (G). Select the Bind Points tool (I) and press the Spacebar to bind the points to the selected bone.

3. Repeat step 2 for each of the remaining bones being careful to only attach the points closest to the selected bone.

4. Click the Manipulate Bones tool (Z) and drag the gingerbread man's limbs. Notice how only the bound points move with the bone, as shown in Figure 26.11.

Figure 26.11
Manually bound points.

> **Note**
>
> If the selected bone already has bound points, then when you select the Select Bone tool (B), the bound points are displayed.

Manipulating Bones

After a layer or points are bound to a bone, you can move the bones around using the Manipulate Bones tool (Z). If you click a bone with this tool, the bone is selected, and you'll be able to rotate the bone tip by dragging in the working area. When this tool is selected, the area of influence of each bone is displayed as a semi-transparent area that surrounds the bone.

> **Note**
>
> When manipulating bones at frame 0, the skeleton is automatically reset when another tool is selected.

Adjusting Bone Strength

The bone strength area is designated by a semi-transparent area that surrounds the bone. This area is visible for all bones when the Manipulate Bones tool (Z) or the Bone Strength tool is selected. This area denotes the bone strength and can be altered using the Bone Strength tool. All points that are contained within this area will be moved with the bone and any points outside of this area will remain in their position when the bone is moved. With this tool, you can drag in the working area to change the influence area of the selected bone. You can change the bone strength using the Bone Strength field in the Options bar. Figure 26.12 shows the bone strength for the left leg being reduced.

> **Note**
>
> The Bone Strength tool is only available when a bone layer is selected in the Layers palette.

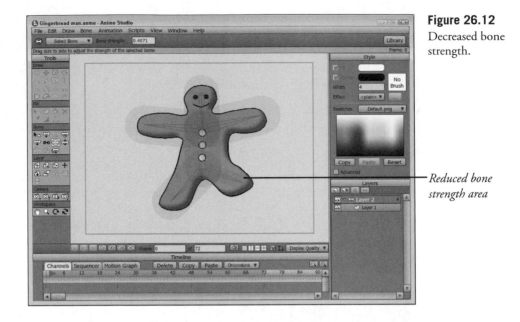

Figure 26.12
Decreased bone strength.

Reduced bone strength area

Releasing Layers and Points

If you select a set of points that you want to release from its current bound bone, you can use the Bone, Release Points menu command or the Bone, Release Layer menu command. Once a layer or a set of points is released, it will no longer be controlled by the bone.

Reapplying Automatic Binding

If you use the Bind Points or the Bind Layer tools to manually bind the bones and then decide that you want to use the automatic binding method instead, you can choose the vector sublayer and select the points to apply a flexible binding to and choose the Bone, Flex-Bind Points or the Flex-Bind Layer menu command. This throws away the manual binding for the selected points or layer and reapplies the automatic flexible binding to the selection.

Chapter Summary

This chapter introduced the bone features available in Anime Studio. Using the Bone tools, you can create bones quickly and connect them to create skeletons. These hierarchical skeletons can then be bound to layers and points to aid in animating a character using either automatic or manual binding features. Now that you understand how to create and bind bones to 2D objects, the next chapter digs even deeper into bones showing how they are used to animate your scenes.

27

Animating with Bones

- Transforming bones
- Resetting and locking bones
- Using bone constraints
- Animating with bone dynamics
- Warping with bones

The previous chapter discussed creating bones and binding the bones to points and layers. This chapter continues the discussion of bones and shows how objects are animated using bones.

Animating with Bones

When animating with bones, it is important to remember that at frame 0, you are only in setup mode. Changes you make to the bone structure during setup mode don't affect the keys or animation. However, if you alter the skeleton at any frame other than 0, then a set of keys will be created for the change. Working with keys and the Timeline palette is covered in more detail in Part IV, "Animating in Anime Studio."

> **Note**
>
> Any bone movement changes made with the Manipulate Bones tool (Z) while at frame 0 will automatically be reset when another tool is selected.

Moving Bones

When any frame except frame 0 is selected, moving, scaling, or rotating bones will result in a new key being added to the Timeline. Moving a bone as part of an animation will cause all the bound points to be stretched away from the rest of the object, as shown in Figure 27.1.

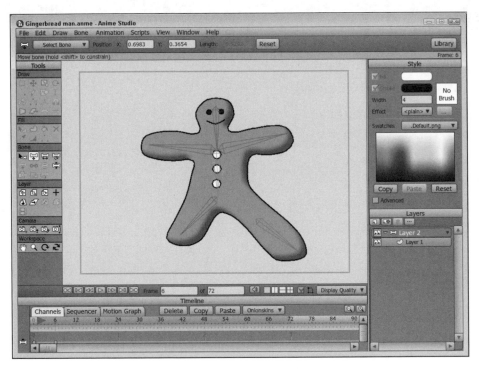

Figure 27.1
Moving a bone.

Scaling and Rotating Bones

When you begin to animate a bone by moving to a frame other than frame 0, the Scale Bone tool (S) becomes active and available. Dragging on a bone with this tool causes the length of the bone to increase, which results in the object being stretched to accommodate the new length, as shown in Figure 27.2.

Figure 27.2
Scaling a bone.

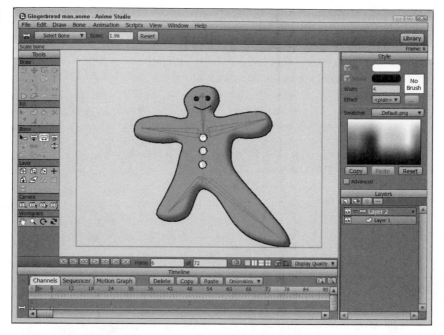

The Rotate Bone tool (R) rotates the bone tip around its base.

Note

When animating bones, the Rotate Bone tool (R) works the same as the Manipulate Bone tool (Z).

Resetting Bones

If you change your mind about the animation of a single bone at a specific key, you can use the Bone, Reset Bone menu command to return the bone's position and orientation to its original location as defined by the setup found in frame 0.

If you want to reset all bones to the default setup, you can use the Bone, Reset All Bones menu command.

Locking Bones

When the Select Bone tool (B) is selected, the Options bar at the top of the working area includes an option to Lock Bone. If you enable this option, the bone becomes frozen in its current position and remains there until you uncheck the Lock Bone option. This option can also be animated.

Handling Overlapping Fills

When a filled object that is being controlled by bones is bent back on itself, the overlapped sections will be cleared of any fill, leaving a gap in the object, as shown on the leg in Figure 27.3. This can be fixed by splitting the single filled object into two filled objects.

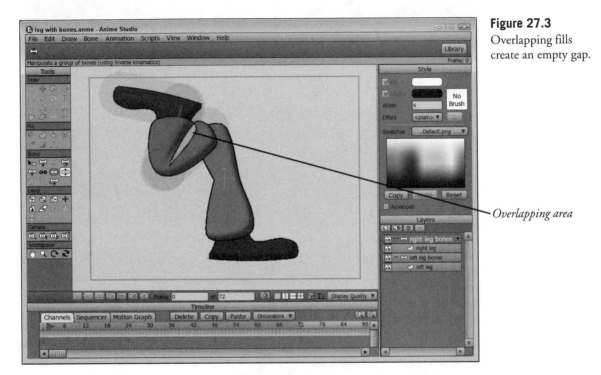

Figure 27.3
Overlapping fills create an empty gap.

Overlapping area

To eliminate an open gap created by overlapping filled sections, follow these steps:

1. Open the Leg with bones.anme file from the Chapter 27 folder on the CD. This file shows a simple set of legs with bones added to the legs for controlling their movement. If you select the Manipulate Bones tool (Z) and bend the leg backward, the fill overlaps itself, thereby producing an empty gap.

2. Select the right leg layer in the Layers palette and hide the left leg and left leg bone layers. Then choose the Add Points tool (A) and draw a new line that separates the leg into two pieces. Make sure the Auto-Weld option is enabled so that the new line is connected to the existing lines.

3. Select the Select Shape tool (Q) and click on the leg's shape to select it. Then click the Copy button in the Style palette to save the existing fill color.

4. With the leg shape still selected, select the Edit, Clear menu command to remove the fill from the existing leg.

5. Select the Create Shape tool (U), click one of the points of the upper leg shape, and hold down the Shift key and select all the points that make up the upper leg. When the checkered pattern appears, click the Paste button in the Style palette to apply the original fill color to the new shape.

6. Repeat step 5 for the lower leg shape.

7. Select the Hide Edge tool (H) and click the line that separates the two leg shapes to remove its stroke.

8. Select the left leg bone layer and delete it from the Layers palette. Then select the right leg bone layer and click the Duplicate Layer button in the Layers palette and rename the new layers "left leg bone" and "left leg."

9. Select the Manipulate Bone tool (Z) and drag the lower leg bone until the leg bends over itself, as shown in Figure 27.4. This time there is no empty gap.

Figure 27.4
Overlapping gap
is removed.

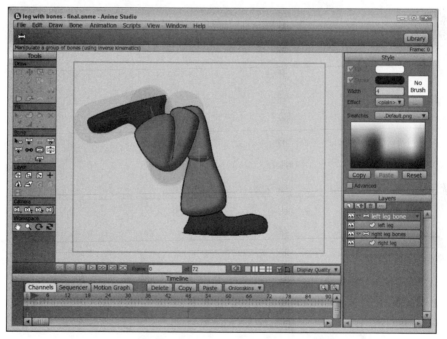

Setting Bone Constraints

Another option that is enabled when the Select Bone tool (B) is selected is the Bone Constraints button. This button opens the pop-up dialog box of options shown in Figure 27.5. The Angle Constraints option lets you set minimum and maximum rotations that the bone can make. This provides a way to limit the movement of the selected bone.

> **Tip**
>
> The Angle Constraints setting is useful for ensuring that legs and arms don't bend backward.

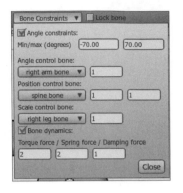

Figure 27.5
Bone Constraints dialog box.

When a constraint is applied to a bone, a red constraint line is placed at the bone joint to mark the bone's limits, as shown in Figure 27.6.

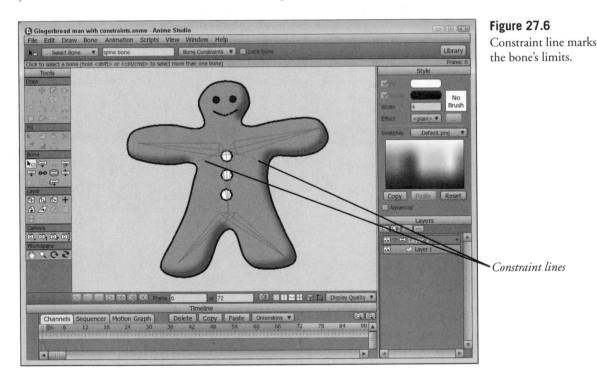

Figure 27.6
Constraint line marks the bone's limits.

Constraint lines

To constrain a leg bone so that it doesn't move unnaturally, follow these steps:

1. Open the Constrain leg bone.anme file from the Chapter 27 folder on the CD. This file shows a simple set of legs with bones added to the legs for controlling their movement. If you select the Manipulate Bones tool (Z) and bend the lower leg bone forward, the leg moves in an unnatural way, as shown in Figure 27.7.

Figure 27.7
The leg bends
unnaturally.

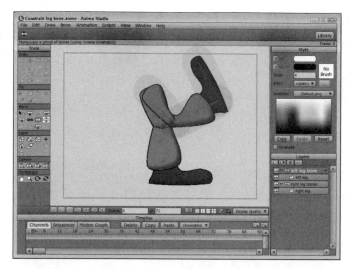

2. Click the Select Bone tool (B) and select the lower leg bone. Then click the Bone Constraints button at the top of the Working Area and enable the Angle Constraints option. When the Angle Constraints option is enabled, two lines are shown at the base of the selected bone to show the current constraints.

3. Change the Min/Max values to –130 and 20. The constraint lines are updated in the Working Area.

4. Select the Manipulate Bone tool (Z) and drag the lower leg bone to test the resulting constraints. If they don't look right, adjust the constraint values until the limits are correct. Figure 27.8 shows the leg being bent to one of its constraint limits.

Figure 27.8
The leg now
has limits.

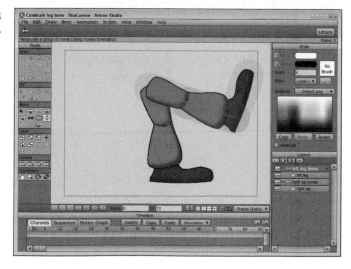

Using Control Bones

Even more powerful are the options to select a control bone to control the angle, position, or scale of the selected bone. The value field to the right of the selected control bone is a multiplier that amplifies the affected change. This multiplier value can be set to 1 for a movement that is equal to the control bone, to 0.5 for movement that is half the control bone, to 2.0 for movement that is double the control bone, or even -1 for movement that is opposite the control bone.

Tip

The control bones will only work for named bones.

The two values next to the Position Control Bone option affect movement in the X direction and in the Y direction separately.

To make the rotation of one bone control the rotation of another bone, follow these steps:

1. Open the Constrained clock.anme file from the Chapter 27 folder on the CD. This file includes a simple clock with large and small hands that are bound to rotate with the clock hand bones. The hands are set to 12 and 3.

2. Click the Select Bone tool (B) and select the large hand pointing to 12. In the Options bar, type in the name "large hand." Then select the small hand pointing to the 3 and name it "small hand."

3. With the large hand selected, click the Bone Constraints button in the Options bar. Click the Angle Control Bone drop-down list and select the Small Hand option and set the value to 12. Then close the Bone Constraints dialog box.

4. Select the Manipulate Bone tool (Z) and drag the tip of the small hand to rotate it around the clock. The large hand rotates along with the small hand, only it spins 12 times as fast just like a real clock, as shown in Figure 27.9.

> **Tip**
>
> When defining control bones, make sure that the control bone is not parented to the bones it is controlling.

To make the position of the hand bone control the kite's position, follow these steps:

1. Open the Flying kite.anme file from the Chapter 27 folder on the CD. This file includes a simple project with a kite and the hand of a person flying the kite. Bones have been added to the kite and the person's hand.

2. Click the Select Bone tool (B) and select the kite bone and name it "kite bone." Then select the small hand, and name it "hand bone."

Figure 27.9
The large clock
hand is controlled
by the small hand.

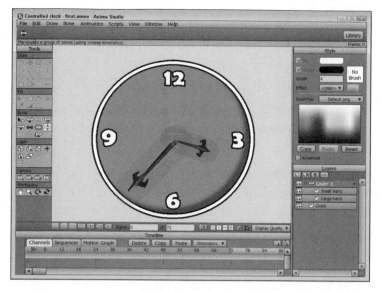

3. With the kite bone selected, open the Bone Constraints dialog box by click-ing the button on the Options bar. For the Position Control Bone, select the hand bone option and set the position values to 10 and 6.

4. With the bone layer selected, drag the Time Slider to a frame other than frame 0; then choose the Translate Bone tool (T) and drag the hand bone around. The kite will move to follow the hand only to a greater extent, as shown in Figure 27.10.

Figure 27.10
The kite follows
the movements
of the hand.

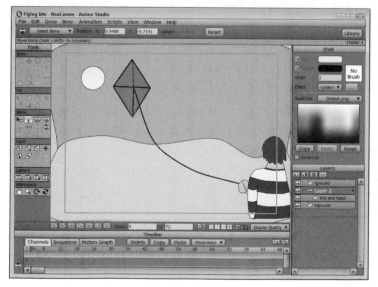

Using Bone Dynamics

The task of animating usually focuses on the main, or primary, motions such as the legs and feet moving when a character walks, but realistic motion can be enhanced by looking for secondary motions like a ponytail swinging back and forth and the jostling of a backpack. These types of motions can be enabled by turning on the Bone Dynamics feature in the Bone Constraints dialog box.

After the Bone Dynamics feature is enabled, all child bones will react automatically with secondary motion when the parent bone is moved. For example, when a dog wags its tail back and forth, the bones at the end of the tail will rotate beyond the small rotation of the parent, causing a wagging effect when dynamics are enabled. The bone chain in Figure 27.11 consists of simply moving the top bone back and forth. Because Bone Dynamics is enabled, the children bones swing back and forth with momentum.

Bone dynamics are controlled by three values:

- **Torque Force:** This is the force applied to the child bone when the parent bone changes direction when moving.

- **Spring Force:** This is the force applied to the child bone when the parent bone changes its rotational direction.

- **Damping Force:** This is the force that limits the motion of the child bone, causing its secondary motion to die out more quickly, like a shock absorber.

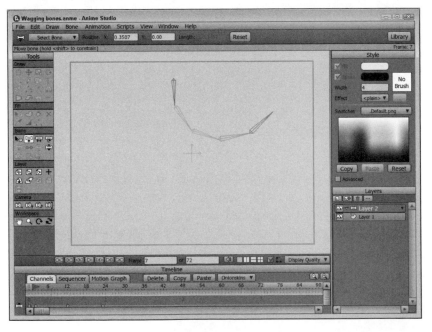

Figure 27.11
Bone Dynamics enabled.

To endow the kite's tail with dynamic bones, follow these steps:

1. Open the Flying kite with tail.anme file from the Chapter 27 folder on the CD. This file is an extension of the previous tutorial. For this project, the kite has been given a tail and four new bones to control the tail's movement. The tail bones are parented to the main kite bone.

2. Drag the Time Slider to frame 1 to see the kite, its tail, and the tail's bones. Then select the bone layer in the Layers palette.

3. Choose the Select Bone tool (B) and select the first tail bone. Open the Bone Constraints dialog box and enable the Bone Dynamics option. Set the Torque Force to 2, the Spring Force to 2, and the Damping Force to 1. Repeat this step for each of the tail's bones. Then close the Bone Constraints dialog box.

4. Select the Transform Bone tool (T). Select and move the hand bone to the left of the working area. Then drag the Time Slider to frame 12 and move the hand bone to the right of the working area. This automatically creates the necessry keyframes to animate the kite, but it also causes the tail to dynamically whip back and forth as the kite moves. Create some additional keyframes for the kite's movement.

5. Click the Play button in the lower-left corner of the main window to see the resulting animation. The kite tail whips around as the kite moves, as shown in Figure 27.12.

Figure 27.12
The kite tail whips around as the kite moves.

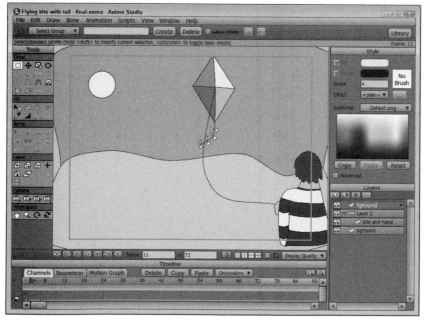

Offsetting Bones

When animating complex bone skeletons that have a lot of bones, it can sometimes be tricky to identify where all the bones and their bound layers are located. The Bone Offset tool lets you enter a mode that defines the beginning positions of all the bones at frame 1. These positions can be different from the bone positions at frame 0.

So using the Bone Offset tool, you can position the bones exactly where they need to be for the animation, and then using frame 0, you can place the bones where they are organized and easy to select with gaps between them.

Note

The Bone Offset tool is only available when the Timeline is set to frame 0.

One common way to set up a character to work with bones is to place each of the different body parts separate from one another, as shown for the default Winsor character in Figure 27.13. Once each of the independent layers is bound to a set of bones and the bone strength areas are set, you can use the Bone Offset tool to position each of the body parts where they should be for animating, as shown pieced together in Figure 27.14.

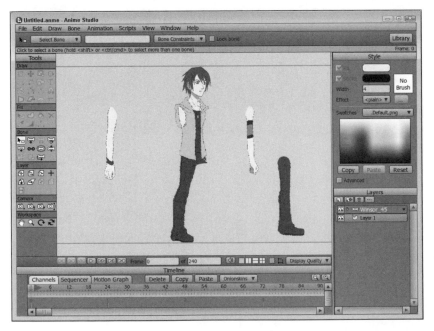

Figure 27.13
The Winsor character as separate parts.

> **Note**
>
> You can find the Winsor character in the Anime Studio 5 Content Library.

Figure 27.14
The Winsor character pieced together.

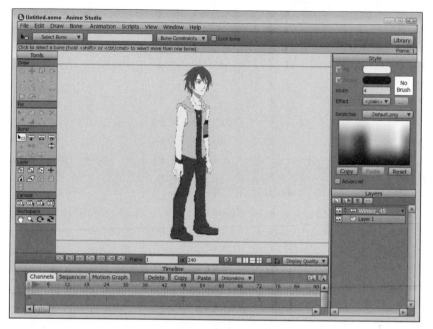

After the Offset Bone tool is used to position the body parts, the character will automatically assume these positions when the Manipulate Bones tool (Z) is active at frame 0 or whenever a non-0 frame is selected. When any other tool is selected at frame 0, the body parts will move to their separated state. This provides a way to work with the bones either together or apart.

Warping with Bones

There are a couple unique ways to use bones to control the warping of a bound layer. Once a layer is bound to a bone system, the bones can be manipulated to create a warp field or to define how the object moves. Although layer warping can be accomplished using a chain of bones, you'll have more control over the warping by using a set of independent bones that aren't parented to one another.

To create a set of independent bones, you simply need to click the background with the Select Bone (B) tool to deselect the current bone after each bone is created. You can check to see if any bones are parented by selecting the Reparent Bone (P) tool. Any parented bones will show a red arrow from the child bone to its parent. To remove any parenting, just select the bone that has a parent and click the background away from the other bones with the Reparent Bone tool.

Creating a Warp Field

The key to defining a warp field is to place the bones at frame 0 to represent an undistorted view of the layer that you want to distort. The bones should be placed so that the bone's base is located at the rotation point for the warp. Then at frame 1, rotate the bones to create the warp. The change between the bone's orientation at frame 1 will automatically be applied to any sublayers under the bone layer.

> **Note**
>
> This technique is similar to the technique presented in Chapter 22, "Adding Image Layers."

To warp a bone sublayer, follow these steps:

1. Open the American Flag.anme file from the Chapter 27 folder on the CD. This file is a simple image layer of a flag.

2. Click the New Layer button in the Layers palette and create a new bone layer. Select and drag the image layer and drop it on the new bone layer to make it a sublayer.

3. Select the bone layer, select the Add Bone (A) tool, and drag from the lower-left corner of the flag to the top of the flag to create a single vertically-oriented bone. Choose the Select Bone (B) tool and click away from the other bone to deselect the first bone. Then with the Add Bone tool, drag from the lower-right corner to the top of the flag to create a second vertically oriented bone.

4. Set the frame to frame 1 in the Timeline palette and choose the Manipulate Bones (Z) tool and drag the tip of each bone to the right. Figure 27.15 shows the resulting warped image.

In addition to changing the bone's orientation by rotating the bones, you can also move the bones from their original position to stretch the image in the direction of the bone's movement. The Bone Strength can also be adjusted to change the area around the bone that is affected by the bone's change.

Figure 27.15
Warped image.

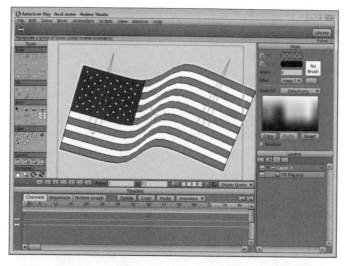

Defining a Motion Path

Since the Bone sublayer will automatically be warped with the bones, you can also use a set of bones to create a motion path for the sublayer to follow. The key is to lay out the original set of bones is a straight line in frame 0 and animate the movement of sublayer with the Translate Layer tool following the set of bones. Then in frame 1, you can move the bones, and the moving sublayer will be distorted to follow the manipulated bones.

> **Tip**
>
> This technique will work with a chain of parented bones or with a set of individual bones. The only difference is that the unparented bones will give you more control over the bone's placement.

To use bones to define a motion path, follow these steps:

1. Open the Following a path of bones.anme file from the Chapter 27 folder on the CD. This file shows a simple amoeba character.

2. Click the New Layer button in the Layers palette and create a new bone layer. Select and drag the vector layer and drop it on the new bone layer to make it a sublayer.

3. Select the bone layer, select the Add Bone (A) tool, and drag from the middle of the character to the left, creating a chain of six parented bones that extend in a straight line to the right edge of the working area.

4. Select the vector layer and drag the Time Slider in the Timeline palette to frame 30. Then move the character across the screen to the right side of the screen with the Translate Layer tool.

5. Select the bone layer and drag the Time Slider to frame 1. With the Manipulate Layer (Z) tool, change the orientation of the bones to create a motion path for the character to follow, like the one shown in Figure 27.16.

6. Click the Play button to see the character follow the path defined by the bones.

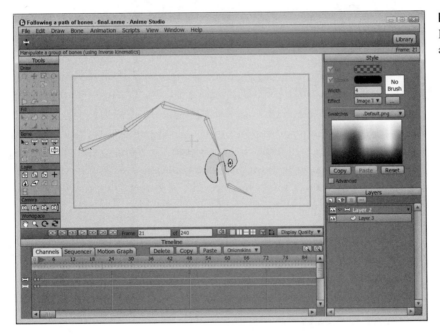

Figure 27.16
Following a bone path.

Chapter Summary

This chapter continued our coverage of the bone features available in Anime Studio, discussing specifically the animating bone features. There are many options for using bone layers and tools, including some advanced features like bone constraints and dynamics. Bones can also be used to create a warp field and to define a motion path.

Using a video backdrop to line up your video helps save a lot of time. Anime Studio includes the ability to track video objects, making the job even easier. These video tracking features are covered in the next chapter.

28

Using Video Tracking

- Loading a reference movie
- Placing tracking points
- Adjusting tracking points
- Setting a layer to follow the tracking

Loading an image or a movie into the background is a great way to use references when drawing objects, but movies that include animated objects can also be used as references by tracking the moving objects. The video tracking features of Anime Studio make it possible to have a specific layer follow the precise animation of an object in a movie.

New Feature

The video tracking feature is new to Anime Studio 6.

Loading a Reference Movie

Before you can use the video tracking feature, you'll need to load in a movie. This is done using the File, Import, Movie menu command. The video formats that can be loaded include the AVI and QuickTime formats. You can learn more about loading movie files in Chapter 22, "Adding Image Layers."

Note

Within the Library, Movies folder are several sample movies that you can try out.

If the loaded movie has a clean, clear background, then the tracking will have an easier time following objects in the movie. Also, make sure that your movie has some action, and it is best if the objects in the movie don't move too fast. Video tracking has a tough time with blurry objects.

Placing Tracking Points

Once a background movie is loaded, the next step is to place tracking points on the main points of those objects that you want to follow. The easiest objects to track are those that have a strong contrast to the background and that are easy to distinguish. Corners and tips of objects make good tracking points.

To place tracking points in the project, you'll need to click the Video Tracking tool in the Layer section of the Tools palette. With the Video Tracking tool selected, you'll be able to click the background movie at a point to track. The tracking points are identified by two circles within each other. The inner circle identifies the item to track, and the outer circle marks the area within which the item moves. Figure 28.1 shows two tracking points.

Caution

If the Show Paths option located at the bottom of the working area isn't enabled, the tracking points will not be visible.

Each tracking point can be named by typing a name in the text field on the Options bar. Each tracking point is given a name by default, but you can enter a custom name. If you plan on tracking multiple points, then giving each tracking point an easy-to-identify name is a good idea.

When placing tracking points, you can place multiple points on the video, but for each layer, you can set two points, a primary and a secondary point. These points are selected in the Motion Tracking dialog box when you set which layer to follow the tracking. The primary tracking point always defines the movement of the layer, and the secondary tracking point can be used to define the rotation or the scale of the layer relative to the primary point.

Figure 28.1
Tracking points.

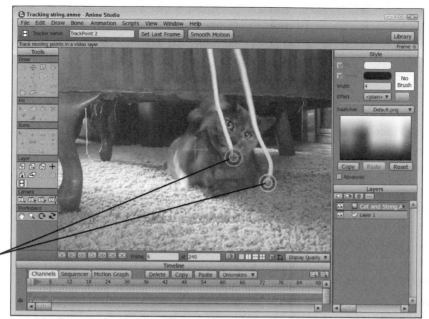

Tracking points

Imagine that you have a video of a friend dancing the robot dance with swinging arms and all. If you were to track this video, then you could place a tracking point at the hand to keep track of the hand's movement and a second tracking point for the elbow to keep track of the rotation of the arm. Then when you create an arm layer, you can set the hand tracking point to the primary tracking point and the elbow tracking point to the secondary tracking point.

Another way to use a secondary tracking point is to keep track of the size of an object. If you had a video that zooms in and out of a scene, then a secondary point could be placed at the edge of the object to keep track of the scale of the object as it changes size.

After you've place the tracking points, you simply need to click the Play button or the Step Forward buttons to progress through the movie frames. Tracking points will place a keyframe in the Timeline palette for every frame of the animation. If the points are easy to track on the background, they will follow the point as the movie plays, but more than likely you'll need to adjust the tracking points.

Adjusting Tracking Points

If the tracking progresses and follows the designated point for a while and then simply just stops, then the tracking point has moved beyond the tracking point's range or the background color is too close to the tracking point and the tracking gets confused.

If multiple tracking points are placed in the scene, then the selected tracking point is the one that is highlighted red. Clicking the Delete button will remove the tracking point from the project.

If the tracking gets lost, there are a couple of things you can do to fix the problems. The first is to adjust the tracking point ranges. To adjust the circles, simply click and drag the circles to expand or shrink them. The inner circle defines the size of the object that you are tracking. Figure 28.2 shows a tracking point sized to fit perfectly over the cat's eye.

Figure 28.2
Matching tracking objects.

Tracking point

The outer circle defines the area within which the movement takes place. For objects that move a lot, you'll want to increase the diameter of this circle. The inner circle cannot be made larger than the outer circle.

If the tracking point gets confused, you can manually move the tracking point back to its correct location and then click play again so that tracking can continue.

Tip

For shorter animation movies, it is easier to use the Step Forward animation control button and adjust the tracking point as needed.

Setting Last Frame

If the object you are following leaves the working area, then you can eliminate the tracking point at the frame where the object leaves by clicking the Last Frame button in the Options bar.

Smoothing the Tracking

Some tracking will be jerky as the tracking points are manually moved between the different frames. This can result in motion that is harsh. If you click the Smooth Motion button on the Options bar, then the motion between successive frames is smoothed, creating a more gradual transition. This also reduces the total number of keys.

Setting a Layer to Follow the Tracking

After the tracking is complete, you can set a layer to follow the tracking using the Animation, Track Layer to Video menu. This opens the Motion Tracking dialog box, shown in Figure 28.3. Using this dialog box, you can select the tracked movie to use and select two tracking points.

The primary tracking point sets the motion of the layer to follow, and the secondary tracking point can be set to control either the angle or the scale of the layer. If no secondary point is used, then you can select None as the secondary point.

Figure 28.3
Motion Tracking
dialog box.

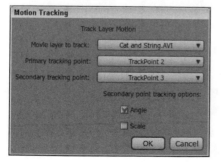

Note

The Animation, Track Layer to Video menu command is only available when a nonvideo layer is selected.

After a layer is set to follow the tracking of a video, the path of the tracked point is displayed in the layer when the layer is selected and the Show Paths option is enabled. This path is displayed in Figure 28.4 where the layer of a hat is placed on the cat's head as it moves chasing a string.

Figure 28.4
Layer set to follow a tracked video.

— *Path of tracking point*

When using the Track Layer to Video menu command, the selected layer is moved so that the origin point moves to the location of the primary tracking point's location. So when drawing the object to match the tracked object, make sure that the object is drawn relative to the origin, so that when the layer is moved, it matches up.

To track the motion of a video, follow these steps:

1. Select the File, Import, Movie menu command and import the Karate kick.avi video file from the Chapter 28 folder on the CD.

2. With the Karate kick layer selected, click the Video Tracking tool in the Tools palette. Then click the corner of the white hem of the left leg to create a tracking point marker. Then drag the outer circle to increase its size.

3. Click again on the video layer at the lower tip of the belt to create a secondary tracking point. Then increase the inner circle to just cover the end of the belt, as shown in Figure 28.5.

Figure 28.5
Primary and secondary tracking points.

Secondary tracking point

Primary tracking point

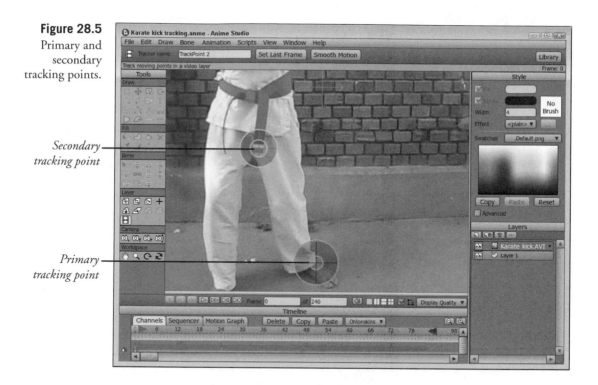

4. Look on the Timeline palette and notice the left-pointing red arrow that indicates where the video ends at frame 85. Enter 85 in the ending frame field at the bottom of the working area and press the Enter key.

5. Click the Step Forward button and notice how the tracking points move to follow the video points. If the tracking point stops tracking, then manually move the tracking point by dragging its center.

6. After tracking is completed, select the Move Layer tool and click the Play button to check the resulting tracking. If you need to make a change, select the Video Tracking tool again and make the change.

7. Select Layer 1 and drag it above the video layer in the Layers palette. Then use the Add Points tool to draw a simple cartoon foot at the layer origin.

8. With the vector layer selected, choose the Animation, Track Layer to Video menu. In the Motion Tracking dialog box, select the Karate kick.avi video and TrackPoint 1 as the Primary tracking point and TrackPoint 2 as the secondary tracking point. Then choose the Angle option and click the OK button.

9. Click the Play button to see the cartoon foot follow the video kick, as shown in Figure 28.6.

Figure 28.6
The cartoon foot follows the video.

Chapter Summary

Using the Motion Tracking features included in Anime Studio, you can track the movement, orientation, and scale of objects within a video and use those same motions to control another layer. The Video Tracking tool includes the ability to create and manipulate tracking points.

Chapter 29, "Using 3D Layers," discusses working with 3D objects.

Part VII

Working with 3D

Using 3D Layers

- Importing 3D objects
- Working with 3D layers
- Manipulating 3D objects
- Using the 3D scripts

Although Anime Studio works with 2D vector layers, it also supports importing 3D models into 3D layers. These 3D objects can be manipulated using the Layer tools, which allow you to rotate the 3D objects to see them from different sides.

Importing 3D Objects

The 3D objects are unique to Anime Studio because they can be manipulated to show several different sides of the 3D object. Anime Studio cannot be used to create 3D objects, but it can use 3D models that are created in other 3D packages and imported into an Anime Studio project.

> **Note**
>
> 3D objects can only be imported and manipulated in Anime Studio Pro.

To import a 3D object into Anime Studio, select the File, Import, OBJ 3D Model menu command. This opens a File dialog box where you can locate a 3D model to import. The File, Import menu also includes several prebuilt 3D objects in its default library. These prebuilt objects are located in the 3D Objects folder. Figure 29.1 shows an assortment of the available 3D library objects.

Note

The Library also includes an assortment of 3D objects in the Anime Studio 5 folder, including several 3D animals.

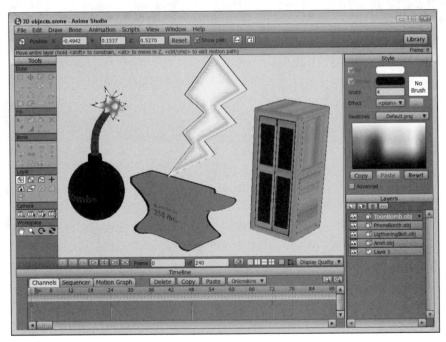

Figure 29.1

Various 3D models.

Imported prebuilt models are automatically placed on a 3D layer, and the name of the layer is the object's file name.

Importing OBJ Models

OBJ is the 3D format that is supported by Anime Studio. OBJ models are common and most 3D programs can output 3D data to this format. You can learn more about this format in Chapter 30, "Using Anime Studio with Other 3D Packages."

Importing Texture Maps

For OBJ models, textures are referenced and stored as separate MTL files. When an OBJ file is loaded, any referenced MTL texture files are loaded along with it at the same time. If you look into the Library, 3D Objects folder where Anime Studio is installed, you'll see several OBJ files along with their associated MTL files.

Caution

There are many options available for exporting 3D objects that are set in the 3D program that is doing the exporting. If you are having trouble importing a 3D object or its texture, try changing the export options in the 3D program.

Working with a 3D Layer

Three-dimensional objects can only exist on a 3D layer. When you import a 3D object, a 3D layer is automatically created to hold the imported object. If you then open the Layer Settings dialog box when you have a 3D layer selected, there is another panel, labeled *3D Options*, as shown in Figure 29.2.

Figure 29.2
3D Options panel in the Layer Settings dialog box.

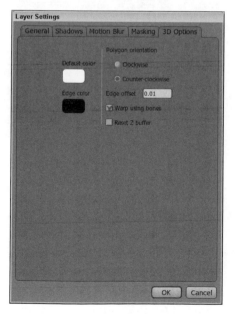

If the imported 3D object has a texture or a defined color, then that color or texture is displayed, but if the 3D object doesn't have a defined texture, the default color and edge colors specified in the Layer Settings dialog box are used. You can alter these colors by clicking their respective color swatches. Figure 29.3 shows two standard 3D objects with different colors. Notice how the cube's color hasn't changed, which means that it is using a texture.

Note

The 3D default and edge Color Pickers don't allow you to select an alpha value for making semi-transparent colors.

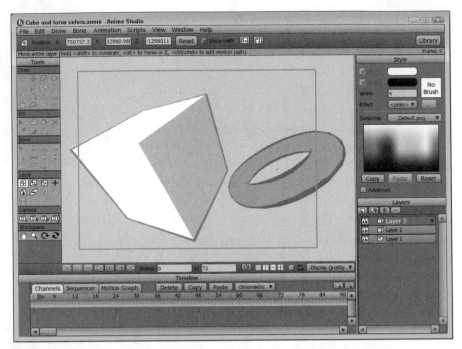

Figure 29.3
3D objects with custom colors.

> **Note**
>
> If the 3D object layer isn't displaying any textures, check to make sure that the MTL file is included in the same folder as the OBJ file. Or you can edit the path to the textures within the MTL file. MTL files can be opened and edited within a text editor.

The Polygon Orientation options can be set to Clockwise or Counter-clockwise. When a polygon is created as part of the 3D object, the edges that make up each polygon can be drawn in either direction. If a clockwise direction is used, then a vector perpendicular to the surface of the polygon, called the *normal vector*, will point away from the camera; if the counter-clockwise direction is used, the normal vector points toward the camera. Generally, normal vectors that point toward the camera are visible and normal vectors that point away from the camera have their backside to the camera.

Using the Polygon Orientation setting, you can alter the direction of these normal vectors for the entire object. If your imported 3D object appears to be turned inside out, the normal vectors probably were altered during the importing process. Altering the Polygon Orientation setting will fix the problem.

> **Note**
>
> Inside out 3D objects will generally look all black or the full edge color.

The Edge Offset value lets you set the offset for the edges to make them appear more cartoony and hand-drawn. A value of 0 removes all lines from the 3D object and a value of 1 will entirely engulf the 3D object in lines. Small values are usually best. Figure 29.4 shows two rabbit 3D objects. The one on the left has an Edge Offset value of 0 and the right rabbit has an Edge Offset value of 0.04.

> **Note**
>
> If the imported 3D object appears blotted out, then check to see if the Edge Offset value is set to 1.

> **Note**
>
> The edge width is also impacted by the Scale Compensation option in the General panel of the Layer Settings dialog box. This option causes that line width closest to the camera to be larger than those farther away.

Figure 29.4
Changing the Edge Offset value.

If the 3D layer is placed within a bone layer, the 3D object can be controlled by bones if the Warp Using Bones option is selected. Be aware that bones in Anime Studio are only 2D; they provide a minimal amount of control over 3D objects. The best way to use bones with 3D objects is to place each individual part on a separate layer; you can then control its rotation relative to the other parts.

If multiple objects are overlapped when viewed from the camera, Anime Studio only draws the one that is closest to the camera. All objects are stored in a buffer called the Z-buffer that keeps track of how far from the camera each object is. This generally works quite well, but if the front object is semi-transparent, then the object behind it that is overlapped will not be drawn. However, if you enable the Reset Z Buffer option in the 3D Options panel of the Layer Settings dialog box, then the overlapped object will be drawn.

Manipulating 3D Models within Anime Studio

When a 3D layer is selected, you can use the Layer tools to manipulate which side of the 3D object is visible. The Translate Layer and Scale Layer tools work the same as 2D layers, but when a layer is rotated, its side and even back become visible. Figure 29.5 shows the rabbit 3D object rotated about its Y-axis.

> **Tip**
>
> The crosshairs in the center of the working area will rotate along with the 3D object and are helpful for determining its orientation.

The Translate Layer tool (1) lets you move the 3D object within the plane that is perpendicular to the camera, but if you hold down the Alt/Opt key, you can also change the 3D object's depth by moving it closer or farther from the camera. The Rotate Layer X Y tool is also useful for changing the 3D object's perspective.

Finally, you can use the View, Direction menu commands to see the 3D objects from the Top, Right, Back, Bottom, and Left views. Figure 29.6 shows the 3D rabbits from the Top view.

Figure 29.5
Rotated rabbit.

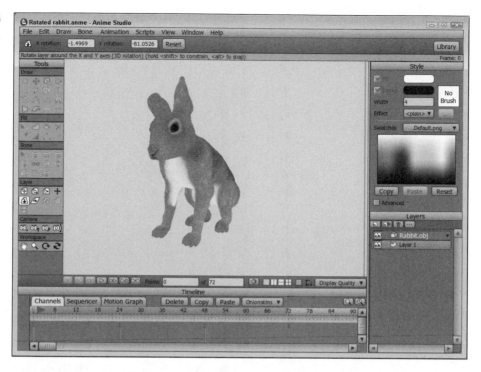

Figure 29.6
Rotated rabbits
from top.

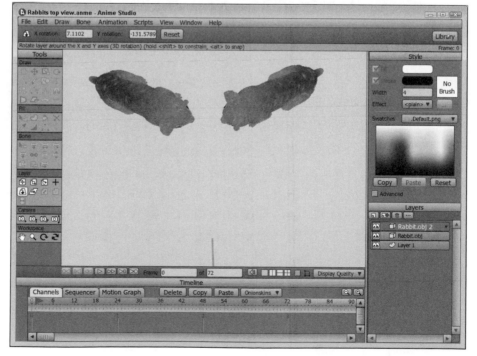

Using 3D Scripts

The Scripts, 3D menu includes several unique scripts for creating 3D objects and rotating the selected 3D layer. The available scripts include the following:

- **Auto-Scale:** Automatically scales the 3D layer so it fits within the working area.

- **Cube:** Creates a simple 3D cube on a new 3D layer.

- **Rotate X:** Rotates the current 3D layer 90 degrees around the X-axis.

- **Rotate Y:** Rotates the current 3D layer 90 degrees around the Y-axis.

- **Rotate Z:** Rotates the current 3D layer 90 degrees around the Z-axis.

- **Torus:** Creates a simple 3D torus object, which looks like a doughnut.

When 3D objects are imported from a 3D program, it is common for the imported 3D object to be either so small that it is invisible or huge compared to the other scene objects. This is caused by a difference in the scale used in the 3D program and Anime Studio, but the Auto-Scale script will quickly remedy this problem and resize the 3D object to fit the current project.

If you need to rotate the current 3D layer, you can use the layer tools to do this, or if you just need to quickly rotate the 3D layer, you can use Rotate scripts to do the work. This is especially handy if you have a bitmap texture that you need to align to the project. Each time one of the Rotate scripts is used, the selected 3D layer is rotated 90 degrees about the script's selected axis.

Finally, if you need some quick 3D objects to test your current scene, you can use the Cube and Torus scripts to create a 3D layer. Figure 29.7 shows the cube and torus objects created using the 3D scripts.

To import and work with a 3D layer to make a hedge, follow these steps:

1. Select the File, New menu command to create a new project.

2. Select the File, Import, OBJ 3D Model menu command. Then select the Hedge.obj file from the Chapter 29 folder on the CD. This file is a simple 3D box with a hedge bitmap applied to it. The hedge texture is saved in a MTL file in the same folder, and it is loaded automatically with the OBJ file.

3. Once loaded, the 3D model looks like a huge black bar because the scale of the 3D object is different from the project's scale. Select Scripts, 3D, Auto-Scale to reduce the size of the 3D object's scale.

Figure 29.7
Cube and torus.

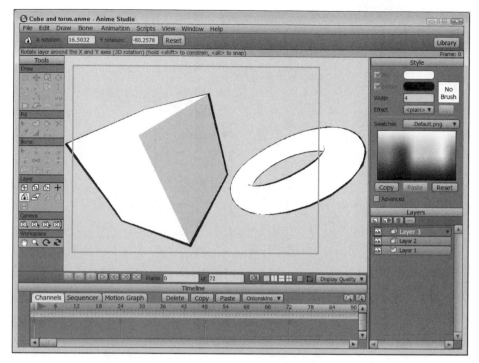

4. Select the Rotate Layer X tool and drag in the working area to change the orientation of the 3D object.

5. As you change the box's orientation, you may notice that the object turns all black. This is caused by the Edge Offset value. Double-click the Hedge.obj layer in the Layers palette to open the Layer Settings dialog box. Select the 3D Options panel and set the Edge Offset to 0.01. Then click the OK button to see the applied texture.

6. Select and drag in the working area with the Rotate Layer Y tool until the hedge object recedes into the back of the project. Then use the Translate Layer tool (1) to drag the hedge to the left edge of the working area. Hold down the Alt/Opt key and drag the layer until it is aligned with the left edge of the working area.

7. Duplicate the Hedge layer using the Duplicate Layer button at the top of the Layers palette. Select the Scripts, 3D, Rotate Z menu command to rotate the new layer. Then use the layer tools to align the new layer opposite of its original, as shown in Figure 29.8.

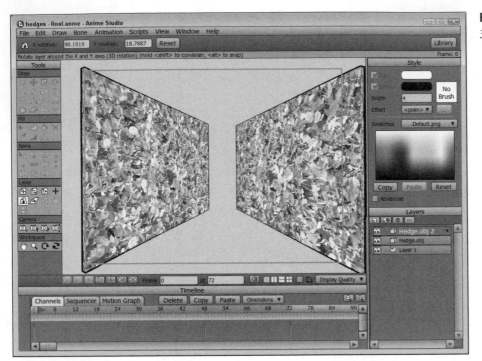

Figure 29.8
3D hedges.

Chapter Summary

This chapter introduced 3D layers and showed you how to import 3D objects and manipulate them within Anime Studio. Once imported, 3D objects can be manipulated using the Layer tools in the Tools palette. There are also a number of useful 3D scripts in the Scripts menu for 3D objects.

The next chapter shows how to create and export 3D models that can be used within Anime Studio using several popular 3D programs.

30

Using Anime Studio with Other 3D Packages

- ■ Preparing 3D objects for exporting
- ■ Exporting 3D objects from Poser and other packages

If you plan to use an external 3D package to create 3D objects that can be exported to Anime Studio, then there are a number of helpful steps you can take to ensure that the 3D objects are exported cleanly. There are also a number of 3D packages that can be used to create 3D objects.

Preparing 3D Objects for Exporting

Taking some steps to prepare your 3D objects for exporting will help your objects make a clean transition to Anime Studio. If these steps aren't taken, you could end up with an item that is resized too large to be useful or that has no color and texture.

Triangulating Models

Some 3D programs can deal with polygon faces that have multiple edges forming a square, a pentagon, or even more. The problem with polygons that have four or more faces is that they might be curved, which often causes trouble during the exporting process. To make sure that no polygons are concave or convex, you can triangulate all the polygon faces in the 3D object.

A triangular face has only three edges, so it is impossible for it to be bent. By forcing all polygon faces to be triangles, you can eliminate any concave or convex faces. Most 3D programs have a simple command to triangulate the entire 3D object. Figure 30.1 shows two 3D sphere objects. The one on the left uses polygons with four edges called *quads* and the one on the right is triangulated.

The drawback to triangulating a 3D object is that it can increase the number of polygons by two to four times the current number. If your model is fairly simple, such as an undistorted sphere, cube, or some other primitive shape, then you may benefit more by forcing the model to be exported using quads. Some 3D packages include an option to export the model using quads.

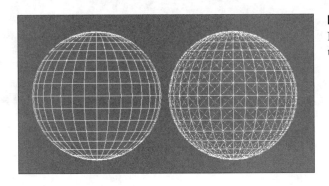

Figure 30.1
Nontriangulated and triangulated spheres.

Sizing Models and System Units

One common error that is often made when exporting a 3D model is to have the system units set to something that is incompatible with the project scene in Anime Studio. Of course, 3D models can be scaled to match the size of the other objects in the project, but doing so can be a hassle. If you make sure that the system units in your 3D program are set to centimeters, then all exported objects should be within scale.

Tip

If your imported 3D object is out of scale, you can use the Scripts, 3D, Auto-Scale menu command to resize the 3D object to fit the project scale.

Baking Textures and Lighting

The OBJ 3D format supports saving texture images with the .MTL image extension, but another way to handle textures is to bake the texture and lighting directly into the model using the vertex color channel. The method for doing this is different in each 3D package, but if you look in the help file for the specific package you are using, you should be able to figure this out.

In addition to texture effects, you can also bake in lighting to the model's vertex channels. Anime Studio has no way of lighting a 3D object, so it is best if you can light the object in its original 3D package and then bake the lighting into the object. Notice how the hawk model in Figure 30.2 has been prelit and the lighting is saved to the hawk's texture.

Figure 30.2
A prelit hawk.

Importing Figures from Poser

Poser supports the OBJ file format and includes a command for exporting 3D objects. The exported 3D objects from Poser can be loaded directly into Anime Studio. However, the default OBJ export feature in Poser doesn't create OBJ files that can be cleanly loaded into Anime Studio, but there is a separate script for automating the exporting process.

Using the Poser OBJ Exporter

3D objects created in Poser can be exported easily to Anime Studio using a freely available Python script that can be obtained from the Smith Micro Web site at http://my.smithmicro.com/mac/poser/updates.html.

Once the script is downloaded and unzipped, you can place it in the Python folder where Poser is installed. You can then execute the script using the File, Run Python Script menu command in Poser. During the exporting, Poser saves the OBJ, MTL, and a number of referenced JPEG files. All of these files need to be in the same folder when importing into Anime Studio.

To export a model from Poser and import it into Anime Studio, follow these steps:

1. Within Poser, open the Poser default man.pz3 file from the Chapter 30 folder on the CD. This file includes the default Poser man in a unique pose, as shown in Figure 30.3.

Figure 30.3

A male character in Poser.

2. Select the File, Run Python Script menu command from within Poser; then locate and run the PoserOBJ_Export_AnimeStudioPro.py file that was downloaded and unzipped from the Smith Micro Web site.

3. In the File dialog box that opens, save the Poser file with the name Poser default man. The script exports all the needed files into the same folder. A message window appears telling you how successful the export was, as shown in Figure 30.4.

4. Open Anime Studio and select the File, Import, OBJ 3D Model menu command. In the File dialog box, select the exported Poser default man.obj file and click the OK button. This same file is located in the Chapter 30 folder on the CD also. The 3D character is loaded into Anime Studio.

Figure 30.4
Script export report.

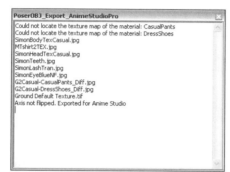

Note

The default Poser figure is quite large and will take some time to load into Anime Studio.

5. Select the Scripts, 3D, Auto-Scale menu command to run the scale script. Scale the 3D object to fit within the working area. Then double-click the 3D layer in the Layers palette and select the 3D Options panel and set the Edge Offset value to 0. This removes the black edge around the 3D model. The resulting model is shown in Figure 30.5.

Figure 30.5
Imported 3D model from Poser.

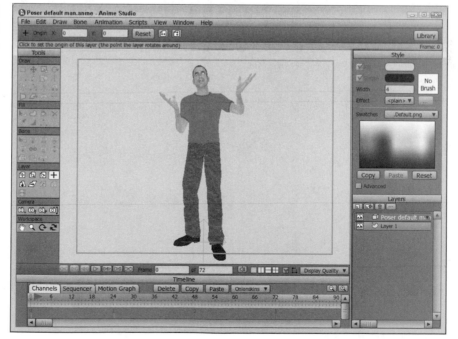

Importing Models from 3ds Max and Maya

Two other popular 3D packages are 3ds Max and Maya, both available from Autodesk. The OBJ export options in each of these packages offer several different settings for customizing the output.

Importing 3ds Max Models

When exporting models created in 3ds Max to the OBJ format that can be imported into Anime Studio, be aware that you'll need to export the model's geometry using the OBJ format and then export the material/texture using the MTL format. If you only export the OBJ format, then the geometry will be imported into Anime Studio, but to get the materials and textures, you'll need to export the MTL file also.

To export a model from 3ds Max and import it into Anime Studio, follow these steps:

1. Within 3ds Max, open the Birdbath.max file from the Chapter 30 folder on the CD. This file includes a birdbath model with a granite texture applied to it, as shown in Figure 30.6.

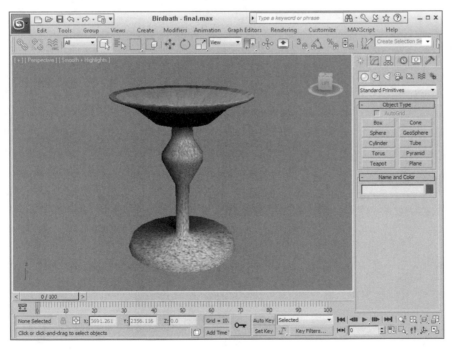

Figure 30.6
3D object
in 3ds Max.

2. Select the File, Export menu command and in the File dialog box that opens, select the Wavefront Object (OBJ) file format, name the file Birdbath.obj, and click the Save button. This causes the OBJ Export Options dialog box, shown in Figure 30.7, to appear. Be sure to select the Export Materials option and click the Export button.

3. When the export is complete, an Export Results dialog box, shown in Figure 30.8, appears with details on the exported items.

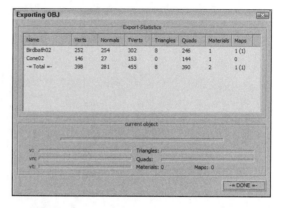

Figure 30.7
OBJ Export Options dialog box.

Figure 30.8
Export Results dialog box.

Note

If you select the Create Material Library option in the OBJ Export dialog box, then the MTL files are automatically exported along with the OBJ.

4. Open Anime Studio and select the File, Import, OBJ 3D Model menu command. In the File dialog box, select the export Birdbath.obj file and click the OK button. The birdbath model is loaded into the working area, and the materials are loaded automatically with the geometry.

5. Select the Scripts, 3D, Auto-Scale menu command to run the scale script. This scales the 3D object to fit within the working area. Then double-click the 3D layer in the Layers palette and select the 3D Options panel and set the Edge Offset value to 0.01. This adds a thin black edge around the 3D model. The resulting model is shown in Figure 30.9.

Tip

If you want to completely eliminate the outlines surrounding the 3D object, just set the Edge Offset to 0.

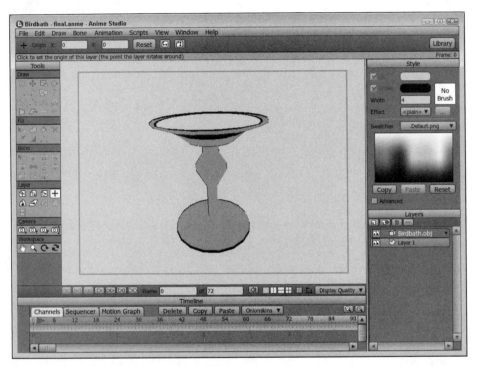

Figure 30.9
Imported 3D model from 3ds Max.

Note

The default OBJ exporter in 3ds Max doesn't handle the exporting of textures very well. If you use a different exporting engine such as Okino's PolyTrans or if you bake the texture within 3ds Max, then you can get textures.

Importing Maya Models

When exporting models created in Maya to the OBJ format, you'll need to download and install an OBJ translation script. Maya doesn't include a default OBJ exporting feature, but you can enable it using the Plug-in Manager. Once enabled, you can select it using the File, Export menu command.

Creating 3D Models Using Free Software

The 3D packages such as Poser, 3ds Max, and Maya are great for working with 3D, but they are expensive and require some time to learn. If you don't need a heavy amount of 3D objects, then a freely available 3D package might be just the ticket. There are several 3D packages that you can download and use. Some of these packages have quite a bit of power, and they all are well supported by active communities.

Of the available 3D packages, these three stand out:

- **Blender**: A full-powered 3D package freely available at www.blender.org.

- **Wings3D**: A full-powered 3D package freely available at www.wings3d.com.

- **Anim8or**: A 3D modeling package freely available at www.anim8or.com.

Chapter Summary

Preparing models for the exporting process will result in a cleaner, easier-to-use 3D model within Anime Studio. Most of the available external 3D packages include the ability to export 3D objects to the OBJ file format.

The next chapter looks at particle layers and how they can be used to add special effects to your scene.

Part VIII

Adding Special Effects

31

Using Particle Layers

- Working with particle layers
- Configuring particles
- Reducing particles on export
- Using particle effects scripts

Some effects, such as snowflakes blowing around during a storm, can be created by making a large number of objects dance and move randomly around the scene. The problem with this is that such a large number of objects can quickly become unmanageable. The answer to this problem is to localize them in a particle layer.

A single particle layer can create multiple copies of any sublayers contained under it. This provides a quick and easy way to turn off or delete all the copies at once. Particle layers also give you access to a settings panel in the Layer Settings dialog box where you can set the total number of particles and several other properties describing the particle's motion. So, let's get going because I detect some snow flurries that are coming.

Working with Particle Layers

A particle layer is a layer that can hold multiple sublayers. From each sublayer a group of particles is emitted from a local source in a specified direction and spread angle. These particles continue along the defined path until the layer is turned off or until some other property interacts with them.

Note

Particle layers are only available in Anime Studio Pro.

To create a particle layer, click the New Layer drop-down list at the top of the Layers palette and choose the Particles option. Now layers can be dropped onto the particle layer to add them as sublayers to the particle layer.

The particles are defined by the objects contained on the sublayer. For example, if you create a small circle on a vector layer that is a sublayer of a particle layer, then the small circle is repeatedly emitted and moved around the scene, as shown in Figure 31.1.

Note

The Library palette includes a folder of sample particle layers including explosions, rain, and clouds.

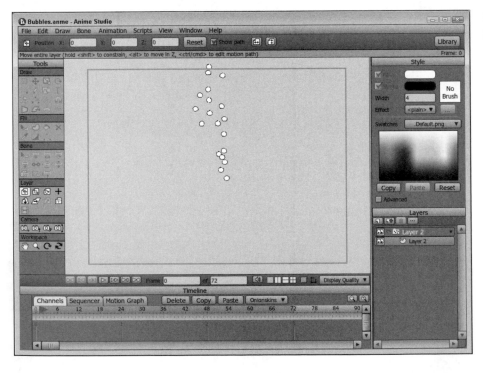

Figure 31.1
Bubble particles.

Configuring Particles

If the particle layer is selected, then within the Layer Settings dialog box is a new panel named *Particles*. Using the Particles panel shown in Figure 13.2, you can define properties for specifying the number of particles, how long they survive, their dimensions, speed and direction, and how randomly they move.

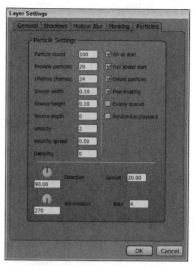

Figure 31.2
Particles panel in the Layer Settings dialog box.

Changing the Number of Particles

The Particle Count value sets the total number of particles that are present in the scene at a given frame. Be aware that increasing this number can slow down the render and export time for the project. The Preview Particles value is the number of particles that are visible within the working area. This value is usually a fraction of the total number, and keeping it small allows some of the particles to be visible without having to wait for a large number of particles to be drawn every time a change is made to the project. Figure 31.3 shows two sets of particles. The left set has a Preview Particles value of 20 and the right set has a Preview Particles value of 60, so many more particles are visible in the working area at right.

Controlling the Particles' Lifetime

The Lifetime value determines how long the particles stay around the scene. It is measured in frames, so if the Lifetime value is set to 12, each new particle will move through the scene for 12 frames before it disappears. If this value is set to 0, the emitted particles will continue to move through the frame without being removed.

Setting the Particles' Dimensions

Particles are emitted regularly from their starting location in a straight line unless you change the width, height, and depth of their source. The Source Width and Source Height values set the width and height that the particles can move from their source. Figure 31.4 shows the particle stream on the left with width and height values of 0 resulting in a straight line; the particles on the right have width and height values of 0.5.

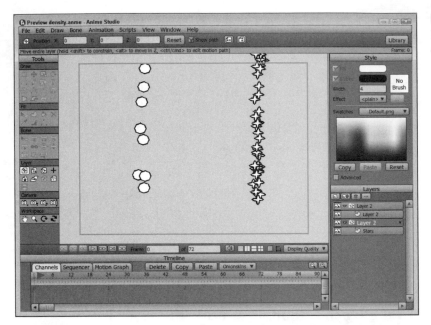

Figure 31.3
Preview Particles density.

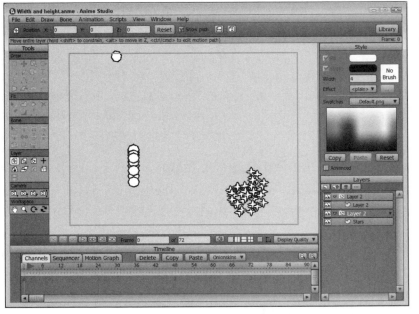

Figure 31.4
Changing width and height values.

There is also a value to change the source depth. Changing this value causes the particles to randomly appear closer to and farther from the camera, which results in smaller and larger particles, as shown in Figure 31.5.

Figure 31.5
Changing source
depth.

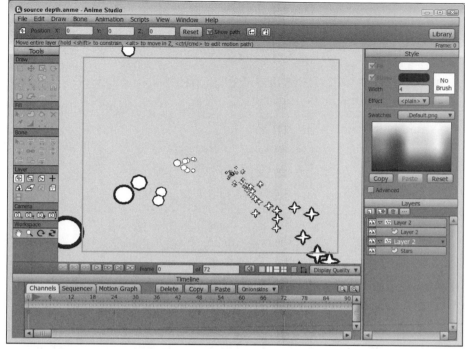

Changing the Particles' Speed and Acceleration

The particles' speed as they are first emitted is controlled by the Velocity value. A value of 2 will cause the particles to move across the entire screen in one second. The Velocity Spread value defines the random variation for the velocity value. A value of 0.1 will cause about 10% of the particles to move at a different speed.

The Damping value causes a resistance to speed and can also contribute to the randomness of the particles' movement. The Acceleration value defines how quickly the velocity is changing; its direction is determined by the pointer dial and value at the bottom of the panel. If acceleration is pointing downward, it simulates gravity. The Rate defines how quickly acceleration is slowing the particles down.

Setting the Particles' Direction and Spread

The direction of the particle stream is determined by the Direction pointer and value. A value of 90 causes the particles to move straight up and a value of 270 causes the particles to move downward.

The Spread value defines an angle that the particles stay within. It is measured in degrees, so a spread of 30 will keep the particles within a 30-degree angle. Setting the Spread value to 360 causes the particles to move in all directions.

Other Options

The Particles panel also includes several other options. The On at Start option causes the particles to begin moving when the animation is first started. If disabled, the particles are turned off. You can enable particles at any time during the animation by right-clicking the particle layer and selecting Turn Particles On.

The Full Speed Start option causes the particles to move at full speed at frame 1. If this option is disabled, the particles will take some time to get going at frame 1. The Orient Particles option causes the particles to rotate to be aligned with the direction they are moving. If disabled, the particles maintain the current orientation throughout the animation.

The Free Floating option allows the particles to move independently of the layer and its movements. If this option is disabled, the particles will move along with the layer as the layer is moved and rotated. The Evenly Spaced option causes the particles to be emitted at regular intervals. If disabled, then the particles appear more randomly. The Randomize Playback option causes the particles to start moving at random times.

To create a firehose using particles, follow these steps:

1. Open the Firehose.anme file from the Chapter 31 folder on the CD. This file includes a hose object that is animated using bones.

2. Select the New Layer button at the top of the Layers palette and choose the Particles option from the pop-up menu. Drag and drop the particles layer on the bone layer. This makes the particle layer part of the bone layer so the particles will move with the end of the firehose.

3. With the Translate Layer tool (1), drag the center origin and position it at the end of the firehose.

4. Select the New Layer button in the Layers palette to create a new vector layer. Change the Fill color in the Style palette to light blue and create a small thin triangle at the end of the firehose to look like a water stream. Drag and drop the new vector layer on the particles layer.

5. Double-click the particles layer to open in the Layer Settings dialog box. In the Particles panel, set the Particle Count to 400, the Preview Particles to 40, and the Direction and Acceleration values to 315. Then click the OK button to close the Layer Settings dialog box.

6. Click the Play button (Spacebar) to see the resulting particles stream from the end of the firehose as it whips around, as shown in Figure 31.6.

Figure 31.6
Particles stream from
the end of a firehose.

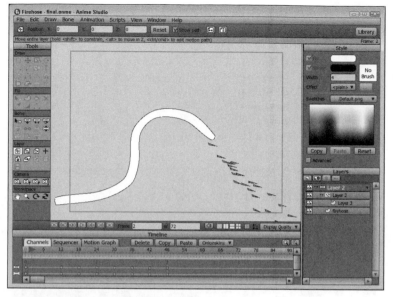

Figure 31.7
Export Animation
dialog box.

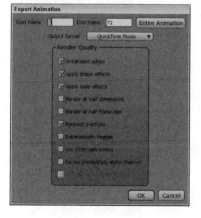

Reducing Particles on Export

If your scene includes a large number of particles, exporting the scene can be slowed down considerably. To reduce the rendering bottleneck, you can enable the Reduced Particles option in the Export Animation dialog box shown in Figure 31.7. This reduces the total number of particles at render time without changing the specified number of particles in the Particles panel.

Using Particle Effects Scripts

The Scripts, Particle Effects menu includes several different scripts that automate the creation of certain types of useful particle layers. The available particle effects scripts include the following:

- **Energy Cloud:** Opens a dialog box where you can choose a color. This color is used to create circles that fill the working area.

- **Explosion:** Opens a dialog box where you can specify a direction and a spread. The effect includes smoke and flames.

- **Rain:** Adds a subtle rain effect to the scene.

- **Smoke:** Opens the Smoke dialog box shown in Figure 31.8, where you can change the smoke color, particle, and flame lifetime, and one of five styles: Cloud, Plume, Narrow, Medium, and Wide.

- **Snow:** Adds slowly falling snow particles to the scene.

- **Sparkles:** Opens a dialog box where you can choose a color. This color is used to create randomly moving particles that extend from the center of the working area and slowly dissipate.

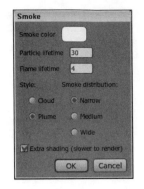

Figure 31.8
Smoke effect dialog box.

Figure 31.9 shows the smoke and rain particle effects.

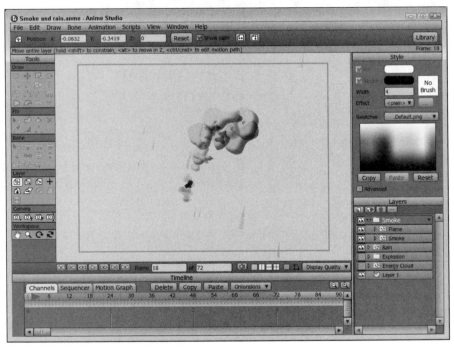

Figure 31.9
Smoke and rain effects.

Chapter Summary

This chapter introduced the particle layer, which enables you to add multiple small objects to the scene that move randomly around the scene. Particles are useful for creating effects like fire, smoke, rain, and snow.

The next chapter covers the depth of field and motion blur effects.

32

Using Motion Blur and Depth of Field

- Enabling motion blur
- Using the depth of field effect
- Adding noise grain
- Using stereoscopic (red/blue) effects

In addition to particles, which reside on particle layers, Anime Studio includes several other common effects that are implemented on the project and layer levels. *Motion blur* is an effect that causes objects moving quickly through the project to appear blurred. *Depth of field* is an effect that allows the "camera" to focus on a single layer and all other layers in the project appear blurred. Using these blur-creation effects, you can give your project a sense of motion and depth. The Project Settings dialog box also enables you to use noise grain and stereoscopic effects.

Enabling Motion Blur Effects

Motion blur is an effect that helps the audience identify which objects in the scene are moving fast. When enabled, objects in the scene that are moving are blurred, thereby giving them the impression of speed. Objects in the project that are at rest are not blurred, which gives a contrast to the moving objects.

Motion blur is enabled at the layer level using the Motion Blur panel, shown in Figure 32.1, in the Layer Settings dialog box. To access this panel, double-click a layer or select a layer and click the Layer Settings icon at the top of the Layers palette.

The Motion Blur On option enables the motion blur effect for the current layer. When enabled, the motion blur effect is created by rendering all the layer objects over a series of frames. These renderings are then combined to create the blurred effect. If the object is moving faster, the distance between each rendered object will be greater than the rendered frames of the slower objects. If the object isn't moving at all, then the successive frames will appear to be on top of one another.

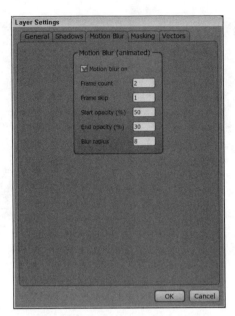

Figure 32.1

The Motion Blur panel in the Layer Settings dialog box.

Note

The motion blur effect is only visible when the project is rendered. It is not visible in the working area.

The Frame Count value sets the number of successive frames that are used to create the blurred object. The default value of 2 is typically enough to give the illusion of motion, but higher values are useful for creating transformation effects.

For objects that aren't moving that fast, a low Frame Count value results in an effect that is barely noticeable, but you can extend out the successive renderings by causing a designated number of frames to be skipped between the successive frames that are rendered.

Another useful technique that makes the motion blur effect work is to gradually make the trailing renderings transparent. These can be controlled using the Start Opacity and End Opacity values. These values mark the beginning and ending percentages where transparency is introduced and where the fading starts.

The final motion blur parameter is the Blur Radius. This value controls the amount of blur that is applied to the successive renderings. Higher Blur Radius values result in a greater blur effect.

To add a motion blur effect to a layer, follow these steps:

1. Open the Rocket with motion blur.anme file from the Chapter 32 folder on the CD. This file includes a simple rocket being animated moving over a moonscape surface.

2. Select the Rocket layer and open the Layer Settings dialog box. In the Motion Blur panel, enable the Motion Blur On option. Then set the Frame Count to 2, the Frame Skip to 1, the Start Opacity to 50, the End Opacity to 30, and the Blur Radius to 8. This creates a nice blur over two frames.

3. Drag the Time slider in the Timeline palette to the middle of the animation and render the project with the File, Preview menu command (Ctrl/Cmd+R). The results are shown in Figure 32.2.

Figure 32.2
Motion blur rocket.

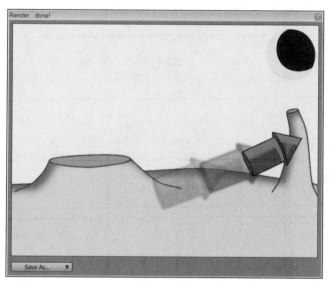

Enabling Depth of Field Effects

The depth of field effect occurs when the camera is focused on one particular object in the scene and all other objects closer to and farther away from the camera than the designated object appear blurry. The amount of blur depends on the distance from the object in focus. For example, picture a football player running down the sidelines. Using a depth of field effect, you could focus on the football player while any players in the foreground and the crowd in the background would be blurred.

To enable this camera effect in Anime Studio, open the Project Settings dialog box, shown in Figure 32.3, using the File, Project Settings menu command. In the Depth of Field section, choose the Enabled option to turn on this effect. You can then set the Focus Distance, which is the distance from the camera where the focus is clear. The Focus Range determines how near and far the focus is clear and the Max Blur Radius sets the highest amount of blur in the scene.

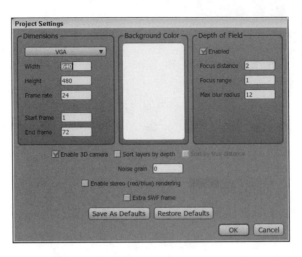

Figure 32.3
Project Settings dialog box.

To enable the depth of field effect for all layers in a project, follow these steps:

1. Open the Butterfly depth of field.anme file from the Chapter 32 folder on the CD. This file includes two layers: the Butterfly 3D layer and an image layer with a background image.

2. Select the background layer and choose the Move Layer tool. Then hold down the Alt/Opt key and drag in the working area to move the background image backward along the Z-axis. Use the Scale Layer tool to scale the layer to fit within the working area borders.

3. Choose the File, Project Settings menu command to open the Project Settings dialog box. Click the Enabled checkbox under the Depth of Field section, set the Focus Distance value to 2, the Focus Range to 1, and the Max Blur radius to 212. Close the dialog box.

4. Select the File, Preview menu command. The scene at the current frame is rendered with the depth of field effect, as shown in Figure 32.4. Notice how the background is blurred while the butterfly in the foreground is in focus.

Making a Layer Immune to a Depth of Field Effect

If you enable the depth of field effect, it is applied to all layers in the scene, but if you have a layer that you don't want to be affected by this effect, you can enable the Immune to Depth of Field option in the General panel of the Layer Settings dialog box. This option removes the selected layer from the depth of field effect.

Figure 32.4
Butterfly with depth of field effect.

Enabling the Noise Grain Effect

Another effect option in the Project Settings dialog box is the Noise Grain value. When set to the default of 0, no noise is added to the rendered image, but by increasing this value, random noise is added to the rendered scene. The best example of noise grain is seen when watching or simulating an old-time movie reel that has lines, streaks, and scratches running through the film. This type of effect can be created with a high noise grain value.

Figure 32.5 shows the butterfly image produced in the last example with a Noise Grain value set to its maximum of 128.

Figure 32.5
Butterfly with the Noise Grain effect.

Enabling the Stereoscopic Effect

The final effect setting to examine is the stereoscopic effect. This effect creates an image that can be made to appear three dimensional when viewed using red and blue stereo glasses that were common in the older 3D movies. The technique is created by the project from one angle using a red channel and from another angle using a blue channel. By combining these two overlapped images, the depth of the image is re-created.

This option can be enabled for a rendered project using the Enable Stereo (Red/Blue) Rendering option in the Project Settings dialog box. The greater the value, the more the red and blue channels are separated from each other.

Figure 32.6 shows the butterfly image produced in the last example with the Enable Stereo option checked.

Figure 32.6
Butterfly with the stereoscopic effect.

Chapter Summary

This chapter covered some specialized effects that are enabled using the Layer Settings and Project Settings dialog boxes. The motion blur effect blurs objects that are moving quickly through the scene by rendering the object over several successive frames. The depth of field effect focuses on a specific object in the scene that is a designated distance from the camera and blurs all other layers in the project. Finally, the grain effect and stereoscopic effects can be enabled in the Project Settings dialog box.

The next chapter shows how a final project can be rendered in all its glory.

Part IX

Rendering and Exporting

33

Rendering the Final Scene

- Creating a preview
- Rendering the scene
- Exporting an animation
- Enabling shadows
- Using the batch export feature
- Using command-line rendering

After all your layers are created, filled, and stroked and all the animation keys are set, you can render out the final results for the current frame using the File, Preview (Ctrl/Cmd+R) menu command. There is also an option to export the final animation to several different formats, including AVI, QuickTime, and Flash.

Rendering a scene provides a way to check your project along the way. Often when rendering a project, you can see that the layer stacking or the fill effect of an object is incorrect and discovering these errors before exporting can save you some time.

Creating a Preview Render

If you're finished with your project and you want to check the look of your resulting artwork for the current frame before exporting, you can use the File, Preview (Ctrl/Cmd+R) menu command. This command renders a quick preview of the current frame, as shown in Figure 33.1. Preview renders include details not visible in the working area, including certain effects and shadows.

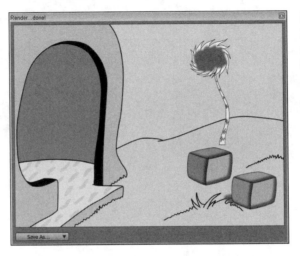

Figure 33.1
Preview render of the current frame.

The preview image appears in a separate window, and you can save the preview image using the Save As button located at the bottom of the window. Clicking the Save As button accesses options to save the image as a JPEG, BMP, Targa, or PNG image. There is also an option to copy the image to the clipboard.

Previewing an Animation

If you want to preview an animation sequence, you can press the F5 key. This creates a temporary preview file that automatically opens within your system's default media player, as shown in Figure 33.2. The preview uses its own default preview render settings regardless of the settings in the Display Quality dialog box. It also renders the project at half the size specified in the Project Settings dialog box.

> **Note**
>
> The Animation Preview command isn't found in any of the menus or palettes. It can only be accessed using the F5 key.

Figure 33.2
Animation preview.

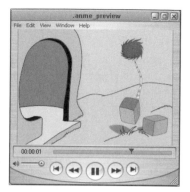

Exporting an Animation

The File, Preview command lets you see what the finished artwork looks like for a single frame, but to view the entire animation, you need to use the File, Export Animation menu command. This command opens the Export Animation dialog box shown in Figure 33.3, where you can specify the range of frames to export and specify the output format.

Figure 33.3
Export Animation dialog box.

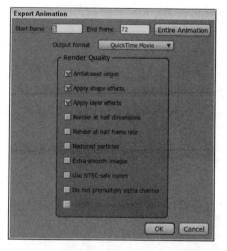

The available output formats include sequential images using JPEG, BMP, Targa, PNG, or PSD formats. You can also output animations to AVI for Windows, QuickTime for Macintosh or Windows, and Flash (SWF). You can learn more specifics about exporting to these various formats in the next two chapters.

Understanding the Render Quality Settings

The Export Animation dialog box includes a number of render quality options that you can enable. These options allow trade-offs between rendering at high quality or reducing quality to speed the rendering process. The render quality options include the following:

- **Antialiased Edges:** Applies a smoothing calculation in order to eliminate any jagged, pixilated edges.

- **Apply Shape Effects:** Applies any designated fill effects such as shading, gradients, and halo.

- **Apply Layer Effects:** Applies any layer effects to the exported animation, including shadows, blurring, and noisy strokes.

- **Render at Half Dimensions:** Renders the project at half the resolution that is designated in the Project Settings dialog box.

- **Render at Half Frame Rate:** Renders only every other frame of an animated sequence.

- **Reduced Particles:** Renders the project using only a fraction of the total number of particles.

- **Extra-Smooth Images:** Enables an additional smoothing pass on images to eliminate jagged edges.

- **Use NTSC-Safe Colors:** Limits the export colors to those colors that will work on a television monitor.

- **Do Not Premultiply Alpha Channel:** Allows the exported animation to use the existing alpha channel transparency for compositing in a video-editing package.

- **Variable Line Widths:** Available only when the SWF format is selected. This option allows variable line widths to be exported to SWF when enabled.

> **Note**
>
> The Antialiased Edges, Apply Shape Effects, Reduced Particles, and Variable Line Widths options are only available in Anime Studio Pro.

Enabling Shadows

Several visual attributes are only visible when the project is rendered, including fill effects, motion blur, depth of field, complex masks, and layer shadows. Layer shadows and layer shading are added using the Shadows panel in the Layer Settings dialog box, shown in Figure 33.4.

When the Shadow On or the Shading On option is enabled, then all layer objects are automatically given a shadow or are shaded when the project is rendered. Note that this shadow is only a drop shadow that helps to raise the object from the surface, as shown by the right rocket in Figure 33.5.

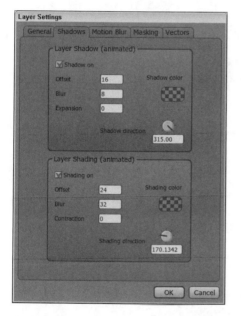

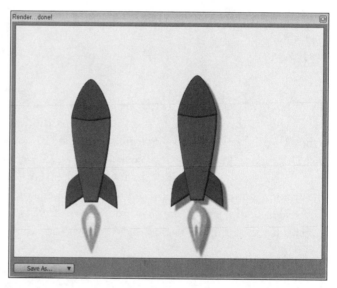

Figure 33.4
Shadows panel in the Layer Settings dialog box.

Figure 33.5
Enabling shadows gives all layer objects a drop-shadow.

When the Shadow On option is enabled, the other settings become active. The Offset value defines the distance from the original that the shadow is moved in a diagonal path. Figure 33.6 shows the shadow on three flowers with Offset values of 16, 32, and 64.

The Blur value defines the amount of pixels used to blur the shadow. Higher values result in a greater amount of blur and a less noticeable shadow. Figure 33.7 shows three glasses with blur shadow values of 0, 16, and 32. Notice how a blur value of 0 leaves a strong shadow line.

Figure 33.6
Shadow Offset values.

Figure 33.7
Shadow Blur values.

The Expansion value sets the number of pixels to increase the shadow. For example, if you set the Offset value to 0 and the Expansion value to 10, then you'll get a nice 10-pixel halo around the entire object. The Expansion value can range from 0 to 30. Figure 33.8 shows four swords with an Offset value of 0 and Expansion values of 2, 4, 8, and 16. The Shadows panel also includes a setting for altering the shadow color. Clicking the color swatch opens the Color Picker where you can select a color and a transparency value. There is also a Shadow Direction control for setting the direction the shadow is cast.

Tip

A good technique is to use layer shadows to create a strong black stroke that surrounds the layer's objects. For this effect, use an Offset value of 0, a Blur value of 0, and an Expansion value of 5. This creates a strong, thick stroke around the objects.

In addition to the layer shadows, the Shadows panel also includes an option for enabling shading. This shading is the same as the Shading fill effect, except it is applied to all the objects in the current layer.

Figure 33.8
Shadow Expansion
values with
different colors.

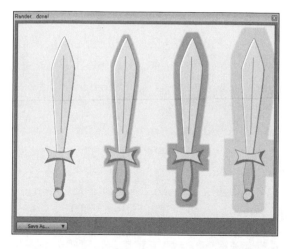

Caution

If the Shading fill effect is applied along with the Shading layer effect, then the effect is doubled on the object.

The Shading settings of Offset, Blur, Shading Color, and Shading Direction work exactly the same as the Layer Shadow settings, but the Contraction is a little different. It defines the size of the shading in pixels and can range from 0 to 30. Figure 33.9 shows examples of layer shading applied to an apple with values of 0, 8, 16, and 30.

Figure 33.9
Shading
Contraction values.

Note

The Layer Shadow and Layer Shading settings can be animated.

To add a layer shadow to a spinning logo, follow these steps:

1. Open the Spinning logo.anme file from the Chapter 33 folder on the CD. This file is taken from an earlier tutorial and features a spinning logo.

2. Select and double-click the single layer in the Layers palette to open the Layer Settings dialog box. Click the Shadows panel and enable the Shadow On option.

3. Set the Offset to 0, the Blur to 8, and the Expansion to 12; then click the Shadow color swatch and change the color to a bright neon green. Then close the Layer Settings dialog box.

4. Drag the Time Slider to frame 24 and select the File, Preview menu command (Ctrl/Cmd+R) to see the resulting glow, as shown in Figure 33.10.

Figure 33.10
Glow added to spinning logo.

Batch Exporting

The process of rendering and exporting animations can take a long time, depending on the complexity of your project and the number of frames to render, but you probably don't want to sit around while your computer crunches away at the final images. Anime Studio includes a batch export feature that lets you select several projects to render one after another while you're away from your computer.

The File, Batch Export menu command (Ctrl/Cmd+B) opens the Batch Export dialog box shown in Figure 33.11. This dialog box includes the same options as the Export Animation dialog box except that it also includes a text area that can hold several Anime Studio files. By dragging all the files that you want to render into the Batch Export dialog box and clicking the Start button, you can initiate a sequence that renders each specified file in turn. The rendered files are saved to the same folder as the original ANME file.

> **Note**
>
> The Batch Export feature is only available in Anime Studio Pro.

> **Caution**
>
> To fill the Batch Export dialog box list, you'll need to drag the files from a file manager interface such as Windows Explorer or Mac's Finder. This can be a problem on some Linux systems that don't allow files to be dragged from a file manager.

> **Note**
>
> Before starting the batch export process, you can remove files from the list by selecting them and pressing the Delete key.

Figure 33.11
Batch Export
dialog box.

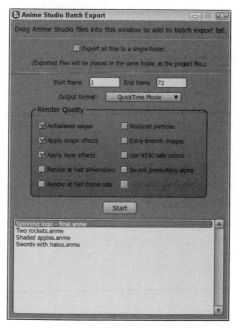

Each file in the Batch Export dialog box can have different rendering settings. To change the settings, simply select the project and its settings appear at the top of the dialog box.

After the Start button is pressed, a percentage value appears next to the file in the list that is currently being rendered. This value slowly counts up to 100%, indicating the progress of the current file. During the rendering phase, the Start button changes to a Pause button so that you can pause the batch export process if you wish.

> **Note**
>
> If you press the close window button in the upper-right corner of the Batch Export dialog box, a warning box appears asking if you want to quit the rendering process. If you choose to quit, then all rendered progress is deleted.

Using MoRen

As an alternative to the Batch Export dialog box, one Anime Studio user created a simple application called *MoRen*, shown in Figure 33.12, which runs external to Anime Studio. This application can be downloaded for free from www.flashpulse.com. The MoRen application is available for Windows and Linux. You can find more information on this tool on the Anime Studio forum at www.lostmarble.com/forum.

Figure 33.12
MoRen dialog box.

Using Command-Line Rendering

Command-line rendering is possible with Anime Studio. These rendering commands let you start a rendering sequence without initiating it from the Anime Studio menu command, making it possible to create a system script that automatically runs at a predetermined time. For example, using the command-line interface, you can create a script to render the completed project for the day during the night when you're away from your computer. Then the next morning, you can see the results without having to wait for each frame to render.

To use command-line rendering in Windows, simply enter the following text command into a BAT file, into the Command Prompt window, or into the Run dialog box:

```
Anime Studio Pro.exe -r filename.anme
```

> **Note**
>
> BAT files are simply text files saved with the .bat extension. This allows you to enter multiple commands in a single file. On Windows machines, BAT files can be executed just like EXE files by double-clicking on them.

Since the Mac system handles applications differently, the syntax needs to be slightly altered.

```
Anime\ Studio\ Pro.exe/Contents/MacOS/Anime\ Studio\Pro -r
filename.anme
```

And on a Linux system, the command-line syntax looks like this:

```
Anime\ Studio\ Pro.exe -r filename.anme
```

This command executes Anime Studio Pro and renders the filename.anme file. If you add the **-v** switch, then the task is run in Verbose mode, which returns information on the status of each frame.

> **Caution**
>
> Verbose mode doesn't work under Windows.

Adding the **-f** switch lets you specify the format to use when rendering. If this switch is not included, then the default format for Mac and Windows is QuickTime and the default format for Linux is JPEG. The available formats include QT (for QuickTime), JPEG, TGA, BMP, PNG, and SWF.

The **-o** switch lets you specify an output file name, such as **-o** outfile.mov.

> **Note**
>
> AVI is not a supported format for command-line rendering because the format requires that you specify the codec to use to compress the video file, which cannot be accessed from the command line.

The **-start** switch followed by a frame number lets you specify the starting frame of the rendered project; the **-end** switch followed by a frame number lets you specify the ending frame. If either of these switches is not included, then the file starts rendering at frame 1 and ends at the frame range.

The rendering options found in the Export Animation dialog box can also be included on the command line using the switches listed below followed by either *yes* to enable the option or *no* to disable it:

- ■ **-aa:** Switch for enabling the Antialiased Edges render option.

- ■ **-shapefx:** Switch for enabling the Render Shape Effects render option.

- ■ **-layerfx:** Switch for enabling the Render Layer Effects render option.

- ■ **-halfsize:** Switch for enabling the Render at Half Size render option.

- ■ **-halffps:** Switch for enabling the Render at Half Frame Rate render option.

- ■ **-fewparticles:** Switch for enabling the Use Reduced Particles render option.

- ■ **-extrasmooth:** Switch for enabling the Extra-Smooth Images render option.

- ■ **-ntscsafe:** Switch for enabling the NTSC-Safe Colors render option.

- ■ **-premultiply:** Switch for enabling the Pre-Multiply Alpha render option.

- ■ **-variablewidths:** Switch for enabling the Variable Line Widths render option.

To export a project using command-line rendering, follow these steps:

1. Locate the file that you want to render and note its path, such as the Doorway.anme file in the Chapter 33 folder on the CD.

2. Open the Run dialog box in Windows by clicking the Start button and selecting the Run option. You can also enter a command in the Command Prompt interface. To open the Command Prompt interface, click the Start button and select the All Programs, Accessories, Command Prompt option. You'll then need to navigate to the Anime Studio Pro directory in order for the command-line commands to work.

   On a Mac system, open the command-line interface, or on a Linux system, access a command-line prompt. For each, make sure that the current path points to the Anime Studio folder where the executable is located.

> **Tip**
>
> Within the Command Prompt interface, you can use the *dir* command (directory) to list the subdirectories of the current folder. The *cd foldername* command can then be used to move into a subdirectory named *foldername* and the *cd* .. is used to move up one directory. Remember that folder names are case-sensitive.

3. In the Run dialog box, click the Browse button and navigate to the Anime Studio Pro executable found in the Program Files/e Frontier/Anime Studio Pro folder.

4. Enter the following command into the Run dialog box or in the Command Prompt interface after the program's path, as shown in Figure 33.13:

```
Anime Studio Pro.exe -r D://Chapter Files/Chap 33/Doorway.anme
-f QT -o C://temp/Doorway.mov
```

Figure 33.13
Run dialog box.

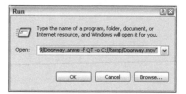

5. Then press the OK button to execute the command: This command opens and renders the Doorway.anme from the CD as a QuickTime movie and saves the results in the temp folder.

Chapter Summary

This chapter showed the various ways to render the final scene, from preview renders to exporting the final animation. This chapter also explained the various render options that let you enable or disable specific features for faster renders. It also covered the layer shadows and layer shading effects along with the Batch Export dialog box and listed the commands for command-line rendering.

The next chapter covers the specifics for exporting a project for use on the Web.

34

Exporting to the Web

- Exporting to Flash
- Optimizing Flash files
- Handling SWF Issues
- Uploading to YouTube and Facebook

If you want to view your animation on the Web, then Anime Studio offers several options, including Flash and direct uploading to YouTube and Facebook. Flash files require a Flash plug-in in order to be viewed in the Web browser, but the Flash player is common and easy to install for users who don't have it installed already. So, let's get started because your fans are waiting.

Exporting Flash Files

To export the current animation to the Flash (SWF) format, select the File, Export Animation (Ctrl/Cmd+E) menu command. This makes the Export Animation dialog box appear, as shown in Figure 34.1. Select the frame range for the animation to export. If you click the Entire Animation button, then the entire defined range of frames will be set to export. Next, select the Flash (SWF) option from the Output Format drop-down list.

When the Flash (SWF) option is selected, several of the Render Quality options are disabled, but you can still choose to render the animation at half dimensions, at half frame rate, to use reduced particles, or to use variable line widths. Details on each of these options are presented in Chapter 33, "Rendering the Final Scene."

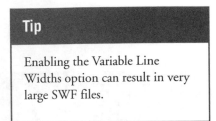

Tip

Enabling the Variable Line Widths option can result in very large SWF files.

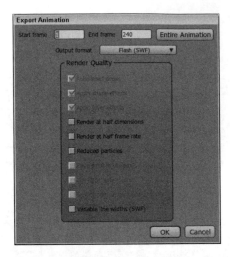

Figure 34.1
Export Animation dialog box.

After clicking the OK button on the Export Animation dialog box, the Save As dialog box opens, and you can name the file to be exported and select a folder where you want the file to be saved. Now the exported SWF file can be opened within a Web browser or within a Flash player to be viewed, as shown in Figure 34.2.

Note

Although SWF files exported by Anime Studio can be loaded into Flash MX and later, Anime Studio exported SWF files cannot be loaded into Flash 5 or earlier versions.

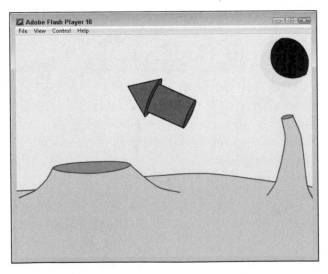

Figure 34.2
Viewing an exported SWF file.

Exporting Limitations

Because some of the features found in Anime Studio are unique, there are some elements that cannot be exported. If you try to avoid using these features, the export animation process will go more smoothly. The following *cannot* be exported:

- **Brushes:** Custom brush strokes aren't exported and are dropped from the project.

- **Nongradient fill effects:** All fill effects with the exception of a simple gradient cannot be exported.

- **Nongradient stroke effects:** All stroke effects with the exception of a simple gradient cannot be exported.

- **Layer effects:** Layer effects, including layer shadows, shading, and noisy strokes are not exported.

- **Motion blur:** Motion blur as defined in the Layer Settings dialog box is not exported.

- **3D movements and cameras:** Flash doesn't understand 3D camera movements and will not export such effects.

- **Images controlled by bones:** Image layers can be exported, but not if they are linked to a bone.

- **Layer masking:** Masking effects are also not exported.

- **Multiple audio files:** All sound files must be included in a single MP3 file in order to exported to Flash.

- **3D layers:** Any objects contained on a 3D layer will not be exported.

Optimizing Flash Files

Since Flash files are typically placed on the Web, the smaller you can make the resulting file, the less of a headache it will be for viewers to download and enjoy them. There are a number of steps you can take to optimize your project so that it will be a smaller final file.

Use Particles Sparingly

Particle layers can be exported to the Flash SWF format, but each separate particle takes up memory, so complex particle layers with hundreds or thousands of particles can very quickly bring the SWF file to its knees. If you plan on exporting the project to the SWF format, try to keep the particle layers to a minimum.

> **Tip**
>
> To limit the number of particles that are exported, simply enable the Reduced Particles option in the Export Animation dialog box.

Use MP3 Soundtracks

Sounds and music can be included in a project that is being exported to the SWF format if the sounds are included in a single MP3 audio file. The audio file must also be saved using the 44100 kHz, 22050 kHz, or the 11025 kHz sample rate. Any other odd sample rate will not be exported.

> **Note**
>
> Anime Studio will only play loaded MP3 files if you have QuickTime installed on your system.

> **Caution**
>
> Although Anime Studio projects can have multiple audio files loaded, exporting the project to Flash only allows a single MP3 file.

Use Optimized Layers

Optimized layers are layers that don't use any Anime Studio–specific features. All new vector and image layers are automatically optimized, but certain features will make a layer no longer optimized. Nonoptimized layers will still export just fine, but they aren't as small as optimized layers.

> **Note**
>
> Optimized layers are indicated by a small red dot in the upper-left corner of the layer type icon in the Layers palette.

The following actions will cause a layer to no longer be optimized:

- **Any 3D camera movements:** Displays the entire figure as if it were cut out and displayed against the gray background. This style is good for isolating edges.

- **Shearing a layer:** Displays just the figure lines that outline the various body parts.

- **Uneven scaling:** Displays all the mesh lines that make up the entire figure.

- **Point animation:** Displays only those lines that are facing the camera. Lines on the back of the figure aren't shown.

- **Bone animation:** A wireframe view that is colored based on the scene lights.

Figure 34.3
Optimized layers are shown in the Layers palette by a red dot.

Nonoptimized layer

Optimized layer

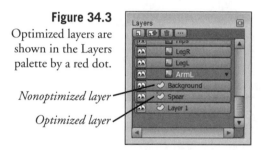

Vector layers that are optimized are exported as Flash symbols making them very efficient within Flash, but nonoptimized layers (the ones that don't have the small red dot next to the layer icon) are exported separately for each frame, resulting in much larger files. Figure 34.3 shows the Layers palette with some optimized and nonoptimized layers.

Reduce the Frame Rate

Slower frame rates such as 12 fps will be adequate for most animations intended to be viewed on the Web, and a lower frame rate results in a smaller SWF file.

Translate a Layer Instead of an Object

Another way to reduce the complexity of a SWF file is to translate objects by translating the entire layer instead of translating the object by moving its points. This may require dividing some objects into several layers, but more layers are easier to optimize than point animations.

Avoid Lots of Points

The more points a project contains, the larger the resulting SWF file. If you can reduce the total number of points, it will help keep the file size small. In particular, avoid using the Freehand tool and the Insert Text feature. Both of these will add a lot of unnecessary points.

Flash Export Issues

Even if you optimize the project, there are some export issues that you need to be aware of, or they can cause trouble for you.

Clearing Animated Content

One problem that can arise when an animated project is exported to the SWF format is that the content on the last frame of the animation remains when the animation loops to start again. This can really disrupt the flow of a looping animation. Figure 34.4 shows this problem with the dancing flower. Notice how the last frame of the flower stays around after the animation has finished and when it loops to start again, the flower is still there.

<table>
<tr>
<td>

Note

This problem is inconsistent. It tends to happen more often with larger files.

</td>
<td>

</td>
<td>

Figure 34.4
Looping SWF animations sometimes don't clear the screen.

</td>
</tr>
</table>

Luckily, Anime Studio includes a simple fix for this problem. In the Project Settings dialog box is an Extra SWF Frame option. This option causes a blank frame to be automatically added to the end of the animation. This blank frame clears the screen so that when the animation loops, the animation starts with a clear screen.

Caution

If your exported animation is a short looping clip, then the Extra SWF Frame option might cause an annoying flicker.

Releasing Bone Control

If an image layer is bound to a bone, then it cannot be exported. You can determine this by looking for the red optimization dot in the Layers palette by the layer's icon. If you have an image layer that is within a bone or a switch layer that you know isn't controlled by a bone that isn't being exported, then you can ensure that it will be exported by selecting the layer and using the Bone, Release Layer menu command. This removes the bone binding for the layer, and the red optimization dot should reappear for this layer.

Working with MP3s

Anime Studio lets you add audio files that are WAV (for Windows) or AIFF files (for Mac), but these audio formats are uncompressed and result in larger file sizes. You can use highly compressed MP3 audio files in your exported SWF files, which helps to keep the file sizes down.

To use the MP3 file, you'll need to add the WAV or AIFF file to the project and then convert the same audio file to the MP3 format. Place the converted MP3 file in the same folder as the WAV or AIFF file and name it the same. When the file is exported to the SWF format, the MP3 file is used in place of the larger WAV or AIFF file.

Anime Studio doesn't include the ability to convert audio files from the WAV or AIFF formats to MP3, but there are several programs that can easily do it, including iTunes and Audacity, as well as the major audio editing packages.

> **Note**
>
> The ability to use MP3s works when exporting to QuickTime also.

To export a project with sound to the Flash (SWF) format, follow these steps:

1. Open the Dancing flower.anme file from the Chapter 34 folder on the CD. This file is taken from an earlier tutorial and features a flower that moves to the beat of an audio file.

2. Convert the TutDrum.wav file to a MP3 file using an audio editing program or iPod software. A copy of a converted file is located in the Chapter 34 folder on the CD. Place the converted MP3 file in the same folder as the WAV file.

3. Select the File, Export Animation menu command (Ctrl/Cmd+E). In the Export Animation dialog box, select the Render at Half Dimensions option to speed up the exporting process. Then choose the Flash (SWF) option from the Output Format drop-down list and click the OK button.

4. In the File dialog box that opens, give the export file a name and choose a location; then click the Save button.

5. To view the exported file, drag the exported SWF file and drop it on an open Web browser. The file will open and play with sound in the Flash player, as shown in Figure 34.5.

Figure 34.5
Exported SWF file playing in a Flash player.

Avoid Large Frame Ranges

The Flash export feature sometimes has trouble when trying to export an animation with a large number of frames. Generally, animations with over 500 frames will have trouble. You can overcome this trouble by exporting the animation using smaller batches of 50 to 100 frames. The smaller sequences can then be recombined using Flash.

Tip
You can render multiple smaller frame ranges at once using the Batch Render dialog box. The Batch Render also lets you do background renders, so you could render frames 1–100 using the File, Export feature and then start frames 101–200 using Batch Render and both will render simultaneously.

Controlling Looping

Animations in Anime Studio that are exported to SWF will automatically loop indefinitely, and Anime Studio doesn't include a command forcing the animation to play only once. If you want your animation to play through only once, you could load the SWF file into Flash and add a stop command to the end of the project, or you could add the **loop=no** command to the HTML page that is calling the SWF file. When the SWF file is playing in the browser, you can right-click the browser and disable the Loop option in the pop-up menu.

Uploading to YouTube and Facebook

Anime Studio includes features that let you upload your animation directly to YouTube. Within the Preferences dialog box, which is opened using the Edit, Preferences menu, is a panel labeled Video Uploads, as shown in Figure 34.6. Using this panel, you can enter your YouTube username and password.

Figure 34.6
Within the Preferences dialog box, you can enter your YouTube log-in information.

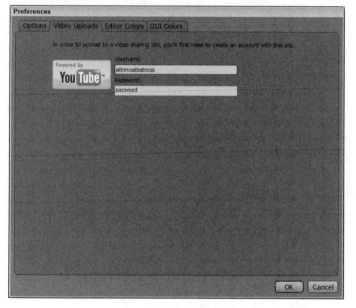

The Project Settings dialog box includes options in the Dimensions drop-down list for YouTube and YouTube HD. Selecting either of these options will format the project resolution for YouTube. Once this information is entered, you can use the File, Upload to YouTube menu command.

New Feature

The ability to upload animations directly to YouTube is new to Anime Studio 6.

The File menu also includes an option to Upload to Facebook. This works by letting you select a rendered movie. You then need to log into your Facebook account and give the Smith Micro Video Uploader permission to upload the video. This is a setting that you can enable in the Edit Applications Page. Once permission has been granted, Anime Studio presents a dialog box allowing you to continue with the upload.

Note

The Upload to Facebook feature was added to Anime Studio in version 6.1.

Chapter Summary

This chapter showed how you could export the current project to the Flash format. There are a number of things you can do to help optimize the exported animation and to overcome export issues. This chapter also showed how an animation can be uploaded directly to YouTube or to Facebook.

The next chapter looks at how you can export to AVI and QuickTime formats.

35

Exporting Movies

- Exporting animations
- Selecting a codec
- Exporting to a DVD
- Exporting limitations

Anime Studio allows animation sequences to be exported as a sequence of images using the JPEG, BMP, Targa, PNG, and PSD formats, but you can also have Anime Studio combine all the frames into a compiled movie file using the AVI or QuickTime formats.

Note

If QuickTime isn't an export option on Windows, you'll need to install QuickTime on your system. You can find a QuickTime installer located on the Anime Studio 6 installation CD.

Exporting Animations

Animated sequences can be exported using several different formats, including JPEG, BMP, Targa, PNG, PSD, AVI, MOV, and Flash (SWF). To export an animation, open the Export Animation dialog box shown in Figure 35.1 and choose the format to use from the Output Format drop-down list.

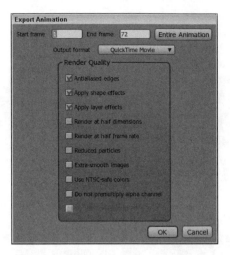

Figure 35.1
Export Animation dialog box.

Exporting to an Image Format

When one of the image formats is selected, each frame of the animation is saved as a separate image file. Each file is given a file name followed by the frame number. These sequenced images can then be imported into a video editing package like Final Cut Pro or Adobe Premiere and recompiled into a movie format.

Note

Exporting to sequenced images is only available in Anime Studio Pro.

Within the Export Animation dialog box are several render options. These options include the following:

■ **Antialiased Edges:** This option eliminates any jagged edges caused by aliasing the lines. This is accomplished by filtering the edges in such a way that replaces the hard edges with smoothed ones.

■ **Apply Shape Effects:** This option includes any designated shape effects added to the project. If this option is disabled, the export process will run much faster.

■ **Apply Layer Effects:** This option lets you include layer effects like shadows and transparency, or they can be disabled for quicker exporting.

■ **Render at Half Dimensions:** This option is helpful for creating quick previews by rendering the results at half the specified size.

- **Render at Half Frame Rate:** This option renders the results at a frame rate that is half the designated amount in order to speed the rendering.

- **Reduced Particles:** This option causes all particle layers to use a fraction of the specified particles in order to speed up the rendering.

- **Extra-Smooth Images:** This option renders all images with an extra sampling pass to smooth out the results. This yields a higher-quality image, but takes longer to render.

- **Use NTSC-Safe Colors:** This option limits the colors used to a palette that is safe for presenting consistent color on television.

- **Do Not Premultiply Alpha Channel:** This option causes any alpha channel not to be added to the image, which can overlight an image in some cases.

Note

The Antialiased Edges, Apply Shape Effects, and Reduced Particles options are only available in Anime Studio Pro.

Exporting to a Movie Format

If you select the AVI Movie (for Windows) or QuickTime Movie (for Macintosh or Windows) options from the Output Format drop-down list in the Export Animation dialog box, then you can export the project using a video format.

New Feature

The ability to export HD Video is new to Anime Studio 6. This feature is only available in Anime Studio Pro.

Setting Movie Dimensions

While the Export Animation dialog box includes options for reducing the size of the output and for reducing the frame rate of the animation, these values can also be changed using the Project Settings dialog box shown in Figure 35.2. The Project Settings dialog box is opened using the File, Project Settings menu command. To reduce the size of the final rendered image, decrease the Width and Height values.

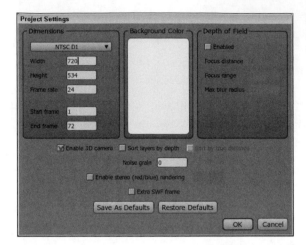

Figure 35.2
Project Settings
dialog box.

Exporting for Compositing

If you plan on compositing your exported movie with a background video in a package such as After Effects or Final Cut Pro, you'll want to include an alpha channel with your animation. Only certain formats support alpha channels.

When exporting to the QuickTime format, look for a codec that offers *Millions of Colors+* as its color depth. The plus sign indicates that the codec supports an alpha channel.

When exporting to the AVI format, be aware that none of the default codecs support alpha channels. If you've installed a video-editing program on your system, however, you may have a codec that supports alpha channels available.

> ### Tip
>
> If you can't find an AVI codec that supports alpha channels, then search the Web for the Huffyuv codec. It is a free codec for Windows that supports alpha.

You can also export the animation to a series of numbered images using the PNG and Targa formats, both of which support an alpha channel.

If you plan on exporting an animation to be composited with another video, make sure you enable the Do Not Premultiply Alpha Channel option in the Export Animation dialog box. This option will enable the composited animation to be cleaner.

Selecting a Codec

When you choose to export an animation sequence as an AVI or a QuickTime movie, one more dialog box appears after you name the movie file in the File dialog box. The Video Compression dialog box, shown for AVI in Figure 35.3 and for QuickTime in Figure 35.4, lets you select, specify, and configure the codec that is used to compress the video.

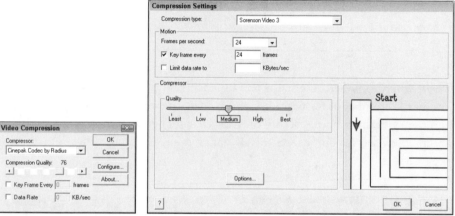

Figure 35.3
AVI Video Compression dialog box.

Figure 35.4
QuickTime Compression Settings dialog box.

A *codec* is a piece of code that is used to compress the unused bits of data in the video to make it a more reasonable size. Codec works in video just like the MP3 format works in music. Some codecs allow video frames to be compressed losslessly and others use a lossy method to compress the data. A *lossless* method of compression maintains the same quality as the original video frames whereas the *lossy* method works to reduce the size more aggressively by removing some of the original pixels.

> **Note**
>
> The JPEG format is an example of a lossy compression method. If you compress a JPEG image to a low-quality setting, the substandard results are clearly visible.

The Compression Settings dialog box, whether you are using AVI or QuickTime, has a number of codec options available from a drop-down list. Some of these codecs are common among a large variety of software packages such as Cinepak, DV, Intel Indeo, MPEG, and Sorenson Video. Others are more specialized.

Tip

The exact codecs that are available on your system depend on the software you have installed, but new codec options can be installed and added to the list.

The Compression Settings dialog box also includes options to set keyframes every designated number of frames. These video keyframes record the entire screen data and nonkeyframed frames record only the changes between the keyframed frame and the new frame. This causes the keyframes to be rendered with minimal compression.

Tip

A good rule of thumb for the Keyframe Every value is to set it to a number that is equal to the frame rate. However, if your animation has a lot of fast-moving objects, you'll want to lower this value to about half the frame rate.

The Limit Data Rate setting specifies the size of the video file per second. The specified size is dependent on the size of the final video, its frame rate, the selected codec, and the complexity of the project. As a general rule of thumb, try using these settings if you intend to stream your video over a network or the Web:

- **Full HD at 1920 by 1080:** Use a data rate of 7,000 to 9,000 Kbyte/sec.

- **NTSC-widescreen at 1280 by 720:** Use a data rate of 5,000 to 6,000 Kbyte/sec.

- **Standard resolution at 640 by 480:** Use a data rate of 1,000 to 2,000 Kbyte/sec.

- **Web resolution at 320 by 240:** Use a data rate of 300 to 500 Kbyte/sec.

- **Mobile resolution (3G) at 176 by 144:** Use a data rate of 150 to 200 Kbyte/sec.

Tip

Several of these options are available in the Project Settings dialog box.

After a codec option is configured and selected, the exporting process begins, and the rendered project frames are displayed in the progress window, shown in Figure 35.5. When the video is complete, it is automatically opened and played in the default media player.

Figure 35.5

Export progress window.

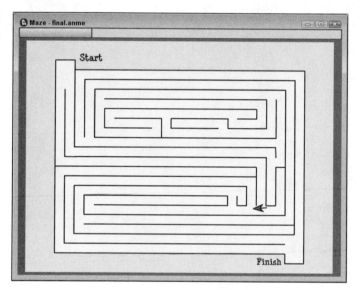

To export a project using the AVI format, follow these steps:

1. Open the Spinning logo.anme file from the Chapter 35 folder on the CD. This file is taken from an earlier tutorial and features a spinning logo.

2. Select the File, Export Animation menu command (Ctrl/Cmd+E). In the Export Animation dialog box, select the Antialiased edges, Apply Shape Effects, Apply Layer Effects, and the Render at Half Dimensions options. Then choose the AVI Movie option from the Output Format drop-down list and click the OK button.

3. In the File dialog box that opens, give the export file a name with the .AVI extension and choose a location; then click the Save button.

4. In the Video Compression dialog box, select the Cinepak Codec by Radius option from the Compressor drop-down list. Drag the Compression Quality slider to 75 and click the OK button.

5. After the export process is completed, the video file opens and plays within a media player, as shown in Figure 35.6.

Figure 35.6

Exported AVI file playing in a media player.

To export a project using the MOV format, follow these steps:

1. Open the Maze.anme file from the Chapter 35 folder on the CD. This file is taken from an earlier tutorial and shows an arrow being animated moving through a maze.

2. Select the File, Export Animation menu command (Ctrl/Cmd+E). In the Export Animation dialog box, select the Antialiased edges, Apply Shape Effects, Apply Layer Effects, and the Render at Half Dimensions options. Then choose the QuickTime Movie option from the Output Format drop-down list and click the OK button.

3. In the File dialog box that opens, give the export file a name with the .MOV extension and choose a location; then click the Save button.

4. In the Video Compression dialog box, select the Sorenson Video 3 option from the Compressor drop-down list. Set the Frames per Second to 24 and enable the Keyframe Every option with a value of 24. Then drag the Compression Quality slider to High and click the OK button.

5. After the export process is completed, the video file opens and plays within the QuickTime player, as shown in Figure 35.7.

Figure 35.7
Exported MOV file playing in the QuickTime player.

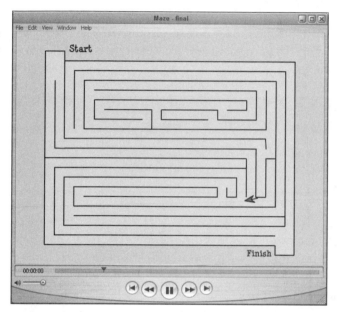

Exporting Animation Files for a DVD

If you're planning on exporting your animation so that it can be played on a DVD player, there are some tips that can make the process run a little more smoothly. Set your animation to use a frame rate of 30 fps for NTSC or to 25 fps for PAL. NTSC is common in the U.S. and Canada, and the PAL format is common in Europe.

For the resolution, you can choose the one of the 1080p presets in the Project Settings dialog box to use a resolution of 1440 pixels by 1080 pixels for HDV or the HDTV preset with a resolution of 1920 by 1080.

Although these presets will work fine, you can actually improve the visual quality of the animation if you double the resolution and then resize it later in your video editing software. The key to doubling the resolution is to keep the ratios between the width and height consistent. For full-screen animations, the ratio is 4:3 and for widescreen it is 16:9. To double the resolution for your animation for television formats, use the following resolutions:

- **NTSC-full screen:** 1280 by 960
- **NTSC-widescreen:** 1280 by 720
- **PAL-full screen:** 1536 by 1152
- **PAL-widescreen:** 2048 by 1152

Within the Export Animation dialog box, make sure you have the Antialiased Edges and the Use NTSC-Safe Colors options enabled. If you have the disk space, try to export the animation uncompressed.

Caution

The tricky part about exporting an Anime Studio animation to DVD is that the computer uses square pixels, but the pixels on a television are rectangular.

Within the video editing software that you are using, apply a blur filter followed by a resize filter if you've rendered the animation at double the resolution, and finally add a gamma correction filter. Then select the DVD output setting and make sure the Interlace option is disabled and render the final output. This will encode the animation file so that it can be played on a DVD. This output file can now be loaded into a DVD authoring package where you can add menus.

Exporting Limitations

If you are exporting an animation using Anime Studio Debut, then the maximum size supported is 768 by 768 pixels. Animation sequences are also limited in Anime Studio Debut to 3,000 frames. If you are using Anime Studio Pro, then you have a maximum size limit of 9,000 by 9,000 with an unlimited number of frames.

Chapter Summary

This chapter dealt with exporting animations to an image format or to a movie format. The Export Animation dialog box includes several options that impact the rendering speed and quality. The chapter also explained how codecs work and covered issues related to exporting to a DVD.

The next chapter shows how you can have complete control over changing the Anime Studio interface.

Part X

Extending Anime Studio with Scripts

36

Customizing
the Interface

- Altering the Tools palette
- Changing menus

The Anime Studio interface seems to work well, but there are some "gotchas" that might be causing you trouble. This is true especially if you've used many other software packages that don't work the same way as Anime Studio. For instance, in other packages like Maya and Photoshop, you can use the Tab key to quickly hide all open palettes, but in Anime Studio the Tab key is used to select connected points.

If learning a whole new set of keyboard shortcuts is slowing you down, you can tinker under the hood and change the tool and menu keyboard shortcuts along with many other configurations. I mean, who wants to use the packaged Anime Studio when you can change it to read, "My Awesome Animation Machine."

Altering the Tools Palette

If you look in the Scripts/tool folder where Anime Studio is installed, you'll find a simple text file named _tool_list.txt. This file controls the sections, names, colors, and keyboard shortcuts of all the tools found in the Tools palette.

If you edit this file, you can change the tool positions and colors, add or alter the keyboard shortcuts for each tool, and even add new tools to the Tools palette.

Caution

The _tool_list.txt file is a system file used by Anime Studio to create the Tools palette. If you make a mistake and delete some of the data from this file, the Tools palette may become corrupted and not work properly.

Tip

Before you change the _tool_list.txt file, create a backup of the original file and name it something like _tool_list_backup.txt so that you can revert to the original file if you need to.

Note

You will need to restart Anime Studio before you can see any changes made to the Tools palette.

Changing Keyboard Shortcuts in the Tools Palette

When you first look at the _tool_list.txt file shown in Figure 36.1, you'll see that the file is divided into groups that hold tools and buttons.

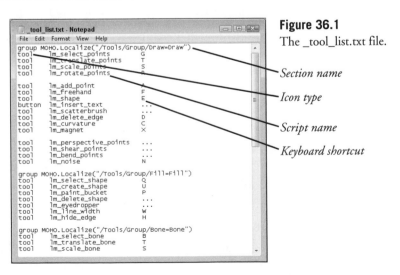

Figure 36.1
The _tool_list.txt file.

Section name

Icon type

Script name

Keyboard shortcut

Within each group are lines for each tool that include its type, the script name, and a keyboard shortcut. To change the keyboard shortcuts for the Tools palette, you simply need to change the letters in this file. If a tool has no shortcut, then it simply has three periods in a row. If you replace these periods with a letter, the tool will have the designated letter as its new shortcut.

Tip

If you change the keyboard shortcut for a tool, be sure that the new shortcut you are using isn't used elsewhere. If two tools share the same keyboard shortcut, then the shortcut automatically defaults to the first tool on the list with that shortcut.

To change the keyboard shortcuts for tools, follow these steps:

1. Open the Scripts/tool folder in which Anime Studio is installed. This folder includes a single text file, several Lua script files, and several .PNG icon files.

2. Locate and double-click the _tool_list.txt file to open it within a text editor.

3. Locate and replace the letter A found to the right of the lm_add_point text with the letter Q. Then locate and replace the three dots to the right of the lm_arrow text with the letter A.

4. Save the file and restart Anime Studio. The keyboard shortcuts for these two tools have been changed.

5. Move the mouse cursor over the Arrows and the Add Points tools and notice that the keyboard shortcut has changed. Select a vector layer and press the A key to see the Arrows tool highlighted and the Q key to see the Add Points tool highlighted.

The keyboard shortcuts in the Tools palette are designed to use only single letters and digits. Entering more than a single letter or digit will cause the shortcut to be ignored.

Changing Group Names in the Tools Palette

Each tool section in the Tools palette is denoted in the _tool_list.txt file as a group followed by a localization string and a name. If you change the group name variable and its name (located to the right of equal sign), then the new name is displayed in the Tools palette. For example, if you change the text *group MOHO.Localize* ("/Tools/Group/Draw=Draw") to *group MOHO Localize*

("/Tools/Group/Draw1=Draw_Cool"), then the section name of Draw is changed to Draw_Cool. If the text is too long, it will be truncated on either end. Figure 36.2 shows my updated Tools palette with unique tool group names.

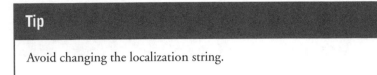

Figure 36.2
New tool group names on the Tools palette.

> ### Tip
>
> Avoid changing the localization string.

Creating a New Group in the Tools Palette

If you copy and paste a group name to the bottom of the _tool_list.txt file, then a new section will be added to the Tools palette. This new section can hold any of the existing tools or any new tools that you add to the tool folder. If you've scripted a new set of scripts, you can add them to the Tools palette by simply adding a type and referencing the script name. If you add a keyboard shortcut to the right of the script name, then the shortcut will be used. Figure 36.3 shows a new section added to the bottom of the Tools palette that contains only selection tools.

Figure 36.3
The Tools palette with a new group of selection tools at bottom.

> ### Tip
>
> Rather than typing in the new group and script names, it is easier to simply copy and alter an existing group and script. By doing this, you can be sure the formatting will be consistent with what Anime Studio expects.

The keyword to the left of the script name is used to designate the icon type. The default Tools palette recognizes three icon types:

- **Tool:** Displays the default icon and allows the icon to be selected. The selected icon is highlighted in yellow.
- **Button:** Displays the icon that is executed immediately when clicked.
- **Spacer:** Leaves an open space instead of an icon.

The Tools palette is set up to have a width of four icons across. Even if you remove the extra row in the _tool_list.txt file, the icons will still be displayed in order using a four icon width.

Figure 36.4
Unreferenced scripts are automatically placed in the Other section.

Figure 36.4
Unreferenced scripts are automatically placed in the Other section.

Adding a New Tool to the Tools Palette

All scripts added to the Scripts/tool folder are displayed in the Tools palette somewhere. If they are referenced in the _tool_list.txt file, they'll appear within the designated group, but if they are not included within any of the groups, then they automatically appear in the Other category. For example, if you delete the _tool_list.txt file from the Scripts/tool folder, then the groups are deleted and all scripts are placed within the Other category alphabetically, as shown in Figure 36.4.

Figure 36.5
Scripts with no icons are shown as question marks.

If a Lua script is added to the Scripts/tool folder, then the script automatically appears in the Other section of the Tools palette. But if the new script doesn't have any associated icon, it simply appears with a default question mark icon, as shown in the bottom row of the palette in Figure 36.5.

> **Tip**
>
> Only certain types of scripts can work in the Tools palette. To learn how to create new tool scripts, see Chapter 37, "Using Scripts and Lua."

To create a new icon for a custom tool script, simply select and edit one of the existing PNG icon images and then save the new icon with the same name as the tool script that it represents. New icons should be 24 pixels by 20 pixels.

> **Tip**
>
> If you make the background of the PNG icon image transparent, the specified group color will show through when viewed in the Tools palette.

To create a custom icon for the Tools palette, follow these steps:

1. Copy the completed tool script into the Scripts/tool folder.

2. Open one of the PNG icon image files within an image-editing application. Create a new icon using the same dimensions as the existing file. Rename the edited PNG image file to be the same name as the tool script and save the file in the Script/tool folder.

3. Open the _tool_list.txt file found in the Scripts/tool folder and copy the first group definition along with one of the icon definitions. Paste the copied text to the bottom of the file. Edit the group name to be the new section name that will hold the new script and change the referenced icon name to match the new tool script name.

4. Save the file and restart Anime Studio. With this change, the new group and the new icon should appear in the Tools palette in the My Scripts section, as shown in Figure 36.6.

Figure 36.6
A new tool and group have been added to the Tools palette in the My Scripts section.

Changing Menus

The Tools palette isn't the only thing you can customize. If you look in the Resources/Strings folder where Anime Studio is installed, you'll find a file named Strings.EN.txt. This file contains all the text strings that appear throughout the program, including the menus. They are all contained here in a single file to make it easy to localize the software for foreign languages, but you can use this file to alter the text that appears in the program, including the menu keyboard shortcuts.

> **Note**
>
> The Resources/Strings folder also holds text files for the German and French languages.

When you open the Anime Studio .strings file in a text editor as shown in Figure 36.7, you'll see a bunch of specific variable names followed by an equal sign and then a text string. These variable names and the strings they represent are divided into categories to make the various types of strings easy to identify. Table 36.1 lists the various variable names and the type of text they represent.

> **Note**
>
> The text string file didn't ship with Anime Studio version 6.0, but a link for downloading this file is available on the Anime Studio forum located at www.lostmarble.com/forum.

Figure 36.7
The Anime Studio strings file.

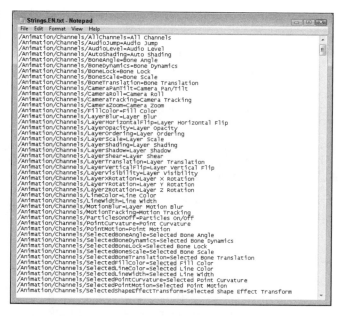

Table 36.1   Types of Strings

Variable Name	Types of Strings
/Animation/Channels	Animation Channels strings
/Application	Application name, manual, and QuickStart names
/Controls	Animation controls
/Dialogs	Dialog box text, including Layer Settings, Preferences, and Project Settings
/File	Import warning text
/Menus	Menu text
/Popups	Text for all pop-up windows
/Scripts	Text for scripts in the Scripts menu and in the Tools palette
/Windows	Main window strings

Changing Menu Keyboard Shortcuts

If you scan through the variable names for the menus, you'll find all the text strings for the menus. At the end of some of these strings is a single capitalized letter that is used to set the keyboard shortcut for that particular menu item. All menu keyboard shortcuts automatically use the Ctrl/Cmd key along with the designated letter to access the shortcut. For example, the menu string for Undo is listed as *UndoZ*. This means that the Close menu command uses the Ctrl/Cmd+Z keyboard shortcut.

If you carefully change this last capital letter, you can alter the menu keyboard shortcuts. After changing the final capital letter, save the file and restart Anime Studio to see the updated keyboard shortcuts. If you want to add a keyboard shortcut to a menu command that doesn't have one, look for a space at the end of the menu name and replace that space with a letter or digit.

> **Note**
>
> Some menu strings end with three periods. This indicates that a dialog box opens when the menu command is executed. The keyboard shortcut can follow these periods with no trouble.

If you change the keyboard shortcut to a letter used by another menu command, then the first menu command to be assigned that shortcut will be accessed.

To edit the Anime Studio Pro strings file to change a keyboard shortcut, follow these steps:

1. Open the Resources/Strings folder located where Anime Studio is installed.

2. Locate and double-click the Strings.EN.txt file to open it within a text editor.

3. Locate and add the letter H after the string variable name for /Menus/File/ProjectSettings=Project Settings...P. This makes the File, Project Settings menu command have the Ctrl/Cmd+Shift+H shortcut.

4. Save the file and restart Anime Studio. With this change, the keyboard shortcut for the selected menu item has changed, as shown in Figure 36.8.

Figure 36.8
File, Project Settings now has a different keyboard shortcut.

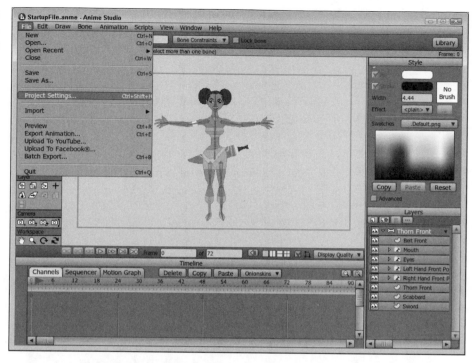

Note

If this example isn't working, then it could be that your software has been automatically upgraded to a newer version and the strings file name needs to be updated also.

Chapter Summary

This chapter showed how you can alter different aspects of the Anime Studio interface, including the Tools palette and the menus, by changing the text setting files. Being able to alter the interface text strings gives you a wonderful sense of power and control even if you never change anything.

If it's power and control you're looking for, the next chapter is right on track. Using the Lua scripting engine, you can extend Anime Studio to have new features that will really set your installation apart.

37

Using Scripts and Lua

- Understanding Lua
- Embedding scripts
- Using script-writing scripts
- Locating and installing scripts
- Writing custom scripts

Lua is a scripting language that can be used to extend the features of Anime Studio. By locating existing third-party scripts, you can save time and energy and take advantage of other users' experience and expertise. If you learn the Lua syntax, you'll even be able to write your own custom scripts.

Understanding Lua

Lua is the name of a scripting language that is supported by Anime Studio. Using the Lua syntax, you can script behaviors for the software that are new and unique and even extend its functionality. Lua isn't unique to Anime Studio. Several other applications use Lua, and it is broadly supported across the Web. Lua is a common scripting language for games. You can learn more about scripting in Lua at www.lua.org.

Embedding Scripts

Scripts can also be added to a layer using the Embedded Script File option in the General panel of the Layer Settings dialog box. When this option is enabled, a File dialog box opens where you can locate a script to execute when the layer is encountered.

Using Script-Writing Scripts

Another category that is helpful as you begin to write scripts is the script-writing scripts. These simple scripts show you how to accomplish certain tasks like making an alert box appear or printing debugging messages to the Lua Console.

> **Note**
>
> The Scripts menu is only available in Anime Studio Pro.

The Alert Test script opens a warning dialog box. You can look at the script syntax to produce this alert box by opening the lm_alert.lua script file found in the Scripts, Menu, Script Writing folder where Anime Studio is installed. It can be opened into a simple text editor. Figure 37.1 shows this simple script.

Figure 37.1

lm_alert.lua script.

The result of this script is shown in Figure 37.2.

Figure 37.2
Alert box.

Some of the other script-writing scripts send messages to the Lua Console, as shown in Figure 37.3. This console is a simple message window that can display messages from the scripting engine. Select the Scripts, Script Writing, Print Test menu to see the Lua Console.

Figure 37.3
Lua Console.

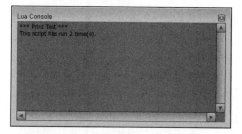

Locating Scripts

Many useful scripts can be found on the Anime Studio forum (www.lostmarble.com/forum), which is a meeting place for Anime Studio users. Many experienced users and script writers offer their scripts to beginners.

Installing Third-Party Scripts

Once you locate and download a script from a third-party source, you can add it to your system by simply dropping it into the Scripts folder where Anime Studio is installed. Within this folder are several subfolders—one for menus, one for tools, and one for utilities.

Menu scripts can simply be placed in one of the menu folders and the scripts automatically will appear in the Scripts menu. Tool scripts require an icon graphic that is named the same as the script. When a tool script is added to the Scripts, Tools folder, it appears in the Tools palette in an Other category. You can learn more about configuring the Tools palette in Chapter 36, "Customizing the Interface."

Useful Forum Scripts

As you read through the Anime Studio forum, you'll find that many power users accomplish their magic using a whole set of advanced tools. Table 37.1 is a quick list of the scripts available on the forum that are particularly useful. The credit for these scripts goes to the user that created it, and I personally cannot vouch for each of these scripts, but they provide a good starting point for upgrading your installation.

Table 37.1   Useful Forum Scripts

Script Name	Creator	Function	Type
hv_copyflipbones.lua	heyvern	Mirrors a set of bones to the opposite side of a symmetrical model.	Menu
hv_bonerenamer.lua	heyvern	Script for renaming a set of bones.	Menu
hv_select_bone.zip	heyvern	Provides an alternative method for selecting bones from a scrolling list.	Tool
Freeze points	genete	Freezes a selection set of points so they can't be edited while working with other points.	Menu
Sort_shapes_by_bonesv2.lua	genete	Creates the bones for a selected vector layer.	Tool
Align shapes by gravity center	genete	Aligns selected shapes by their X and Y gravity center.	Tool
cc_reverse_layer_keyframes.lua	crashcore	Reverses all layer keyframes on X and Y gravity center.	Menu
cc_list_external_files.lua	crashcore	Lists all external files used in a project.	Menu
cc_sf_MegaMagnet.lua	crashcore, 7feet	Features new tools that attract all points within a range to the mouse.	Tool
fa_add_point.lua, fa_bind_points.lua, fa_create_shape.lua, etc.	fazik	Features a complete set of replacement tools that have many new and useful additions.	Tool
Spiral script	myles	Creates a spiral curve.	Tool

Writing Custom Scripts

Custom scripts can be written using the Lua scripting language. Lua scripts can be written in a standard text editor; you simply drop the new scripts into the Scripts directory to make them available in the Scripts menu after Anime Studio is restarted.

There are many resources for learning Lua on the Web, and the Anime Studio forum also includes a Moho Scripting Reference that you can download and use. You can find the Moho API documentation at www.lostmarble.com/moho/extras/scripts/moho_scripting.zip.

Chapter Summary

This chapter introduced the Lua-scripting language and showed some resources that you can use to get more information.

This concludes the chapters. I hope that you've been able to find some useful information. For more information, please go to the Anime Studio forum at www.lostmarble.com/forum. This forum is a wealth of information and has a strong community.

Index

License Agreement/Notice of Limited Warranty

By opening the sealed disc container in this book, you agree to the following terms and conditions. If, upon reading the following license agreement and notice of limited warranty, you cannot agree to the terms and conditions set forth, return the unused book with unopened disc to the place where you purchased it for a refund.

License:

The enclosed software is copyrighted by the copyright holder(s) indicated on the software disc. You are licensed to copy the software onto a single computer for use by a single user and to a backup disc. You may not reproduce, make copies, or distribute copies or rent or lease the software in whole or in part, except with written permission of the copyright holder(s). You may transfer the enclosed disc only together with this license, and only if you destroy all other copies of the software and the transferee agrees to the terms of the license. You may not decompile, reverse assemble, or reverse engineer the software.

Notice of Limited Warranty:

The enclosed disc is warranted by Course Technology to be free of physical defects in materials and workmanship for a period of sixty (60) days from end user's purchase of the book/disc combination. During the sixty-day term of the limited warranty, Course Technology will provide a replacement disc upon the return of a defective disc.

Limited Liability:

THE SOLE REMEDY FOR BREACH OF THIS LIMITED WARRANTY SHALL CONSIST ENTIRELY OF REPLACEMENT OF THE DEFECTIVE DISC. IN NO EVENT SHALL COURSE TECHNOLOGY OR THE AUTHOR BE LIABLE FOR ANY OTHER DAMAGES, INCLUDING LOSS OR CORRUPTION OF DATA, CHANGES IN THE FUNCTIONAL CHARACTERISTICS OF THE HARDWARE OR OPERATING SYSTEM, DELETERIOUS INTERACTION WITH OTHER SOFTWARE, OR ANY OTHER SPECIAL, INCIDENTAL, OR CONSEQUENTIAL DAMAGES THAT MAY ARISE, EVEN IF COURSE TECHNOLOGY AND/OR THE AUTHOR HAS PREVIOUSLY BEEN NOTIFIED THAT THE POSSIBILITY OF SUCH DAMAGES EXISTS.

Disclaimer of Warranties:

COURSE TECHNOLOGY AND THE AUTHOR SPECIFICALLY DISCLAIM ANY AND ALL OTHER WARRANTIES, EITHER EXPRESS OR IMPLIED, INCLUDING WARRANTIES OF MERCHANTABILITY, SUITABILITY TO A PARTICULAR TASK OR PURPOSE, OR FREEDOM FROM ERRORS. SOME STATES DO NOT ALLOW FOR EXCLUSION OF IMPLIED WARRANTIES OR LIMITATION OF INCIDENTAL OR CONSEQUENTIAL DAMAGES, SO THESE LIMITATIONS MIGHT NOT APPLY TO YOU.

Other:

This Agreement is governed by the laws of the State of Massachusetts without regard to choice of law principles. The United Convention of Contracts for the International Sale of Goods is specifically disclaimed. This Agreement constitutes the entire agreement between you and Course Technology regarding use of the software.